3 23

STRAND PRICE

5 00

D1212038

STEPS ON MY
PILGRIM JOURNEY

CARDINAL CAHAL B. DALY

STEPS ON MY PILGRIM JOURNEY

MEMORIES AND REFLECTIONS

VERITAS

First published 1998 by
Veritas Publications
7/8 Lower Abbey Street
Dublin 1

Copyright © Cardinal Cahal B. Daly 1998

ISBN 1 85390 319 1 (cased)
     1 85390 476 7 (paper)

British Library Cataloguing
in Publication Data.
A catalogue record for
this book is available
from the British Library.

Scripture extracts taken from the *Jerusalem Bible* are published and copyright
1966, 1967 and 1978 Darton Longman & Todd Ltd and Doubleday and
Company Inc., used by permission of the publishers; extracts from Seamus
Heaney's *Death of A Naturalist, North, Door into the Dark* and *Wintering Out*
are published and copyright Faber & Faber Ltd. Reproduced with
permission. All other quoted material is as credited in the text.

The portrait reproduced on the jacket is by David Hone PPRHA and
is used by kind permission of the Royal Hibernian Academy of Arts.

Cover design by Bill Bolger
Printed in the Republic of Ireland by Betaprint Ltd, Dublin

CONTENTS

ACKNOWLEDGEMENTS

I gratefully acknowledge my indebtedness to all who helped me in the production of this book: to Mrs Frances Doran, formerly of my office staff in Lisbreen, Belfast, and to Mrs Alice Warde, of my current staff in Ard Mhacha, Belfast, who so efficiently typed the material at various stages of its redaction, Mrs Warde also carefully checking the proofs; to the staff of Veritas Publications and particularly to Maura Hyland, Product Development Manager; to Fiona Biggs, Managing Editor, who so carefully prepared the material for publication and so patiently endured the repeated amendments, additions, insertions and breaches of deadlines involved; to Brian Lynch, Marketing Co-ordinator, who expeditiously handled all the arrangements for promotion and launching of the book; also to Ms Ann Hanley, Director of the Research and Development Unit of the Irish Episcopal Conference, for much assistance with statistics of religious practice; to Rev. R. F. S. Poots, Deputy Clerk of the General Assembly, for information regarding Presbyterian clergy born in Loughguile. The list of those who helped me in the checking of details relating to facts, dates, etc., is too long to be included here. To them all, I offer my very sincere thanks. Any errors which remain are strictly my own.

I dedicate this book to the memory of my parents:
Charles, who died in 1939,
Susan, who died in 1974.

PROLOGUE

This is not an autobiography; it is rather an assortment of somewhat random memoirs, not arranged in chronological order, compiled in odd moments snatched from busy schedules, with the obvious omissions, repetitions and imperfections which result. I have perhaps indulged myself in these recollections, especially in what concerns Loughguile; but everyone has his or her own 'Loughguile' somewhere and my memories of 'home' may strike a chord with others.

As someone who for twenty-two years of life taught philosophy, I may be forgiven for quoting from 'The Epistle to the Reader', which prefaces John Locke's 'Essay Concerning Human Understanding', for I find the words very appropriate to this book of mine. Locke writes:

> Some hasty and undigested thoughts ... gave the first entrance into this Discourse; which, having been thus begun by chance, was ... written by incoherent parcels; and after long intervals of neglect, resumed again, as my humour or occasion permitted.... This discontinued way of writing may have occasioned, besides others, two contrary faults, viz. that too little and too much may be said in it. The further I went the larger prospect I had; new discoveries led me still on, and so I grew insensible to the bulk it now appears in. I

will not deny, but possibly it might be reduced to a narrower compass than it is, and that some parts of it might be contracted, the way it has been writ in by catches, and many long intervals of interruption, being apt to cause some repetitions. But to confess the truth, I am now too lazy, or too busy, to make it shorter.

I should not, however, be presumptuous enough to say what Locke says:

> If thou has but half so much pleasure in reading it as I had in writing it, thou wilt as little think thy money, as I do my pains, ill-bestowed.

I can, however, sincerely say:

> Mistake not this for a commendation of my work; nor conclude, because I was pleased with the doing of it, that therefore I am fondly taken with it now it is done.

For one thing, it is hard to be 'fondly taken' with writing which is constantly repeating the word 'I'. Egotism is so boring. But how else am 'I' to write about 'my' pilgrim journey? I can only try to be as 'objective' as a 'subject' can be.

Another philosopher, one of our own time, Jean-Paul Sartre, once said that a writer is in bad faith who claims that, if he had taken longer time, he would have written a better book. 'A writer', Sartre says, 'is as good as his book, no more, no less.' With that rather chilling thought, I now launch this book.

In June 1991, I celebrated the golden jubilee of my ordination as a priest, which occurred on 22 June 1941. In July 1992, I celebrated the silver jubilee of my ordination as bishop, which occurred on 16 July 1967. These celebrations prompted me to recall some of the steps along the road of a pilgrim journey which has brought me, after thirty-one years of episcopate, to three different dioceses as bishop; three arrivals, three leavetakings. To aid my recall, I reread the text of homilies preached and addresses given on these various occasions. These texts served for me as an exercise in personal examination of conscience on the responsibilities of the episcopal ministry and on my own shortcomings in the actual living out in practice of the aims and ideals I had verbally expressed on the occasion of my arrival in and departure from each of these dioceses.

Jubilees are times of memories, and I found myself recalling earlier parts of my life's story which were for me occasions of grace and growth and reasons for thanksgiving, and often reasons for salutary sorrow and repentance. On reliving these periods and re-reading these texts, I also came to feel that the recollections and the texts had perhaps sufficient unity to be offered to a wider public as possible themes for reflection on the pastoral ministry of a priest and bishop in the post-conciliar world and in an Irish Church of rich promise and great opportunities, but also of very grave problems, an Ireland of rapid social change and new uncertainties, of deep-seated inequalities and injustices, and, in the North, of what has long seemed intractable conflict and violence, and yet an Ireland of immense spiritual resources and of earnest searching for deeper and more authentically lived faith and prayer, justice and peace.

In Part One of this book I have put together some memories of and reflections on my experience as a boy in Loughguile, a student in St Malachy's College and Queen's University, and later in Maynooth and still later in Paris, then as a young priest and (relatively) young bishop, together with memories of subsequent life and experience as bishop.

In Part Two, I bring together texts relating to my episcopal appointment to and departure from Ardagh and Clonmacnois, and then Down and Connor, my appointment to Armagh and my appointment as Cardinal, and finally my retirement and departure from Armagh. In the concluding chapter, which I call 'A Future Full of Hope', I permit myself some thought about future directions for the Church in Ireland.

Experience of fifty-seven years of priesthood and thirty-one years as bishop in three dioceses convinces me that, despite all appearances to the contrary, we are living through a 'second spring' of the Church in Ireland. I develop this thought more extensively in various parts of the text.

Personally, despite my own failures and disappointments and setbacks along life's pilgrim route, I have always drawn strength and hope from the conviction of having been called to the priesthood by God; a call objectively authenticated, firstly by the sacrament of priestly and later of episcopal Holy Orders and, secondly, by the call of our Holy Father, the Pope, to pastoral care as bishop of three successive dioceses. I have also constantly taken courage from a number of scriptural passages, particularly from St Paul.

The first is the passage from the Second Letter to Timothy, from which my former Professor of Theology and my predecessor as Bishop of Down and Connor, Bishop William Philbin, took his episcopal motto, *Scio cui credidi:*

> I have not lost confidence, because I know who it is that I have put my trust in, and I have no doubt at all that he is able to take care of all that I have entrusted to him until that day (1:12).

The second is from the Letter to the Romans:

> May the God of hope bring you such joy and peace in your faith that the power of the Holy Spirit will remove all bounds to hope (15:13).

The third is from the Letter to the Ephesians:

> Glory be to him whose power, working in us, can do infinitely more than we can ask or imagine, glory be to him from generation to generation, in the Church and in Christ Jesus, for ever and ever (3:20-21).

The fourth is from the Letter to the Colossians:

> The mystery is Christ among you, your hope of glory; this is
> the Christ we proclaim, this is the wisdom in which we
> thoroughly train everyone and instruct everyone, to make
> them all perfect in Christ. It is for this that I struggle wearily
> on, helped only by his power, driving me on irresistibly.
> (1:28-29)

The fifth is the passage from the author of the Letter to the Hebrews
from which I selected my own episcopal motto, *Jesus Christus, heri
et hodie:*

> [Let us] keep running steadily in the race we have started
> ...Let us not lose sight of Jesus, who leads us in our faith and
> brings it to perfection... Jesus Christ is the same today as he
> was yesterday and as he will be forever. (12:1-1; 13:8)

Finally, the sixth is St Paul's farewell address to the presbyters of the
Church at Ephesus, near the end of his apostolic journeying. It is a
passage which is cited more than once in the text that follows. It
has been a constant inspiration to me in my life; I pray that it may
be a strength and not a reproach to me at my death:

> Life to me is not a thing to waste words on, provided that,
> when I finish my race, I shall have carried out the mission
> the Lord Jesus gave me – and that was to bear witness to the
> Good News of God's grace. (Ac 20:24)

PART ONE

THE ROAD WHICH HAS BROUGHT ME HERE

Let us go forward on the road which has brought us
to where we are.

Philippians 3:16

CHAPTER ONE

COUNTRY BOY IN LOUGHGUILE

On 22 June 1991, I celebrated fifty years of priesthood. Earlier, on 11 June 1991, I joined twenty-six of my fellow golden jubilarians in a concelebrated Mass of thanksgiving in the College Chapel in St Patrick's College, Maynooth, where we had all been ordained to the priesthood on 22 June 1941.

For all of us who were celebrating that Mass together it was a day of memories. Each priest had his own particular memories of home, of boyhood and of seminary life in Maynooth, of ordination day and of his life as a priest. If I recall my own memories on that day and record some of them here, together with the memories which they in turn subsequently recalled, this is because it is good to remember and because some of my recollections may strike chords of memory in the minds of others too, or at least record for a later generation scenes from a rural culture now almost disappeared.

Earliest memories
I was born on 1 October 1917. My earliest memory is of being in my father's arms in my night attire, outside our house in Ballybradden, a townland of the parish of Loughguile, County Antrim, and pointing up at the fire on the roof and trying, in whatever words I then knew, to ask who lit the living-room fire up on the roof of the house. This event obviously and naturally made

a deep impression on the mind of a child. I was then aged about four and I have no clear memory of anything that happened from then until many years later.

The facts were that our house had been set on fire as a result of an 'operation' by the North Antrim IRA during the Irish 'Troubles' of 1916-22. It became known that the 'Auxiliary Police' had decided to move back into a disused barracks in Loughguile, presumably in response to rumours of IRA activity. The IRA promptly burnt down the barracks. A first attempt in 1920 was only partially successful; a second attempt, also in 1920, completed the destruction. The fire-scorched walls of the old barracks, like those of our house, remained standing for many years. The Auxiliaries then commandeered the vacant house which formed part of a double house, the other part of which my parents had rented as their first home after their marriage in 1912. The IRA retaliated by setting fire to our house, and so driving out the police who were quartered next door. For this to happen, our house had to be evacuated, and this was done summarily in the middle of (I think) a winter night in 1921. There were then four small children; John (aged 8), Nicholas (6), myself (4) and Margaret (2). Three more children were born subsequently: Sheila, Rosaleen and Patrick.

All my parents' wedding presents, all their first pieces of furniture and possessions, went up in flames. Only one article was salvaged by my mother – a gold necklace which my father had bought her as an engagement present. It remained among her most treasured possessions and it still survives. It must have cost my father many months, if not years, of savings out of his modest teacher's salary. He used to speak of his starting salary as a teacher of £80 a year.

Half a century after the event, when I was Bishop of Ardagh and Clonmacnois, I met a man called Walter Burke, who had taken part in the 'operation'. He came from County Galway, from a poor family. At the age of fifteen or sixteen he went to the 'hiring fair' in Ballinasloe and was hired by a Protestant farmer from Mallaboy, in the parish of Loughguile. As a young man he joined the IRA of that time and this was his first 'operation'. He claimed to have lifted me out of my cradle and carried me outside after ordering my parents to evacuate the house in great haste. He left Loughguile after the Anglo-Irish Treaty and never returned. I was amazed at his accurate memory of names and events after the long lapse of nearly sixty years.

I have very vague memories, coming from the mid-1920s, of the holding of a political rally in front of the old disused school in Loughguile, addressed by Mary McSwiney, sister of the famous Lord Mayor of Cork, with 'B-Specials' in the background, at whom the orator hurled fiery defiance.

Tales of 'the Troubles' of the 1920s were part of the folklore of my boyhood. Stories of the IRA and the 'Black and Tans' were accompanied by stories of the atrocities of the RIC, 'B-Specials' and loyalist gun gangs who were murdering innocent Catholics in the streets of Belfast during those same years. The murdered families of the McMahons and the Duffins, the 'Halfpenny triple murder' victims and many others, including Joseph Murray of Omerbane, shot in Corkey South as he returned from evening devotions in Loughguile 'Chapel' on a Sunday in 1921, were among the litany of names of victims killed in those times simply for being Catholics. Their names were recalled by Catholics; but sadly the names of Protestant victims of parallel killings were scarcely noticed. Doubtless the reverse happened in Protestant communities. Folk memories can be dangerously selective. The trails of bloodshed were interrupted for periods, then resumed in the mid-1930s, the 1940s and the late 1950s; they then became continuous from the end of the 1960s until 1994. To pray and work to end this recurring cycle of violence and misery was to be one of the main concerns of the Church and one of my own major preoccupations during all of my years as bishop.

At the same time, however, Catholics in Loughguile had excellent relationships with the Protestants, a small minority, who lived in their midst. 'Morrowing' (exchange of machinery and labour) at peak times of farming activity went on with them just as between Catholics. Around the Twelfth of July Protestants did seem to us to assume a more stern and 'door' (dour) look than at other times; but we felt that this was out of a sense of stern 'Protestant duty' rather than by choice! Several Protestant families had sons studying for the ministry as I was studying for the priesthood, and I formed friendships with many of these, friendships which were maintained throughout later life and were greatly cherished. They included Reverend William Hanna, Presbyterian, later Minister of Randalstown O.C., and then of Windsor, and Reverend Robert Hanna, Reformed Presbyterian, of Loves Corkey, who had also an uncle, Reverend Tom Hanna, a Reformed Presbyterian minister. William and Robert were no relatives of one another but were both neighbours of the Dalys when we lived in Ballybradden. There were also Reverend Professor Adam Loughridge, Reformed Presbyterian, of Friary, and Reverend James Hamilton of Tober. Reverend John Young, Presbyterian, later Minister of Belmont, was a son of Hugh Young, our 'breadman', of Ballymoney. He used to accompany his father on his weekly rounds to Loughguile and often called at our house in Tully. John was one year older than I and we compared notes of secondary school and theological college days and remained lifelong friends, particularly during the years of 'the Troubles'. Another well-known Loughguile clergyman was Reverend Samuel Hanna, also of Ballybradden, who was long-serving Reformed Presbyterian (or Covenanter) Minister in Berry Street, Belfast, who died in 1944. He had the unusual qualification of completing his medical studies and conducting a medical practice while still in active ministry. He was the uncle of Reverend William Hanna. At the time of my ordination, there were five living Catholic priests from the parish of Loughguile. Loughguile was manifestly a community of lively faith, both among its Catholic majority population and its Protestant minority.

Even then, the *Coleraine Chronicle* and the *Coleraine Constitution* were much more cross-community than was usual in those days and were read as avidly by Catholics as by Protestants, as indeed are their contemporary counterparts. There was no sectarian tradition in Loughguile or in North Antrim generally. A former IRA man whom I knew resigned from the movement in 1922 because, as he recalled, he was ordered by his organisation to be part of a unit assigned to kill a local Protestant businessman. The operation was fortunately not successful. It has been a source of great satisfaction to me that Loughguile and North Antrim never became involved in any significant degree in the recent Troubles.

Just as the first memories of my life are of armed conflict in Ireland, so the experiences of the last three decades of my life have been associated with renewed armed conflict. These memoirs of mine were written down at different times and in odd moments over the last five years and in no particular order. Such order as they have was imposed later. It brings me great happiness to record that the present lines are being written in the first week of May 1998, after the signing of the Good Friday Agreement. If the necessary restraint and responsibility are exercised by all concerned and if the Agreement is allowed to operate in all its aspects, then, by God's grace, we could be close to the formal ending of the longest campaign of insurgency in our island history, but could also be at the beginning of the healing of one of Europe's longest-lasting and most bitter conflicts – that between Ireland and Britain and between Irish and British traditions in Ireland itself. For this we hope. For this we pray.

After the burning of their home the Daly family received temporary accommodation in my grandparents' home in Glenbush. I remember its open hearth with the 'pit' for ashes in front and overhead the soot-covered and smoke-blackened crane, on which hung the chains and hooks for cooking pots and for the 'griddle' on which my grandmother baked her soda farls and her special delicacy, oaten cakes. A dish which we children ate more out of duty, because she insisted it was 'good for us', than by choice, was a bowl of 'sowans'. This was made from the seeds left over after the corn had been ground at the mill into oatmeal. The seeds were steeped in water, then strained, and finally cooked into a kind of porridge. This was guaranteed to give protection against the ills and chills of winter. The chirruping of crickets around the open hearth was a special excitement, and on cold evenings the seat nearest the fire, called the 'hob', was much coveted.

My grandmother, Maggie, was tall and straight and stately in her long black dress, which was regulation dress then for older ladies.

Over it was a working apron on ordinary days and a black silk apron for Sundays and for visitors. She was a woman of immense charity for the poor. She was what in many areas was called 'the handy woman' for the whole neighbourhood, that is, the untrained but experienced midwife who delivered most of the babies in the homes of Glenbush, and always kept a supply of linens and baby clothes for poor families. All deliveries of babies were at home in those days, medical help being called only in emergencies; in those days of crude obstetric instruments and before anaesthetics, medically assisted deliveries were dreaded. On her hurried way on foot to the expectant mother, my grandmother prayed for a safe delivery, and the prayer continued for the mother-to-be and the baby during the labour. In later life my mother sometimes spoke of the agonising experience of her own first childbirth. Clumsy use of forceps by the local doctor (a good man but not particularly sensitive to patient pain) left, she told me, permanent scars and recurrent memories of the pain. In later years, she sometimes also shyly recalled for me the distinct memory she had of the morning when I was born.

From Glenbush the Daly family then moved to a farmhouse in Tully, which, with a small farm, had passed into my father's possession. It is with this house that my next childhood memories are associated. Both grandparents used to come to our house in Tully each First Friday weekend in the month for monthly confession and communion. My grandfather's best suit with frock coat and my grandmother's best black silk dress were carefully kept in moth-balls for these occasions. My grandfather would carefully 'walk the fields' on the Saturday afternoon to see how his son's (my uncle's) crops were faring and doubtless to deplore the decline in standards of farming since his own day!

My memories include a visit by my father's youngest sister, Beasie (Brigid) Jane, from my father's home in Keadue, County Roscommon. In her honour, a kitchen dance was organised and brought a packed house. My father sang and danced that night, as he rarely did afterwards. He had a lovely tenor voice and his songs were all of Roscommon and the West.

It was also here at the age of eight or nine that I spent several months in bed with pneumonia. This pulmonary weakness was to recur in the form of tubercular pleurisy at the end of my first postgraduate year in Maynooth, entailing several months of rest, and it recurred again in the form of TB a couple of times in the 1950s and the early 1960s, brought on each time, I have to confess, by overwork. Eventually, in 1963, I was advised to have surgery to remove the infected lobe of my lung. I was still convalescing from this when the Second Session of the Second Vatican Council opened in September 1963. Because of these illnesses and because of my father's death at the rather early age of sixty, I myself never expected to be a long liver. It was while in my bed with pneumonia in 1926 that I said goodbye to my Uncle John, leaving on his long journey to New Zealand, at a period of world economic depression leading to wholesale emigration from North Antrim and indeed from all the Northern counties, comparable to what was happening in the West of Ireland until quite recently. That uncle seems to have talked, sung and dreamt of Loughguile during the whole quarter century he spent in New Zealand. He used to have his boots made in Loughguile and mailed out to him; in his eyes, nowhere in New Zealand were there to be found boots to compare with those made by John Watt of Corkey North. John's son, Laurence, still carries on the craft, handed down in the Watt family in Corkey North for more than eighty years. Farmers' boots in Loughguile in those days were made for rough roads; they were hob-nailed or reinforced by sparables on the leather soles and iron protectors on the toes. They were laced with leather thongs or 'whangs'. Later these boots were replaced by the all-purpose (and unisex) 'wellington boots'. My uncle returned to Loughguile in the 1950s and died there, in what he often sung of as his 'lovely home in sweet Loughguile'.

Another of a long line of local craftsmen was a tailor, Johnny Dowds of Corkey. He used to 'measure' for his suits in the Chapel precincts on Sunday, and 'fitting-on' was done in the disused stables on the ground floor of the old school. His suits of worsted cloth had narrow trousers, reinforced around the bottom hems with extra strong thread for good wear. I remember seeing him reclining on his wooden sofa at the narrow window of his neat little house, busy with the scissors and needles of his trade, his tongue as occupied with 'craic' as his fingers were with needles.

In our first house in Tully we had as next-door neighbour a celebrated Loughguile wit called Daengel (Daniel) McIlhone. He constantly but good-humouredly grumbled and scolded about the misdemeanours of the young Daly 'spoiled brats' and their destructive and wasteful ways. Listening to him considerably enlarged the expletive vocabulary of some of the young Dalys – to the amusement of our curate, Father Bob Rogan, and to the deep embarrassment and chagrin of our parents.

Many tales of Daniel's ready wit are still told in Loughguile. Once, during a parish mission, there were two 'missionaries' and, as folk memory often had it in reference to old-style parish missions, one was a 'hard' preacher and confessor and the other a 'soft' one. Daniel came for confession and enquired at the chapel gate as to which of the two was the 'easygoing' one. The 'experts' directed him to the 'hard' one and eagerly awaited the result. After a considerable time, Daniel emerged and was asked how he got on. Daniel replied, 'I'll warr'nt you (warrant you) this; thon man will hear the cuckoo a quare wheen o' times before he hears me again!' 'Hearing' was a common name for confession; 'Is he still hearing?' meant, 'Is the priest still hearing confessions or has he finished?'

A brother of Daniel's, Charlie, was one of the very few of his generation who had some formal schooling and who bought and read books. He had worked as book-keeper in a shop in Ballymoney. He left behind some books which became part of my early reading, including one which fascinated me, a book about nature, plants and birds, illustrated with drawings, called *Goldsmith's Natural History*. My first exposure to literature came through this and through another of Charlie's books abandoned as useless at his death. It was called *The Cabinet of Irish Literature,* edited by Charles A. Read and published in New York in 1903.

After Charlie died, Daniel, finding no one left of comparable good sense to talk to, used to go every day and sit on his grave in the cemetery and retail to Charlie in vivid terms the gossip and scandals of the parish. The one-sided conversation was conducted in a loud voice (because Charlie was deaf!); and Daniel was never aware of the living audience he sometimes attracted, one hidden here and one there behind neighbouring tombstones, themselves anxious to 'listen in' to the local gossip. Daniel himself died some years after Charlie, being, in his own words, 'in the nick o' ninety'.

I remember Daniel's wake, with his kitchen full of people for all of two days and two nights. As a small boy of perhaps ten, I passed round the large plate stacked with tobacco for the pipe smokers to help themselves to a good 'fill', while some grown-ups passed round the whiskey ('port wine' was usually served to the ladies, who invariably sat with the corpse or in another room). The proceedings were not always wrapt in mourning! The repertory of Daniel's quips passed around on those nights was unending. Then and from other occasions I recall the 'pipe of hospitality', when the pipe, once it was well lighted, would be passed from one man to the other for a few good 'pulls'. There were no qualms or hesitations about hygiene, much less about passive smoking! Indeed, it was impolite to decline a 'draw' on the pipe, and the smoker would commend the quality of the tobacco. As children, we sometimes dug up in the garden a cache of white clay pipes, discarded after some funeral of earlier times. Sometimes we found among them pipes decorated with the emblem of the harp.

We later moved to another house in the same row in Tully and this remained our home until the family moved to Belfast in the late 1940s, following my appointment to Queen's University. Belfast, however, never became 'home' for us, in the sense in which Loughguile was and still is. To this day, 'going home' for me still means home to Loughguile.

Boyhood in Loughguile

Boyhood in the country brought one very close to nature and its seasons and rhythms, its colours, scents and moods. Memories come back to me still of nature's endless variety. We experienced it on our own or our uncles' farms: the smell of clay upturned in neat furrows by horses and plough; the rhythm of the fiddle-like appliance with which a man sowed seed for grass or corn, recalling Our Lord's parable of the sower; the bitter cold of October potato-digging time, when the 'gatherers', including ourselves as children, jumped up and down and clapped hands to restore circulation to freezing limbs, for, as Seamus Heaney remembers, 'fingers go dead in the cold' (*Death of a Naturalist*, 'At a potato digging'). I still recall the experience on frosty mornings of digging through the protective clay cover of a potato pit, to bring home a bucket of potatoes. It was the women's job to cut the seed potatoes. I remember seeing women, much as Heaney remembers them, sitting 'under the hedge in a half circle', their 'sharp knife.../ lazily halving each root that falls apart/ in the palm of the hand', while animated conversation continued uninterrupted (*North*, 'The seed cutters').

There were more pleasant scenes and scents in warmer seasons, like those of new-mown hay, as one raked it into heaps to form 'laps' or 'huts', trying not to seem a cissy by complaining about blisters formed on hands more used in student days to wielding pens than rakes or forks; or the delightful feeling on a balmy September evening, when the year's last 'stook' of corn had been 'stacked' and we lay exhausted on the ground and watched the harvest moon rise majestically in the sky.

An exciting experience was that of twisting 'ropes' of hay with an appliance which wound the dry hay into quite a strong rope, as long as was needed, the length extending as far as the winder walked backwards from the clump of hay, working the appliance in his hands as he walked. The rope was used to tie down the 'rucks' of hay in the field. In due time they would be hauled in a sled or 'slipe', a horse-drawn vehicle with a tip-up fitting and a pulley and rope to pull up and tie down the 'ruck' and draw it into the hay yard to be built into a haystack for winter feeding of cattle and horses.

Tractors began to displace horses in the 1950s. Sometimes they were used for passenger journeys, particularly for bringing people to Mass. This was illegal but no one was ever brought to court. Soon horses in the fields became as rare as the once familiar corncrake, another victim of mechanised and technologised farming. Seamus Heaney's very first published poem, which appeared in the *Belfast Telegraph* in 1962, was called 'Tractors', and it deplored 'their melancholy spouts that never have been broken in' (unlike the horses that preceded them).

The arrival of 'thrashing' day each year was awaited with a mixture of fear and excitement. The mighty steam-engined threshing machine puffed and snorted and cranked its way up the lane and through the gate into the field where the stacks of corn stood. The sheaths were forked into its maw and then the corn spilled out into waiting bags, while the battered chaff piled out of a larger aperture. As the stack became lowered towards the ground, one waited excitedly but fearfully for the fleeing rats or for the sight of baby rats, rudely expelled from their cosy nest. There was pity for the terrified baby rats; one thought of Robbie Burns' poem 'To a Mouse': 'Wee, sleekit, cowrin', tim'rous beastie/ O what a panic's in thy breastie.' The threshing gathered a large army of helping neighbours, and there were drinks and celebration at the end, as winter food for 'man and beast' was now secure. The 'morrowers' would reassemble tomorrow at the next neighbouring farm, until the threshing in the townland was completed for the year. The threshing machine replaced water-mills used earlier; a decaying large black wooden wheel, once driven round by water, still survived on a neighbour's farm in my boyhood, and was all the more attractive because we were strictly forbidden to go near it.

For dinner, everyone sat round the big deal kitchen table, free of table cover but frequently washed and clean; a mound of potatoes was piled in the centre and a plate with knife, fork, mug and spoon was set in front of each diner. Copious helpings of cabbage and bacon (often home-cured), with ample butter and mugs of buttermilk, made man-sized meals. The meal might end with tea, sometimes cooled by being fanned with one's cap or else poured into a saucer and back into the mug several times. Sugar was stirred and stirred and stirred again, lest any be wasted.

One of my early recollections is of my Uncle Pat doing his own threshing on his barn floor with a flail, a home-made instrument composed of a long pole and a shorter stick attached to it with a leather thong. With this, he pounded the sheaths and separated the corn from the chaff; and my uncle was no slouch as a 'thrasher', spitting on his hands from time to time as he flailed away mightily. The method had not changed since the time of 'Matt the Thrasher'. Indeed, it had not basically changed since Araunah the Jebusite did his threshing on the threshing-floor on which King David erected an altar, as described in the Second Book of Samuel (24:16). Recalling my uncle's exertions now, I can discern what a pummelling and buffeting the Lord foretold for Peter and his successors when he said that Satan would have his way and would 'sift' Peter 'as a farmer separates the wheat from the chaff'.

One of the more unpleasant experiences on the farm was of gathering lint (flax), which had none of the glamour or fragrance of new-mown hay or corn. It was also hard on the hands. A school principal in those days was expected, in addition to 'marking the roll', to keep a record of absentees, noting the reason given for absence. Necessary farm work was benignly regarded as a legitimate excuse for absence from school, even though the school attendance officer, who visited the school regularly, used to repeat on each visit the ritual phrase, which we all knew by heart, that next time he would accept no excuse, 'good, bad or indifferent', for absenteeism. I was recorded as absent several times for 'pulling flax'. I suspect there may have been some economy with the truth in the excuse. The 'retting' or rotting of the flax in an artificial 'dam', the lifting out of the rotted flax from the foul-smelling dam by men standing up to their waists in putrid water, with rough meal-bag aprons on top of their clothing, the spreading and drying of the 'lint', must have been among the most unpleasant of drudgeries of farming life in those days. A flax mill was still in operation in Corkey in my youth, and closed down finally only in 1957.

Then there were the annual weeks of turf-cutting in 'the moss'. The turf-cutter, with many a spit on the hand in the process, first cutting away the top layer of 'scraw' with a special spade (sometimes called a 'flaughtering' spade) and then slicing through the wet peat with another type of angled spade, and throwing the cut 'peats' up on the bank where we waited with graip in hand to

load them on to our wheel-barrow. I remember the wheeling of the
wet peat, the spreading them to dry, later the 'footing' and
'clamping' which were part of the drying process; and finally the
loading on to carts for the rocky transport on pot-holed bog tracks
home to the turf shed. Time on the bog was measured for young
boys by hunger and homesickness, not by watches. 'Champ'
(mashed and creamed potato, mixed with scallions, and generously
dosed with butter) was brought along in lieu of dinner; but 'the
moss' was a hungry and a lonely place, and to children the hours
seemed like days. I recall one summer day when my brothers and
I toiled all through the long day, had our 'champ' and resumed
working for 'hours' more until we were convinced that it was near
nightfall, and then trudged wearily home for supper, only to find it
was not long after mid-day.

I can still see 'Wee Paddy' McCluskey, our occasional turf-cutter,

> nicking and slicing neatly, heaving sods
> over his shoulder, going down and down
> for the good turf. Digging.

I can still hear what Seamus Heaney calls 'the squelch and slop/of
soggy peat' as the wet peats landed on the bank above (*Death of a
Naturalist*, 'Digging').

Of memories such as these are many of Seamus Heaney's finest
poems 'dug'. Between his finger and his thumb 'the squat pen rests'.
He digs with it, as he immortalises his Mossbawn, where

> the ground itself is kind, black butter
> melting and opening underfoot.
> (*Door into the Dark*, 'Bogland')

Indeed my Loughguile in many ways resembles Seamus
Heaney's Mossbawn, and no one recalls for me its 'feel' and sights
and sounds and tastes as vividly as Heaney does. The preservative
properties of wet peat, so memorably explored by Heaney in
'North', were well known in generations before ours. We once

found, deep below the bog's surface, a firkin of butter which, down the ages, had turned solid as stone. Evidently placed there for preservation, it had been forgotten by its owner, and solidified as the bog water drained away, through time and turf-cutting.

Childhood was marked by the daily trip to the 'spring well' for buckets of drinking water; I recall the climb over the 'stile', the bolder ones among us lying down to 'lap' the water, in terror of falling into what to us children seemed its bottomless depths. A familiar 'dare' for the young water-carriers was to see who could spin round fastest with a bucket of water (or, for the greatly daring, two buckets), without spilling a drop. Like Heaney, we found that two buckets were easier to carry than one; they balanced one another. It took Heaney's poetic genius to see in this an analogy with the North's two traditions and the need to give equal weight to both (cf. 'Terminus', *The Haw Lantern*).

Great was the disillusionment when I visited the well again long years afterwards and found that it was only a little shallow pool, with a trickle of water from a mountain stream; but its taste was as fresh and as pure as of old. There was a thorn-tree in a field near the 'well-field', and we children stayed well clear of it for fear of disturbing the fairies who might be dancing unseen around it. These 'fairy trees' stand in many fields, and no farmer ever dared to cut them down, but carefully ploughed around them, leaving the trees untouched.

A little stream (we called it 'the burn') ran past our house. Such streams in part determined the siting of houses in country areas that had no piped water. To us as small children it seemed a great river. We sometimes gave toy boats their maiden voyage on its waters. In front of the house the stream was covered over. A deed of 'derring-do' for older boys was to crawl under the long bridge, braving the terrors of the deep before emerging as heroes on the other side – an exploit never attempted by the faint-hearted. At a point near the front door, a man-made mini-waterfall had been created to facilitate the filling of buckets with water for washing; for small children it had some of the wonders of the Niagara Falls. Below the house was a meadow where we played hurling and football.

My sister Margaret had a sweet soprano voice. She sometimes sang a sentimental ballad about 'The Old House' revisited in memory:

Here's where the children played games on the heather ...

Here's where we sailed our wee boats on the burn ...

Gone is the old house, the place stands deserted, ...
Gone are the old folks, the children are scattered,
'Tis time I was leaving, 'tis time I passed on.

Sentimental at all times, the words took on a new poignancy at Margaret's early death.

Then there was the familiarity with animals and their ways. Most of our small farm was let to the uncles; but we kept the 'grazing of a cow' for our own use. The annual calving was an exciting event, and watching the new-born calf struggle to stand up on its spindly legs was an object of fascinated wonder. No less wondrous was the art of coaxing the calf to drink the 'beestins' (the first milkings of the newly-calved mother cow) out of a bucket without letting the calf, wild with excitement and hunger, spill the lot. At the end of the season the calf was ready for sale. A certain crafty professional cattle-dealer would usually call, riding bareback on his pony. After a first parley with my mother about a price, he would give up in disgust and with a flourish charge down the lane on his pony like a Wild West cowboy riding angrily out of town. Soon, however, he would return, saying he came back because he genuinely 'felt bad' about letting my mother miss the chance of a 'great offer', which was in truth far too high, given the 'hard times that were in it', and which was offered really because the seller was a lady. Bargaining would begin again. The exercise of riding off in dudgeon and returning might be repeated several times before the deal was finally struck, the price paid in cash and the calf collected. Once my mother proudly told of how she had got nine pounds into her hand for a nine-month-old calf.

I never had personal experience of attending a market fair in Ballymoney or Ballymena, our nearest towns, where they were held on fixed days of each month. But I heard graphic descriptions of the ritualised and choreographed drama of the 'dealing' process. This process prevailed virtually all over Ireland and has parallels, particularly in Middle Eastern markets, to this day. The dealer and the seller respectively would propose, and angrily reject, an offer and then walk away in disgust. A 'middleman' in the crowd would bring them together again and swap offer after offer in view of reaching agreement between two 'decent men'. Meanwhile, a knot of bystanders would play the part of a Greek chorus, shouting words of encouragement and reproof to dealer and seller respectively. The 'middleman' would eventually urge them to 'split the differ'. He would at a certain point clasp the hands of both disputants and clap them together, crying 'It's a deal'. There still remained the question of the indispensable 'luck penny'. Once this was settled the beast was marked as sold and the drama ended with the principal actors and the middleman and the chorus of bystanders repairing to the pub to celebrate. I recall my aunt remarking about my uncle who sold a mare at a horse fair in Ballymena, that he had come home from the fair 'with £20 and the full of himself'.

'Trard Lane' ('Trard' being probably a corruption of 'Tullyard' or 'High Tully') passed by a farmhouse occupied by a family called 'the McAleeses of Trard', to distinguish them from several other McAleese families. The house had a large yard, over part of which a flock of geese, presided over by a proud and jealous gander, exercised proprietorial rights. Once, as a small boy, I had to carry a hen from Glenbush to Tully past this house, the hen enclosed in a bag with a hole for the bird's head to protrude. As I skirted the yard, the gander swooped towards me, wings flapping and long neck extended, screeching furiously. The hen was terrified and tried wildly to escape. I was still more terrified and ran for dear life all the way home. This kind of experience is, of course, the origin of the Irish phrase, 'I'll leave you past the gander'.

The phrase recalls the hospitality ritual followed universally in

Loughguile at that time. When a visitor called and was profusely (and genuinely) welcomed, he or she would at a given time make signs of leaving, but would be told 'You're time enough; sure it's early yet'. When at length the visitor was moving towards the door, be-coated and be-hatted as occasion required, the conversation was continued standing, and further continued at the door. Then when he or she eventually did leave, a member of the family 'convoyed' the visitor part of the way home. Even then, farewells were continued at the parting point. All these gestures were meant to symbolise the household's welcome for the visitor and reluctance to see him or her depart. When later the family acquired a car, the ritual was observed by my mother asking my younger brother, Patrick, to drive the visitor home. In boyhood in Tully, it was often my task to 'convoy' the visitor 'past the turn in the lane'. It was, of course, unheard of that a visitor be allowed to leave a house without at least a cup of tea 'in your haun' (hand), or occasionally 'something stronger', 'port wine' being offered to ladies.

Later, when, as a young priest, I visited the homes of the parish on my bicycle, I was given a special seat by the open hearth, newly dusted for me, while immediately preparations were set in train for a meal. This consisted usually of tea, with fresh soda farls and two boiled eggs, crowned by fruit cake. The meal was served in 'the room', namely the parlour, which was used only on special occasions. The table was covered with the best spotless linen and the willow-pattern tableware was similarly preserved for special visitors. I was left to eat alone, with only occasional visits from the hosts to make sure that the tea was still hot and that there was still plenty to eat.

Bringing, or helping to bring, the cow from our byre up Trard Lane to the bull was an unremarkable event for a country boy. Like Seamus Heaney, I remember, though it takes Heaney's genius to find the right words for it, how from a safe distance, as the bull emerged clumsily from its shed,

> I watched the business-like conception
> The door, unbolted, whacked back against the wall

> The illegal sire fumbled from its stall
> Unhurried as an old steam engine shunting…
> Just the unfussy ease of a good tradesman;
> He slammed life home, impassive as a tank.
> ('The Outlaw', *Door into the Dark*)

Holding the cow's tail as my mother milked the cow was not a popular chore, nor was sweeping out the sewage of the byre into the nearby 'midden', which was separated from the byre by the cobble-stoned 'street' or 'cassey' (causeway) which fronted the out-offices of the farm. Churning milk to make butter was mostly fun, unless it went on too long, and then it was wearisome; for as Heaney recalls, 'arms ached / hands blistered. Cheeks and clothes were spattered / with flabby milk' (*Death of a Naturalist,* 'Churning Day'). Our neighbour, the above-mentioned Daniel McIlhone, would look in from time to time to see how the churning was progressing. Once, when the exercise went on and on with no butter surfacing, he was heard to mutter, 'How in hell can they hae' butter when the weans ('wee yins' or 'small ones') drink a' the crame?'

After the churning followed the next stage of the butter-making, when the 'gold flecks' were gathered into a wooden butter-bowl and my mother produced little corrugated butter-spades with which she shaped the butter with the pat and slap of the small spades, turning it into slabs by means of a round instrument which made the imprint of a swan on the slab; or, for stylish occasions, she made little round pats, ready for table use. Shop butter or 'creamery butter' when it first became available seemed insipid compared with the home-made variety; although the heavily salted butter served in some houses was dreaded by us children. Visits with my mother to the houses of her friends were also sometimes feared, because of the form which special delicacies occasionally took. One old lady in particular could think of no greater treat to offer each of her visitors than a large duck egg, very lightly boiled. I was and am in dread of any lightly boiled egg, but a large duck egg caused greater revulsion. In spite of the nausea, I had to eat it, so as not to let her and my mother down. I remember once being offered and enjoying what the folklorist Michael J. Murphy describes as a treat offered to a child in County Tyrone in the 1940s, 'a lick of a damp spoon dipped in sugar'. No child, says Murphy, however often it came, was ever allowed out of a house in that region without that delicacy, or failing that, a biscuit or a sweet. Murphy says the custom came from fairy beliefs.

Thatched houses were becoming rare in the Loughguile of my boyhood, but the thatcher's craft had not died out. I remember watching a thatcher at work on the roof of Mrs Currie's house, not far from our own. The sheaves of straw and bundles of 'sally rods' had been delivered in readiness for his coming. He brought with him on his bicycle his light roof ladder and his sharp knives. The knives were for trimming the sheaves and cutting the rods to the length required to pin down the sheaves and hold them firmly in place against the wind. The art lay in the even spread of the thatch along the roof, the tidiness of the coping at the top, the neatness of the eaves projecting over the walls. The fresh thatch gave the house a mellow golden finish, which Heaney beautifully calls the thatcher's 'Midas touch' ('Thatcher', *Door into the Dark*).

I have a distant memory of a house with a floor of hard-packed clay, the 'hearthstone' in front of the open fire being the only stone in the floor, a pit dug in the floor and closed with a grated cover in front of the fire for ashes. In one corner of the living-room was the settle-bed, with a white curtain in front. In another corner was the piled-up turf. Against a wall was the standard dresser with delft, the larger plates, decorated in willow-pattern, kept for display at the bottom and the plainer items for daily use at the top. Above the settle-bed was the half-loft under the thatch, with other beds for the children. It was a direct descendent of the earlier mud-cabins of the Famine era. The mattresses in my boyhood were still often stuffed with goose feathers. Quilt-making from squares of many-coloured stuff was a cultivated home craft and a matter of competition between the mistresses of the craft. Crochet work of a highly skilled quality was done in some homes, the craft passed on from mother to daughter. A beautiful alb was chocheted by a dear old lady, 'Ma' Kane, herself the mother of a priest, for my first Mass.

The open hearths and their attendant fittings were aesthetically pleasing, if perhaps cumbrous in use. They did involve much heavy toil for the women of the house. They began in my boyhood to be replaced by the range, one of the first signs of modernity in the traditional rural living-room. This was a more efficient form of heating and of cooking, but, in contrast to the open hearth, it was distinctly unaesthetic and unhomely. We did not gather round it in quite the same way was round an open fire. There was no hob on which to sit for privileged nearness to the heat. There was warmth and the luxury of hot water on tap; but unlike the open hearth, the range gave no warm heart to a room. There was heat but no longer any chirruping crickets.

The range in the house and the tractor in the fields were perhaps the first steps towards the virtual disappearance of a form of rural culture which had persisted through centuries. Indoor toilets and bathrooms were non-existent in rural houses in my time and up to when I began living in Belfast in the 1940s. We never had such a facility in Tully nor, of course, had we electricity. The only toilet was a dry closet (called the 'wee house') hidden discreetly away behind the outhouses. The little houses of the mill-workers in Belfast had only outside closets until the 1960s. The quality of housing all over Ireland is now happily transformed. The human being, however, shows remarkable capacity to retain the core of a culture, while shedding its outward ligaments. I believe that rural culture can preserve and has largely preserved many of its core values in spite of material changes. These values are still the stuff of literature and food for the soul, a God-loving, Christ-centred, lived and 'earthed' spirituality.

One of many childhood memories is of visits to the little shop, where a gentle old lady, Miss Annie McKillen, presided behind the counter. A pennyworth of 'black balls', 'liquorice allsorts' or 'conversation lozenges' was a large amount of delight for a child then. Greedy appetite was whetted as we watched Miss McKillen weigh a handful of sweets on her weighing machine, adding a couple of extra sweets for good measure, then deftly fold a piece of yesterday's newspaper into a cone-shaped packet or 'poke', and hand it over in exchange for the coin. Miss McKillen's shop doubled as post office. There was a brace of scales and a wide variety of weights, from square pounds for heavier goods to little round ounces and half-ounces for letters.

Another shop of more general character, presided over by Lizzie, sister of the postman, Paddy McGowan, had a more varied stock, both of goods and of 'craic'. I remember the cuts of dried fish (ling) suspended from the ceiling; this was staple food for many, supplemented by the 'Ulster fry', often of home-cured bacon and, at a later period, sausage. Lizzie was a woman of warm heart with an honest tongue; she 'told it as it was', or as she saw it. To a brother of mine, without a thought of giving offence, she said, 'Some people tell me you're all right; but someway I cannae lake (like) you.' Large meal-bags, flour-bags, onion boxes, a big container of paraffin oil (then in constant demand) and 'carbide' for carbide-fuelled bicycle lamps, provided a rare variety of scents and sights for childhood wonder.

The mail was collected at exactly the same time each evening by Robert Murray from Killagan, a genial and popular Protestant, who came by horse and side-car. Occasionally, a lift for one or other of us returning to college was arranged with him to Killagan railway station or to the 'broad line' at Kennedy's Corner for the bus to Belfast. The post was delivered daily by the postman, Paddy McGowan, on his bicycle. It was said that Paddy had difficulty reading addresses but knew who were likely to get letters and could accurately guess at the handwriting. He also undertook delivery of the two or three copies of the *Irish News* then reaching the parish. By arrangement, the copy was sometimes left under a stone to be collected. In my early boyhood, the recipient would sometimes read out the news for the neighbours who called in at night. Copies of the *Coleraine Chronicle* and the *Coleraine Constitution* were delivered by the bread van and were read from cover to cover, particularly the reports of court cases, then mostly to do with disputes about land, fences, stray cattle, etc!

One of the gruesome farmyard rituals was the annual slaughtering of pigs on my uncle's farm. By any standards it was a primitive and barbaric performance. The pigs were dragged by the ears, squealing pitifully, to the place of slaughter. The local butcher began by felling the pig on the forehead with a sledgehammer. Presumably, this was intended as some primitive way of trying to lesson the animal's pain. Sometimes the hammer missed and the squealing intensified. Then came the huge knives, specially sharpened for the occasion. The blood, the squeals of terror from the pigs, the evisceration which followed, added up to a horrible experience, even for a child who was kept at a distance from the gruesome scene. The pig was then washed in scalding water, shaved, ribs parted by wooden struts, and finally suspended from the kitchen ceiling, ready for transport to the market. Very early next morning, sometimes long before dawn, the uncle set off on horse and cart with his pig carcasses for the market in Ballymoney or Ballymena, to return only late the following night, sometimes, as the phrase had it, a little 'the worse for wear', having celebrated the deal in one or more pubs in town. One or two pigs were kept for salting and curing, to provide bacon and ham for the household, with portions given as special gifts to relatives and friends.

Servant boys, as hired farm-workers were called, sadly did not rate highly on the social or financial scale. They were hired by the half-year and paid a pittance, though 'keep' was provided, the quality of the food and the accommodation depending on the decency or meanness of the farmer. I can still see in my memory's eye one such, 'wintering out', in Seamus Heaney's words, 'the back-end of a bad year / swinging a hurricane-lamp / through some outhouse' in a farmyard where we used to visit, 'a jobber among shadows' (*Wintering Out*, 'Servant Boy').

It was still in considerable measure a subsistence economy, with most of the food needs being produced on the farm and cash being a feature in only a few transactions. It was a way of life in which it came naturally to thank God before and after meals for food which visibly came from his bounty and not from a supermarket, and in which it made immediate sense to offer to God at Mass the bread 'which earth had given and human hands had made'. There were annual farm 'paraliturgies', in which children delighted to participate, and which later they loved to conduct; notably, the blessing of the fields, outhouses and animals with Easter water on Easter Saturday; and, for some, the bringing of blessed salt to the animals. The origin of these rituals in the Paschal liturgy of the Easter Vigil was not clearly understood at the time, but they indicated the way in which liturgy could merge easily with daily life in that rural culture. Some rituals, which may well have had a pre-Christian origin but which had become 'inculturated' into the Christian year, included the eating of apples and nuts at Hallowe'en and the fires and hard-boiled eggs of Easter, coloured from being boiled in water to which had been added the blossoms of 'whins' (gorse).

We live now in a culture of the disposable. The culture of my childhood and boyhood was a culture of the reusable or recyclable. In a half century, we have gone from an economy of saving to an economy of waste and of debt. In my boyhood, there was shame and stigma attached to being in debt: the slogan was 'save for the rainy day'. Now, the economy at all levels presupposes borrowing and encourages going into debt: the slogan is: 'live now, pay later'. Furthermore, for all the contemporary talk about ecology, society at the time of my boyhood was much more environment-friendly and planet-conserving than is today's society. The words ecology and recycling had not yet been coined, but the realities were practised and taught in homes and families. 'Waste not, want not' was an overriding principle. Everything was saved for actual or possible re-use. Empty flour-sacks were washed and bleached to become work-aprons, dusters, bandages, poultices. Empty meal-bags became overalls for the rougher farm tasks like lifting rotten lint out of 'the dam', or for cleaning the out-houses. Corks were saved and stored to serve for unspecified future uses. Bottles were kept for carrying milk to school for lunches or to the fields for the farm-workers. Jars served as vases for flowers or for home-made jam or honey. Empty onion boxes were 'bespoke' from shops and served as bedside holdalls, or in my case as DIY bookcases. Old newspapers lined drawers, covered bedsprings under the mattress, served as insoles in boots and shoes when they were a size too big or when a sharp nail began to break through the sole of a well-worn shoe. Goosewings chased dust and ashes and cleared away cobwebs. Downy goose-feathers went into the making of feather-bed mattresses, quilts and cushions. Jerseys or 'ganseys' were knitted. Socks with holes in heels or toes were darned. Needles and thread or knitting needles and yarn were in constant use. The culture of the time could be expressed in the familiar jingle: 'use it up / wear it out / make it do / or do without'. Instinctively, people seemed to know that we lived in a finite world with limited resources and that we had to live within these limits. It is a lesson that people will increasingly be forced to learn again, but which contradicts many of the patterns of thinking and living which we have developed in the more affluent Northern hemisphere.

Traditional farming patterns, handed on from farming father to son, for unnumbered generations, also embodied sound ecological principles. There was a regular sequence of crops; and fields would, in their turn, be left fallow and be allowed to 'rest' for a year before being brought into crop production again. Instinctively, people close to the land knew that land has limits and should not and could not be pushed artificially beyond those limits. Agriculture has in our days become an industry, highly dependent on technology; but it is at its own and humankind's peril that agriculture fails in respect for God's 'good earth'.

Every house in my boyhood had a box or chest filled with assorted standard medicines for a variety of ailments. Iodine was the immediate response to cuts, with peroxide as back-up. Cascara pills and Epsom Salts or Glauber Salts or baking soda were at hand in case of indigestion. Castor's Little Liver Pills or Cod Liver Oil were sure to 'build you up' when feeling unwell, or, as Loughguile parlance had it, feeling 'donsy'. Sloan's Liniment was 'your only man' for arthritis or for when 'the ould pains were at you again'. 'Kali Water' and 'Tonic Wine' were by every sick bedside. Hot poultices were remedies for chest infections or for boils or 'beeling' fingers. As children saw it, the principle was, 'if it hurts and if it tastes bitter, it must be good for you'!

'Holy Wells' are found all over Ireland, usually named after the Blessed Virgin Mary or one of the Irish saints, and are frequently associated with 'cures' of various ailments. These were often the focus of pilgrimages or 'patterns'. Pins, coins or pieces of stuff were often left around the well. An object of curiosity in my boyhood was a well known as the 'Pin Well', in hill country above Drumkeel. Pins were still to be seen there, but no one remembered the history of the well or the origin of the custom.

The 'Pin Well' was just off the hill path (or 'pad') by which we used to walk to an aunt's house in Upper Glenbush. It took us up narrow lanes and steep hills, over stiles and through gaps (or 'slaps') between fields and turf banks, but was a shorter journey, as well as better fun, than going by road. One hazard, however, was the knowledge that badgers (or 'brocks') lurked in their lairs along some of these lanes and were dreaded by children as well as, presumably, by local fowl. A further subject of curiosity *en route* was the one reservoir we knew, a minuscule one from which water was piped to the parish priest's house, or 'the parochial house', as we called it. This was the only house in the parish to have running water or an indoor toilet, except perhaps the local doctor's. From the top of our climb we had sight of a glint of the sun on the waters of distant Lough Foyle, with Malin Head dimly outlined beyond.

In Drumkeel itself, above Tully, there was a Mass Rock, one of many in the parish, where Mass was said by hunted priests in the Penal Days. In the same townland there was still to be seen a rough stone carving of a human head and shoulders, which tradition called 'the pagan man', and which is reputed to have been a pre-Christian idol. Drumkeel had, before human memories, been a village, as the cluster of ruined wall-steads showed. Presumably the Famine had brought an end to habitation there. Ridges or 'rigs' were still visible in the hillside fields above Tully, as a sign of earlier cultivation for potatoes on land since given over to rushes and whins.

There was (and still is) a well-known clearing-house in Loughguile for news, views and pints; it is 'the Pound'. The name came from the old legislation requiring stray livestock or livestock seized by the bailiff for non-payment of rent to be 'impounded' until reclaimed. The reclaiming was effected by the owner's producing the broken-off part of the 'Tally Stick' in the possession of the 'Keeper of the Pound'. If the broken portion fitted the original and the prescribed fine or rent was paid, the owner could reclaim his impounded animals. Fairs were held in the Pound 'every quarter', where horses, cattle, pigs and linen yarn were sold and bought. These had ceased long before my time, as had the stabling for horses and ponies for Massgoers in the ground-floor part of the old school beside the Chapel. This school, built in 1841, had long been disused. It was of the upstairs/downstairs style, with outside stone steps to the upper floor. I found a couple of examples of this design in the diocese of Ardagh and Clonmacnois. There was a public house at the Pound, the only one for many miles around. It now has as an annexe an excellent restaurant.

In the Pound area was the old forge. I remember the boyish excitement of that forge, with what Seamus Heaney calls the 'unpredictable fantail of sparks' (*Door into the Dark*, 'The Forge') when the blacksmith, with his leather apron, predictably a McGowan, plied his bellows and hammered the red-hot iron horseshoe into shape on his anvil; the hissing steam which formed when he plunged the blazing iron into a tub of water to cool it, and then the acrid smell of a horse's hooves burning (I can still smell it seventy years later) as the hot new horseshoe was fitted and nailed in place. It was truly what Heaney calls 'a door into the dark', but a dark interior of great excitement and endless thrills for a small boy. The forge was a great communications centre, where parish news was exchanged, prices of animals discussed, Irish politics debated, and the world in general put to rights.

In a rural parish, the same family names frequently recurred and tradition required that Christian names be passed on from grandparents to grandchildren in a rather fixed pre-determined pattern, the first boy 'called after' the paternal grandfather, the first girl after the maternal grandmother, etc. This determined the naming of my brothers and sisters: John, then Nicholas; I was 'called after' my father and was christened Charles, but 'Cahal' was used because it was the Irish equivalent of Charles; then Margaret, 'called after' my maternal grandmother, etc. The tradition was, however, becoming less binding over the course of time. It was necessary to have ways of distinguishing people with the same name from one another. Hence we had 'Nellie's John' and 'Nellie's John's Paddy' etc. Nicknames, too, were common, some surviving from the Irish, like 'the Bochall'. My mother's name was Susan, but my father was constantly vexed by hearing her called 'Shusan' in the old Loughguile pronunciation. For this reason, my sister Rosaleen, baptised Susan Rose, was always called Rosaleen instead of Susan.

Family life was close and kinship was very important and extended to distant cousins. I remember ritual family visits on my grandfather's pony and trap exchanged on a two-way basis with cousins in Glenravel. Rarely were children born out of wedlock, but the few who were were brought up at home by the mother and grandmother and were treated at school and in society just like other children. A strict moral code was not in conflict with charity and tolerance.

Loughguile can broadly be called part of the Glens of Antrim; it is separated from the Glens by the moderately high range of hills called Trostan and Orra Mountain. Holidays from college and university brought the opportunity to explore by bicycle many of Nine Glen, as well as the famous North Antrim Coast Road from Glenarm to Portrush. We pushed our bicycles uphill past Omerbane and through Glenravel to the top of Glenariffe and then coasted easefully into Waterfoot; or else took the harder push up past Toor by what was then a pot-holed bog road (now a scenic route) to the top of Glenaan and Glendun, crossing, like John Hewitt, 'by lonely Orra round the Glen', and sometimes 'stopped with men at turf upon the moss' before descending without touching a pedal downhill into Cushendun. I know no better souvenir of those days than *The Day of the Corncrake*, with poems by John Hewitt and paintings by the great painter of the Glens, Charles McAuley (The Universities Press, Belfast, 1984).

Often my brothers and I, with our friend Archie McMullan (later Principal of St Joseph's High School, Crossmaglen), cycled to

Ballintoy, either by the inland road via Ballinlea or along the coast from Ballycastle, and then sometimes further round past Dunluce Castle, Dunseverick, Carrick-a-Rede, Portrush and Portstewart. Fishing off the rocks at Ballintoy was a special experience for me, even though I was as surprised as the fish was when once I made the only sea-fishing catch of my angling life. A good 'Ulster fry', with added fish, in McShane's hospitable house made the cold of an evening's fishing more than worthwhile. My brother Nicholas was the family's angling expert and possessed our only proper fishing rod. I never got beyond the homemade variety, but sometimes joined him fishing for trout, with worms as bait, up the mountain burns which flowed, and after rain, cascaded, down the slopes of Orra. Heavy rain following dry weeks left the trout greedy for the meanest worm and easy catch for even the dumbest of anglers, which I was. We were often drenched (we said 'drooked') by these rain showers, but this was all part of the fun, as well as pleasing the fish which escaped our hooks.

Primary school
Going to school in North Antrim was not dissimilar to going 'to school through the fields' in Alice Taylor's County Cork. In summer, most of the boys went barefoot. Sometimes it was out of necessity, boots being saved for winter and for Mass on Sundays. Often it was because this was the 'macho' thing to do. Some boys were proud to show off how they could kick stones with their bare feet, calloused from long exposure. Everybody walked to school, carrying their books and 'a piece', with maybe a bottle of milk, in a schoolbag. On wet or cold days, when children arrived at school in wet clothes or were cold, they were allowed to take turns at standing in a semicircle around the open turf fire in the school grate, toes just touching a line drawn in white chalk on the floor. In school, one had to talk 'polite' to the teacher; but in the playground one talked the local 'patois', which in North Antrim was close to Lowland Scots. The poems of 'Rabbie' Burns were immediately intelligible to a North Antrim child; and I used to love hearing my uncle, Pat Connelly, recite

them in the natural Loughguile dialect and accent, which doubtless would have been not too unlike the accent of their author 'Rabbie' himself.

I can still hear him recite faultlessly, as he remembered it from his schooldays, the long poem 'Tam O' Shanter', a fearsome tale of how Tam, 'weel mounted on his grey mare, Meg', but drunk, was pursued by 'auld Nick in shape of beast', with attendant warlocks and witches, and made a desperate dash to reach the bridge over a river, knowing the evil spirits could not cross water. His fate depended on reaching 'the key-stane o' the brig' before they seized him; otherwise, he well knew,

> Ah Tam, ah Tam, thou'll get thy fairin'
> In hell they'll roast thee like a herrin'.

I listened as a boy in delight and trepidation to this tale of a perilous brush with a fate worse than death. The language was pure Loughguile-speak as well as Lowlands Scots. It is now disappearing fast, more is the pity; for it is a rich tongue, once shared by 'Gael and Planter' all over the nine counties of Ulster. Reputedly this language often preserved the Elizabethan pronunciation of English words.

For many rural children, particularly boys, school represented imprisonment or even punishment more than opportunity. Some could scarcely wait to be released from obligatory schooling and literally counted the days until their fourteenth birthday when they would be freed from school. Farm work was their life and education was not seen as having any relevance to it. My own interest in books began early. My father was a keen reader. Few people in the parish had much interest in reading; Loughguile's was an oral culture much more than a literate one, but there were the makings of literature in that oral culture. Indeed, when I read Patrick Kavanagh's prose and poetry I am struck by the similarities of language, of Ulster sayings and idioms and customs, country wit and wisdom and deep but unsentimental faith, between Kavanagh's Inniskeen and Monaghan and my boyhood's

Loughguile and North Antrim. It is interesting that it is two poets, Heaney and Kavanagh, who are for me the outstanding witnesses to the culture of my boyhood. The same kind of culture, I was later to find, was still common in places like North Longford and Leitrim, and South Armagh and East Tyrone or South Derry in the Archdiocese of Armagh. I have always felt quite at home in that kind of culture and appreciate its rich human and Christian qualities.

When I was a boy, some of the older generation still had a certain fear of books and reading. First of all, it seemed they feared that reading books would be a waste of the precious time needed for genuine work, which meant farm work. Secondly, books were thought to be 'bad for the eyes'. When, from an early age, my head was, as my grandmother said, 'always stuck in a book', she would warn me, 'You'll ruin your eyes'. This, I assume, was a relic of the time of rush candles, when reading by feeble lighting did put a strain on the eyes. Indeed, a quaint couple, Barney and Mary, a brother and sister who lived near our home, never used artificial light at all. Until what Loughguile people called 'their dying day', they went to bed when darkness came and awoke at the light of dawn. The interior of their kitchen itself was impervious to the sun, being always dense with smoke from their turf fire and smoky chimney. In their house, visitors, particularly the priest, were treated to tea and an egg, the egg boiled in the same little pot in which the strong tea was 'drew'.

The desire for 'book learning' in the parish was, nevertheless, slowly growing from the beginning of the century. In the early 1900s my father organised classes for adults, and these were well attended. They were held in the upstairs room of the disused school of which I have spoken. My father often told of the eagerness of grown men and women to learn how to read and write and count. On the other hand, as I have remarked earlier, I used to marvel at the ability of my Uncle Pat to recite long passages of poetry and prose which he had learned long before in the old 'Fourth Book' used in senior classes in the school of his time.

Many farmers in the early years of the century, however, could not cope with measurements and complicated calculations. One of my father's extra-curricular activities early in his time in Loughguile was measuring fields for local farmers. This was done by 'stepping the land' and translating the steps into units of length. My father also had measuring chains for that purpose. This service was often required in connection with disputes and sometimes litigation covering farm boundaries, rights of way, etc. Heaney recalls it in his poem 'Land', in *Wintering Out*.

Another task which my father completed at the request of his new parish priest when he arrived in Loughguile was that of entering details of baptisms in the parish baptismal register. Previous parish priests had apparently been somewhat haphazard and remiss in entering the data. Baptisms, it seems, were often performed by the priest in the homes of the parents and details would be entered on slips of paper which may have got lost later. In any case, my father went round the houses of the parish, collected names of children, parents and sponsors, and entered them in the register. Many pages in the Register of Baptisms in Loughguile Parish are therefore written in my father's copperplate handwriting.

Memories of my father
My father came to Loughguile in 1903 as a young teacher, aged twenty-four, from Keadue, County Roscommon. Many years later, when I was Bishop of Ardagh and Clonmacnois, I met a man, well into his eighties, then living in Dublin, who had been a fellow student of my father in De La Salle Training College, Waterford. His name was John O'Rourke. He was from Drumshanbo, near Keadue, and my father and he had known each other before they went to college. John was a first-year student while my father was in his second and final year; my father had left the college, therefore, when John began his second year, and was applying for teaching posts wherever he heard of them.

John O'Rourke described how one of the college professors, whom he remembered as a Mr Kerr from Glenravel, County

Antrim, announced in class early in the first term, that a Father David Burke, parish priest and school manager in Loughguile, was seeking a principal teacher for a national school in Corkey in that parish. The school had just been built and was opened in 1903. Mr Kerr said that, coming from neighbouring Glenravel, he could thoroughly recommend the school, the parish and the manager, and asked the students to pass on the information to any recent graduates who might be interested. John O'Rourke passed the information on at once to his friend, Charlie Daly, who immediately applied for the post and was appointed. John O'Rourke later left the teaching profession and became a civil servant. As in the case of Walter Burke, I was again struck by his perfect recall of names and events of seventy years earlier.

When he first came to teach in Corkey, my father obtained lodgings in Walsh's house on the Lough Road, and cycled each day to and from his school in Corkey, passing Loughguile school on the way. My father had great difficulty in understanding Loughguile's ways with the English language and in making himself understood with his Western *blas*. One person, however, came quickly to understand him in the years that followed. She was a young monitress, or trainee teacher, in the school in Loughguile. Her name was Susan Connolly, and she was some nine years younger than my father. Once when, as Bishop of Down and Connor, I was celebrating Confirmation in Glenravel, I met a lady who had been a child at Loughguile school when my mother was a monitress. She remembered how embarrassed she was when my father would dismount from his bicycle and furtively and blushingly hand her a note to be delivered to Miss Susan Connolly. Presumably, the letters were carefully kept but were burned in the fire in Ballybradden. We have a photograph from the year 1906 of the children and teachers in Corkey school. My father is wearing a neat little moustache, but this disappeared before the next school photograph. I suspect it did not please his fiancée and was discarded early on in their romance. My parents married on Christmas Day 1912, when my mother was twenty-four and my father thirty-three. In later life, my mother could not remember why they were married on Christmas Day but occasionally, in answer to our probing, she would recall with pride how happy they felt when the parish priest called for 'three cheers for the young couple', as they were driven away in a pony and trap from Loughguile Chapel to her mother's house in Glenbush for the wedding meal. The honeymoon consisted of a few days spent in Keadue with the paternal family.

On Christmas Day, 1972, in Longford, sixty years after my parents' marriage, my sister Sheila and I had a quiet family celebration of the diamond jubilee of my mother's wedding. My mother was in a wheelchair following the amputation of her leg, necessitated by circulation problems; Sheila and I had brought her home from hospital for the occasion. She radiated happiness all through that Christmas feast. Memories of boyhood Christmases filled my mind that day: the whole family coming home up Tully 'rodden' in frost, with the sound of ice cracking on the pot-holes (we called them 'puddles') under our feet while we sang all the Christmas carols we could remember. As a college boy learning Latin, I loved to 'show off' by singing 'Adeste Fideles' and other carols in Latin.

After some years teaching in Corkey, my father moved to a different school in the parish, at Magherahoney, beside the parish's second church and next to the river Bush. This school was built in 1899. I and the older members of the family attended the 'new school' in Loughguile, because it was nearer. It was built in 1889. When my father acquired a car, a Ford 10, in 1934, the younger members of the family travelled with him to Magherahoney. At the risk of digression, may I remark that the word 'travelled', in the Loughguile of my boyhood, meant 'walked'; so that the question, 'Did you get a lift?' (i.e. in a pony and trap or motor car) could be answered by the reply, 'No, I travelled'. It is worth noting that three new schools were built in the parish within five years at the turn of the century, at a large financial cost to the parishioners. This is surely a tribute to the hunger of people for education and to the zeal of the parish priest, Father David Burke.

My father's motor car was one of the very few in the parish at the time. Having learned to drive late in life, and being already unwell and nervous, he regarded twenty m.p.h. as dangerous driving. In my boyhood in the 1920s, the only car in the parish, a Ford 'Tin Lizzie' owned by Jim McKee and driven as a 'hackney car', was scarcely capable of this speed. I remember as a small boy being in this car with some adults on the road to Glenbush when the car was unable to 'make it' up the 'Black Gate Brae', and all the passengers had to get out and push the vehicle up this little incline, which to my boyhood eyes seemed a steep hill.

Memories of my father are still vivid in my mind. I remember the 'ceremony' of the lighting of the lamp at night, which was always reserved to him. At first, it was a double-wicked oil lamp. Then we graduated to a tilly lamp, and finally to an 'Aladdin' lamp, with its very fragile mantle but what seemed on first experience to be brilliant light, making possible much longer reading sessions, particularly for me; during my university and seminary years I spent nearly all the holiday nights reading until a late hour.

But it is memories of my father's faith which have stayed most clearly with me. When Pope John Paul was in Poland in August 1991, on the occasion of the World Day of Youth at Czestochowa, he visited the grave of his parents in Krakow. There he remarked: 'Sometimes, when I wake at night, the image of my father appears before my eyes. He taught me the mystery of the infinite majesty of God'. I feel that I could say the same thing about my father. He had great reverence for the presence of God at Mass and in the tabernacle and deplored talking or any irreverence in Church.

His was a deep but unostentatious faith. He would not have thought of himself as a pious person. As was the custom with many men of his generation, he would have gone to confession and received Holy Communion once a month, usually on the first Sunday. On those weekends, however, everyone was aware that something very special was happening to him. On the Saturday night, there would be in the house an unusual awareness of preparation and expectation, carrying over to the Sunday morning a sense of occasion and an atmosphere of quiet. The eucharistic fast required abstinence from all food or drink from midnight on the night before receiving Holy Communion. Holy Communion was, therefore, administered only at 'first Mass' at 9.00 a.m. on Sundays, not at 'second Mass', or 'late Mass', at 11.00 a.m. Only a section of the congregation received Communion, or 'went forrit', as was the expression then used. The comparative infrequency of Holy Communion in those days was surely compensated for by the seriousness and the fervour with which it was received. The reception of Holy Communion by virtually the whole congregation nowadays is certainly a great blessing; but there is a danger of a certain casualisation of Holy Communion, with a declining awareness of the stupendous reality of what we are doing when we receive the very Body and Blood of Jesus Christ.

My father's nightly role in preparing his children for sleep was to do the round of the bedrooms, sprinkling the children with holy water, reminder of baptism, of the Blessed Trinity, of Christ's death for us on the Cross: surely a truly fatherly office. A particular feature of his sense of God's majesty was the slow and careful way in which he made the sign of the cross. He disliked the perfunctory and half-hearted way in which many made the sign of the cross: for him, it was something to be done thoughtfully and reverently. I associate this with visits which I would have made with him each day at lunch-break to the chapel in Magherahoney, beside the school where he taught after leaving Corkey. Magherahoney, of course, was part of the parish of Loughguile. I often spent the summer vacations relieving him of some of his classes during the later years of his life, when he was in failing health. He remarked more than once that the best prayers he ever said were said before the Blessed Sacrament in Magherahoney chapel. He disliked rushed prayers and wanted us always to say our prayers slowly and meaningfully.

It is to my father that I owe my introduction to two saints for whom in later life, as priest and as bishop, I was to have a special devotion, namely Blessed Oliver Plunkett, for whose canonisation he prayed every day, and St Thérèse of Lisieux, a saint whom he greatly loved.

My father imparted to me at an early age his own love for reading and his own sense of the importance of study. He was conscious also, before this was common, of the need to prepare oneself to explain and defend the faith in an intelligent manner. Cuttings from newspapers and journals which he sent to me in Maynooth showed his sense of the need for a Catholic 'apologetic' in the modern world.

Marked, as everyone in his generation had been, by World War I, then called 'the Great War', my father seemed to sense the inevitability of another war. I recall being in front of the main entrance to Queen's University on 1 September 1939, probably on my way back to Maynooth to begin my 'Third Divine' year, when I learned that war had been declared. My father's health was already declining then and he no longer followed world news.

His death came two months later. He died in the morning of Hallowe'en, at the early age of sixty, and was buried on All Souls Day, 1939. I received permission to come home to our house in Loughguile before his death, and I spent the last days and nights by his deathbed. We did not analyse then the importance of the ritual of bereavement: it was simply part of the way of life. But I was already aware of how much the support of the priests and of a whole community, during the days and nights of an Irish wake and at an Irish funeral, can mean to a grieving widow and children. In that tradition, which still survives and which can now be given more appropriate liturgical expression in the revised Rite of Funerals, one lives the truth of St Paul's words:

> No one lives for himself or herself alone, no one dies for himself or herself alone; whether we live or whether we die we are for the Lord. (Rm 14:8-9)

There was a community aspect to dying as well as to living. When the word passed round that someone was gravely ill, relatives and neighbours set up a spontaneous rota of people to sit up through the night with the members of the family, taking it in turns to sit by the bedside of the dying person. A dying person was said to be 'a-waitin'-on'. Rosaries were recited and prayers for the dying repeated. There were always experienced people on hand who knew the signs of impending death; and there were also experienced women who knew how to 'lay out a corpse'. Each house carefully kept washed, starched and ready the linens needed for the communion table, with the other requisites for the communion of the sick or the viaticum of the dying. Each house also took care to have its 'blessed candle' carefully kept since the previous Easter Vigil or Candlemas Day, to be held by the dying person as he or she departed with the lighted candle of baptism in hand, on life's last journey to meet the Bridegroom of us all, the Risen Lord.

Such a community was certainly one which verified Heidegger's dictum that 'man is the only creature who knows he has to die'. Indeed, Heidegger came close to making this part of the definition of the human being. It should be still more true of the Christian.

When the death occurred, the chapel bell was tolled and the news spread rapidly round the whole parish that a member of the parish community had 'gone to his or her eternal reward'. Of a pious and charitable person who had died, it was said that he or she 'had a good errant to die'. Truly, alive or dying or dead, each parish member knew that he or she belonged to the community and belonged to the Lord.

Prayer in the home

Like so many homes in Loughguile at that time, ours was a home of prayer. Our nightly family rosary was supplemented by the Litany of Loreto and, according to the season, by the Thirty Days Prayer, prayers to Our Lady and St Joseph in October, the May Altar and special prayers to Our Lady in May, special prayers for the dead in November, special prayers for Lent. It was always supplemented by invocations for the sick, the dying and the deceased among our relatives and friends and in the parish. There was a real liturgy of the home, with prayers at the bedside night and morning, the sign of the cross with holy water on leaving and entering the house, prayers at the beginning of every journey and the rosary during it, and, naturally, prayers before and after meals. Holy pictures were on view throughout the house, and lights burned before the pictures of the Sacred Heart (to whom every home was consecrated) and Our Lady.

Spiritual votive lights were lit at examination times or when one of us was travelling or for other special needs. It was a simple but expressive way of indicating a desire for uninterrupted prayer or for continuous remaining in the presence of God. Thus, by simple means, ordinary people followed the paths which led so many saints and mystics to the heights of contemplation.

The 'trimmings on the rosary' were sometimes too long for sleepy children – or for neighbours more anxious for the 'craic' that followed the rosary than for the rosary itself! A story was often recalled of two regular but somewhat less pious callers at my grandparents' house in Glenbush, which was a famous céilidh-house in its time and one frequented by a great local seanchaí, John McCormick, alias 'The Laddie'. These two gentlemen used carefully to time their visit to coincide with the ending of the family rosary. Always, however, they listened attentively at the keyhole before entering, to make sure that the coast was clear. On one occasion, they heard the praying still going on. One remarked to the other, 'We forgot that a quare "lock" o' people died this last wee while, and the trimmins'll be a brave sight longer the night!' On another occasion, at the same house, the 'scout' at the keyhole reported back, 'We'd better houl' (hold) on a while; they're only at the First Gospel!' (Up to the liturgical changes following the Vatican Council, the Prologue of the Gospel of John was read as a 'second gospel' in every Mass.)

Gatherings at a céilidh were occasions of excitement and also terror for children; for the tales, like those of the folk tradition all over Ireland, were of ghosts, headless horses, fairies, changeling babies, and other horrors of the dark. Hospitality was naturally part of the céilidh culture. 'Céilidhers' were offered a cup of tea and 'a piece' (of bread) or, at an earlier time, a bowl of porridge from the ever-simmering porridge-pot. Earlier still, a bowl of 'sowans' (described elsewhere) was served. The oral culture of the céilidh was first threatened by the wireless in the 1930s. Listening to storytellers while watching their expressions and gestures was replaced by listening in to faceless voices. There was no electricity, and for years we carried the 'wet' batteries the two miles up the

Corkey road to John Sayers for recharging. The advent of radio was quickly followed by the outbreak of the Second World War, and wartime news bulletins filled the airwaves. In the early days, radios were few and neighbours gathered in a house which possessed one to 'listen in' together. Conversation was replaced by listening to the 'sound-box'. The final blow to traditional oral culture was television, introduced in the 1960s and soon virtually universal. Gathering round a hearth and talking is a community experience. Gathering round a television screen is a collection of individual experiences. The more we are together in front of a television screen, the lonelier we can be! However, I still believe that neither radio nor television nor the internet can kill the Irish gift for conversation and for story-telling and for making drama and poetry and epic story out of everyday experience.

Memories of my mother

At the time when my father died, none of the family had finished their education, and my mother insisted that all should continue their studies, while she remained alone at home in Tully. Her health was not good at the time, and I marvelled at her courage in spending the winter alone following my father's death. In September 1941, returning to Maynooth at the beginning of my first postgraduate year there, I accompanied my mother to Belfast and left her in hospital for medical tests. A week later I received the shattering news that she had inoperable and terminal cancer, and might have only a year or eighteen months to live. By God's goodness, in what I regarded as divine intervention, she recovered and was to live for another thirty-three years.

It was only long afterwards that I realised that she had known about the cancer at the time, but concealed her knowledge of it so as not to increase our worries. My father had died two years before, and she was still alone at home in Tully, convalescing from the effects of the rather primitive radiotherapy of the time. Years later she confided that she had been able to 'make it' to Mass every day, even though she regularly had to sit and rest on a stone by the side of the lane (we Loughguile people called it the 'rodden' or the 'loanan') leading from our home to the church. Later on, while she was living in Belfast, much of her day was taken up with assisting at Masses, whether in the parish church or in the nearby convents of Nazareth House and the Good Shepherd Sisters. Often, having returned from Mass and having just sat down for breakfast, she would hear another Mass bell ring and immediately get up again, leave her breakfast behind and hurry out for that Mass. Her life, for as long as I can remember, revolved around the Mass. Mass was, of course, set in the context of personal and family daily prayer and self-denial. She fasted on all Wednesdays, as well as all Fridays of the year. During Lent the prayers and penance were intensified. She 'did' the Way of the Cross every day in Lent. When the children were young and her days were taken up with the work of the house, the church would sometimes be closed for the night by the time she was free. On such evenings she followed 'the Stations' around the outside of the church through the cemetery, in the dark, taking one or other of us by the hand as she did so. When I was her companion, my childish fear of ghosts got in the way of my devotions as we made our way past the tombstones.

I went to Longford in July 1967 as Bishop of Ardagh and Clonmacnois. In October of that year, my mother suffered a heart attack. As quickly as possible, I rushed home to Belfast to be with her. Her first words were, 'You know why this happened to me? It was because you had to leave.'

Her convalescence following that attack was completed in Longford. By the spring of 1968 she was able to go outside, then take short walks with assistance in the grounds, then walk down the avenue of the bishop's house, St Michael's, to the road. Each day she lengthened the distance of the walk. It all had a purpose and found its climax one day in early summer when she came back, tired but triumphant, saying 'Do you know what I did today? I got as far as the Cathedral and said my prayers there!'

From that year on, my mother used to spend the winter months with me in Longford. At first, she felt lonely at leaving her friends in Belfast and Loughguile, and felt that at her age she would never be able to make new friends in a strange place. In fact, she made many new and dear friends in my new diocese and came to feel completely at home in Longford. Always, when I was leaving the house for pastoral visits around the diocese or for whatever reason, she insisted on my naming a time for my return. Never sure as to the precise time of return, I would always add a few hours to the expected time, so that she would not be over-anxious at a later return. Nevertheless, I was often unavoidably detained until an even later hour. I noticed that she was sometimes agitated and distressed when I returned home later than promised. She could not sit, but kept going from chair to window and back to watch and listen for the sound of my car. It was only afterwards, near the time of her own death, that she told me that, ever since I was ordained a priest, she had prayed that I might be with her when she died. Her fear all along had been that death might come suddenly in my absence, and that was the reason for her restlessness and anxiety.

The closing years and months of life she spent in Longford were for me among the most blessed moments of my life. They brought me closer than ever to her and gave me a new insight into the trials and at the same time the special loveliness of old age. They gave me new insight into the holiness of her life.

Eighteen months before her death, having developed circulation problems, she had had her leg amputated and from then on was confined to bed and to a wheelchair. This was a severe blow, which she accepted with remarkable serenity. She spent the last fourteen months of her life in my house in Longford, cared for lovingly by my sister Sheila, helped, in the later stages, by my sister Rosaleen, For Sheila, who slept in the same room with her during these months, this meant never having a full night's sleep and staying by her side, night and day. My faithful 'houseman', James Donnelly, was also tirelessly attentive to her every need.

My mother's holiness expressed itself in many ways, and particularly in her love of prayer, her charity for the poor, and with all this, a strong sense of her own unworthiness. Months before she died, when my sister had settled her down for the night, I heard a loud sobbing in her room and rushed to her side. The sobbing was uncontrollable. When eventually she calmed down and I asked what was wrong, she replied that she suddenly saw how sinful her life had been and asked how she could possibly appear before God in view of all that sinfulness. It was only shortly before Sheila herself died that she told me that one of the things that worried my mother most at the time was the thought that she had been unfair to Sheila by 'keeping her at home' when the other members of the family had independent lives. Sheila, of course, never felt this way about her own life and constantly said she had no regrets whatever. It took me some time that night to restore my mother's serenity by recalling that God is above all the Father of love and mercy and compassion and that he is our Saviour before being our Judge. But I remembered too that it is characteristic of truly holy people that, the closer they come to God, the more conscious they become of their own sinfulness. Indeed, the Lord himself, from the very beginning of his public ministry, linked faith in his Gospel with the sense of one's need for repentance and conversion. I recall with wonder the fact that during my life as a priest, indeed since shortly after my ordination, my mother frequently insisted on making her confession to me: proof, surely, of the depth of her faith. The intensity of sincerity in her confession and sorrow in her contrition were profoundly humbling for me.

My mother was able to assist at Mass in my Oratory in Longford every day until the day before her death. On that day itself, I celebrated Mass in her bedroom. Two days before she died, she said to me, 'Every day since you were ordained I prayed that God would keep you always pure and holy. I want you to help me to pray. I want you to help me to die.' She died at 3.00 on the morning of 28 January 1974 with all five of the surviving members of her family praying around her bed. She was aged eighty-five, having been born on 12 December in what she called 'the year of the three eights', 1888. All during the previous day, she had seemed unconscious; and yet a flicker of a smile showed on her face every time she heard my voice as I prayed with her, and she bowed her head slightly in recognition each time the name of Jesus was spoken.

My father's and mother's influence

My father and mother are so much one in my mind and memory that I do not find it easy to determine which of them influenced me the more. My father's health was always fragile and he had increasing bouts of illness in his later years, arising chiefly from high blood pressure. My mother was more robust, always ready for a hard day's work in the home and around our small stock of cow, calf and hens. Someone once remarked facetiously about his parents that 'father took all the major and important decisions, like those touching on world affairs, war and peace, politics, the state of the country, the educational system, etc, whilst mother was left to look after the minor matters like running the home, conducting the purchasing for all, managing father's salary, balancing the family budget etc.'! This was something like the system I remember in my boyhood home. My father normally referred all decisions to my mother, but they came to us children as shared decisions.

My father and mother loved each other deeply, but it was not done in those days to display married affection publicly, even before the children. Yet, without even being aware of it, we felt totally secure in our parents' 'two-in-oneness' with one another. Surely nothing is more needed by a child than the security of knowing that that two-in-oneness will always be there.

My mother, while gentle in voice and in manner, had a powerful strength of spirit and will and character, an indomitable determination which carried her bravely through the crises of my father's death, her widowed aloneness in the subsequent winters, and, in succession, the illness of cancer, heart attack and amputation. Each priest, I feel sure, thinks his own mother and father 'the greatest'. I may be pardoned for being proud and grateful for mine and for applying to them both the poem which concludes the Book of Proverbs:

> Her husband is respected at the city gates…
> Her sons stand up and proclaim her blessed,
> Her husband too sings her praises…

It gives me great satisfaction to know that still in Loughguile, at least among older people, my mother's 'works tell her praises' at the chapel gates (cf. Proverbs 31: 23, 28, 31).

I think of her in the words of Kavanagh's poem, 'In Memory of My Mother':

> I do not think of you lying in the wet clay
> Of a [Loughguile] graveyard; I see
> You walking down a lane among the poplars
> On your way to the station; or happily
> Going to second Mass on a summer Sunday –
> You meet me and you say:
> 'Don't forget to see about the cattle' –
> Among your earthiest words the angels stray ....
>
> O you are not lying in the wet clay
> For it is a harvest evening now and we
> Are piling up the ricks against the moonlight
> And you smile up at us – eternally.

Mothers and vocation

A vocation to the priesthood is, of course, a gift of God. I recall the words of the prophet Jeremiah, to whom the Lord, in calling him to be a minister of his Word, said:

> Before I formed you in the womb I knew you,
> Before you came to birth I consecrated you,
> I have appointed you as prophet to the nations. (Jr 1:4-5)

Humanly, God's call is often mediated through a mother. This was certainly so in my case. Some months before her death, my mother confided in a nun whom she greatly loved that ever since my birth she had prayed and hoped that I would be a priest. Yet, this wish of hers was never put into words. She would have been afraid to influence my decision. She would also have been afraid to 'spoil' her son, and was always particularly careful to correct in me or in any of her children, any tendency to pride or self-importance. I like to think that my mother's hope and prayer for a vocation to the priesthood for one of her sons began while I was still in her womb. We are justified by the findings of modern embryology and psychology in reflecting on the mysterious interchange between the mother and her unborn child. A person's vocation is, in the will and plan of God, already decided when he or she is still in the womb, and the father and mother are part of that divine plan. We know nowadays that a child's whole future begins to be shaped already in the womb. Psychology, and particularly depth psychology, show us how the child is being influenced while yet unborn by the lifestyle and attitudes and personality of the mother. We Christians would add, by the faith and prayers of the mother also.

I like to apply this to the mystery of the Annunciation and the time that the child Jesus spent in Mary's womb. In some parts of the world, including, I understand, the Isle of Man, the Feast of the Annunciation is referred to as 'The Feast of the Whisper'. This alludes to the angel's whisper to Mary at the moment of the conception of her son, Jesus Christ. It recalls the whispered prayer of Mary to God, who had now brought her, under the overshadowing of the Holy Spirit, into such immediate physical and spiritual contact with his all-holy Presence. The prayer of an expectant Christian mother for her unborn child becomes one with Mary's prayer during her pregnancy. It used to be the conventional wisdom that an expectant mother had to eat for two, herself and her child. Surely we can, with still better reason, say that an expectant mother has to pray for two, herself and her unborn child. More properly, she prays for three, the child, herself and her husband; for he too is expecting their child. The mother prays for the safe delivery of a living, healthy, normal child. A Christian expectant mother prays for a child who will by baptism share in the life of Christ and be a full and active member of the Church, the community of those who believe in Christ. She wants Christ to live in her child, and knows that the life already in her womb comes from Christ and belongs to Christ. Mary Beckett, in one of her short stories, 'The Mother and the Bomb', puts into the mouth of one of her characters, an expectant mother, the words:

> At Christmas I was so besotted that instead of talking to Christ in the stable I talked to him as if he were the child moving in my own womb. (*A Belfast Woman,* Poolbeg, 1980)

Such insights, which only women can have, need to be shared more in today's Church, and only women can share them.

The delivery of the child, as experienced by the mother, surely does not end when the child is physically born, with all the pain and often distress which accompany that delivery, and all the joy and sense of fulfilment which follow it. The child, and later the adult, have still to be 'delivered' by the mother, to school and, in my mother's day, perhaps later to boarding-school; to the adult world, to the world of work. In the case of the seminarian, he has to be 'delivered', perhaps, to boarding-school, certainly to seminary, then to ministry in different parishes; and always there is the parallel sense of pain in the parting, loneliness in the separation, fulfilment through the pain. Indeed, each time the growing child, adolescent and adult begins for the first time to exercise free will, to give signs of a will of his or her own, to develop a personality which, however much it may resemble the mother's or father's, is nevertheless independent, I imagine that the mother must experience a new kind of 'delivery', with the attendant pang and pain of separation, and the accompanying satisfaction and fulfilment.

Families and vocation

It is the home which is the first seminary. The word 'seminary' means 'seed-bed'; a seminary is a seed-bed of vocation, a seed-bed of formation. Formation for priesthood is an ongoing process, continuing literally from the womb to the altar. During all of that process the future priest is being formed and moulded, long before entry into seminary, by the prayer and faith of his family, the love and unity within his family, the influence of teachers and schools, the influence of neighbours and the example and prayer of the community of adult Christians in the parish. We are all of us meant to be a support group for one another in the faith. We all have the responsibility to be a faith-support system for one another. I was blessed to have such a faith-support system in my family.

I do not remember a time when I did not think of becoming a priest. My first thoughts of priesthood were, of course, naive and romantic. In 1925, when I was seven-and-a-half, extensive renovations in St Patrick's Church, Loughguile, were completed under the direction of the parish priest, Father John Healy. To prepare for the rededication, a parish mission was held, conducted by two Augustinian priests, Father Frank Dempsey, a native of Loughguile and a cousin of my mother, who spent much of his priestly life in Austrialia, and Father McCoy. As a small altar-boy I was fascinated by the Augustinian habit and briefly fantasised about becoming an Augustinian.

Father Healy died unexpectedly in 1928. He had been born in Loughguile and became one of its best-loved pastors. His photograph, with dog and gun and fishing rod, is still seen in many homes in the parish. I was a boy of eleven at the time of his death and I distinctly recall the shock and grief which gripped everyone as the news of his passing spread rapidly around the parish.

In the same year in which Father John Healy died, 1928, the See of Down and Connor was vacant through the elevation of Dr Joseph MacRory to the Primatial See of Armagh. There was a year of interregnum before the appointment of Bishop Daniel Mageean to the See of Down and Connor. During this period, Loughguile had the unusual experience of having two curates and no parish priest; the two curates being the late Father Robert Rogan and the late Father (later Canon) Gerard H. McNamara.

The boyish enthusiasm of these young priests had an exhilarating effect in the parish. Both of them would speak all through their later lives of their time in Loughguile as a golden time in their priesthood. Like all priests who have ministered in Loughguile, they were overwhelmed by the friendliness and hospitality and welcome of the people of the parish and, above all, by their deep faith and piety.

Father Rogan took a special interest in his altar servers, with a particular care to look out for signs of a possible vocation to the priesthood. Before I went to St Malachy's College, I received my first introduction to Latin from him in his sitting-room in the parochial house. I did not fully realise it at the time but clearly this was part of his pastoral 'strategy' for fostering vocations.

As children, the young Dalys sometimes played at 'going to Mass', erecting and dressing little altars and dressing up appropriately, each one for the assigned role. My brothers and sisters always took it for granted that I would 'role-play' the priest!

Gone before us with the sign of faith

My sister, Margaret, next younger to me in the family, a teacher, returned to Loughguile to teach and she married there. She was diagnosed as having cancer in April 1961, a few weeks after the birth of her youngest child. She told me after the birth of her first child, of how moved and helped she had been throughout the experience of childbirth to remember the words of Our Lord:

> A woman when she is in labour has distress because her hour has come, but when she has given birth to the child, she no longer remembers the anguish, in her joy that a child has been born into the world. (Jn 16:21

After cancer was diagnosed, I accompanied Margaret to Lourdes, together with her husband, Charlie, and some other members of the family, in June of 1961. Only later did I realise that, while naturally hoping for a miracle, Margaret was also consciously preparing for death. In long moments of silent prayer before the Grotto, and in prolonged periods of prayer in Bernadette's Cachot, that silent self-offering continued. Months afterwards, when a priest pretended to her that he was 'cross' with Our Lady for not curing her, Margaret replied, 'She did not cure me; but she is showing me how to die, and maybe that is better.'

She died on the feast of the Birthday of Our Lady, 8 September 1961. Her baby was six months old. I was touched by the coincidence of date when, so many years later, I was allowed to choose 8 September as the date for the announcement of my nomination as Bishop of Down and Connor in 1982.

My eldest brother, John, died in 1966, the year before I became bishop. A son of his, Brian, is a priest serving in our native diocese of Down and Connor. John was working as a pharmaceutical chemist in London when war broke out, and had to do military service, but as a non-combatant in the army medical service. He crossed into Normandy not long after D-Day. He visited Lisieux shortly after its liberation, and later described the near-total devastation caused by Allied aerial bombing of Lisieux during the Normandy campaign. He visited Lourdes later on. In 1945, having been appointed Lecturer in Scholastic Philosophy in Queen's University, I was beginning to specialise in philosophy and was anxious to have some of the works of Jacques Maritain which had not yet been translated into English and were unavailable at home. John was able to send me from France my first volumes of Maritain in the original French. He had himself imbibed my father's love of books, and we often shared books with one another, particularly in the religious domain.

The unexpected death of my sister Sheila, on 27 January 1993, was another time of great sorrow and loneliness and loss. After the death of my mother, Sheila had taken over from her the care of the Belfast maternal home and of 'mothering' me. Her friends will know what I mean when I say that she looked after me with a 'fierce protectiveness'! She had a severe coronary attack in Holy Week 1980, and nearly died. She had, as it turned out, more than twelve years of active life still before her. In the last six months of her life, however, progressive deterioration of the heart muscle caused increasingly severe angina and breathlessness, which made movement or activity difficult. Happily, she was still in good form at the time of the Consistory of my Cardinalate and enjoyed the ceremonies in Rome immensely. My going to Armagh in 1990 was a great blow to her, since she knew that my new responsibilities were going to be much more onerous. But she kept her feelings carefully concealed from me lest they should upset me. I miss her sorely. My brother, Nicholas, a retired psychiatrist in Littlemore, Oxford, who was two years older than I, died in 1996. As sometimes happened in those days, he had spent some years of his boyhood in Glenbush to 'do messages' and provide company for my aged grandparents. He returned to Tully in 1930, when my grandmother died. He spent most of his life in England. Visits with him and his family in Littlemore brought me the added joy of visits to Newman's Cottages as well as of browsing in Oxford bookshops.

Two members of the family are happily alive with me today, my brother Patrick and my sister Rosaleen, both retired teachers. Patrick lives near me in Belfast and Rosaleen in Toronto, where she taught in the Catholic school system. I cannot express in words the gratitude I feel towards all of them, who have shared with me days of joy and days of sadness, times of 'partying' and times of parting, times of sickness and death in the family, and times of new birth and celebration. In a very special way, they and my 'in-laws' have supported me all through my seminary and priestly life and through my life as bishop. I could venture to say like St Paul that they have 'shared my work in establishing and defending the Gospel'. I thank them and I thank God for them.

In an important sense, the parish community of Loughguile have been an 'extended family' for me and helped to form me in the faith, supported my vocation, were a 'support system' for me in my early years of priesthood and have continued to 'carry' me by their prayers and their lives of faith all through my life. I am very fortunate – and very proud – to be a Loughguile man.

Love of neighbour

My parents' love for God found outlet in love for others, and particularly for the aged and the poor. There was much poverty, and frequently dire poverty, in Loughguile in the time of my boyhood. The decade of the 1920s in the North of Ireland was a time of deep economic depression. Hundreds of people emigrated from Loughguile and the surrounding parishes before the end of the decade. Some of those who remained lived in very poor conditions. We were taught as children to have a great respect for them and to be willing to share with them, and to avoid waste ourselves, realising that what we might waste would be eagerly welcomed by those who were poor. Initiation into the spirit of charity was not just by words but by example; it was not just theoretical but practical. Often we would be sent on errands of mercy, bringing food or clothes discreetly to poor families, but always with the insistence that we must not 'put on airs' or think that we were any better than anyone else. A teacher's salary in those days was modest and rearing and educating a family was a struggle for my parents. We were very conscious of limits on spending, the necessity for 'saving up', the need to avoid waste. Children were taught not to leave food on their plates because poor people would be glad of it. Such lessons are no less relevant in our affluent world today.

This was admirable preparation for a life intended to be lived in imitation of the Good Shepherd, who knows his people and keeps them always in mind, with a special care for the weak and the bruised and the abandoned. My happy experience, then and since, is that it is indeed 'more blessed to give than to receive', and that one always receives more than one gives. The pastor is kept close to Christ while trying to be close to Christ's people, and especially to the poor and the suffering.

Prayer and preaching

As a young priest and since, the influence of my parents has given me a strong sense of the indispensable place of prayer in the life of a priest. St Luke tells us that the Lord himself, even when large crowds would gather to hear him and when large numbers of people were waiting to have their sickness cured, would always go off to some place where he could be alone and pray (Luke 5:16). Preaching that does not flow from prayer soon becomes hollow and empty. It carries the hollow sound of the preacher's ego rather than the voice of the living God. It becomes a 'gong booming' rather than words which are spirit and life.

Equally, the prayer of a priest naturally issues in preaching which expresses a longing to draw others into the conversation with God which nourishes that preaching. My mother was saddened when a priest did not preach. I recall her chiding me quite firmly, early in my priestly life, for not having preached on a particular Sunday when I said Mass in Loughguile. It was the feast of the Holy Name of Jesus, and she was conscious, even then, of the way in which the Holy Name was abused and misused. Her disappointment was great that I had omitted to preach that day. I never forgot that lesson.

Hurling

To end a chapter on Loughguile without mentioning hurling would be like reading or watching *Hamlet* without the Prince. Loughguile and 'the Shamrocks' are inseparable. I shared the passion with everybody else, both as supporter and as combatant. I never 'made it' to membership of any of the Shamrocks teams; I never won gold or glory as a player, in spite of many knocks and bruises, for I tried to make up in sheer doggedness and stubbornness what I lacked in style and skill.

I had a few short-lived moments of glory on the football field. Once, playing for some St Malachy's College junior team, I scored a difficult point (by accident more than by accuracy) from a midfield position. A sports journalist next day described young Daly as a 'thorn in the side' of the opposing team's midfield. This earned for me for a period the nickname 'Thorny'.

Contrasting Loughguile hurling then with now I note and marvel at a dramatic improvement in the game and in its amenities at all levels. In my boyhood, there was no permanent hurling field. One was rented from year to year. Sometimes the grass was cut, but unevenly so, and sometimes hardly at all. Hence, I presume, the phrase: 'We'll get them next half in the long grass'. Players changed into their 'togs' behind the hedge. Most wore caps as they played – one famous Loughguile hurler always wore his hat. Training was desultory. Yet some players were brilliant, with sheer native talent.

Nowadays, while losing none of its essential and precious

amateur quality, hurling has become more 'professional', practising and training are taken very seriously, pitches and clubrooms are of high standard. The schoolroom where I went to school is now extensively refurbished, to serve as a Shamrocks clubhouse. Loughguile and the Antrim County Team, although still not quite at the level of the great Irish hurling parishes and counties, are at least now able to compete with the best with honour and sometimes with distinction; and their determination is still undiminished that they will one day take home the vaunted 'Cup' to Antrim. One of my first engagements after my return to Down and Connor as bishop was to attend the All-Ireland Club Final match between the Loughguile Shamrocks and the Banagher, Co Offaly, St Rynagh's. The game was played in Casement Park. It was, in fact, the first game played there since the beginning of 'the Troubles', the British Army having commandeered it in the early 1970s. After a splendid display of hurling by both sides, Loughguile won handsomely. Banagher is in my former diocese of Ardagh and Clonmacnois and, meeting the two teams before the match, I found that most, if not all, of the Banagher team had been confirmed by myself. This, however, did not avail to keep my loyalties neutral during the match!

Loughguile has undergone radical changes since my boyhood. In the 1920s there was a deep recession and much hardship in the parish. Farm prices, after a relative boom during the First World War, slumped disastrously. Money was extremely scarce. Emigration offered the only hope of a decent future, and it rapidly assumed massive proportions. Not just individuals but whole families emigrated from Loughguile in their scores, especially to Canada and New Zealand. They often left their farms unsold behind them, because there were no buyers. New communities of Loughguile people were formed as far away as Edmonton in Mid-Western Canada and Christchurch and Dunedin in New Zealand. Some of my school classmates were to return later as servicemen in the Australian and New Zealand or US and Canadian forces during the Second World War. Almost the only employment opportunities available at home for many years were in the shirt factory established in the 1930s in Cloughmills by the enterprising and public-spirited McGuckian family. It was the only establishment of its kind in the area, and was know simply as 'the Factory'. Scores of girls cycled for many miles to work there. It enabled many families to remain in Loughguile who would otherwise have had to emigrate.

Very few boys and girls had the opportunity of secondary education and fewer still had the chance of proceeding to university education. The right to 'free education' and to free school transport were still far in the future. Buses were never seen in Loughguile. The nearest bus stop was on the 'narrow line' at Tober or on the 'broad line' at Kennedy's Corner. During our years at college we walked or cycled the two or three miles to the bus stop. The 'education explosion' of the 1950s and 1960s, with free second-level education open to all, was perhaps the most dramatic factor for the transformation of society in parishes such as Loughguile in those and the following decades.

A community in which all have received second-level education and many are university or third-level graduates, is significantly different from the community of my youth. A community in which a much wider range of professional and career opportunities is available is notably different from the community in which I grew up. Today's community is inevitably more questioning, faced with new challenges to faith and needing more adult formation in faith and new ways of expressing that faith, open to new forms of involvement in the life and mission of the Church, and called to find new ways of living their Christian faith. Above all, it is a community with a wide range of skills and talents and experience, and therefore capable of taking a more active part in the building of a truly Christian community in the conditions of the late twentieth century.

What impresses me most about the people of Loughguile is that, through all the radical changes of the past half century, their faith is as deep, their love of the Church as strong, and their attachment to their priests as firm and faith-filled as it was when I was an altar-boy in the newly renovated St Patrick's Church seventy years ago.

Today, I can say to the people of Loughguile, as Bishop Henry, the last Loughguile-born Bishop of Down and Connor, would have said, and as all the priests who have ministered in Loughguile would say, in the words of St Paul: 'What do you think is my pride and my joy? You are.'

Remembering the parish Masses of my boyhood, the place in the chapel where my mother always knelt and the expression on her face as she prayed, the silence at the Consecration, broken only by the threefold tinkle of the bell for the elevation of the Sacred Host and then of the Chalice; recalling also the animated group conversations and discussions at the 'chapel gates' after Mass; and recollecting the silent visits to the Blessed Sacrament, often in the evening after work, with the light of the Sanctuary lamp flickering in the twilight, and what Heaney calls

> the whispered calls
> [which] take wing up to the Holy Name,
> ('Poor Women in a City Church', *Death of a Naturalist*)

from people 'dropping in' from time to time for an evening 'visit' to the chapel, I can find no words to describe the Loughguile of my youth more aptly than those of Patrick Kavanagh in his poem 'The Great Hunger':

> The tension broke. The congregation lifted its head
> As one man and coughed in unison.
> Five hundred hearts were hungry for life –
> Who lives in Christ shall never die the death.
> And the candle-lit Altar and the flowers
> And the pregnant Tabernacle lifted a moment to Prophesy
> Out of the clayey hours....
> God is not all
> In one place, complete
> Till Hope comes in and takes it on his shoulder –
> O Christ, that is what You have done for us:
> In a crumb of bread the whole mystery is....

Men build their heavens as they build their circles
Of friends. God is in the bits and pieces of Everyday....

CHAPTER TWO

COLLEGE BOARDER

Entering St Malachy's College as a boarder was my first formal step towards priesthood. For those desiring Catholic education at that time, St Malachy's was the only college offering second-level education for boys in the diocese of Down and Connor and it was consequently necessary for boys from the country to board. Boarding was, anyhow, obligatory for intending seminarians. I first came to the College in August 1930, a homesick thirteen-year-old country boy turned boarder. The homesickness was not in the least lessened by the fact that two elder brothers were already there as boarders. (A third, the youngest member of the family, was to follow later, his time there overlapping with my own short time as a member of the teaching staff.) If I remember correctly, the day of my arrival was 25 August, for I associate my first day with the feast of St Louis of France. At night prayer, Father John McCaughan, the President, led us in prayer and included a prayer for our parents and for all at home. Our response was muffled, spoken into handkerchiefs, quickly produced to catch the tears. The handkerchiefs were needed again in the 'wee dorm', as boys tried to sleep, 'perchance to dream', and, if they dreamt, perforce to dream of home.

Another memory from that first night was the solemn reading of the College Rule: no delay of time was left for non-obligatoriness of a *'lex ignota'* or a *'lex dubia'*. Further announcements were made, including the information that students who might be considering a vocation to the priesthood should take Greek as their second language, in addition to the obligatory Latin which was prescribed for every student throughout the school. We still lived then in the days when Latin was considered the foundational intellectual discipline for any properly educated person, clerical or lay. During all of my student days, there were two obligatory forty-minute periods of Latin every day for every boy throughout the entire four years of study in the College. This showed an excessive emphasis on Latin; but personally I never regretted the excellent foundation in Latin and Greek which I received in St Malachy's.

Ancient Classics

Classical Latin and Greek were, both at College and later at University, my subject of predilection. At the Junior Certificate examination in 1932, I secured high marks and modestly felt that my Latin teacher in Junior I, Dr James Hendley (alias 'Wee Jimmy') might compliment me on my performance. Dr Hendley had also taught me Mathematics. In the meantime, he had become College President, Father McCaughan having been appointed Parish Priest of St Paul's, Belfast. I met Dr Hendley on the stairs on my return to the College at the end of the holidays. His greeting was, 'Well, Daly, you didn't do very well in Mathematics. You'd better pull up your socks and work harder.' He obviously discerned – quite rightly, I freely admit – that I was in danger of a 'swelled head', and he wanted to prick the ego-bubble and make sure the cap would continue to fit!

Despite his many-sided greatness, Dr Hendley was, frankly, a bad teacher of Mathematics. It might also be the case, however, that I was a bad pupil! The first person who taught me that Mathematics is rational and makes sense was Dan McKeon ('Wee Dan'). Much of his class would indeed be taken up with expounding philosophy or drama or with mock-sarcastic jibes directed at 'my colleague in the next room', namely 'Big Jim Casey'; but, in the twenty minutes or so that remained, he illuminated for me in my fourth year for the very first time the meaning and the rationality of Mathematics, which 'wee Dan' would often describe as 'organised common sense'.

Father Eddie Crossin was another great influence in the College in my time. A dedicated missionary, whose health did not permit him to serve on the mission overseas, he founded, with Bishop Mageean's help, the Apostolic Work, which now has branches all over Ireland. The Apostolic Work was part of the great missionary movement in the Catholic Church of Ireland in the early part of this century. As the name suggests, this was an organisation aimed at enabling lay people at home to become workers for the missions, making liturgical vestments, collecting money for a variety of uses in mission lands, above all praying for the missions and creating missionary awareness at parish level. It was composed of women and gradually spread all over Ireland. It could be called a precursor of the later movements for motivating and forming lay missionary workers.

Father Crossin taught Geography, and he brought a new dimension to it by establishing a geographical museum, with objects collected from Irish missionaries working in Africa and elsewhere. Seeking to extend the Kingdom of Christ had for Father Crossin the side-effect of extending the frontiers of the teaching of Geography, which at the time was often a dry and uninspiring subject.

Father John McMullan was my first Greek teacher. His enthusiasm for Greek was infectious. Rather than putting Greek into us, he drew Greek out of us by his own childlike enthusiasm and his kindly encouragement. I still remember my small boy's thrill at receiving his plaudit for being the first in the class to use the genitive absolute, *pollon apothanonton,* to translate the English phrase, 'with many casualties'. For some reason Father McMullan inherited in College lore the initials of a great pioneer of Catholic lay involvement in the Church's life and of action for social justice, Canon J.K. O'Neill, and was consequently called by the boys 'J.K.', or 'Jakey'. He had the ability to make Greek battles of long ago as exciting as contemporary news and to make Xenophon's men's first sight of the sea as thrilling as my own first glimpse of the sea as a small boy from the top of the hill above Ballycastle.

At senior level I enjoyed the excellent Greek teaching of Seamus Campbell, who had joined the staff in my second year in the College. The reputation of St Malachy's in Classics in those days was outstanding. Successive professors of Latin and Greek in Queen's University readily acknowledged that a steady flow of their best pupils came from St Malachy's. Father McMullan often referred to 'the great Father P. J. O'Neill', whose pupils frequently went on to Honours Classics studies in Queen's. My own Professor of Latin, R.M. Henry, always had a special welcome for students from St Malachy's.

There was, of course, corporal punishment. It is with sorrow that I say 'of course'; for corporal punishment was the rule rather than the exception in most schools at the time. We called it 'flippering'. Most teachers carried canes into class, but many rarely if ever used them. One institution was, if rarely resorted to, all the more dramatic for that; namely a 'public flippering'. It was reserved for what were deemed particularly grave breaches of rule. The whole school was summoned to the Study Hall by a special tolling of the bell, and waited in taut silence and tension for the President's entrance.

The President mounted the rostrum, solemnly rebuked the culprits and then administered the punishment, which on such occasions was 'six of the best' on the tips of the fingers of each hand. Memory of the only occasion when I experienced this drama remains vivid to this day. The experience was particularly painful for me, since my eldest brother, John, was one of the culprits. The offence was smoking. The outcome was, I felt, one early proof that punishment is not an effective deterrent; John continued smoking heavily all his life from then until his death from cancer of the lung in 1966. Perhaps still more painful for him was the fact that he was also on that occasion deprived of his status as senior monitor. This was the only experience of public 'flippering' in my seven years in the College. It was one experience too many and was probably the last ever administered in St Malachy's College.

As I remember it, a prime place in the student scale of values at that time was reserved for fairness and impartiality. Punishment was acceptable to most boys, provided it was just and fair and unaffected by any favouritism. But there were then, as always, students who were more perceptive and more sensitive to the sheer wrongness of physical punishment, its abuse of power, its assault on the human dignity of young boys. I instance writers like Brian Moore, a younger contemporary, and Bernard Mac Laverty, of a later generation, whose descriptions constitute sufficient indictment of the practice. This, however, did not for me make St Malachy's any less of a happy place or anything other than a great college, of which I cherish the fondest and most grateful memories.

Dean James Hendley

I have mentioned Dr Hendley, who, more than any other, dominated St Malachy's College in my experience. President of the College, in succession to Father McCaughan, he later became Parish Priest of St Paul's and Dean of the Diocese and Vicar General to the late Bishop Mageean. The 'President' of the College (which in fact is recognisably St Malachy's College) in Brian Moore's novel, *The Feast of Lupercal,* is in part a fictionalised conflation of the characters and some of the characteristics of Father John McCaughan and Father James Hendley. In real life, by what he was, even more that by what he said, Dr Hendley made a deep impact on me and my contemporaries, whether as teacher or as President, or later as senior and most respected and revered and trusted priest of the Diocese of Down and Connor. He was a strict disciplinarian and feigned to be stern; he was indeed personally austere; but several things we knew about him turned respect into admiration and soon into respectful affection. We knew from experience that he was strictly fair and impartial, he had no favourites. We knew that he practised what he preached and never asked small boys to do what he was not doing and living himself. We knew that he led a disciplined and even ascetic personal life. We knew that he was a man of God. In time, we came to appreciate the kind and compassionate heart which beat beneath the somewhat rugged exterior. He had always a special kindness for the lame duck student, the trier, the plodder or the person from a poor background.

One example springs to my mind. All importation of chocolate and sweets was strictly forbidden under dire penalties. Yet 'slabs' of twopenny Cadbury's chocolate were openly or semi-openly sold by the College barber, 'Wee' Paddy McCall, who came in to the College once a week. Haircuts were extraordinarily popular and frequent – and not necessarily for the sake of hair grooming; supplies of Cadbury's milk or milk-and-nut ran out quickly among the crowd awaiting a haircut. Dr Hendley pretended not to know why there were always queues at the barber's door! But then 'Wee Paddy' was a man after 'Wee Jimmy's' own heart – a working man of modest circumstances who worked hard to rear a large family in North Queen Street. His chocolate trade 'on the side' usefully supplemented his modest income. One of his sons later became a priest of Down and Connor.

It was when I was a university student, a 'Queensman', as we were then unofficially called, that I and my contemporaries came specially under the direction and influence of Dr Hendley. Once a week he gave a spiritual talk. We gathered in the back seats of the College Chapel. Dr Hendley sat against the back of one of the seats and gave his message with unforgettable conviction and earnestness, gestures of his closed right hand with a thumb upraised and head lowered seeming to drive the message deep down into our consciousness and our memory. The message reflected his own concern for truth and his scorn for what he called humbug; his total integrity and honesty, his impatience with hypocrisy or playacting, his desire to be sincere with God and before God. Many of his often repeated sentences have remained fresh in my memory for more than sixty years:

> You are here for one purpose and one purpose only: to love and serve God.

> You are what you are in the sight of God, nothing more and nothing less. All the rest is only humbug.

> You have only one time in which to serve God, and that is

the present moment, not yesterday, not tomorrow, but now. Everything that you have, everything that you are, God has given you. You have nothing on your own; don't go strutting around boasting of what you have done or what you own: that is all God's giving and God's doing. Don't try to take credit to yourself for what God does for you or what God gives you.

Don't think that the ordination to the priesthood is going to make you into a different human being or a better person. After ordination, you will still be the same old 'tuppence ha'penny' that you are now.

His detestation of humbug and of half-hearted Christianity found expression in a favourite quotation of his from the Book of Revelation:

I wish you were either hot or cold, but since you are neither cold nor hot but only lukewarm, I will spit you out of my mouth. (3:14-45)

Dr Hendley was a pioneer of lay involvement in the life and mission of the Church long before the concept became familiar. He conducted voluntary study groups amongst students, with fortnightly meetings, at which students would prepare papers on particular topics of religious interest. I remember a year's group discussions on the life and worship of the Orthodox Church and the Eastern Uniate Churches – a topic then neglected but of much actuality at the present time. Another course concentrated on the great Councils of the Church.

Dr Hendley gathered around him a group of lay people, for whom he conducted a study circle, for the purpose of reflecting on the Church's social teaching and on what was then, in Pope Pius XI's time, called 'Catholic Action'. The aim was to prepare these lay persons to live their professional lives in the spirit of the Gospel and act as a leaven in society, so as to renew society by the standards of the Good News of Jesus Christ. This group included lay members of the teaching staff of the College, like the late Seamus Campbell and Maurice Drinan, and professional lay people like Joe Cooper and architect and poet Padraig Gregory.

This was in the early days of Bishop Daniel Mageean's episcopate in Down and Connor, and Dr Hendley was a close friend and trusted adviser to Dr Mageean then and until the end of his life. He helped Bishop Mageean to make Down and Connor the leading diocese at the time in Ireland in terms of Catholic Action, the Catholic Lay Apostolate, the Apostolate of the Press, the Social Teaching of the Church, and, to use Pope Pius XI's phrase, taken up from Pius X, 'the renewal of all things in Christ'. The lay people formed by Dr Hendley played a leading part in the organisation of a movement of Catholic workers set up by Bishop Mageean and in a series of great Conferences in Belfast, organised by Bishop Mageean in the 1930s, on Catholic Action, on social justice and on the press (or what we now call the media).

Dean Hendley admired St Paul – above all the 'manliness' of St Paul (the title taken from a pamphlet by Dr Walter McDonald of Maynooth, which Dr Hendley recommended to us). Typical of this 'manliness' is that one of his first actions as President of the College was the provision of the first College gym.

The serious dimension of Dr Hendley's life and teaching must not, however, give the impression of someone above human emotion and playfulness. At football matches in the 'big field', he could be seen moving excitedly up and down the side of the pitch, unashamedly partisan in his support for the home team.

Dr Hendley embodies for me the spirit of St Malachy's, caught in the poem composed by Michael Hilton, English teacher in the College, for the Sesquicentenary of the College in 1983:

> A place of learning
> Informed by faith,
> Finally mortised, nerved
> And living.

Among distinguished past pupils were four well-known writers, Michael McLaverty, Brian Moore, Bernard Mac Laverty and Robert MacLiam Wilson, and, in Irish, Father Patrick McKavanagh.

St Malachy's has a long and honoured history. I was a third-year student at the time of the celebration of the College's centenary in 1933. On that occasion, for the first and the last time, I sang in a choir. I deliberately say 'in a choir', rather than 'with a choir', for my note was not always in tune! I remember coming up from Loughguile by bus for the Thanksgiving Mass, at which we sang the Gregorian Chant, directed by Father Eddie Crossin.

Much had changed by the time of the 150th anniversary, celebrated in 1983, during my first full year as Bishop of Down and Connor. The college had grown from under 200 boys, mainly boarders, in 1930, to over 1100 boys with no boarders in 1983. The unprecedented expansion of second-level education introduced by the revolutionary 1947 Education Act called for phenomenal and rapid extension of classroom space, increase in staff, introduction of new subjects, unprecedented broadening of the curriculum and introduction of new teaching methods. The College staff of that time rose to the challenge with remarkable courage and resourcefulness. My classmate and close friend, the late Father Walter Larkin, displayed his hitherto rarely revealed qualities of organisational and administrative talent in equipping the College to face a new future, retaining the best of its great tradition, while opening mind and heart and doors to a vastly increased student enrolment, a new and wide-ranging curriculum, a new world order following the Second World War, and a renewal of the Church through the Second Vatican Council. As a former student, indeed, for fourteen months, from September 1944 to Christmas 1945, a former Classics teacher in the college, I could only look on in wonder and admiration at the new St Malachy's. But now, as then, its glory was not in buildings and externals, but in its inner spirit, moulded of grace and faith and prayer, as we are reminded by the College motto, *Gloria ab intus*, 'Glory from within'.

CHAPTER THREE

UNIVERSITY STUDENT

My formal commitment to preparation for the priesthood took place when I became a seminarian or, in the term popularly used at the time, a 'Queensman', beginning my undergraduate studies in Queen's University, Belfast, in September 1934. Then, as now, Down and Connor seminarians continued to reside in St Malachy's College. The President of the College had responsibility for the seminarians as well as for the lay boarders and day pupils of the school.

Dr Hendley, President for all but the first of my student years and all of my seminary years, took a close personal interest in the formation of the seminarians. He believed in strict discipline. The story went round that he made a test walk, watch in hand, from St Malachy's College to Queen's University, to find out how many minutes the walk required. The 'Queensmen' were expected to leave the College exactly that number of minutes before their first lecture of the day, and 'check in' to the College again the same number of minutes after the end of their last lecture. Additional time for visits to the University Library, particularly for honours students, could be negotiated! Time for less scholarly pursuits, like visits to cafés for ice-cream (still a novelty then) could be bought by travelling surreptitiously by tram. Our regime would nowadays be considered strict, but for most of us the walking trip to university and back each day was sufficient liberation, and in any case, study required all of our time. I have already referred to the dominant influence which Dr James Hendley had over me and my fellow-seminarians during those years of formation.

For my university studies, I naturally chose to take the honours course in Ancient Classics. I found the literature and the whole culture of the Greek and Roman worlds most exciting. One professor in particular, Robert Mitchell Henry, Professor of Latin, had a great impact on me, both as a teacher and as a man. He inspired awe as he strolled along the cloister to his classes, cane in hand and black cloak flowing out on either side. Hush followed his mounting the rostrum to begin his class.

Henry set exacting standards and was severe, particularly on students from whom he knew that he could expect better performance. He would fix the monocle in one eye and give a look which could set students quaking. A lady student in the honours class wrote on the first page of her Latin prose book:

> I had as lief not be
> as live to be in awe
> of such a man as I myself.

I have seldom experienced a discipline more intellectually challenging, more demanding of sheer hard thinking, than Professor Henry's Latin prose classes. His philosophy of translation into Latin was that one should read the English passage, find out what the writer was trying to say, and then say it as an educated Roman of, say, Cicero's time would have said it. This meant seeing through mere verbiage or 'verbal padding' and discarding it, and thinking through the words to the exact meaning. It was an exercise in thinking, an insight into words and their precise meaning and use, for which I have always been grateful. The structure of the Latin language at its best, its economy with words, its precision of meaning, the rhythms of its classical prose and poetry, have always fascinated me. One never reads or writes English in quite the same way again after the study of the Latin language in its best period.

Henry, like Cardinal Newman, was a believer in a broad liberal education. For an additional or 'supplementary' subject, I wished to take Roman Jurisprudence. Henry said, no, I should read English or Modern History. I chose the latter. I asked his advice about reading during the summer vacation, expecting to be directed towards non-prescribed Latin texts. Instead, he advised that I read Milton's *Paradise Lost* and other English classics.

Reading and writing Latin and reading poetry have been a passion with me all my life; and the two are not unrelated. Each shares a commitment to working with words (Seamus Heaney's 'digging' comes to mind), a patient search for the right word in the right place, a fascination with the sound of words. The habit of reading silently is relatively modern, and it makes for loss as well as gain. Cicero's Latin was written for speaking, for declamation, not for silent reading; so it is with poetry. I can modestly say that I share something of that compulsion for finding the word that feels right and sounds right and is right. Not seldom it surfaces just at the moment one was about to fall asleep, and then the word or phrase has to be written down at once, lest it be lost before morning; and the thought of sleep is banished. Someone spoke of poetry as being akin to the craft of the Mourne stone-worker, searching patiently for the right size and shape of stone to fill a vacant spot in building one of those dry-stone ditches which are unique to Mourne's stony hillsides; where each stone is right for its place and no other stone would do. Pope Paul VI, himself a Latinist and a classical stylist, is quoted by Jean Guitton as having said that being Pope was 'rather like being a writer'.

To return to Professor Henry, 'R.M.' had a very human heart beneath the austere exterior. His wife had died before I knew him, and he married again during my years in Maynooth. His bride was a former student; the story was that when she failed her finals she came to talk to Professor Henry about her results. When she broke down in tears, Henry's heart was touched, and so began a beautiful romance. That lady is still alive and some years ago I had the pleasure of visiting her and finding her room filled with photographs and mementos of 'R.M.'. They were souvenirs of the intellectual, literary and artistic giants of the Ireland of his time, with photographs of his brother, Paul Henry, the painter; William Conor, a Belfast painter; Robert Lynd; Seán O'Faolain and many others.

I was privileged not only to be Henry's student but also to become in time his friend. He was not a professed Christian, but was a genuine humanist, a man of great integrity, sensitivity and tolerance, a man who hated humbug, filled with indignation against injustice, compassion for the underdog. These qualities led him to take a particular interest in Catholic students at the University, who, Henry saw, as seemingly few of his peers saw or cared to see, had lacked equal opportunity and who deserved special encouragement. Politically, he was an Irish nationalist, when such a stance was extremely rare and 'politically incorrect' for a person of Protestant background. Henry supported my vocation to priesthood and took care to include some reading in early Church Latin as part of the course. I still cherish the 'Henry Medal in Latin Studies', newly struck in his honour at his retirement. I was the first recipient of this medal at my graduation in 1937.

To facilitate for me the transition to theology, Henry recommended that I study for a Master's Degree and take for my topic, 'The Church in North Africa in the Time of Tertullian'. I read for this during my first theology year in Maynooth and completed my thesis during the summer vacation of 1938. I virtually confined myself to my bed-sitting room in Tully during all of that summer, working without interruption and with the minimum of sleep from the end of June to the end of August, and completing my thesis on 23 August, Feast of St Rose of Lima. There were no typing facilities in or near Loughguile at that time and arrangements had to be worked out to send the manuscript material to Belfast for typing. I developed an ingenious system for sending each day's output to Belfast on the daily evening Portrush-Belfast bus, care of a kindly conductor, who took the precious envelope to the typist (at J. A. Irvine's in College Square North, a short walk from the then Smithfield bus depot), and who picked up the previous day's typing for me to collect at the bus stop at 'Kennedy's Corner' next day. The only interlude for me (apart from morning Mass) in that summer's relentless grind was that once-daily trip to the bus stop and back. I drove my father's car, which he had recently had to purchase and learn to drive because failing health made cycling to school impossible. When I hear Blanaid Irvine's beautiful poetry readings on RTE Radio I recall that early association with her late father's typing pool. Incidentally, this daily trip was my only chance for a surreptitious smoke, for I did smoke in these days, but not at home, fearing it might upset my parents.

Once there was a crisis in the daily system. My father's car, which I was driving, refused to start. The deadline for finishing my thesis was near. My material simply had to be got to Belfast. Quietly, my mother said, 'I'll go.' This meant cycling the two or three miles to the bus stop and back. She did not know Belfast. Undeterred, she set out, caught the morning bus and returned triumphantly with the precious envelope of typescript that evening.

My mother's cycling trips often saw her more heavily laden. She cycled on shopping trips to the bus for Ballymena and came home pedalling slowly up the lane, with bags and parcels hanging from each handlebar and others tied on the pillion. On her outward journey down the lane, she would call back at me, 'Don't forget to feed the hens', or 'Remember to take in fodder for the cow' (cf. Patrick Kavanagh, 'In Memory of My Mother', quoted earlier).

The winter graduation in 1938 fell on the first day of the Christmas vacation from Maynooth. My train was delayed by snow and I arrived at Queen's too late for the graduation ceremony. Henry, who was acting Pro-Chancellor, conferred me with my Master's degree in his study, with the registrar as witness. Many years afterwards, when I had become a bishop, the registrar, J. M. ('Maxie') Freeland, told me that after I left the room on that day, Henry had said to him, 'Mark my words, that young man will be a bishop one day.' Happily I knew nothing about this at the time and would not have taken it seriously if I had. All I wanted, then or later, was to be a priest.

Catholics in Queen's
Apart from two fellow-seminarians, all the other classmates in the

Honours Classics class were Protestants. I formed valued friendships with many of them. One in particular was a dear and lifelong friend – Gordon Borrows, brother-in-law of Ray Davey, founder of Corrymeela. We corresponded until his death a few years ago. I was touched when he invited me to be present at his daughter Alison's wedding a couple of years earlier; I was Bishop of Down and Connor at that time.

Nevertheless, the experience of Catholics in Queen's University at that time was one of 'precarious belonging', to borrow Dr John Dunlop's phrase. Catholics were then a small minority of the student body; this reflected the economically disadvantaged condition of the Catholic community in Northern Ireland at the time. The number of Catholics at any level in the teaching, administration or auxiliary staffs, was minuscule. It was still, frankly, a Protestant place, in which Catholics could not feel completely at home. Its culture was unionist and British, in that order. Unionist and British symbols were honoured on its ceremonial occasions, including graduation, and graduates of Irish nationalist tradition endured the ceremony because of the degree conferred but could not identify with its spirit. Apart from R.M. Henry, the academics who were interested or seemed aware of the problem were few indeed. Later, as a university teacher, I was aware of a certain 'chill factor' experienced by Catholic members of the teaching body. Gradually, however, more people in the university became conscious of the need to create a more inclusive university community.

I hasten to add that I was always treated with the utmost courtesy and kindness and welcome by fellow-members of staff, as I had been earlier as a student. I was very generously treated by the University in terms of leave of absence to attend three full sessions of the Second Vatican Council and the opening and closing of the Fourth Session, as well as sabbatical study leave and sick leave. I have always been an admirer of my University and am proud to call myself a Queensman. But my pride in Queens was increased by the recent decision to take steps to make the University a more inclusive community, with symbols which express unity and not division or exclusion. What could be more worthy of a university? By this decision Queen's has given leadership to the wider community in Northern Ireland. This is surely an important part of what society has a right to expect from people who enjoy the privilege of learning or teaching in a university. R. M. Henry would have strongly supported the Senate's decision and been proud that Queen's was mature enough to take it, in spite of the criticisms it was likely to evoke.

CHAPTER FOUR

MAYNOOTH SEMINARIAN

Going to St Patrick's College, Maynooth, Ireland's national seminary, in September 1937, began the last chapter in my preparation for priesthood. I begin my recollections of Maynooth as a seminarian, with its conclusion and climax, the day of my ordination to the priesthood on 22 June 1941. I was one of one hundred young men who filled the sanctuary of Maynooth College Chapel on that day. We still cherish the framed photographs of the rows of white-albed prostrate figures covering the floor of the great sanctuary of the College Chapel during the singing of the Litany of Saints in the course of the liturgy of ordination. Thirty-five of us were still alive to celebrate our Golden Jubilee and twenty-six joined in the Maynooth Jubilee Reunion in June 1991.

I remember a phrase from Psalm 102 which formed part of Vespers or evening prayer on the eve of ordination day:

> You will arise and have mercy on Sion
> for this is the time to have mercy;
> yes, the appointed time has come!

This verse expressed my feelings on the night before ordination.

We began the ordination liturgy by taking our places in the front stalls, normally reserved to the Professors. I remember standing on the right-hand side, just opposite the painting representing the

First Station of the Way of the Cross, It shows Jesus standing handcuffed before Pilate. I mentally tried to put my hands into the handcuffs with Jesus, so as to follow him wherever he might lead. At the beginning of the liturgy of ordination, Father John Lane, the Senior Dean, called each of the ordinands in turn by name. The names were called in Latin, since the liturgy was, of course, then celebrated entirely in Latin. Each candidate, when his name was called, answered 'Adsum', and immediately stepped forward from his stall to take his place around the sanctuary. The word and the gesture recalled the calling of Isaiah in the great chapter 6 of his prophecy:

> I heard the Lord saying 'Whom shall I send? Who will go for us?' I said: 'Here am I! Send me' (Is 6: 8-9).

I felt this to be the beginning of a pilgrimage in the company of Jesus Christ to continue his journey and his work in the world. I did not know where the journey might lead, but wanted it only to be in his company, having freedom only to be by his side and do what he asked. I was to remember this often in later life, when the journey took surprising directions and when it was not by any means as easy or as consoling to follow as it seemed in the emotional fervour of ordination day. In October 1990, when asked by the Pope to go to Armagh, I had occasion to remember that moment and to associate it with Our Lord's words to Peter:

> When you were younger you fastened your belt about you and walked wherever you chose; but when you are old, you will stretch out your arms and another will put your belt on you and lead you where you have no wish to go. (Jn 21:18)

The tide of war
Before ordination day we had just spent eight days in retreat in preparation for ordination. Retreats in those days were times of solemn and total silence. The world was at war. The Battle of Britain raged in the air over British cities. Ireland had just had its first taste

of war when Belfast was subjected to an air raid the previous Easter. But after Dunkirk there had been an uneasy kind of comparative calm in terms of land armies, what the French called the *'drôle de guerre'*, the 'phoney war'. The silence of the retreat kept most of us unaware of the great event of that very date, the opening of the Eastern Front, when Hitler launched 'Operation Barbarossa' against Soviet Russia. One of our classmates, Matthew ('Mattie') O'Rourke of Meath, however, had somehow got news of the event. During the ordination liturgy, after the anointing of hands with chrism, when we went into the sacristy to have the oil washed off, this man, an inveterate news-gatherer and war-watcher, announced in a loud whisper that 'he [Hitler] was into Russia and was expected soon to be near the gates of Moscow!'

I have already mentioned that my eldest brother, John, who was living in London, was drafted into the Army Corps as a pharmaceutical chemist. For the rest of the family, the nearest exposure to the war was when some of them came with my mother to Maynooth on a pre-ordination visit during Easter Week 1941. We did not then have a car, and a car had to be borrowed for the journey to Belfast (petrol coupons having been begged and borrowed for the purpose, for it was a time of strict petrol rationing). The car was left in Belfast, while the rest of the journey was continued by train. They had just collected the car on their return journey and had driven well clear of Belfast, when the first of the German air raids unleashed death and devastation over the city.

Normally at that time all priestly ordinations took place on one 'Ordination Sunday' in Maynooth College Chapel, with a limited number of family members present for the ordination and for the first Mass on the following day. War-time conditions were the reason given for a decision that family members would not be permitted to attend the ordination liturgy in June 1941. As a compensation, the newly ordained were exceptionally permitted to journey home on Ordination Sunday, so as to celebrate their first Mass in their home parish on the next day. So it was that I secured a 'lift' to Dunloy on that afternoon in the car of the priest brother of a classmate, Pat McFerran, and from Dunloy a neighbour took me, with the help of carefully hoarded petrol coupons, to my home in Tully. The whole parish seemed to be present for the first Mass in 'Loughguile Chapel' next morning. Rationing did not prevent my mother, with the help of several neighbouring ladies, from providing copious helpings for all at tables in every room in our Tully house, in relays of sittings, following that first Mass.

Maynooth in retrospect

Maynooth itself was marked during my years there by the consequences of war. The students of the Irish College at Salamanca had to be evacuated from Spain at the outbreak of the Spanish Civil War in 1937. They were transferred to the Irish College in Paris. At the outbreak of the Second World War, all the seminarians of both Paris and Salamanca were transferred to Maynooth. Maynooth, therefore, had, during the war years, one of its highest ever number of students, and the class ordained in 1941 was one of the largest ordination groups ever to be ordained in the history of the College.

The Down and Connor contingent entered Maynooth in September 1937, accompanied by a group from Dublin, who had studied in UCD. There were ten students from Down and Connor, who had completed their studies in Queen's. In 1939 the ten were joined by two others from Paris. The classmates with whom we were to spend the next four years had already been closely bonded by three years of residence and study in the College, but they quickly assimilated the newcomers.

For young men who hitherto, for the most part, had had fairly restricted experience and limited travel, life in Maynooth represented a great broadening of horizons. We met there young men from every diocese and every county in Ireland, and formed friendships which took us out of the rather narrow confines of our own diocese and parish. I remember the first time I boarded a bus from the railway station to the College, and sat behind two students from Kerry, fascinated to hear them talk in fluent Irish. Only later did I discover that they were talking Munster English! They, however, had similar difficulties with understanding our Ulster English.

The effects of food rationing and the rationing of petrol and oil, together with the virtual absence of coal, made life in the College in the years 1939 to 1941 even more austere than it normally would have been. Even though the College had its own generator and its own central heating system, turf, often wet, was a poor substitute for coal. Light was strictly rationed and heating was minimal and often less than minimal. I remember in one very cold winter piling the floor-mat on top of the bedclothes for warmth at night and breaking the ice in the water jug before ablutions in the morning.

Yet, for most of us, Maynooth was a happy place; a certain austerity was, after all, supposed to be a characteristic of the life for which the seminary was preparing us. The spirituality of that time gave a special importance to mortification. The books officially issued to every new student on arrival included, of course, the Bible; then *The Imitation of Christ* by Thomas à Kempis; *The Soul of the Apostolate* by Dom Chautard; *The Ways of Mental Prayer* by Dom Vital Lehodey, translated from French by 'A Monk of Mount Melleray'; *The Eternal Priesthood* by Cardinal Manning; *The Introduction to the Devout Life* by St Francis de Sales. All of these stressed the place of asceticism in the spiritual life, and especially in the life of the priest. Included also was a quaint book by the Christian Brothers, called *Christian Politeness and Counsels for Youth,* designed presumably to teach raw country youths like myself some elements of polite manners! Finally, each student had to acquire the *Liber Usualis,* the indispensable reference point for Gregorian chant in those days, and indeed never replaced, though considerably less used, since then. Modern writers, however, were also recommended, including such precursors of modern theology as Karl Adam and Abbot Anscar Vonier. Dom Columba Marmion's works were also read by many seminarians in that generation. Father Crossin had already introduced us to Marmion in St Malachy's College.

Some of this reading might, of course, seem strangely dated to people of a later generation. I wonder, however, whether the ascetic dimension of spirituality may not be due for revival. In fact, it is already being stressed afresh in much of contemporary theology and spirituality. How, after all, could one have a Christian or a priestly spirituality which is not based on the Gospel and on the paschal mystery of Christ, and how can one have the Gospel without the Passion, or the paschal mystery without the Cross? As students we were, unfortunately, better at reading about this than living it (aren't we all, or most of us, still the same?); but most of what we priests profess makes little sense and most of what we preach lacks credibility unless the Cross of Christ is somehow reflected in our lifestyle, in the form of a certain restraint and simplicity, a disregard for personal wealth and worldliness, and an avoidance of love of power or misuse of authority.

The great sorrow of my Maynooth days was of course the death of my father on 31 October 1939. I still remember the long, lonely train journey home. It was already wartime; trains were cold, dark, bleak, befitting my state of mind and my pleading *de profundis* with God for my father's recovery but also for the grace to accept and to help my mother through the difficult and lonely years ahead. I remember too the tremendous support of my fellow-seminarians and also of the professors and deans, people who in those years were kept at a distance but who now showed to me their human face and heart.

Study of theology in Maynooth was a new intellectual and spiritual experience. The quality of teaching varied, and was occasionally too closely tied to the conventional 'Latin Manuals' of theology of that time. However, several professors chose to break free of the manuals and introduce us to their own original research. I was particularly stimulated by the lectures of Dr William Moran in Dogmatic Theology, Dr John F. O'Doherty in Church History, and later by a post-graduate course of lectures by Bishop William Philbin in the early history of Penance. I have never found myself so intellectually 'stretched' as by Dr Moran's theology lectures (and I include R. M. Henry in that assessment). In my last examination in theology in my Fourth Divinity Year, I recall sitting for seventy-five minutes of the two-hour period simply thinking my answer through, before lifting my pen to write. Clarity and conciseness counted for more with Moran than verbal 'padding'. It was an exhausting but exhilarating experience.

The Second Vatican Council was still far off in an unforeseen future. But I was later to find that a Maynooth priest of that generation was by no means unprepared for the Council and could trace the continuity between Council's teaching and what he had learned in his college days.

The Maynooth tradition in theology at its best engendered a healthy scepticism about the standard 'manuals' of theology then in use. It stressed the importance of situating the definitions of the great Councils of the Church in the history of their time and in the context of the theological debates out of which they grew. This gave a sound grasp of the laws of development in doctrine, never to be separated from total fidelity to the 'deposit of faith' and to the Church's teaching authority. My own earlier work on Tertullian alerted me to the need to verify 'proof texts' from the Fathers of the Church, which were a feature of the Latin Manuals and were listed as 'Proofs from Tradition'. I saw the need to place these texts in the context of the work cited, the author's other writings, and also the wider context of the culture of his time. All this, and the best of the Maynooth professors of theology of the time, stressed the importance of the historical perspective. I name only some of my own teachers when I say that the treatment of the theology of the Eucharist by William Moran, of the theology of the episcopate and presbyterate and of collegiality by himself and Gerard Mitchell, of the theology and history of Penance by Bishop William Philbin, of Scripture by John O'Flynn and especially by Edward Kissane, and of Church History by John F. O'Doherty, all helped me in advance to see the documents of the Vatican Council when they came as a development, not a rupture, and to find in them a return to deeper sources of the faith 'once delivered to the saints'.

Maynooth at that time certainly had its limitations. With few exceptions, none of its Professors had studied abroad. Few of them read or spoke French or German. The college was academically too closed, too self-sufficient. Several Professors recognised this and recommended post-graduate study abroad. Classes for students in French and German began to be introduced in later years. However, the sheer intellectual brilliance of men like Kissane, Moran and O'Doherty made Maynooth an academically as well as a spiritually stimulating place.

I look back on Maynooth as a deeply formative experience, which I should not wish to have missed and for which I have always been grateful. The style of formation then had its faults and was even then in many respects in need of updating. Nevertheless, it was a good formation for the kind of society into which Irish priests were being sent in the 1940s, and it was flexible enough to send out many alumni of great verve and innovativeness. They pioneered new pastoral methods and introduced concepts of community development which were new to Ireland in the 1940s and 1950s and which proved beneficial also in Britain, where they were introduced through the Irish Chaplaincy scheme initiated by the Irish bishops in the 1950s. Maynooth priests could confidently take their place in the very different cultures and conditions of England and Scotland, the United States and Canada, Australia and South Africa, and often took leadership positions in their new dioceses. The name of Maynooth was respected throughout the English-speaking world and a Maynooth-trained priest could hold his head high wherever he went.

CHAPTER FIVE

THE SOCIAL JUSTICE IMPERATIVE

The priests ordained in Maynooth College Chapel on 22 June 1941 took a decision before leaving Maynooth to found a society of priests, dedicated to the study and diffusion of the Church's social teaching and to the encouragement and assistance of priests in all forms of work for social justice. The society was soon given the name 'Christus Rex'.

The publication of *Rerum novarum* in 1891 had stimulated a number of Irish clergy to further study and action in the area of social justice. Canon J. K. O'Neill and Father Robert Fullerton in Belfast, Monsignor John Kelleher in Waterford, Monsignor Patrick Lyons in Drogheda, later Bishop of Kilmore, and Canon John Hayes of Cashel, were only a few among those who in the first decades of the twentieth century tried to keep the spirit and the teaching of *Rerum novarum* alive and to incarnate it in concrete initiatives in their different spheres of ministry.

One of the most interesting of these was Father Robert Fullerton. Born in Maghera in South Derry, he studied Arts and Philosophy in St Malachy's College, at a period when that College was authorised to offer university courses for examinations set by the Royal University of Ireland. Ordained priest for the diocese of Down and Connor in 1903, he spent most of his priestly life on the Falls Road, moving from a curacy in St Paul's parish to become the first parish priest in the newly created parish of St John's, where he died in 1938. He was prominent in the Irish language revival movement in the early years of this century and indeed up to his death. He was deeply committed to social justice and demonstrated this commitment by publishing in 1911 a book entitled *Socialism and the Working Man*, printed by P. Quinn, Belfast, and published by M.H. Gill, Dublin. It was an unusual venture by a young curate into what was then a controversial field. It won for him a letter of congratulation from the great Canon Sheehan of Doneraile. Father Fullerton also published many articles on subjects of debate between the Church and contemporary thought in his time, touching on such issues as evolution, materialism, psychology, etc.

Another pioneer was Canon J. K. O'Neill, parish priest in the Sacred Heart Parish in Belfast. He was one of the first to see in the early 1900s the need to involve lay people in study and action for the renewal of society in the light of the Gospel. He organised study circles and discussion groups in the Sacred Heart Parish in the Oldpark area of North Belfast, for the purpose of study and the application of the Church's social teaching in the harsh working conditions of workers in Belfast in the first quarter of the century. In time, Canon O'Neill saw the need for a more structured organisation for lay people, and he founded the Knights of St Columbanus, with the general aim of 'renewing all things in Christ'.

In the 1930s the Knights, at the invitation of the Irish bishops, collected funds for the endowment of a chair in Maynooth for the study of the social teaching of the Church. The Bishop and the college authorities had already introduced a series of annual lectures on social questions, with visiting lecturers coming to Maynooth to address the students. The new chair was to supersede these occasional lecturers and provide more systematic study of Catholic social teaching. The choice of a name for the chair was influenced by Pope Pius XI's concept of the apostolate of the laity in society: it was named the Chair of Catholic Action. The first Professor appointed by the Trustees was Father Peter McKevitt, a priest of Armagh, then curate in Ardee. Father McKevitt went for further studies to Louvain, where he obtained his doctorate in philosophy. He took up teaching duties in Maynooth in 1937. The

1941 ordinands were, therefore, the first group of seminarians to receive his lectures. The members of that class were the first audience to benefit from the teaching which was later embodied in Peter McKevitt's book, *The Plan of Society*.

Earlier than this, the greater part of that class, who had entered Maynooth in 1934, had the experience of sitting at the feet of Dr Cornelius Lucey, later Bishop of Cork, and had been stimulated by the strong social and community emphasis in his lectures on ethics. Dr McKevitt and Dr Lucey were the two priests whose influence and guidance played a key role in the foundation of Christus Rex.

The idea of a society of priests grew directly out of a study circle formed by a group of members of the class of 1941 for the purpose of studying the Church's social teaching, as expounded principally in the papal encyclicals, *Rerum novarum* of Pope Leo XIII, and *Quadragesimo anno* of Pius XI. We had the desire and we saw the need to continue this interest after ordination, convinced that this was a vital need for the Ireland of our time and an integral part of the proclamation of the Gospel which we were ordained to live and to preach.

The first meeting of the group after ordination was held in Dublin in September 1941. At that meeting, it was decided that a committee should be elected with the object of keeping our study circle in being as an interim measure, while we would deliberate further about its future development. For some years, some members of that ordination class, including myself, remained in Maynooth for postgraduate studies. Consequently, the meetings of the committee were held in Maynooth. In 1942, the idea of a permanent social study society for priests was beginning to take clearer shape. Each succeeding class of seminarians was invited to select one of its members, who would undertake to enrol members of his class in the nascent but still unstructured movement. The time for formally inaugurating an organisation did not yet seem favourable. We were still living in wartime and restrictions on travel and other difficulties made meetings at national level impracticable.

It was in 1945 that the Christus Rex Society was finally instituted. The Bishops' approval was obtained and the name

Christus Rex was chosen as the official title. Cardinal MacRory became its first Patron and Cardinal D'Alton soon succeeded him in this capacity. The first Annual Congress was held in Galway in 1946. The themes and sub-themes chosen for successive annual congresses reflect a wide range of interests and concerns. I name only a few of them here: 'Justice for the Worker', 'The Service State', 'Emigration', 'Trade Unionism Today', 'Industrial Relations', 'Rural Organisations', 'Rural Community Development', 'Irish Agriculture', 'The Priest and Social Action', 'Youth', 'Voluntary Institutions in the Modern State', 'The Mass Media', 'Television and Irish Youth', 'The Faith and National Revival', 'The Provision of Employment', 'The Christian Layman in the Modern World', 'The Vatican Council and Women', 'The Church in the Modern World', 'Pastoral Aspects of Emigration', 'Censorship of Books'.

The Christus Rex Society can, therefore, claim to have had a role in the renewal of the Church in Ireland in the lead-up to the Second Vatican Council and in the diffusion of the Council's teaching in the 1960s. Christus Rex was one of the first organisations of priests in Ireland to involve laity directly with priests in discussion of pastoral and social issues. It was among the first organisations to question the rather philistine operation of our censorship of books legislation in the 1950s. It was one of the first to raise the question of the place of women in the Church. It inaugurated annual seminars for women religious, with a view to helping their ongoing formation in theology, scripture, liturgy and pastoral skills. Christus Rex sought to be relevant to the needs of the Church and of society in the Ireland of the 1950s and the 1960s and thereby it succeeded in anticipating many of the issues which continued to be of concern in the Church in the 1970s and in helping to prepare for the challenges of the 1980s and the 1990s. All this can be traced back at least indirectly to *Rerum novarum*.

Rerum novarum was a watershed in Catholic social teaching and has served as a point of reference for subsequent seminal papal statements of that evolving teaching. Many later encyclicals took their occasion and in many cases their title from successive anniversaries of this encyclical. Thus we had *Quadragesimo anno* for the fortieth anniversary in 1931, *Mater et magistra* for the seventieth anniversary in 1961, *Octogesima adveniens* for the eightieth anniversary in 1971, *Laborem exercens* for the ninetieth anniversary in 1981, and *Centesimus annus* for the centenary in 1991.

I should like to recall some trenchant passages from the sermon preached by Bishop Michael Browne of Galway at the very first Christus Rex Congress, held in Galway in August 1946. Dr Browne's words would still constitute a ringing challenge, if not indeed a sensation, were they spoken today. He said:

> There is one objection which many find to be disconcerting. It is that priests have really no business to be dealing with these things at all. Their kingdom is not of this world.... The proper sphere of the Church is in religious and spiritual matters – the relations of the soul with God. Priests have not the knowledge of industrial and economic affairs and their interference in them is impertinent and unhelpful. When a clever economist or bank director lets himself go on this theme he can be very effective – and pious as well. He can show a very high respect for the 'true' functions of clergymen and an earnest desire to keep them 'unspotted' from this world.
>
> What kills the poor social enthusiast is that many of his own brethren will agree with the bank director and economist. They shake their heads at all such activities as social study clubs, social weeks, meetings and discussions: they keep within the safe circle of confessional, sacristy and armchair: and pride themselves that they are attending to the real work of a priest....
>
> It is of interest to examine the reasons why the Catholic Church and its priests have a duty and a right to concern themselves with the social question.
>
> In the first place they are bound by charity to defend and relieve the poor and the working class who are the victims of unemployment, low wages, bad housing, high

prices, and all the other evils of the modern world. Charity is the fundamental Christian virtue: it is going to figure prominently at the Last Judgment. It means that each single priest and layman is bound to do what he can to remedy the defects of the social system....

The second reason is because the Church is bound to save souls. Her critics are always telling her that this is her job and she should keep to it. Quite: but the most potent influence at present for the perversion and destruction of souls is economic and social disorder....

The third and most important reason is that the Church was given the right and the duty to teach the doctrine of Christ; she was made custodian and teacher of the truth. She has the truth and must teach it, proclaim it, and apply it to the modern world and its condition....

But there is a proposition which may need some defence: it is that every priest on the pastoral mission should know the social teaching of the Church thoroughly. It may be asked what need there is for the priest in the small towns or villages or in the countryside of Ireland to bother his brains with this subject. What good can he possibly do? The cynical and pessimistic brethren will assure him that he is wasting his time, for he can do nothing to bring about social reforms and may burn his fingers badly; only statesmen and politicians can bring about social reform. Quite true, only legislators can change the laws. But they generally do so only in response to public opinion. And the education of public opinion on the social teaching of the Church is the right and duty of the priest. It depends on him whether the Catholic people – men and women of every class – will understand the issues and perform their duties at local and general elections and in their political clubs as Catholic citizens, or whether they will be ignorant and indifferent to everything but their narrow selfish interests....

Young priests may say that they will find few such demands in their country curacies where the young vegetate. But if they do not develop knowledge of this subject when

they are young they will not have the time or interest when
they have reached an urban curacy....

These words still retain all their force of prophetic challenge,
even in our time of liberation theology and preferential option for
the poor. The words are, of course, based upon *Rerum novarum* and
Quadragesimo anno, which were then the main inspiration for
Catholic Social teaching and action.

It has been a very persistent but very puzzling prejudice among
some critics of the Church that Christianity is so much concerned
with the other world, the next life, the supernatural, the worship of
God, that it turns its back on this world, the natural life, the service
of the poor, and that only now, after the Second Vatican Council, is
it discerning the importance of the horizontal, this temporal world,
this present life, the service of our fellow men and women. This
was and is a gross misunderstanding. For Christianity, eternity is
worked for and prepared for in time. Supernatural life requires an
elevation and transformation in Christ of the natural. And God is
not truly worshipped unless people are also loved and served.
Indeed, at the Last Judgment an important part of what we shall be
examined on is our treatment of our fellow human beings. Christ,
our Judge, will say to us:

> 'I was hungry and you never gave me food.... I was sick and
> in prison and you never visited me'. And in amazement, we
> may answer: 'Lord, when did we see you hungry... or sick
> or in prison...?' And he will answer: 'I tell you solemnly, in
> so far as you neglected to do this to one of the least of these,
> you neglected to do it to me.' (Mt 25:41-46)

This teaching of Our Lord himself is the foundation for the
whole social teaching and action of the Church. The Church cannot
be silent about the morality of business, industry, finance, credit,
taxation, wages, work; because these are the raw materials of
eternal destiny for all who are concerned with them or affected by
them. These are the arenas of soul-making or soul-destroying in

time and for eternity. Morality is social and not just individual; and society must be moral or else it is anti-social. We cannot cultivate 'the garden of [the] soul' selfishly or in isolation; for the tools of this gardening are charity and justice, and these engage us inescapably in the woe and weal of the community. Cardinal Suhard liked to repeat that 'Catholicism is social or it is nothing'. He declared that 'the Christian duty is to create favourable conditions in this world for living the Christian life'. He found somewhere in St Thomas Aquinas the phrase: 'When a man is hungry, you give him bread, not a speech'. Bishop Helder Camara's well-known words are relevant here: 'When I say, 'Give alms to the poor', they call me a saint; when I say 'Give justice to the poor', they call me a communist.' There is a reality called 'social sin' or 'the sin of structures', or 'structures of sin', as Pope John Paul II puts it, as well as individual sin. The Rite of Penance brings home to us the community dimension of sin and of repentance and reconciliation.

Pope Pius XII said in 1953:

> It is not possible to separate social reform from the religious and moral life of individuals and of society, because it is not possible to split this world off from the next, nor to break into two parts man, who is a living unity. (Speech to Italian Christian trade unionists)

But many years earlier, in the document which stands among the great social-revolutionary documents of modern history, the encyclical *Rerum novarum*, Pope Leo XIII said:

> It is plain to us and to everyone that the majority of the poor, through no fault of their own, are in a condition of misery and wretchedness which call for prompt and well-chosen remedy. The traditional workmen's guilds were abolished in the last century; no form of protection took their place; in its laws and institutions, the State disowned the ancestral faith. Hence by degrees we have reached a time when working men, isolated and unprotected, have been delivered over to

the brutality of employers and the unchecked greed of competition. To make bad things worse, rapacious usury, condemned by the Church time after time, is practised still by grasping and covetous men, who have changed its guise but not its nature. Lastly, the giving of employment and the conduct of trade generally, have passed so completely into the hands of the few that a small body of excessively rich men have laid on the teeming multitudes of the poor a yoke which for all intents and purposes is the yoke of slavery.

That was 1891 – a long time before the welfare state. If Christian people had listened to that ringing voice of Christian justice in the seventy years between, how much injustice, intolerance and enslavement – whether from unbridled capitalism or from communism – would have been averted, how much bitterness and sorrow avoided. For it is in anguish and grief and remorse that we have learnt the harsh lesson that 'unless the Lord build the house, they labour in vain that build it' (Ps 126:1).

Christus Rex: 1946-96

Christus Rex, therefore, with the challenge of Bishop Michael Browne, got off to a rousing start with its first Congress in 1946. For the next twenty years, it was to hold annual congresses in most of the cities and major towns of Ireland. These were held in Easter Week and, although at first reserved to priests, were soon opened to lay people. I have indicated above the wide range of topics addressed at the congresses, whether as the main themes or as major discussion topics. The society established a quarterly journal with the same name, whose pages provided a useful guide to the evolving trends in Catholic social teaching in the Ireland of the period preceding and leading up to the Second Vatican Council.

The society from its foundation set about creating branches of Christus Rex in every diocese in Ireland. Many of these long maintained a high level of activity. A sister organisation with the same name was set up in Malta, operating on similar lines; it flourished for many years.

As chairman of the society for twenty-five years, up to my retirement as Chairman in 1966, I found a great deal of my time being devoted to the task of organising the annual congresses and promoting the diocesan branch activities of Christus Rex. The Silver Jubilee year of the society in 1966 seemed an appropriate year in which to withdraw from the Chair. The Vatican Council appeared to promise a fruitful period in the development of the study and implementation of social justice. *Gaudium et spes*, the great Constitution on the Church in the Modern World, itself broke new ground in many areas of Catholic social teaching. It brought this current of Christian teaching into the mainstream of the Church's life. Commissions for Justice and Peace were established in Rome and at national and often diocesan level across the world. All this gave great satisfaction to the members of Christus Rex. After my appointment as bishop in 1967, I found it impossible, because of the pressures, to be any longer involved in the society in an organisational capacity.

Unfortunately, the society was not to continue actively for much longer. It was never formally dissolved but simply lapsed into inactivity. In one sense, it could be said that other areas of Church renewal (liturgy, catechetics, etc.) took precedence. In another sense, and more positively, it could be said that other forums for discussion among priests and between priests and lay people superseded Christus Rex. However, I believe its disappearance was regrettable and left a vacuum which has not been filled. Bishop Browne would certainly have deplored its passing.

Happily, however, a Trust has been set up to perpetuate the society's name and to promote its aims. This is called the Christus Rex Trust, and its objectives are to promote the social teaching of the Catholic Church in Ireland by the giving of lectures, to be called the Christus Rex Lectures, or by seminars and any other suitable forms of education. The Trustees are the four Archbishops of Ireland. So the name Christus Rex lives on and the work of the society will continue in a new form.

CHAPTER SIX

THE FRENCH EXPERIENCE

My teaching in philosophy in the first years was rather conventional and pedantic, depending too much on traditional textbooks and too little enriched by personal exploration of philosophical problems.

A great 'breakthrough' came for me when the University gave me a sabbatical year in 1952/3, and I elected to spend the year studying philosophy in Paris. France was still recovering painfully from the war and the occupation and from the bitter scars left by the *épuration*. It was still unwise to talk about these events. I kept meeting priests and monks who had served in the First World War, or in the Second World War or the Resistance. Their war service helped to gain new respect for priests in public opinion and to loosen the grip of French anti-clericalism.

Most of my time was taken up with courses in the Institut Catholique, the Sorbonne and the Collège de France. It was a most interesting time to be in France and to be studying philosophy in Paris. Existentialism, whether in its secular humanist variety, with Sartre, Simone de Beauvoir, Camus, or in its Christian expression, represented in France particularly by Gabriel Marcel, was flourishing. I attended several public lectures given by Gabriel Marcel in Paris during my year there. Merleau-Ponty lectured in the Collège de France, where Henri Gouhier also gave lectures, inspired by the Christian humanist tradition in philosophy.

Jankélévitch lectured in moral philosophy at the Sorbonne. Jean Wahl organised the Collège Philosophique, where distinguished philosophers, French and foreign, gave lectures from time to time on the major issues then engaging philosophers on the European continent. Paul Ricoeur and Emmanuel Lévinas were writing and lecturing. Jacques Maritain had gone to the United States but his influence continued and a dedicated disciple of his, Professor de Monléon, lectured in moral philosophy at the Institut Catholique. It was broadly the Paris which both Paul VI and John Paul II knew and which influenced them so profoundly. During this year, I was also able to attend some lectures on theology by Father Yves Congar in Le Saulchoir, and by Father Jean Daniélou, Father Louis Bouyer and others in the Institut Catholique. I also took the opportunity to spend some weeks in the Catholic University at Louvain, with its outstanding scholars in medieval and thomistic philosophy, and in the Catholic University in Fribourg in Switzerland.

At the same time, the writings of Sartre and Camus were appearing. Sartre's novels offered a key to his philosophical thought, as well as insight into contemporary secular culture in France. His plays were coming on stage, while his journal, *Les Temps Modernes,* was exploring contemporary issues from the standpoint of Sartre's version of Marxist humanism. Emmanuel Mounier's journal, *Ésprit*, the Jesuit *Études*, the Dominican *La Vie Intellectuelle*, the journal *Dieu Vivant,* were examining similar issues from a Catholic standpoint. Simone Weil's writings were appearing. An epic triangular debate between Francis Jeanson, Sartre and Camus took up much space over several issues of *Les Temps Modernes* in 1952. Sartre accused Camus of ignoring 'the direction of history'; Camus retorted that Sartre 'never pointed anything but his armchair in the direction of history'. Sartre accused Camus of 'moralism'; in a fine apostrophe he addresses Camus as Sisyphus: 'You are condemned to condemn, Sisyphus'. This was French intellectual polemic at its rhetorical and dramatic best.

At the same time, Paris offered endless interest in the fields of theatre, art, architecture, and cultural life generally. I still remember the excitement of Samuel Beckett's *En Attendant Godot* at the

Comédie Francaise and of Bernanos' *Dialogue des Carmelites* at the Theâtre Hébertot. Later, when I first met the artist Ray Carroll, I was intrigued to find that he had spent the same year in Paris as I. He was working at the school of Fernand Léger, and enjoying, as I did, the artistic and intellectual delights of Paris. It was exciting to have coffee in Les Deux Magots, where Sartre used to do much of his writing. A writer did not need a study; he could write all day in a café for the price of a few *cafés noirs*. Truly I feel that I could use the words penned about Paris by Wordsworth in his youth, and say with him:

> Bliss was it in those days to be alive
> But to be young was very heaven.

French Catholic revival

At the same time, I was following with keen interest the many-sided revival which was in progress in the Church in France. France was then leading the whole Church in terms of theology, liturgical renewal, pastoral innovation and evangelisation. It was an exciting time to be in Paris. We did not yet know it, but the great renewal of the Church which was to be brought about by the Second Vatican Council was already being prepared in France during those years. This period has been described as 'one of the springtimes of the Church in France'. Paul VI, addressing the French bishops at the end of the Council, said that the 'intellectual bread of the Church is baked in France'. There was no better preparation than a year in Paris for what was to come in the universal Church ten years later.

Like all genuine renewal, this began with the Bible and theology. St Paul spoke of putting the intellect at the service of Christ. Great theologians like de Lubac, Congar, Chenu, Bouyer and Daniélou were doing just that in the Paris of the 1950s. To meet these men, to sit at their feet in college rooms or lecture halls, to read their books or articles straight from the printing presses, was the privilege of a lifetime. To become the friend of one, the later Cardinal de Lubac, was a special grace. Cardinal Suhard's magistral pastoral letters were still fresh: *Essor ou déclin de l'Église?* ('Rise or decline of the Church?'), issued in 1947, and *Le prêtre dans la cité* ('The Priest in the City'), issued in 1949, being the best known. The Mission de France, founded under Suhard's inspiration by the French bishops in 1941, was still young. It took St Thérèse as its first patroness and its seminary was still in Lisieux when I first visited there in 1952.

Things were not always easy for theologians and pastors with new ideas about novel liturgical and pastoral methods. The Roman Curia was sometimes suspicious of the new ideas being proposed and the new initiatives tried. Fathers de Lubac, Congar, Chenu, each in turn came under suspicion and were variously restricted or for a time forbidden to teach or publish. What was so impressive about them was their love for and loyalty to the Church, even when, and perhaps particularly when, they suffered unjustly at the hands of Church authority. I vividly remember a time of great tension in the Church in France, when the priest-worker movement came under suspicion. One of the movement's thinkers, the Dominican priest Father Montuclard, writing in the journal *La quinzaine*, and in his book *Jeunesse de l'Église*, was clearly moving away from the Church and from Catholic theology into a radical left-wing ideology. He later left the Church. In summer 1953 Father de Lubac published an advance chapter from his coming book, *Meditation sur L'Eglise*, in the Jesuit review, *Études*. This was published in English as *Splendour of the Church*. The previewed chapter had the title 'Mater Ecclesia'. The serenity, the loving and conscious submission to the Church as Mother, the prayer-filled faith of Father de Lubac had a wonderfully calming impact at that critical moment, especially coming as it did from one who had himself been misjudged and wronged. Posthumously published papers by de Lubac show how deeply hurt he had been; but his love of the Church came first. It has also to be said that de Lubac afterwards admitted that, following the intervention of Rome, he had come to recognise that certain uses of language in his writing could have led to misunderstanding and obscured his own true meaning. An outspoken article by Cardinal Saliège of Toulouse, with the title 'Pour l'honneur de la théologie', came to the defence of these scholars in a way which took real courage at that time. The love and fidelity to the Church of these great creative theologians are a silent rebuke to the bitterness apparent in some 'radical' theologians of today. Due tribute to such theologians was paid by the Pope when he created Daniélou a Cardinal and when he similarly honoured de Lubac and, later, Congar. Pope Paul VI first asked de Lubac to accept the honour, and de Lubac declined, feeling in his humility that Daniélou would be a better communicator with the contemporary world than himself.

In May 1953 I was present at the 'defence' of Father René Laurentin's doctoral dissertation in theology at the Institut Catholique. Father Laurentin later became a prolific writer on mariological and other theological topics. His dissertation was on priesthood and the Blessed Virgin Mary. The theological renewal of the time was deeply rooted in Scripture, in the theology of the early Fathers of the Church and in the Church's tradition. The new scriptural scholarship then in progress brought the whole Church back to its foundations in the Word of God. New patristic scholarship showed how similar in many respects the modern world of the 1950s and 1960s was to the Greco-Roman world in which the Gospel was first preached. The great patristic collection, *Sources Chrétiennes*, was bringing the Church back to its origins in the Church of the early centuries. It helped people to see how the first contact of the Gospel with the surrounding pagan culture of Greece and Rome could inspire and equip the Church today to re-evangelise the secular culture of the modern and 'post-modern' western world.

One of the weaknesses in some theological writing today is that it often lacks that contact with the rich doctrine of the early Greek and Latin Christian writers. The sense of tradition and the perspective of Church history were a great strength of the French Church then. After the Council Father Congar spoke of the renewal of the Church as being, not a break with tradition but the return to an earlier and purer tradition. He also remarked that few things were so much needed in the contemporary Church as an historical perspective; for this shows the Church's fidelity to unchanging truth in the midst of development of doctrine, and the unchanging permanence of truth throughout changing formulations.

My 'home' in Paris then and since was the guest-house of a monastery of Benedictine nuns at Vanves in the south-western suburbs of Paris, near the seminary of Issy-les-Moulineaux. This was then a new foundation, representing a departure in the Benedictine tradition, in so far as it envisaged the establishment of monastic life for women in what we then called mission lands and now prefer to call the new Churches. When I came, the community was still young. It had been founded in the 1920s by an English convert, a married woman, Madame Waddington-Delmas, who entered religion as Sister Bénédicte after her husband died and her children were reared. She was helped in her project by Dom Besse of Ligugé. She herself died on 1 February 1952, a few months before I came to Vanves in the following September. The congregation had already by then made foundations in Vietnam and Madagascar. The monastery and the monastic church were designed by a Benedictine architect, Dom Bellot of Solesmes, with the collaboration of a distinguished sculptor, Charlier, who designed the high altar. The buildings are a good example of the religious architecture of the 1930s in France. A plaque inside the church commemorates its consecration in 1949 by the Apostolic Nuncio in France, a certain Monsignor Angelo Roncalli, later to be Pope John XXIII. He was in fact 'standing in' at this ceremony for the Cardinal Archbishop. It was typical of his wit that at a reception afterwards he remarked, with a gesture at his rotund figure, that he was 'good at filling gaps'! This monastery has been my home during many weeks of study and writing in the long weeks of my university vacations as philosophy teacher at Queen's and for much shorter but welcome periods of reading and writing in my years as bishop.

At that time the monastery was a centre of liturgical and monastic renewal, housing at various times the Centre of Pastoral Liturgy, the Aid to Work Projects for Enclosed Nuns, a studium for further study for apostolic sisters. It maintained an atelier for liturgical vestments and a workshop for materials in plastic. Since the 1960s it has housed an organisation called AIM – Aid for Monastic Implantation – which has been a powerful instrument at the service of monastic foundations in developing countries. It has always had a busy guesthouse facility for visitors seeking prayer, silence and peace.

Liturgical renewal

The liturgy in this monastery was impressively celebrated in the classic Benedictine manner of the time. Liturgical renewal was a mark of Church life in France during those years. There were abundant opportunities for experiencing at first hand new approaches to liturgical celebration, new efforts to encourage active participation by the laity, new pastoral initiatives and experiments in team ministry (*équipe* was one of the 'buzz words'), all of them inspired by the liturgy and aimed at the building of living Christian communities centred on the Eucharist.

These new ideas were wisely guided by the French Centre of Pastoral Liturgy (the title in itself suggested a new way of looking at liturgy), directed by the Dominican Father A. M. Roguet and others and with a magnificent series of published liturgical studies to its credit. I met with several pioneers of liturgical renewal, such as the French Father Gy OP, and the Belgian Father Thierry Maertens. Visits to churches such as Saint Séverin, Saint Germain des Près, Saint Étienne du Mont, the Catholic Chaplaincy at the Sorbonne, brought a sense of excitement and of new life and new possibilities for a renewed liturgy. At L'Hay-les-Roses, a brave Benedictine, Father Féligonde, laboured to build a new kind of parish community around the liturgy. After such experiences, I could never again think of liturgy as 'rubrics', or fail to recognise its enormous potential for catechesis, for evangelisation and for Church renewal in all its aspects.

Renewed liturgy was soon seen to require new approaches to the design of liturgical space. With characteristic thoroughness, French liturgists (often with inspiration from Germany) set themselves to study new architectural models of church design and new expressions of religious and liturgical art. The reviews, *Art Sacré* and *Art D'Église,* were products of this search.

My interest in social justice, aroused first in Maynooth and sustained by Christus Rex, as recalled in the previous chapter, was further stimulated in Paris by frequent visits to the Jesuit Centre, Action Populaire, whose *Cahiers* and other publications were making a significant contribution to the development of Catholic social teaching. Father Bigo SJ, its Director, whose lectures I attended, was immensely impressive. He later went to Latin America. Father Heckel SJ, another member of the Action Populaire staff, later became a member of the Justice and Peace Council in Rome, and later still became Auxiliary Bishop of Strasbourg. Contacts with priests involved in the priest-worker movement and in movements stemming from Canon (later Cardinal) Cardijn's Jocistes, such as ACO (Action Catholique Ouvrière), JOC, JAC, JEC (Young Christian Workers, Young Christian Agricultural Workers, Young Christian Students respectively) etc., showed the enthusiasm and thoroughness with which the Church in France was taking up the challenge of evangelising the world of workers, of rural dwellers, of students, of young people. The sociology of religion, then being pioneered by priests like Chanoine F. Boulard, revealed how deeply dechristianised France had become; but, rather than giving up in discouragement, the French Church was gearing itself for a new evangelisation of France, now increasingly seen as 'mission territory'. Books like Maisie Ward's *France Pagan,* based on Father Godin's *France, Pays de Mission?,* made the new French pastoral initiatives known to English-speaking audiences. New experiments in evangelisation and parish renewal associated with such names as Abbé Michonneau and Père Loew were also arousing interest outside the country as well as in France itself.

The findings of Canon Boulard in religious sociology and the writings of Fathers Godin, Michonneau and Loew, which confirmed from pastoral experience the pessimistic findings of Boulard in terms of French religious practice, deeply influenced Cardinal Suhard. But they did not move him to pessimism; instead they filled him with enthusiasm to 'leave nothing untried for Christ'. His boundless hope was still animating the Church in France through the 1960s. In 1960/61, I again had a sabbatical semester in Paris and once more became immersed in and inspired by its great intellectual creativity and the tremendous commitment, energy and enthusiasm of the Church in France.

My fascination with France did not lessen in the intervening years. A year without some visit, however brief, to Paris always seems to me *'une drôle d'année'*, a 'funny year'. At Easter 1997, for the first time in years, I made time to stroll the streets of the Latin Quarter and travel the métro in the directions so familiar to me forty years earlier. Paris had lost nothing of its magic – even if one of the restaurants I used to visit had become a McDonalds! It is always a pleasure in Paris to be able to use a métro ticket from a *carnet* purchased two or three years earlier, to revisit a familiar café and be greeted by the garçon one hadn't seen for two years with a cheery 'comme d'habitude?', 'the usual?', which for me was always tea and a 'tartine de beurre' – bread with butter. Such friendly cafés, in Paris as elsewhere, become fewer and McDonalds-type outlets more common. I believe that even these will become acclimatised and take on a French style and taste in time. France has a way of culturally assimilating its imports!

A changing Ireland

France has been a source of inspiration for me in my life as priest and as bishop. The experience was an excellent preparation for the Vatican Council when it came. More immediately, it transformed – or so I hope – my whole approach to the teaching of philosophy. In the early years of my teaching it was not always easy to get students to ask themselves the questions which serious philosophers ask. In my first years of teaching philosophy we still lived in a society where custom and tradition were highly valued and where radical questioning was rarely encountered. It was an age which, broadly speaking, expected things to remain more or less the same as they had been and which did not anticipate radical change in society or in the Church. In university teaching the traditional type of didactic lecture still prevailed and dialogue between professor and student was not yet common.

Compared with France, ours was a very muted '68, yet things

began to change in the 1960s. Universal free second-level education and greatly expanded third-level educational opportunity, together with the beginnings of new industrial development, and the advent of television, were among the factors working for changed attitudes. Ireland began to share the new mood of questioning of what had been and of greater confidence in what could be. We began to move from a society based largely on stability to a society more oriented towards change.

The problematic of French and German existentialism began to make sense to Irish students. I had found in the writings of people like Sartre and Camus and other 'secular' existentialists remarkable articulations of the religious and spiritual and moral consequences of the social and cultural changes then progressively influencing society in continental Western Europe. I found also in the writings of Kierkegaard, Martin Buber, Karl Jaspers, Max Scheler, Gabriel Marcel and other humanist and Christian existentialists, powerful evidence of how closely the Christian faith meshes with the deep human needs revealed by these same social changes and persisting through them. Corresponding cultural and social changes were soon to make their presence felt in Ireland. Teaching philosophy to young people in Belfast in the 1960s showed how remarkably relevant the Council was to the questionings already coming to the surface of intelligent young men and women in Ireland at that time. One could say that the Council, guided by the Holy Spirit, was helping us to read in advance the 'signs of the times' which were increasingly to mark Irish society in the coming two decades.

Side by side with this, I was constantly discovering in my own reading of Aquinas, how remarkably he had anticipated much of the existentialist way of thinking, strongly influenced as he was by St Augustine, who could rightly be described as an existentialist philosopher *avant la lettre*.

I became impatient with many of the descriptions then current of Thomas Aquinas as an 'essentialist' thinker and of thomistic philosophy as being 'deductivist' and as standing in radical contrast with any existentialist approach, and, indeed, as totally divorced from human experience, if not from human existence. I also became convinced, however, that one version of philosophy commonly taught as 'thomistic' and current in the scholarly manuals was in fact a distortion of St Thomas. Thomas Aquinas was not, in that sense, a thomist! Van Steenberghen and other thomists in Louvain used to speak with scorn of the 'palaeo-thomism' of the manuals and contrast it with 'neo-thomism' or the authentic modern development of the thought of St Thomas himself.

The 1950s and 1960s were exciting times in which to be teaching philosophy, and sharing it with university colleagues at home and in Paris. New methods in university teaching were much more demanding, but at the same time more challenging and rewarding. Some people did, and some still do, regret, condemn or criticise the questioning mood of the young, but teachers who had long striven to evoke questioning and response from reluctant students were hardly likely to resent the questioning, or try to suppress it, when it came. From the religious point of view, one remembered St Anselm's phrase about '*fides quaerens intellectum*', 'faith seeking understanding', and '*intellectus quaerens fidem*', 'intelligence seeking faith'. It is not the questioning or the questioner who deserve rebuke, but rather someone like Pilate who flippantly asks, 'What is truth?', and does not wait for the answer.

In parenthesis, I add that if there was and is regret, it is that much of the questioning nowadays is selective and partial. The traditional is questioned, the contemporary is often swallowed whole. The assumptions of contemporary culture too often remain unquestioned. Plato described philosophy as 'the challenging of the hypotheses' or assumptions of the pervading culture. He declared that 'the unexamined life is not worth living'. The youthful Jesus in the Temple was listening to the Jewish teachers but also asking them questions. He led the rich young man to confront the question of how to enter the Kingdom of Heaven, which is in fact the fundamental question about the ultimate meaning of human existence, the ultimate existential question; and he then challenged the young man with the radical existential choice between earthly possessions and eternal life. A great need in the Church today is to get more people and especially more young people to be intellectually inquisitive about human origins and human identity and destiny, about the meaning and purpose of our life on earth and about the response of the faith to these questions; and at the same time to convince them that Christ is the ultimate answer to all their questioning and to all human searching. The tragedy sometimes is, however, that their God, their Christ, inadequately known, is 'too small'. One of the great needs of our time is a theology commensurate, as true theology is, with the vastness of the universe and the interiority and mystery in the depths of the human heart, with its perpetual discontent with the 'already' and its insatiable longing for the 'not yet' – what Sartre called the *'creux toujours futur'*, 'the ever future void' which is human existence. A fully developed anthropology, an integral humanism, to use Maritain's phrase, shows that only God is enough. Pope John Paul II is one of the greatest modern exponents of that anthropology and that integral humanism.

Faith under question

My experience as bishop from 1967 on quickly reinforced my conviction that there are enormous spiritual resources in the Church in Ireland, and that many of these resources still remain to be fully exploited. The more questioning mood of a better educated laity is not a danger but a strength. We bishops and priests know that Christ is the answer, that Christian faith is the answer, to all the deep needs and questions of humankind. But we must listen to the questions that people ask, and particularly the questions that young people ask; we must be sensitive to the needs that people express, in order to lead them to feel in their own personal experience how relevant Christ and faith in Christ are to them, where they are. We must lead people to a real experience of God, to a personal encounter with Jesus Christ, for it is there that questioning will end in the actual experience that 'only God is enough', and at the same time the unending search will continue in endless exploration into the question of Aquinas, *'Quid sit Deus'*, 'What or Who is God?'

A questioning laity shatters any temptation on the part of priests or bishops to complacency. When I look back on my first contacts with the Church in France, I blush at the smugness and superiority which marked some of my early reactions. The problem of the Church in France at that time seemed to many Irish priests – and I, for a time and to my shame, was one of them – to arise from the unfamiliarity of the French with Irish pastoral methods and to require for their solution little more than to learn from the achievements and successes of Irish pastoral experience!

It was not long before I came to realise that the problems of the French Church came in great part from the profound cultural changes taking place in France in the post-war period and especially in the 1960s. Quickly, too, I reached the conviction that the same changes would affect Irish society too before long, and would consequently confront the Church in Ireland; and that French pastoral experience would be illuminating for us and French pastoral strategies beneficial for us when that time came. Ireland was still shielded from some of those challenges by a certain geographical isolation and a time-lag. But I felt even then that the isolation would rapidly diminish and the time-lag contract. One of the paradoxes, however, of a society in process of change is that it is difficult, in advance of the actual change, to evoke the sense of urgency that the situation requires; and, by then, methods which would have been relevant earlier may have lost some of their effectiveness. Furthermore, the expected change, when it comes, rarely takes the precise form anticipated, and methods of pastoral response have to be constantly adapted to meet the new and fluid social situations as they emerge.

The 1950s and 1960s were exciting times also in Ireland, and especially in the North. The first generation of 'Butler-Act' undergraduates was arriving at Queen's and beginning to change the University's traditional and somewhat staid and middle-class and definitely unionist atmosphere. Since a large proportion of these students were Catholic, and several of them politically conscious, the religious/political balance in the University began to change. The University's willingness and capacity to respond to this challenge were put to the test. It was mainly from these new undergraduates that leaders in the civil rights movement and later in the SDLP were to emerge; and from them came also some of our best poets and writers, including Seamus Heaney. Many of them were students of a dynamic and inspirational lecturer in English, Philip Hobsbaum.

Meanwhile, Pope John XXIII's sunny smile and warm heart were beginning to melt Northern Ireland's ecumenical ice, even if Dr Ian Paisley was also beginning to breathe out icicles and bellow anathemas against 'Papists' and 'Romanising Protestants'. Orange parades were beginning to take on, at least for a short time, something of the character of folklore and fun which all could enjoy. In the early 1960s I remember standing happily in the centre of Shaftesbury Square, watching the Lodges pass and enjoying the music (most of it, paradoxically, traditional Irish music). Change was in the air. Was Northern Ireland ready? Or would 'No' prevail, again … and again?

CHAPTER SEVEN

THE SECOND VATICAN COUNCIL

1962 was a year of new beginnings, both in the Church of Down and Connor and in the Church universal. Bishop Daniel Mageean died on 17 January of that year, after thirty-three years of episcopal ministry. He was one of the great bishops of his time in Ireland, and a pioneer in many spheres of pastoral activity. He saw the importance of modern means of communication, and organised conferences on the Church and the Press. He promoted Catholic Action, which was the term used for lay involvement in the mission of the Church in the times of Popes Pius XI and Pius XII. He saw the need for pastoral presence in the world of industry and work, and was one of the founding members of a pioneering inter-Church group called the 'Churches' Industrial Council'. His funeral was a tribute to the affection in which he was held by priests and people.

On the following 9 June, Bishop William Philbin of Clonfert was named as the new Bishop of Down and Connor. He was my greatly admired former Professor in Maynooth College and we had remained on very friendly terms ever since. He and Bishop Michael Browne of Galway, both natives of Tuam, were regarded as the leading Catholic theologian-bishops of the time. I looked forward greatly to having him as my bishop.

Bishop Philbin 'took possession' of his new diocese on 23 July, and three days later he gave me one of the greatest privileges of my life in inviting me, along with Monsignor Arthur Ryan, to accompany him as theological adviser at the First Session of the Second Vatican Council, which was to open in October. The Vice-Chancellor of Queen's University very readily and generously granted me leave of absence for the purpose. On 20 August, Bishop Philbin was installed as Bishop of Down and Connor. Monsignor Ryan, in his inimitable style, extended an enthusiastic welcome to our new Bishop in the name of the priests and the people of the diocese. Cardinal D'Alton presided, although already showing signs of age and infirmity.

Meanwhile, in the preceding months, I had already been studying several of the draft texts, called 'Schemata', for the coming Council, which had been prepared by the Ante-Preparatory Commission and its various sub-commissions. They were passed on to me for comment by Bishop William Conway, then Auxiliary to Cardinal D'Alton. I have to confess that I found these texts, and particularly the 'Theological Schema', frankly depressing. They were dry, academic, negative, apparently more concerned with condemning 'erroneous opinions' than with proclaiming the truths of faith in language more accessible to the people of today's world. They were much too reminiscent of the Latin manuals which most of us priests had left behind with relief when we left the seminary. These texts seemed to me to be directed against some of the theologians and scripture scholars whose writings I had found so stimulating and spiritually enriching when I first encountered them in Paris. The rejection of these 'pre-packaged' schemata was to be one of the exciting events of the First Session of the Council.

On 9 October 1962 I left Belfast for Rome. Cardinal D'Alton, aged eighty-two and braving his infirmities, came with his fellow-bishops, but was the guest of the nursing order of the Sisters of the Little Company of Mary (the 'Blue Nuns') for the duration of the session. Another guest of theirs was Bishop James Joseph MacNamee, aged eighty-six, whom, in a future then unthought of, I was to succeed some years later as Bishop of Ardagh and Clonmacnois. With them came their respective secretaries, Father Frank Lenny, later Auxiliary to Cardinal Conway, and Father Thomas Carroll, who later welcomed me as his bishop to Longford.

The other Irish bishops, with their secretaries or advisers, were lodged in the Irish College. The College, which, through lack of money, had never been fully finished interiorly and was certainly never 'upgraded' since its erection in the 1930s, was considerably refurbished and redecorated in preparation for the Council. Never before had the bishops of Ireland lived together for an extended period in the College, or indeed in Ireland; it was for them, as many of them were later to remark, a new and fruitful experience of episcopal collegiality in action. Concelebration had not yet been introduced, and one of the organisational problems was the provision in the College basement of individual altars for such a large residential body, and the arrangement of rotas of times for individual celebration of Mass each morning.

The Council was solemnly opened with Mass in St Peter's Basilica on 11 October 1962. It was an unforgettable experience to watch more than 2,500 bishops moving processionally through the piazza, and then taking their assigned seats in the tiered rows of seats which filled the entire nave of the vast Basilica. Pope John XXIII was carried in, in the custom of the time, on his Sedia Gestatoria, or palanquin, carried shoulder-high by attendants. The Mass, celebrated by the Dean of the College of Cardinals, the robust French Cardinal Tisserant, was solemn and impressive. Some of those present, however, already familiar with 'dialogue Masses' and more lay participation, regretted that it was a Mass without congregational responses and without Holy Communion (except for the celebrant). A solemn Profession of Faith then followed, first made by the Holy Father alone, and then by the assembled bishops. Then came Pope John XXIII's historic opening address, the echoes of which continued to resonate all through the four sessions of the Council. It was dramatic to hear these words, on a day which was to be not only the opening of the Second Vatican Council but the opening of a new and exciting chapter in the two-thousand-year history of the Church. I quote some of the salient paragraphs:

> Our duty is not only to guard this treasure (of doctrine) as though we were concerned with antiquity alone; we must

further be alert and fearless in dedicating ourselves to the task which the present age imposes on us.... The deposit of faith itself, or the truth which is contained in our time-honoured teaching, is one thing; the manner in which it is set forth, in full integrity of its sense and meaning, is another.... This is to say that ways and means of exposition must be sought which are more in harmony with the magisterium whose character is predominantly pastoral....

In this present age [the Church] prefers to apply the balm of mercy rather than take up the arms of severity and punishment. She is convinced that present-day needs are more wisely served by explaining the value of our doctrine more fully than by condemning the errors which contradict it. This is not to say that we do not encounter hazards and false doctrines and opinions today. There is no lack of them. We must guard against them and dispel them....

Under these circumstances, the Catholic Church ... through this Ecumenical Council, seeks to show herself the loving mother of all people, kindly, patient, and filled with mercy and goodness towards the children separated from her. ... For nothing is so effective in eradicating the seeds of discord and promoting harmony, peace, justice, and universal brotherhood. ...To achieve this, you will need minds serene in their possession of peace, the spirit of brotherly harmony, moderation in your reproach, dignity in discussion, and wisdom in all your deliberations.

On hearing these words, one could not doubt but that the Lord was indeed doing 'a new deed' in his Church, and that the Holy Spirit was truly at work, 'renewing the face of the earth'. The whole scene was indelibly imprinted on the minds of those who were present, even if, like myself, they were there under false pretences. Theological advisers, apart from the officially appointed Council *periti*, or 'experts', were not admitted to the opening of the Council or to its sessions. However, ingenuity found a way, and Irish College students had a long tradition of ingenuity in finding their ways to the 'best places' in St Peter's Basilica on great occasions and in advising and helping others to do likewise. Spare robes of domestic prelates, or '*monsignori*', were unearthed and distributed, well-fitting or otherwise, and Vatican stewards were reluctant to challenge persons in monsignorial soutanes and sashes. More monsignori in borrowed plumes entered the great doors of the Basilica on that day than ever before or since, and certainly more than were ever listed as monsignori in the *Annuario Pontificio*.

Later on, it often proved possible, especially after the first weeks, to get past the stewards with the help of a well-stocked briefcase and the purposeful look of a man on important conciliar business. Once or twice, however, after being challenged inside and having no *documenti* to show, I was quietly ushered outside, although with exquisite courtesy, by an attendant. Needless to say, I offered no resistance.

There were days in the first two sessions when I had reluctantly to stay at home in the Irish College. I recall re-reading on such days many of the writings of Abbot Anscar Vonier, formerly Abbot of Downside Abbey. I was struck by the way in which Vonier's theology, published many years earlier, was already in line with the theology of the Council documents. The same was true of Abbot Marmion, whom many were still reading avidly in those years. It was not without significance that both these men were Benedictines, and arrived at much of their theology from a starting-point in Holy Scripture, in the Liturgy and in the early Church Fathers, extracts from whose writings frequently recur as readings in the Office of Readings in the Breviary. As I have remarked earlier, our theological formation in Maynooth was already a good preparation for the renewed theology of the Council.

Meanwhile, the work of the Council began with the first General Congregation of 13 October. An impressive ceremony at the beginning of each sitting was the processional carrying in of the Book of the Gospels and its 'enthronement' on the altar. This was followed by daily celebration of the Eucharist, which, in turn, was sometimes conducted in one of the Eastern Catholic rites. Each sitting began with the recitation by all present of the prayer, 'Adsumus', which goes back to Isidore of Seville in the eighth century and which has been used at Church Councils since early medieval times. It is still recited daily at the beginning of each session of the Synod of Bishops and is also said before each meeting of the Irish Episcopal Conference.

Following this day's opening session all the talk was of a 'sensational development': Cardinal Frings of Cologne and Cardinal Liénart of Lille had proposed, and the Council Fathers had agreed, to ask for an adjournment to allow more time for reflection on the names proposed for membership of Conciliar Commissions for the various topics to be debated. This implicitly meant rejecting the lists already prepared by the Preparatory Commission, which had a strong Curial representation. This was the first public sign that the Council would follow its own way and not simply 'rubber-stamp' prepared plans or documents. It was also a sign of the Franco-German theological co-operation, which was to prove so important later. The French and German bishops were joined in later weeks by those from Belgium and Holland. These bishops had already been making very thorough preparations for the Council, with the active involvement of the Catholic Theology Faculties of Germany, the Theology Faculties of the French Instituts Catholiques, the Catholic University of Louvain and the Catholic University of Nijmegen in Holland.

The spirit of 'brotherly harmony, moderation in approach and dignity in discussion', which Pope John XXIII had called for in his opening address, was not always evident in the academic corridors of theologians in Rome. When we arrived in the Irish College, we found ourselves plied with copies of articles emanating from Fathers Spadaforo and Romeo of the Lateran University, which were bitterly critical of the Biblical Institute, commonly known as the Biblicum, in Rome, and particularly of Fathers Lyonnet and Zerwick. These two scripture scholars were accused of denying the historicity of the Gospels, and of 'neo-modernism' in general. There were even intimations of nationalistic rivalries, between Italians and Germans, for example, anticipating the slogans which later became familiar, about 'the Rhine flowing into the Tiber' or 'la bruma Nordica', the cold mists of the North, moving in to cloud the clear blue skies of Rome! A few days after our arrival in Rome Fathers Malachi Martin and Frank McCool from the Biblical Institute arrived at the College to give us the Institute's view of the Lateran University articles. I had read some of Lyonnet's writings, and found them excellent, so I was shocked to read the accusations levelled against him. There was little doubt, however, but that Cardinal Bea, who had earlier been Prefect of the Biblicum, was the real target of the Lateran onslaught. Bea had become synonymous, in the eyes of some senior members of the Curia, with suspect 'progressive' trends in the Church.

On the following Sunday, I visited San Clemente to meet Father Conleth Kearns, the distinguished and highly respected Irish Dominican. He confirmed me in my view of the complete orthodoxy of Lyonnet and Zerwick, and of the outrageous nature of the accusations levelled against them. The controversy, however, rumbled on. It had a sequel during the Second Session of the Council, when the recently elected Pope Paul VI visited the Lateran University for the opening of its academic year and pointedly exclaimed: 'Never again, but never again, must there be such disedifying polemic' between Catholic academies. His 'Non mai ... non mai', was received with enthusiasm by the Irish contingent present on that occasion.

I was able in these first weeks to have long talks with Fathers de Lubac, Congar and Daniélou. It was clear that they were among the theologians who were already working with bishops from France, Germany, Holland and Belgium, on new drafts for a doctrinal document to replace the proposed 'Theological Schema' which had been prepared by the Preparatory Commission. They were agreed that the Schema, as it stood, was quite unacceptable, and did not conform to the aims of the Council, as these had been outlined by Pope John XXIII in his opening address. I also met with Monsignor Etchegaray, then secretary to the French bishops, later to be Cardinal and then President of the post-conciliar Pontifical Council for Justice and Peace. A consummate organiser, this young Basque priest arranged a meeting of bishops' secretaries for an exchange of information. It was decided at this first meeting that further meetings should be arranged, and these became a feature of all four sessions of the Council. I had the privilege of attending them. These meetings were invaluable for keeping oneself informed, not only about the official proceedings of the Council, but also about what Etchegaray called the 'petite histoire', a genre of 'insider knowledge' which is more reliable than gossip, but less certain than official information – though much more interesting!

Meanwhile, lectures by theologians and bishops were being organised all over Rome. The young Hans Küng drew large attendances. In 1961, he had already published an excellent book about the coming Council, outlining his hopes for its deliberations. This book appeared in English as *The Council and Reunion*. The Council did in fact fulfil many of Küng's hopes. However, as the Council progressed, it was already possible to discern in his lectures and writings some of the traits which were later to make him an *enfant terrible* of the Church. I confess that he seemed to me, even then, to be an 'angry young man', scathing in his criticism of those with whom he disagreed, and tending to be aggressive and polemical in style.

The Dutch, with their natural talent for organisation, soon set up an information centre, I-DOC, which issued regular bulletins in the principal languages during the Council Sessions. This centre became a great clearing-house for news of the Council and a favourite rendezvous for journalists. Irish and other English-speaking journalists frequented it. Seán Mac Réamoinn, one of the most popular of them all, organised a group which met for Mass daily and experienced the intimacy of Mass celebrated with a small but deeply involved congregation and with active lay participation. Among them were T. P. O'Mahony and the late and great Kevin O'Kelly. I met Tom O'Mahony in St Peter's Square many years later; he had come on a visit to Rome to retrace the memories of those years when, for both of us, the world and the Church were young. Later still, the United States bishops set up an information centre, issuing regular bulletins. Michael Smith, then a seminarian in third year theology, now Bishop of Meath, was assiduous in collecting these bulletins on every working day and distributing them among the bishops and *periti*. Michael acted as one of a team of note-takers (*minutanti*) at the Council and is perhaps the only remaining Irishman who attended every session. He shared this distinction with the late Thomas Morris, formerly Archbishop of Cashel, until the archbishop's death last year.

Where there are journalists, there is news, official and unofficial. News, speculation, rumour and gossip abounded in Rome in those Council years. Council jokes were circulated and were sometimes pointers to developments within the Council Sessions. On 20 November the Council voted by majority to reject the Preparatory Theological Schema, and Pope John XXIII confirmed this the next day by establishing a new Theological Commission, chaired jointly by Cardinals Ottaviani and Bea. These two came to symbolise the two trends emerging within the Council, the 'conservative' or 'traditional' trend, represented symbolically by Cardinal Ottaviani, Prefect of the Congregation of the Holy Office, and including most of the senior members of the Curia, and the 'progressive' trend, represented by Cardinal Bea, Head of the newly created Secretariat for Christian Unity. Promptly the joke spread around Rome that the 'progressives' were 'flying BEA'. (In Italy, British European Airways, as it was then called, used the advertising slogan: 'Volate BEA', 'Fly BEA'.) On a later date, Ottaviani was addressing the Council and was in full flight, when Cardinal Alfrink of Utrecht, who was presiding at the session, cut him off for exceeding the time limit. This caused a sensation and was taken as a serious rebuff to Cardinal Ottaviani and his supporters. Some wit spread the joke that a sign had been put up overnight at the Holy Office building, reading: 'Affitasi', 'To Let'.

It is worth recording that Monsignor John Quinlan, who was then studying at the Biblicum and was later to become Professor of Sacred Scripture at Maynooth, was sole begetter of many of the best Council jokes. It was possible to establish, indeed, the average length of time which it took for a joke to complete the whole circuit of clerical Rome and return to its starting-point; one had only to calculate how long it took for a John Quinlan joke to be told back to himself. One of the words featured in the first two sessions of the Council was 'midrash', the Hebrew word for a literary genre in which biblical facts or events were elaborated or embellished for theological or catechetical purposes. John Quinlan would ask, 'Is there a cure for Midrash?' The answer was, 'Yes; rub the affected part against the door of the Holy Office on three successive days!' At the end of the Fourth Session, when the Irish bishops said goodbye to Rome and together took the same plane back to Dublin, John had prepared a special menu card in Latin for the in-flight meal. It was a *tour de force*. Headed 'Minutum', the Latin original of 'menu', it featured soup as 'jus canonicum', with a pun on 'jus', 'juice'. 'Brussels sprouts' appeared as 'Ephemerides Lovanianses' ('Louvain Daily'); 'petits fours' became 'Quod Jacobi Dublini fecit' , or 'Jacob's best of Dublin'; smoked salmon became 'salmo, re nicotanea intinctus', or 'salmon exposed to nicotine'. Coffee was 'potio arabica'. Even Archbishop McQuaid was seen to laugh as he read the bill of fare.

Many of the debates of the First Session centred on the Liturgy. These debates were a great learning experience for those who had not been familiar with the liturgical renewal which had been in progress in countries like France and Germany in the two decades preceding the Council. It became clear as the debates proceeded that this renewal was by no means arbitrary or 'gimmicky', but was, at its best, a return to the older and more authentic liturgical tradition of the Church. One veteran Irish bishop who found in the debates the fulfilment of what he had long been advocating was James Joseph McNamee, Bishop of Ardagh and Clonmacnois. He had long been promoting, by sermon and by pastoral letter, the cause of what the Council was later to call 'the full, conscious and active participation' of the laity in liturgical celebrations.

In the dramatic closing week of the First Session, Bishop de Smedt of Bruges, speaking in the name of the Secretariat for Christian Unity, which had been set up by the Pope in 1960, made what was to be one of the most quoted speeches of the entire

Council. A superb orator, with a fine command of Latin, de Smedt denounced three wrong attitudes which he found in the Preparatory Theological Schema, and too often in the Church, namely: triumphalism, clericalism and juridicism or legalism.

The First Session also heard the first speech at the Council by the Auxiliary Bishop of Krakow, Karol Wojtyla. It was a very significant speech on the relationship between scripture and tradition. The speech already made it obvious that Karol Wojtyla had a very important contribution to make to the Council and to the Church.

At the same time, the conviction was growing among a small group of bishops that the Council procedures needed revising, and that the Council itself lacked a coherent, comprehensive and logical plan. The conviction was also growing that completely new texts were needed, texts very different in tone and content from those proposed by the Preparatory Commissions. One of the chief movers in this regard was Cardinal Giovanni Battista Montini, then Archbishop of Milan and soon to be Pope Paul VI. In a letter dated 18 October 1962, addressed to the Secretary of State, but intended for the Pope himself, Cardinal Montini expressed a fear that 'there is not a pre-established plan' for the Council. He outlined a plan which was in fact quite close to that later followed by the Council, although nothing was known publicly about the letter and its contents until long after the Council. John Quinlan, well informed as usual, said to me, three days after the date of that unknown letter: 'Watch out for Montini; he is the barometer of the Council'.

Cardinal Montini had worked closely on this plan with Cardinal Léon-Joseph Suenens. Suenens had been appointed Auxiliary Bishop of Malines-Brussels in 1945 at the age of forty-one; he became Archbishop in 1961 and was named Cardinal by the recently-elected Pope John XXIII in 1962. He tells us himself in his memoirs that the Pope's reason for naming him Cardinal was so that he could become a member of the Central Preparatory Commission of the coming Council.

Cardinal Suenens had been preparing actively for the Council well before its opening. He had been working closely with theologians from the University of Louvain and in particular with

Monsignor Gerard Philips, Professor of Theology. Philips became the Cardinal's personal theologian during the Council and was undoubtedly a major contributor both to the outline plan of Suenens and Montini, and to the principal conciliar documents, *Lumen gentium* and *Gaudium et spes*. These two Cardinals were supported in their planning by Cardinals Bea, Doepfner of Munich and Lercaro of Bologna. The overall plan won the approval of Pope John XXIII. It was in conformity with the Pope's own general vision of the Council, as pastoral, as ecumenical and as missionary, and was in harmony with his own aim of presenting the Church to the modern world in the splendour of its truth and holiness and of proclaiming the Gospel as the sacrament of unity and peace for the whole human family.

This plan obviously entailed the rejection of the seventy prepared texts and the drafting of entirely new texts grouped in a coherent and logical structure. The plan was to distinguish between the Church in its own inner nature and structure and mystery, or as Suenens liked to call it, the Church *ad intra*, and the Church *ad extra*, namely the Church's mission to the nations, its relations with other Christians and with other religions and with non-believers, and its application of the Gospel to the great problems of modern men and women. Intensive further work on the plan of the Council was carried on by Suenens and his collaborators between the First and the Second Sessions. A residential group of theologians convened by Suenens worked between sessions in the Cardinal's residence in Malines on drafts for the Council's texts on the Church and on the Church in the modern world.

From September 1962, before the First Session, Pope John XXIII had known that he had cancer and that his days were numbered. He strongly hoped that he might have been able to see the Council completed, and for a time, thought that this could be accomplished in one session. This was wildly optimistic. However, as the Pope himself remarked, 'So far as Councils are concerned, we are all novices.' The last weeks of the 1962 session were clouded over by signs of the Pope's terminal illness. In November the *Osservatore Romano* let it be known that the Pope was ill. On 5 December he asked that that day's meeting of the Council be terminated early, so that he could greet the bishops and the faithful in St Peter's Square from the window of his apartment at noon, the time of the daily Angelus. It was an emotional moment for all, and notably for the Pope himself. He spoke to the assembled crowd, bishops, priests, nuns, brothers, lay men and women, in a voice that was weak and faltering; but we could catch his words, obviously spoken impromptu:

> What a spectacle we see before us here today: the whole Church [*tutta la chiesa*] in all its fullness. Here are its bishops. Here are its priests. Here are its faithful people. The whole family is here, the family of Christ.

On the next day, the Pope addressed a letter to the Council announcing the setting up of a new Co-ordinating Commission to continue the work on the Montini-Suenens plan in advance of the Second Session. The letter was greeted with enthusiastic applause. I observed Father de Lubac among the *periti tribune*; he could not conceal his delight. The next day the Pope attended the Council in person, and it was painful to observe how weak and ill he was. He was able, however, to attend the final meeting on 8 December and to give a concluding address. He asked people not to be discouraged by the slow pace of progress. It was necessary, he said, for bishops to get to know one another, to 'understand each other's heart', to learn about the diversity of pastoral situations in the Church, and above all to enter spiritually 'into the heart and substance of the divine plan'.

The Second Session
On 22 January 1963, Cardinal Godfrey of Westminster died. Cardinal D'Alton, in spite of his age and infirmity, insisted on going to the funeral. 'I'll go', he said, 'should it be the last thing I do.' It nearly was the last thing he did; it certainly was the last time he was to leave Ara Coeli. Cardinal D'Alton died on 31 January. The funeral, on 6 February, took place in arctic

conditions, which those who took part could never forget. The chief sees in England and in Ireland, Westminster and Armagh, were vacant together.

On 3 June, the day on which Pope John XXIII died, I was admitted to hospital for thoracic surgery. The recurrent tuberculosis from which I had suffered was now dormant; but the doctors agreed that recurrence was always possible so long as the infected area, the top lobe of the left lung, remained in place. They therefore strongly recommended lobectomy. The few days after surgery were days of intense pain, in spite of pain-reducing drugs. I remember noting at the time how pain absorbs consciousness; it is not that one *has* pain, one *is* pain. I found strength in daily Holy Communion and comfort in repeating the words of St Paul: 'Christo confixus sum Cruci', 'With Christ, I am nailed to the Cross'. My suffering, I well knew, was minimal in comparison to his, but it was good to know that I shared, in however small a way, in the pain of Christ which redeemed the world.

On 21 June, Cardinal Montini was elected Pope and took the name of Paul VI. Next day, I was discharged from hospital. For several weeks I was housebound and listened a lot to the radio. I was able to follow President John Fitzgerald Kennedy's historic speech in Berlin and then his triumphant progress across Ireland and the magnificent oratory of his address to the Oireachtas in Dublin. In August, I went to Paris to complete my convalescence. It was there that I heard the news of the appointment of John Carmel Heenan as Archbishop of Westminster, and, a week later, on 15 September, of the appointment of William Conway as Archbishop of Armagh. Four days later, I received a telegram from Archbishop Conway, telling me that he was very anxious that I should come with him to the Second Session of the Council as his theologian, and that Doctor Philbin approved this suggestion. Naturally, I was excited at this, for I had thought that the First Session would be the last and only session I could hope to attend. I was hesitant about asking permission from Queen's University for a second term of absence, but the Vice-Chancellor replied immediately to my telegram and most generously granted the permission. On 28 September I arrived again in Rome, and on 29 September the Second Session opened.

In his opening address, Pope Paul spoke mainly of the complementary roles of papal primacy and episcopal collegiality in the Church. Concerning his own pontificate, he alluded to a mosaic in the apse of St Paul's Outside-the-Walls and said:

> We recognise ourselves in the figure of our predecessor, Honorius III, who is represented [in that splendid mosaic] as a humble worshipper, tiny and prostrate, kissing the feet of a Christ of gigantic dimensions, who, as a kingly teacher dominates and blesses the people gathered in the basilica which symbolises the Church.

Addressing his remarks towards the observers from other Churches, he said:

> If we are in any way to blame for our prolonged separation, we humbly beg God's forgiveness and ask pardon too of our brothers who feel themselves to have been injured by us.

It was the first time a Pope had asked forgiveness for Catholic sins against the unity of Christians. His example has been repeatedly followed by Pope John Paul II.

There was much speculation as to how the Council would fare under a new Pope. It was very soon made clear that the Pope and Cardinal Suenens would continue to work closely together and that the Council would proceed along the lines of the overall plan elaborated by both of them. The cumbrous system of having ten presidents chair the meetings in rotation was replaced by the appointment of four moderators to undertake this function. The four were Cardinals Agagianian, Doepfner, Lercaro and Suenens. Of these, the latter three were seen as the key men of the Council; they were dubbed the 'Three Synoptics'. Cardinal Agagianian was known in Ireland, having visited Dublin for the 1961 celebrations in honour of St Patrick.

A month after the Second Session opened, Cardinal Suenens was asked by the Pope to preach the homily at the memorial Mass for Pope John XXIII in St Peter's Basilica, on the anniversary of his election as Pope. Cardinal Suenens rose to the occasion superbly. His homily was a masterpiece of evocation of the memory of one of the most loved popes of all time. He was applauded many times in the course of that homily. He himself called this 'one of the greatest moments of his life'.

Cardinal Suenens

I may be allowed at this point, at the risk of digression, to say something more about Cardinal Suenens. Undoubtedly, he was one of the great figures of the Second Vatican Council; this was undeniably his finest hour. I fear, however, that he fell short of unqualified greatness, and this because of some less admirable traits in his personality, and particularly because of an almost childish vanity. He needed popular attention, he loved public acclaim. He made the most of his friendship with Pope Paul VI. Peter Hebblethwaite reports how, immediately after the Conclave which elected Cardinal Montini as Pope, when, according to custom, the new Pope appeared on the balcony to give his blessing, Cardinal Suenens appeared alongside Paul, as though he were the 'king maker', thereby incensing those conservative cardinals who had not voted for the new Pope (see *Paul VI: The First Modern Pope,* HarperCollins, 1993). The Suenens version of this event is different. According to his account, this incident happened on a different occasion, when he was having a meeting with the new Pope and the time came for the mid-day Angelus. He says that the Pope, by a gesture, indicated that Suenens should come out to the balcony with him.

During the Council sessions, Suenens gave quite a number of public lectures in various venues. I attended several of these and noted how, in each case, Cardinal Suenens brought the session to a close by looking at his watch and saying, 'You must excuse me now; I have an appointment with the Holy Father.'

Suenens passed through a series of successive enthusiasms in the course of his long life: among these were the Legion of Mary, the renewal of religious life for women, the Council itself, the post-conciliar period of 'contestation', and, finally, the charismatic renewal movement. There were of course admirable constants which remained unchanged throughout all these phases, chief among which were his devotion to Our Lady, his concern for evangelisation, and his commitment to ecumenism.

It was the post-conciliar period which brought into the open tensions between himself and Pope Paul VI, which were felt by some to have begun already during the Council. I happened to be present at an international gathering of European bishops at Chur in Switzerland in 1969, where Suenens seemed to take a very public stand on the side of the post-conciliar 'protesters' and against Pope Paul. This was an anticipation of the series of symposia of bishops which were later to be organised under the auspices of the Council of European Episcopal Conferences (CCEE). Cardinal Conway had asked me to accompany him to this meeting, at which about a hundred bishops took part. The meeting evoked unusual public interest and media coverage, mainly because of an 'alternative symposium' which was being held at the same time in the same city by about a hundred priests from different European countries. These were assembled in a common demand for a number of changes in the Church, and especially in a demand for 'optional celibacy' for priests. They were given the title of 'prêtres contestataires', 'protesting' or 'dissenting' priests. They demanded a meeting with the bishops; and though a formal meeting did not take place, informal contacts were established. The priests, with lay men and women supporters, were admitted to the public session on the opening and again on the closing day of the symposium, and these days were also open to the media.

The closing session of the symposium was a time of high drama. An unprecedented number of journalists, print and electronic, from the world media, were present. The final address was given by Cardinal Suenens. He raised the question of priestly celibacy. Early in his address, he dramatically drew from his pocket a letter which he said he had just received from Hans Küng. This was by way of being a *cri de coeur*, said to come from hundreds of unhappy priests for whom compulsory celibacy had become an intolerable burden, and who insisted on their right to marry and to remain in active priestly ministry. The priests and their supporters, who thronged the gallery above the meeting hall, applauded wildly during the speech. I closely watched the rows of bishops in the hall; not a single bishop applauded. The contrast between the stony silence of the bishops and the frenetic applause of those in the gallery was very striking. Suenens' own Belgian bishops looked straight ahead in studied silence. The Cardinal, who was such a strong advocate of collegiality, was completely isolated from his brother bishops, even those of his own Episcopal Conference. Many commented on the fact that Suenens had not shown the Küng letter to any of his fellow bishops, although all of the journalists had the text in their hands in advance, and it was reported in full in the world's media that evening and the next day. Suenens gives a sanitised version of this event in his memoirs, claiming that he was attempting to build bridges. His fellow bishops clearly felt that the bridge did not reach their shore. Cardinal Suenens himself, in his memoirs, speaks of a period of tension within the Belgian Episcopal Conference, when he found himself blamed for acting unilaterally and without dialogue or consultation with his own bishops.

In the same year as the Chur symposium, 1969, Cardinal Suenens gave a celebrated interview to the journal *Informations Catholiques Internationales*, on 'The Unity of the Church in the perspective of Vatican II', which included veiled criticism of Pope Paul's alleged centralising tendencies, which contrasted, so Suenens claimed, with the Vatican Council's teaching on collegiality. In the next year, 1970, Cardinal Suenens was in the limelight again with an article published in the leading French newspaper, *Le Monde*. In this article, Suenens spoke of the 'deadlock' concerning priestly celibacy, and explicitly blamed the Pope for not allowing the subject to be discussed at the Council, thereby, he again claimed, breaching the spirit of collegiality.

This article drew from Pope Paul the sharpest response he ever made to anyone, a response which undoubtedly reflected the pain he felt at this very public criticism coming from a personal friend. The Pope robustly defended his role on collegiality, pointing to the establishment of the Synod of Bishops as evidence of this. He declared emphatically that he was not a prisoner of any single theological school. He expressed his 'amazement and sorrow' (*nostro doloroso stupore*) at claims to the contrary, which were not, he said, 'in keeping with the fraternal style required for collegiality' (quoted by Peter Hebblethwaite, op. cit.).

Pope Paul's subsequent relations with Cardinal Suenens were models of what I can only call saintly forgiveness. Suenens, however, as Hebblethwaite remarks, always left himself 'escape routes'. On controversial issues such as birth control, celibacy, etc., he always protested that he was personally in agreement with official Church teaching and was not demanding change, but was only asking for debate. He spoke frequently, at the Council and after it, about birth control, but he never made clear where he himself stood on this matter. His 'dissenting' period, in any case, was not too prolonged. It was replaced by a new enthusiasm, this time for the Charismatic Renewal Movement. He first experienced this in the United States in 1972, and it was to be the most enduring enthusiasm of his life. This movement attracted most of his attention from 1972 until his death in 1996, at the age of ninety-two. He said he had been commissioned by Pope Paul to assume responsibility for the worldwide Renewal Movement and to guide its development in close unity with the Church. In conformity with this commission, Suenens published a series of *Malines Documents*, with the aim of providing solid theological underpinning for the whole charismatic movement. These documents certainly provided a very valuable service to the movement and to the Church.

Peter Hebblethwaite speaks of a 'transformed' or 'recycled' Suenens, and notes his abandonment of the 'liberal' or 'progressive' camp. Suenens himself, in his memoirs, speaks of a 'turning-point' in his relations with Pope Paul VI, 'since the problems of the Council were from here onwards increasingly replaced by new concerns: ... [including], in particular, plans to revive the

Charismatic Renewal Movement'. This period, however, was probably the manifestation of the most authentic sides of Cardinal Suenens' complex personality. He chronicles this phase of his life in a book entitled *The Hidden Hand of God*, which records his lifelong collaboration with Veronica O'Brien, the remarkable County Cork woman who founded the Legion of Mary in France and Belgium, and who shared Cardinal Suenens' enthusiasms during fifty years, particularly his earlier enthusiasm for the Legion of Mary and his later enthusiasm for charismatic renewal. She survived the Cardinal by two years, and died in February 1998, at the age of ninety-three. May they rest in the peace of Christ, and may Cardinal Suenens be far removed from any hurt that could come from presumptuous criticisms of certain aspects of his career by people like myself!

A most impressive side of Cardinal Suenens was shown on the occasion of a visit he made to Armagh and to Belfast in January 1986 to preach at ecumenical services for the Week of Prayer for Christian Unity. St Anne's Cathedral in Belfast had the usual picket of protesters from the Free Presbyterian Church outside the Cathedral. What we did not know as we passed them was that little pockets of protesters were posted at various points inside among the congregation. Each time Cardinal Suenens approached the lectern and tried to speak, protesters jumped up, waving bibles and protesting loudly. When they were quietly ushered out by stewards, and the Cardinal again attempted to speak, another group in another part of the Cathedral repeated the performance. This happened several times before order and quiet could be restored. Cardinal Suenens was able to say only a few sentences. The calm and unperturbed demeanour of the Cardinal, then aged eighty-one, was most impressive. He has the kindness, in his memoirs, to recall that I, who was Bishop of Down and Connor at the time, said to him on that occasion that the title of one of his books, *Nature and Grace in Unity*, would be an appropriate motto for himself.

Outside the Cathedral, as we left, some Free Presbyterians were distributing tracts. These contained vile attacks on the Catholic Church, and various and, indeed, sick calumnies against the

Cardinal himself. This sad episode was a vivid illustration of the need for all of us in Northern Ireland to join our Christian energies together to eliminate the repulsive and malign disease of sectarian bigotry from our society.

When all the possible criticisms have been made, it must be repeated that Cardinal Suenens was a dominant figure of the Second Vatican Council. He helped to design its overall plan, reducing the seventy preparatory documents to the actual sixteen which it issued, and giving them a logical structure and a sound theological and spiritual content. With the help of Monsignor Gerard Phillips and other theologians, he was the main author of several chapters of *Lumen gentium*, especially those on the universal call to holiness, the charisms of the laity, episcopal collegiality and the role of the Blessed Virgin Mary, Mother of God, in the Mystery of Christ and the Church. Cardinal Suenens had been the first to raise at the Council the question of the retirement of bishops at age seventy-five. Loyally, when he reached that age in 1980, he offered his retirement to Pope John Paul II, and it was accepted. His successor, Cardinal Danneels, tells us that Pope John Paul II remarked to him that 'Cardinal Suenens played a crucial role during Vatican II and the Universal Church owes much to him'. The last word about Cardinal Suenens can be left to Pope John Paul. In a letter addressed to Cardinal Danneels, which was read at Suenens' funeral, the Pope said:

> I remember with emotion the place which Cardinal Suenens held in the theological and pastoral reflection which took place during the sessions of the Second Vatican Council, and also the ability with which he conducted the debates, with a great openness to the work of the Holy Spirit and an attitude of attentive listening to the Conciliar Fathers. I ask the Lord to receive into his peace and his light one who was a pastor in love with Christ and with his Church of [Malines-Brussels], which he guided with the concern that it should remain faithful to its Lord and that it should, at the same time, be present to the world of this time.

The Council debates

After that long digression, I return to the work of the Second Session of the Council. The schema on the Church, *De Ecclesia*, which was eventually to become *Lumen gentium*, occupied the first weeks of the session. At the end of the first week, I became the proud possessor of a *biglietto personale*, obtained for me by Cardinal Conway; this was a document authorising me to attend all sessions of the Council as his personal theologian, and it carried the right of admission to the Periti Tribune (to which I had frequently sneaked access already without a biglietto!). This tribune was at the top of the left-hand end of the nave, under the Tribune of St Andrew. This was where I was to stay during all sessions from then on. Father de Lubac was frequently in the seat beside me, and I often found myself also side by side with Monsignor Carlo Colombo, who was personal theologian to Pope Paul VI himself. The observers from other Churches were in a tribune on the opposite side of the central aisle. Having a *biglietto* meant that I could look all men in the eye and fear not any Vatican steward!

Early in the third session, Dr Gerard Mitchell, Professor of Theology at Maynooth, visited the Irish College to 'get a feel' of the Council. He gave a lecture in the College on collegiality, and quite rightly pointed out that the ratification by the Council of the doctrine of episcopal collegiality would not require him to 'change a single line of his lectures'. One former student, with a pungent but not too unkind sense of humour, whispered that 'Mitch' never changed a line of his lectures anyway! But Dr Mitchell's point was well taken. Collegiality was standard teaching in Maynooth long before the Council.

On 22 October Archbishop Heenan vigorously criticised 'certain periti', who, he claimed, were using bishops as spokespersons to air their own private and erroneous views. This was not John Carmel's best shot! He succeeded in wounding both the theologians, who resented the criticism, and some of his fellow bishops, who were irked at being represented as mere 'mouthpieces' of the opinions of theologians. Next day, the Council Secretary, Monsignor Felici, in a surprising move, praised the theologians, 'many of whom', he said, 'in silence and by hard work, rendered great service to the Council'. We were left wondering who among us were included in Felici's 'many', and whether the praise was more for our 'silence' than for our work!

Cardinal Conway had been assigned to the Council's Commission for Clergy. He made an important speech on 9 October, asking for a special document on the ministry and spirituality of priests, pointing out that much was said in the draft text on the Church about bishops and their ministry, but that priests were in danger of being neglected. His speech was widely welcomed and supported. It helped to bring about a decision that a separate Decree on the life and ministry of priests be prepared. A small number of drafting committees of theologians and bishops was set up to work on various sections of this document, and I became a member of one of them. I found myself working with great theologians like Yves Congar and Joseph-Marie Le Guillou, both Dominicans, each of whom I had known since my Paris days ten years earlier. The group also included Archbishop Villot, later to become Pope Paul VI's Secretary of State, Bishop Renard of Lille and Bishop Schmidt of Metz. The chief drafters in the group were Congar and Le Guillou. The document eventually issued as *Presbyterorum ordinis*, on the ministry and life of priests. However slight my own contribution to its drafting, I have always felt a certain pride in being associated with this document.

To give more momentum to the Council debates, five crucial propositions were put to the bishops on 29 and 30 October, to ascertain the Council's views on the most keenly debated issues, notably collegiality and the restoration of the permanent diaconate. On 30 October the Council voted by a large majority to accept all five propositions. This was hailed as a resounding victory for the 'progressive' side. In retrospect, it is clear that this marked a decisive moment for the whole work of the Council. Nevertheless, as we shall see later, the session still had some difficult moments to come.

Early in November, we learned of the death of Archbishop Daniel Mannix of Melbourne, at the very advanced age of ninety-nine. In the same month, one of the 'firebrands' of the Council,

Maximos V Saigh, Melchite Patriarch of Antioch, who on principle, as an oriental, refused to speak in Latin (the official language of the Council) and always spoke in French, pressed for the introduction into the Latin Church of Synods of Bishops on the oriental Christian model. After an audience with Pope Paul, he complained about the slowness of progress of Council and about the difficulties of getting consensus. He was reported as having said that Pope Paul replied:

> Send me your papers. I do not promise to be able to implement them immediately. But I ask you to have patience. I know men and I know how hard it is to get agreement. One must learn to wait. Some problems are solved only by death.

I must say that I strongly doubt that Pope Paul would have spoken the last sentence. It is quite uncharacteristic of him to speak thus about anyone. There may be an element of 'progressive midrash' here, due to the French Marist priest who was Maximos' theologian and who was the source of the above report.

A dramatic moment in the Second Session was the entrance of Cardinal Josef Slipyj, recently released from a Soviet prison. A bishop of the Ukrainian Church, he was tangible evidence of the sufferings of modern confessors of the faith in the Churches of Eastern Europe. He spoke to the Council for more than half an hour, but no one felt that he was exceeding the time limit.

During the last weeks of the session, Pope Paul gave an audience to the French bishops. He spoke warmly of the theological development and pastoral initiatives which had characterised the Church in France, and said that 'the intellectual bread of the Church is baked in the ovens of France'. Nevertheless, he pointed out, France's place in the Church brought great responsibilities with it for the bishops, and he asked that they exercise due vigilance over these developments. He pointed out, significantly, that if the proper vigilance were exercised by bishops at local level, there would be less need for recourse to the Offices of the Roman Curia and for intervention by them. This address obviously gave encouragement to the French bishops, as well as to the 'progressives' of the Council generally. It also revealed Pope Paul's sense of indebtedness to France, many of whose Catholic intellectuals and theologians he valued highly, particularly theologians like Léonce de Grandmaison, de Lubac and Congar, and laymen like Maritain, Bernanos and Guitton.

On 19 November, Cardinal Bea introduced at the Council a statement on Catholic relations with the Jews. The document eventually became part of the Decree *Nostra aetate*, 'In our times', which deals with the Church's relations with non-Christian religions generally. The sections on relations with the Jewish people opened a new chapter in Catholic-Jewish relations and was warmly welcomed by many Jews. It brought special joy to my fellow-peritus, Monsignor Arthur Ryan, who was already an esteemed friend of the Jewish community in Belfast. He spoke about it in a lecture to the Belfast Jewish Institute in 1964.

A question frequently asked is, 'Where were you when President Kennedy was assassinated?' I do not have to search for an answer. I was walking along the cloisters in the Irish College, Rome, on 22 November 1963, at 7.25 p.m., on my way to supper, when I caught up with Bishop Patrick Dunne, Auxiliary Bishop of Dublin, who gave me the news. It was a shocked and hushed dining-room as we ate our evening meal.

The last week of the Second Session was marked by confusion, both within the Council and outside it. The Council rumour mills went into overdrive. The week was dubbed by the 'progressives' as the '*settimana nera*', the 'black week'. Pope Paul was said to have 'lost his nerve', 'given in' to conservative pressure and 'back-tracked' on collegiality and other issues. The Council was said to be as good as dead; all that the Pope now wanted, it was claimed, was to find a plausible pretext to pronounce the Council ended. During that week I met with Raffael Sabbatini, and heard the 'inside story'. It went like this: Yes, the Council had failed and only needed the curial pathologist to pronounce it dead. The pretext which Pope Paul had thought up was to announce a pilgrimage to the Holy

Land. ...And so the story went on, in all its melodramatic detail. The story was, of course, sheer fantasy; it appeared in a more elaborate form some months later in the shape of a book called *The Pilgrim*.

Such rumours bore out the account of the different phases of a Church Council which was given in a lecture at this time by Monsignor Pietro Pavan, specialist in Catholic social teaching at the Lateran. There are, he said, three 'times' in a Council's life: 'first there is the time of the devil; then the time of human agents; and last the time of God'. Sometimes, however, the first and the second times overlap!

Pope Paul VI did announce his pilgrimage to the Holy Land, which was to take place in January 1964. But this was no last-minute face-saving device. It had been planned by the Pope from a long time before. It had far-reaching ecumenical repercussions. As a return to the sources, to the Bible, to the land of the common Lord of all Christians, it appealed to Protestants. As an occasion for two meetings between the Pope and the ecumenical Patriarch, the great and saintly Athenagoros, it marked a historic point in the search for the restoration of unity between the Catholic Church and the Orthodox. It emphasised the reality of Christian life as pilgrimage, as exodus, through this world, with Christ, to the Father.

But first, the Second Session was concluded; and in spite of the rumours, it ended on a note of hope. After the concluding Mass, celebrated by Cardinal Tisserant, in the presence of the Pope, the *Constitution on the Liturgy, Sacrosanctum Concilium*, which had been approved at the last sitting by a virtually unanimous vote, was promulgated. Pope Paul greeted it as showing that the Council had the 'right order of values; God in the first place; prayer our first duty; the liturgy the first school of spirituality'. The other document promulgated on the same day, the document on social communications, *Inter mirifica,* was a hopelessly inadequate document; indeed, it was an embarrassment. It was eventually redeemed in 1971 by the Pastoral Instruction *Communio et progressio, The Means of Social Communications*, published by the post-conciliar Pontifical Commission on Social Communications, and described as 'written by order of the Second Vatican Council'. *Inter mirifica* led to protests from journalists in the Square, and to the unedifying spectacle of Council Secretary, Pericle Felici, attempting to grab protest leaflets from the hands of a journalist. Hebblethwaite reports John XXIII as having spoken of Felici as '*questo ineffabile Felici*'! Felici certainly had better moments than this one. Nevertheless, his name is remembered with a certain affection by Council veterans, and his voice is still heard in memory, intoning, after each day's opening Mass and before each sitting of the Council, '*exeant omnes*', asking all to leave except the Council Fathers and those authorised to stay, and '*audiant omnes*', asking for silence to begin the sitting.

Pope Paul's address at the closing of the Second Session was faulted by 'progressives' for two things: firstly, his uncompromising reassertion of papal primacy; and secondly, his declaration of the Blessed Virgin Mary as Mother of the Church. With regard to papal primacy, however, he stressed that primacy was at the service of and in the interests of unity. He said:

> The episcopacy is not an institution independent of and separate from, still less antagonistic to, the Supreme Pontificate of Peter; but, with Peter and under him, it strives for the common good. The coordinated hierarchy will thus be strengthened, but not undermined.

He was to reiterate this at the opening of the Third Session.

With regard to the Marian title, 'Mother of the Church', there was criticism that this was contrary to the decision already taken by the Council, to place the doctrine of Mary within the doctrine of the Church, not above it or outside it. Pope Paul rejected the criticism. It is worth noting that Gerard Philips, theological adviser to Cardinal Suenens and one of the main architects of the *Constitution on the Church, Lumen gentium*, in one of his public lectures, responded that the mother is both part of the family and above the children of the family; and equally, Mary is part of the

Church and also in some sense, and by the grace of Christ, above the Church, as Mother of the people of God who are the Church. He also stated his conviction that mariology cannot be totally contained within ecclesiology.

So ended the Second Session of the Council, the first under the leadership of Pope Paul VI. There was much speculation during the session as to where Papa Montini stood. He was, at various times, criticised by the 'conservatives' for being too 'progressive', and by the 'progressives' as being too 'conservative', and by most as dithering and too slow to make up his mind. To Father Daniel Pezeril, a well-known French parish priest and writer, and later Auxiliary Bishop of Paris, he said:

> I am perhaps slow, but I know what I want ... I have to respect the rights of the [conservative] minority. I could not simply ignore them. (quoted by Peter Hebblethwaite, op. cit.)

Canon Bernard Pawley, who represented the Archbishop of Canterbury in Rome, wrote to his Archbishop in 1964, reporting on his impressions of the Third Session and on his own farewell audience with Paul VI. He quotes the Pope as saying to him:

> I must show that I understand the aspirations of the two sides when they disagree, that I love them personally and that I respect their institutions and their ways of thinking. As captain of a ship, I have to keep her on a steady course ... so you bring all along with you. I am not going to act in a hurry. We have made great strides, but we have made them together.... It is better for me to go ahead slowly and carry everyone with me than to hurry along and cause dissension. Especially when I speak in public, I must show that I love all of my sheep, like a good shepherd. (cited by Hebblethwaite, op. cit.)

It was this spirit and this method which enabled Paul VI to bring the Council to such a successful conclusion and to guide the Church forward surely and preserve its unity during the very turbulent thirteen years of his Pontificate which were to follow the Council. It is worth pointing out that Cardinal Conway, who was close to Paul VI and who admired him enormously, followed a similar course in the post-conciliar period in Ireland.

Third Session

Cardinal Conway kindly again asked me to accompany him to the Third Session of the Council, which opened on 14 September 1964. With exceptional generosity, Queen's University again granted me leave of absence.

Pope Paul, who had always been strongly committed to liturgical renewal, was quick to implement the changes made possible by *Sacrosanctum Concilium*. The opening Mass of the session was concelebrated by himself and twenty-five bishops of different nationalities. For almost all those taking part, this was our first experience of concelebration, and it was an impressive experience. The Pope, in his opening address, dealt again with the relations between Pope and bishops, between primacy and collegiality. He pointed out that Vatican I had dealt only with the primacy and infallibility of the Pope, but had not had time, because of the onset of the Franco-Prussian war, to deal with the role of bishops and their relationships with the Pope. It was now necessary, he said, for this new Council to complete the unfinished task of Vatican I and to do so in a way which neither diluted Papal primacy nor diminished the episcopate. He invoked the sixth-century Pope Gregory the Great as emphasising that the papal office, far from diminishing the authority of bishops, 'asserted, confirmed and vindicated' that authority. He quoted Gregory as saying:

> I do not consider anything an honour to me by which my brother bishops would lose the honour due to them. ...My honour is the united strength of my brothers. (cited by Peter Hebblethwaite, op. cit.)

There is little doubt but that Paul VI had been reading Father de Lubac's *Meditation on the Church*, and was deeply impressed by it. Indeed, much of de Lubac's work found echoes in the Council's final *Constitution on the Church, Lumen gentium*. However, 'conservative' theologians continued to urge serious theological objections against the concept of collegiality, which, they argued, conflicted with Vatican I's teaching and with other affirmations of previous Councils and of theologians. It was not going to be easy for the Council 'progressives', even though they were now clearly in the majority, or for Pope Paul himself, to resist this pressure.

On 21 September I was named an official Council peritus, which brought easier access to Council texts and drafts, and I had no further need to devise strategies and stratagems for obtaining copies! I should like to remark at this point that, right through the Council sessions, I marvelled at the speed and efficiency of the Vatican Printing Press. A draft text could be still in process of being amended and voted on up to the close of one day's sitting, and then come back at the beginning of the next day's sitting, freshly printed in its amended form, and bound, and ready for distribution; and I never once detected a misprint. I felt that the staff must surely turn the night into day. Modestly, I would have to say that the Council theologians often had to do the same.

On 22 September the Council approved the text on collegiality by 1,918 votes to 322. Father de Lubac, sitting beside me in the tribune, was immensely relieved and pleased. Next day, the Council began its debate on religious liberty. There was no debate on which the United States bishops were more personally committed than this one; for them, it was the litmus test of the credibility of the whole Council. Father John Courtney Murray played an important role in the preparation of the various drafts of this text.

At the same time, work was proceeding on the text which was to become the Pastoral *Constitution on the Church in the Modern World, Gaudium et spes*. At this stage in the numbering of Council schemata, it was known as Schema XIII, 'Schema Treize'. Cardinal Suenens and his collaborators once more had a major input into this text. Their draft became known as the 'Suenens draft'. Bishop Ancel, Auxiliary of Lyon, gave a public lecture on this draft. He was a priest of a congregation known as the 'Fils de la Charité', who were committed to the evangelisation of the working class and the poor, and Ancel was one of those who kept promoting, right through the Council, the concept which we now know as the 'option for the poor'. This group had a considerable input into *Gaudium et spes*, and into the outreach to the poor of the world which has marked the whole post-conciliar period in the Church. While in general approving of the draft text, he was also perceptive in criticising some of its language and content. Interestingly, he detected a 'triumphalism of modesty' in its style, finding it too apologetic and too self-effacing in tone.

Others criticised the Suenens or Franco-Belgian draft for being much too optimistic, too slow to recognise the forces of evil in the world and in each human being, too silent about the reality of sin and the need for redemption. It would seem that a group of German theologians, who, perhaps more than any others, had close contact with naked evil under the Nazis, reworked the text in an attempt to redress its melioristic imbalance. The Schema had a vitally important place in the Council's overall plan, being the Church's main message *ad extra*, the framework for its dialogue with the modern world. It was a long text, and needed a protracted debate. In the end, it was this schema, together with the text on religious liberty, which required a Fourth Session. Cardinal Conway gave an important intervention on Schema XIII on 21 October, which was warmly applauded by the assembly.

The Schema on the *Church in the Modern World* had a section on marriage and the family. A dramatic debate on this section took place on 29 October. Cardinal Suenens caused quite a sensation by his speech, calling for a revised theology of marriage and for re-examination of the traditional teaching on contraception. The speech was memorable for its highly quotable phrase in reference to the contraceptive pill: 'One Galileo affair is enough'. As often, Suenens did not state where he himself stood on this matter; he merely called for re-examination.

Indeed, some days later, speaking on a different topic, he offered a 'clarification' of his speech of 29 October. Speaking in the debate on missions, Suenens said that 'misunderstanding in public opinion' had occurred about the interpretation of his position on contraception. He had spoken, he declared, 'not with a view to changing anything in the Church's doctrine, which had been already authentically and definitively proclaimed', but only with a view to 'asking for research in this whole area'. Later, he emphatically denied a rumour that he had been asked by, or on behalf of, Pope Paul to 'clarify' his speech. De Lubac was highly critical of Suenens' speech, which, so he said to me, smacked, according to him, of 'pastoral opportunism'. I shall return to this whole question when dealing with the Fourth Session.

Cardinal Suenens' speech inevitably evoked widespread coverage and comment from the world's media. The *Times* of London, still in its thundering mode, declared the next day that 'yesterday's debate swept away much of traditional Roman Catholic thinking'. The *New York Times* called it a 'watershed in Roman Catholic theology'. Father Bernard Häring CSsR was being much quoted at the time in connection with birth control, and I arranged a meeting with him in the Redemptorist House at San Alfonso. In the course of a long interview, he spoke very disparagingly of the traditional teaching of the Church in this regard, claiming that it rested on a false biology and on an almost animal view of sex. He was dismissive about traditional views on natural law in the sphere of marriage and procreation. He claimed that the 'pill' regulated, not vitiated nature. Many of these arguments were to become standard elements in the argumentation against Paul VI's *Humanae vitae* when it appeared. I have to say that I perceived Father Häring as being dogmatic in his views and as having a closed mind, at least on this question. I admit, of course, that one should not form judgements of a person on the basis of a single interview. Häring had made a most significant contribution to Catholic moral thinking in his three-volume study, *The Law of Christ*, which I greatly appreciated. His views on many matters seemed to have changed since the publication of that work.

On 6 November Pope Paul came to the Council in person, sat at the table of Moderators, and gave an address on the missions. In the course of this, he announced his upcoming visit to India. Meanwhile, I continued working with the sub-committee on priesthood. This group had now been enlarged by the addition of Gustave Martelet SJ, later credited with being one of the drafters of *Humanae vitae*, Henri Denis of Paris and Joseph Lecuyer CSSp (who later succeeded Archibishop Lefèbvre as Superior General of the Holy Spirit Congregation). The group was united in the positive view of priestly celibacy which was later reflected in paragraph 16 of *Presbyterorum ordinis*. Pope Paul had written a letter to the Council asking that celibacy be not debated in the Assembly. He feared that a debate, and especially media reporting of a debate, might give the impression that a change in the Latin Church's discipline was being considered, and that this could have a destabilising effect on some priests. He planned to publish a document on this matter himself at a later time; this promise was fulfilled in his encyclical, *Sacerdotalis coelibatus*, published in 1967. As it was, the Council warmly applauded his letter asking that the question of celibacy be not debated, and later, by a very large majority, approved the paragraph of *Presbyterorum ordinis*, to which I have referred, which included the words:

> [The obligation of celibacy], to the extent that it concerns those who are destined for the priesthood, this Holy Synod again approves and confirms.

I feel it important to note at this point a media invention concerning Pope Paul and the question of celibacy. It was widely reported that, following *Sacerdotalis coelibatus*, he had 'ordered' every priest in the Catholic Church to renew his commitment to celibacy at the Mass of Chrism on Holy Thursday. This story is repeated to this day. It is a falsehood. There is no reference to celibacy in this rite of 'renewal of commitment to priestly service'. I find this an interesting example of how the media can create 'facts' by unfactual assertion and then by copying one another in uncritical repetition. Norman Mailer coined the term 'factoids' for such products of journalists' imagination.

I ask permission to add here two further examples of media 'factoids'. Both bear the label 'made in Ireland'. It was claimed in one report, to which I refer elsewhere, that the Holy See rebuked the Irish bishops for their 1992 statement on the abortion referendum. This is absolutely false. Another story, still current, is that the dress of President Mary Robinson on the occasion of her visit to the Pope was discourteous to the Holy Father and caused offence in the Vatican. This is total fiction. There never was any question either of offence taken or of discourtesy intended. Happily, however, in spite of everything, many journalists still believe that facts are sacred.

Pope Paul VI also asked that a *Nota Praevia*, a Prefatory Note, be appended to the *Consitution on the Church*, as an authoritative norm for the interpretation of the chapter on episcopal collegiality, and that this be published with the text of the Constitution. The Note is chiefly concerned with the reconciliation of episcopal collegiality with papal primacy, but does not in any way alter the conciliar text.

The Third Session closed on 21 November on a very positive note, with the *Constitution on the Church* (*Lumen gentium*), and the *Decrees on the Eastern Churches* (*Orientalium Ecclesiarum*), on ecumenism (*Unitatis redintegratio*), and the *Declaration on the Relations of the Church to Non-Christian religions* (*Nostra aetate*), in which special attention is called to the relationship of the Church with the Jewish people, which it describes as 'the spiritual bond linking the people of the New Covenant with Abraham's stock'.

The next day, Sunday, saw our return to Ireland, and for me Monday morning meant return to lectures at the University and business as usual.

Fourth Session

The year 1965 brought a consistory and a new Irish Cardinal. On 25 January, Archbishop Conway was named Cardinal, sharing the honour with Cardinal Heenan. It was the same day as that on which Winston Churchill died. The first Sunday of Lent of that year was the day that had been fixed for the celebration of the first Masses in the vernacular in Ireland. For reasons that will be apparent later, I wish to mention also that, during Easter week, the usual annual Congress of Christus Rex was held in Cahir, County Tipperary, and I read a paper at the Congress, with the title: 'Natural Law Morality Today'. The text was later published as an article in Ireland and in the United States, and eventually in a small book.

I did not need leave of absence to attend the Fourth Session. The first four weeks fell outside of term, and rescheduling of lectures made it possible for me to return to Rome for the closing week of the Council. The Session opened with Mass in St Peter's Basilica on 14 September. Pope Paul was obviously anxious to introduce, without unnecessary delay, the liturgical reforms authorised by the Constitution on the Liturgy, and also to update papal ceremonial in the same spirit. He entered the Basilica on foot, wearing an episcopal mitre rather than the papal tiara or triple crown, and with a new crozier, which he had had specially designed, with, at its top, the crucifix which became so much associated with him, and then with his successor, Pope John Paul II. He enthroned the Book of Gospels himself. In his address to open the session, the Pope spoke of the need for charity and unity; he announced the setting up of a new institution, the Synod of Bishops, as an instrument of collegiality; and he announced his intention of visiting the United Nations in New York before the end of the Council. He also paid tribute to the journalists who were covering the Council for their assiduous work and important role.

The most animated debates of the Fourth Session were to be those on religious liberty and on the Church in the modern world. The United States bishops continued to press for a strong statement on religious liberty. It was first to be included in the document of ecumenism, but later was assigned a separate document with the title *Dignitatis humanae*. Cardinal Meyer of Chicago had written to Pope Paul in January 1964, pleading, 'as strongly as words permit me', for a clear and strong statement. He wrote:

> The question of religious liberty is the number one most
> important question in the whole schema [on ecumenism]....
> [Without such a document] the cause of the Catholic
> Church in the United States, I am afraid, will suffer greatly
> (cited by Peter Hebblethwaite, op. cit.).

Work on the statement had continued, with involvement by
Father Courtney Murray, during and between sessions. Cardinal
Conway addressed the Council on this subject on 17 September.
There were many days of feverish rumour: would the document be
'blocked' by the 'conservatives' or not? More than sixty speeches
had already been made in the Council on the issue, but serious
difficulties of opinion had developed and questions of wording
were very keenly debated. In spite of dire predictions that the draft
text on religious liberty would be rejected, the Council voted on 21
September by a large majority that the draft be adopted as the basis
for an eventual definitive text. Afterwards, Monsignor Pavan and
Father de Lubac each assured me that Paul VI had personally
intervened to urge that a vote be taken and to state that he was
satisfied with the text.

In the course of the discussions on Schema Treize during the
Fourth Session, there was keen debate on the section on marriage
and the family, including the question of procreation, where,
naturally, the question of birth control arose. I was appointed a
member of a sub-committee to work on this question. The sub-
committee met several times during the month of October. The
meetings were held at the Belgian College. Other members of the
group were Fathers Schillebeeckx of Nijmegen, Delhaye of Lille,
Van Dodeward of Louvain, Lambruschini and Zalba of the Lateran
University, Joseph Fuchs SJ of the Gregorian University, and
Monsignor Carlo Colombo. There was intense discussion about the
wording of what was to become paragraph 51 of *Gaudium et spes*,
the paragraph on 'harmonising conjugal love with the responsible
transmission of life'. It was agreed that 'the moral aspect of any
procedure does not depend solely on sincere intentions or on an
evaluation of motives [but] must be defined by objective standards'.

During one of our meetings, there were sharp differences of opinion about what these objective standards are. Monsignor Carlo Colombo, who had joined the meeting somewhat late, read a text which he had prepared in advance. It ran:

> These [objective standards], based on the nature of the human person and his or her acts, preserve the full sense of mutual self-giving and human procreation in the context of true love. Such a goal cannot be achieved unless the virtue of conjugal chastity is sincerely practised.

No one in the room had any doubt that the wording came from Pope Paul, whose personal theologian, of course, was Carlo Colombo. The wording was adopted by the group and is now part of the Council document. I have often seen these words used, however, to defend the use of contraceptives in marriage. It is, I think, important to put on record that the wording came from the Pope who issued *Humanae vitae* in 1968.

Meanwhile, the round of lectures in Domus Mariae, a conference centre on the via Aurelia, and other venues throughout Rome continued. There has rarely if ever been such a great concentration of the world's leading Catholic theologians in Rome at the same time, and there were unrivalled opportunities for 'refresher courses' in theology. Two outstanding lectures were 'billed' to be given on the same day, 22 September, one by Father M. D. Chenu, at the I-DOC centre, and the other by Monsignor Gerard Philips at the Domus Mariae. Father Chenu spoke on the Church in the Modern World, referring particularly to the draft known as Schema Treize. I was struck by the many citations he gave from the writings and statements of Pope Paul VI and by his very favourable comments on them. Father Chenu's daily notes on the Council were published in 1995, as *Notes Quotidiennes sur le Concile,* but, unfortunately, they only reach the beginning of the Second Session.

Monsignor Philips lectured on the Constitution on the Church, *Lumen gentium.* As one of the leading drafters involved in its redaction, Philips knew more about this document than anyone else ever could. He conceded that the difficulties raised in the various debates by the 'conservatives' about collegiality were justified, since the reconciliation of the concept of collegiality with the concept of papal primacy is neither simple nor easy, and yet both are constitutive elements of Catholic faith about the Church. He recognised that the *Nota Praevia*, inserted at the express request of Pope Paul as a corollary to *Lumen gentium*, was necessary and helpful. He remarked that the patience of Pope Paul had been essential in securing a balanced text and a majority vote of approval, and that his patience was well rewarded.

In the same week, Father Congar lectured at Domus Mariae on Schema Treize. He pointed out that the text was now in its fourth draft, that he found the present draft a considerable improvement on its predecessors, and said that the improvement was in part due to the involvement of lay people in its drafting. He spoke of the dualism, Church and world, which had often been found in Catholic theology in the past, saying that this could lead to 'a world-less religion confronting a God-less world'. This dualism, he went on, must be overcome. The solution of the problem, he argued, must be to reunite anthropology with theology; for the Christian as a human being has a twofold identity, belonging both to the Church and to the world. Church and world are distinct entities, but the human being, who belongs to both, is one. The Bible, he said, is the story of God's relationship with the world and with humanity: it can be called 'the anthropology of God', and not simply the theology of God. Another dualism which must be avoided, he went on, is the excessive duality sometimes placed between nature and grace; grace transforms nature, does not eliminate it; the supernatural elevates the natural, but does not dispense with it. He noted that the earlier drafts of the Schema were criticised as being too 'optimistic' about human nature, and he conceded that there was some force in this criticism. Everything human, he said, is ambiguous, and this ambiguity needs to be stressed. The New Testament as a whole, and particularly the Letter to the Romans and the Apocalypse, stress the reality of the need for

Christian struggle against the evil inclinations within, the need to lose one's life in order to save it, the reality of sin and of evil and of judgment. He noted that some conciliar texts had benefited from the observations of Protestant theologians who were studying them closely and offering comments to their Catholic colleagues. Like all Congar's lectures and writings, I found this exposé most stimulating.

On 30 September Cardinal Conway spoke again at the Council, this time on marriage. His speech was very well received. On 4-5 October Paul VI made his 'lightning visit' to New York for a meeting of the United Nations General Assembly. In the course of a hectic thirty-six-hour day, he left Rome airport at 5.40 p.m. on Monday 4 October and arrived back in St Peter's Basilica at 12.50 p.m. on Tuesday 5 October. After that gruelling schedule, he was still able to address the Council for thirty minutes.

Before the United Nations, in a thirty-minute speech, which Hebblethwaite called 'the speech of his life' (a phrase which he had also used of the Pope's first address to the Roman Curia two years earlier), Pope Paul spoke of the 'two universalities' which met in that assembly hall, the Church and the United Nations. Each had its distinct sphere, but each shared a common commitment to the good of humankind. Paul told the assembly that he had come to 'deliver the letter entrusted to him' by the poor, the disinherited, the suffering, those who hunger and thirst for justice and human dignity; this was a plea for peace. He spoke of the millions of dead in two world wars and other conflicts, and cried: 'Never again war! Never again war!' He called for a new strategy and pedagogy of peace, whose elements would be: a new international order, based on justice, dialogue and negotiations; disarmament and the replacement of the arms race by development aid and relief, and, as the essential moral underpinning of all this, respect for human rights and human dignity.

During October 1965, in the course of one of the debates on the section on marriage and the family in the draft text of Schema Treize, an important speech was made by the relatively young Archbishop Karol Wojtyla of Crakow. At the end of the speech

Father de Lubac whispered to me, 'What a wonderful Pope that young Archbishop would make!' Thirteen years later, the conclave, the Church, and soon the world, came to agree with de Lubac. On the same occasion de Lubac recommended that I read Wojtyła's book, *Love and Responsibility,* which had just been published in a French translation and was soon to appear in English.

On 15 October I returned to Belfast for the beginning of the new term of lectures. Shortly after my return, I had a request from Bishop John Wright of Pittsburgh, who later became Cardinal Prefect of the Congregation for Clergy in Rome, to send him copies of the text of my lecture on 'Natural Law Morality Today', delivered at the Christus Rex Congress the previous April. The text had been published as a booklet and was later expanded into a small book, with the title *Natural Law Morality Today* (1965). On 17 November *The Irish Times* reported that severe criticism of this text had been made by Gregory Baum at a press conference held under the auspices of the United States bishops. The text of Baum's 'refutation' of my arguments was printed in *The Irish Times* on the next day.

It seemed that, at the press conference, one of a series held from time to time by the United States bishops, a journalist asked the panel for comment on my booklet. The panel was nonplussed; they had no knowledge whatever about it; but Gregory Baum quickly got up and read from a prepared script a criticism of my booklet, which, among other uncomplimentary things, he called 'a superficial study'. I did not feel flattered. I felt that a response was called for, since his criticisms were in the public domain in Ireland. I therefore wrote a response, which was published in *The Irish Times* on 25 November. First, I argued that my booklet was not, as it had been described, 'a pamphlet on birth control', but had for its purpose the defence of the moral tradition of natural law against misrepresentations of that tradition and mistaken views about natural law as understood in that tradition. The misunderstandings and the mistaken views which I was criticising had featured strongly, to my mind, in the abundant literature published in those years advocating a change in the Catholic Church's traditional teaching on contraception, and most of my references were to this literature. I had outlined my purpose in the opening paragraph of my booklet. I repeat part of that paragraph here:

> Much criticism of the traditional natural law approach to morality has been expressed lately in the context of writing on contraception. It is in the framework of this writing that my remarks will be set. It would not be realistic to discuss natural law morality today in any other setting. I shall not, however, be intending directly to discuss the arguments for or against the condemnation of contraception as such. Much less shall I be discussing the 'Pill'.... It is the theology of the popular writing on contraception, rather than the problem of contraception itself, which is my immediate concern.

Professor Anthony Hanson, Professor of Theology in the University of Hull, reviewed *Natural Law Morality Today* for *The Irish Times* of 26 November. He was one of a pair of outstandingly brilliant brothers, the other one being Richard Hanson, Professor of Theology in Manchester, and one-time Church of Ireland Bishop of Clogher. Hanson's review was fair and, in many respects, critically sympathetic.

This episode is of very minor importance in itself, but I report it here simply because it is part of my experience of the Council, and particularly because it illustrates the passion, and sometimes near paranoia, which surrounded the discussion of contraception at that time. It was a foretaste of the fury which, in many quarters, outside and inside the Church, was to greet *Humanae vitae* in 1968, when Paul VI reiterated the Church's traditional rejection of contraception.

I referred earlier to the fact that Cardinal Suenens never stated clearly where he stood on this question himself. Lest I be accused of a similar 'opt-out', I wish to state clearly that I was convinced before *Humanae vitae*, and remain convinced since *Humanae vitae*, that the Church's traditional teaching is true. I believe that Paul VI's enunciation of it was courageous and prophetic. I do not, however, intend to discuss the matter any further here, but I do see a need for further reflection and research on the whole issue, not with a view to reversing the teaching, but with a view to deeper understanding of it and to further pondering of the reasons for the persistent opposition to it and the apparent widespread rejection or ignoring of it. In this ongoing reflection, the voice of women must be heard and their experience taken into account, in order that the teaching may be more effectively promoted and defended.

As I have said earlier, I returned to the University at the end of the first month of the session to resume my lectures, and then on 3 December I returned to Rome for the close of the Council. I again made contact with Father de Lubac and found him very pleased with an extremely friendly conversation he had had with Pope Paul. Next day saw the official promulgation of the text on religious liberty, on the missionary activity of the Church, on the life and ministry of priests, and on the famous Schema Treize, which had become *Gaudium et spes*. This public session was also marked by the historic event of the formal withdrawal of the mutual excommunications of 1054 between Rome and Constantinople. On the same day, and at the same time, the declaration of withdrawal was being read in the Church of the Ecumenial Patriarch in Constantinople. It was a moment of great symbolic significance and intense emotion. Pope Paul brought the final public session to an end by asking forgiveness for and promising forgiveness of whatever faults had been committed during the four-yearly duration of the Council. In that spirit, the bishops exchanged with one another the Sign of Peace. The Te Deum was chanted and the session ended at 12.45 pm.

That evening Pope Paul granted a farewell audience to the periti. He spoke in French, and after reading his prepared text, expressing thanks to the theologians for their hard work and their contribution to the success of the Council, he continued with unscripted remarks. His message to us was this:

> Your work is only beginning. There faces you now the great
> task of communicating the ageless doctrine of the Church to

the modern world. You are now, as it were, well trained for that work. Believe in the importance and the value of your work for the Church and for God. Love the Church, love her with passion. Trust the Church, believe in the Church, as you would in Christ. Let this love for the Church light your desks, your books, your writings; this is my wish, this is my hope, this is my blessing.

He then gave each of us a specially bound copy of the New Testament in Latin, in the Vulgate translation, remarking that this was 'not much, but it was prepared specially for you'. I have treasured this as a very special memento of those wonderful four years. The dedication is in Latin and it reads:

> Paul VI, Pope,
> to his dear sons who as periti
> gave generous service to the Second Vatican Council,
> wishes this volume to be a sign
> of his personal gratitude
> and a reminder of his prayer for them
> to Christ, our God, Founder of the Church,
> for all that is holy and grace-giving.
> 7 December 1965

The next day, 8 December, the Feast of the Immaculate Conception of the Blessed Virgin Mary, saw the solemn closing of the Second Vatican Council. I was very happy to find myself again beside Father de Lubac. The Pope's concluding address was a quiet and eirenic meditation on the fruits of the Council. Gifts were symbolically set aside for the poorer countries of the world. Messages were read to different categories of persons representative of humankind in the modern world: to rulers; to people of thought and science; to women; to the poor, sick and suffering; to workers; to youth. Scrolls in which the various messages were written were handed over to representatives of these categories. Jacques Maritain and Jean Guitton were among those representing intellectuals. The whole ceremony was conducted in St Peter's Square in magnificent sunlight. Everything was in tune with the mood of joy and hope which filled all hearts on that day. I felt that the promise of the Lord to his people long ago was being fulfilled for his Church in our day: 'I now create Jerusalem "Joy" and her people "Gladness" ' (Is 65: 18).

Then came the farewells. Bonds had been forged between bishops from all corners of the world, who sat side by side during two months for each of four years and who now would probably never meet again, and there was sadness in the parting. For the periti it was the same. A strong sense had been formed of solidarity in a common task and in serving the unity of the Church amid the diversity of cultures and traditions. These feelings, however, were soon overtaken by the more mundane tasks of packing and preparing for departure. Next morning came the coach ride to Fiumicino. A cartoon published in some newspaper showed mitred bishops dancing in a circle beside a waiting aeroplane, and singing 'Arrivederci Roma'. I suspect that the last thing the bishops were looking forward to at that moment was the prospect of meeting again in Rome. That was over, and the future was going to be a new country to be evangelised in a new spirit and by new methods.

The journey into that future was, in the event, to be much more turbulent than our smooth flight back to Dublin. There had already been some early signs during the Council of troubles to come. As I have indicated, it had become habitual to speak of 'conservative' and 'progressive' camps. Both terms, however, were becoming flexible and loose in meaning. It was becoming evident that some people on the edges of each 'camp' had agendas of their own, which became clear only later. 'Conservatives' were emerging who would refuse to accept the Council's decisions; and 'progressives' were emerging whose agenda for reform went far beyond, indeed sometimes against, the Council's clear mind and explicit word. I had myself often felt impatient, in the course of the Council's debates, with what seemed to me to be the niggling and boring concern of the 'conservatives' about words and phrases which they wanted to see withdrawn or changed. In retrospect, I came to see how often they were right to be concerned. Words and phrases did come to be interpreted in senses totally different from those intended by the Council, or to be quoted out of context and given a meaning different from the original. Gradually, the text of the Council came to be dismissed by some as unimportant, and the 'spirit of the Council' became stressed as alone having significance. Pope John Paul has been accused, for example, of having a 'fundamentalist' fidelity to the text of the Council, while betraying its spirit!

Some of the theologians who had contributed most to the Council were sadly disappointed afterwards by what they perceived to be serious misinterpretation of the Council's teaching. Father de Lubac was one of these. I kept in regular touch with him in the post-Council years and up to his death. I visited him each year, first in Lyon-Fourvière, then in Paris at the rue de Sèvres, later at the rue de Grenelle, and finally, following a stroke, at the Little Sisters of the Poor in the avenue de Breteuil. He was deeply disappointed at the direction which some theologians, even among those he had himself taught, were taking. He felt very unhappy about how the journal *Concilium*, founded to pursue the work of conciliar renewal, began to develop. He had been a founding member of its editorial board, but came to feel that he could no longer be associated with the journal. He asked that his name be removed from the list of members, but told me that he had to write letter after letter before he succeeded in having this done. De Lubac, indeed, went through a period of depression after the Council, and it took some time for him to recover his characteristic serenity and confidence. That he did so in his latter years was due in large measure to his admiration for the leadership of Pope John Paul II.

As I shall indicate in a later chapter, I believe that the Church is now moving out of the worst period of turbulence, and that the spirit of the Council is now being rediscovered in its texts, rather than in appeals to the 'signs of the times' alone. Perhaps the diversity of interpretations of the Council is related to the point of view from which one approaches it. Some seem to begin with *Gaudium et spes*, on the Church in the Modern World, and give priority to the world, to which the Church has to be related.

Perhaps they need to rediscover that the Church which has to relate to this world is the Church whose first duty is to worship God and seek his face (*Sacrosanctum Concilium*), the Church of *Lumen gentium*, the Church whose mission is to proclaim God's word to the world (*Dei verbum*). Correlatively, then, critics of today's 'progressives' need to resist any temptation to retreat into what Congar called 'world-less' spirituality and sanctuary-bound and sacristy-confined clericalism. The true message of Vatican II rejects both extremes.

I take my concluding words about the Council from Pope John Paul II. He was most actively involved in the work of the Council, he was closely implicated in the drafting of some of its texts, particularly *Gaudium et spes*, he is intimately familiar with its whole corpus of documents. He has made the renewal programme of Vatican II the theme of his pontificate, as he had already made it the theme of his episcopate. As Cardinal Archbishop of Krakow, he had produced one of the first studies of the Council's programme of renewal written by a bishop. It is translated into English as *Sources of Renewal*, a study of the implementation of Vatican II. This is a study entirely directed towards pastoral action in his diocese, having been prepared, in fact, for a pastoral synod of the diocese. He writes:

> A bishop who took part in the Second Vatican Council feels the need to acquit himself of a debt.... These men took an active part for four years in the proceedings of the Council and in drafting its documents, and at the same time derived great spiritual enrichment from it. The experience of a world-wide community was to each of them a tremendous benefit of historic importance ... an extraordinary event in the minds of all the bishops concerned.... [It was] an exceptional and deeply felt experience.

As one who played a very minor part on the edge of the Council, I too have felt, in writing this chapter, the 'need to acquit myself of a debt of gratitude'.

CHAPTER EIGHT

SIX POPES

I have no pretensions to write a history of the modern Popes, much less of the modern Church. I speak of the Popes whose pontificates fell within my life-span, and I speak of these only in so far as their persons or works affected my life, or in so far as I had some personal contact with them. Pope Benedict XV (Giacomo della Chiesa), the Pope of the First World War, was elected in 1914 and died in 1922. The Great War had already been raging for three months when he was elected Pope, and much of his pontificate was taken up with the tragedy of the war and the problems of post-war settlement. His first encyclical was issued on 1 November 1914; it is a sustained plea for peace. He tells how deeply distressed he is by the 'spectacle presented by Europe, indeed by the whole world, perhaps the saddest and most mournful spectacle of which there is any record'. His denunciation of the war as 'useless slaughter' was rejected by all sides amid the war hysteria which seemed to grip Europe at that time. In 1917 he offered mediation in view of a peace settlement, but was rebuffed. His proposals for the Versailles Conference were ignored. Had they been followed, the history of the post-war period might well have taken a different direction. In 1920 he wrote a moving encyclical on *Peace, God's beautiful gift*, appealing for reconciliation between enemies. All through the war he carried on an extraordinary range of works of relief of the manifold misery caused by war, particularly the misery of children and the plight of prisoners and their families. Amid all these concerns, he never ceased proclaiming the Gospel of Jesus Christ. Since I was only five years of age when he died, I cannot count him among 'my' six Popes.

Pius XI

Pius XI (Achille Ratti) was elected in 1922, four years after 'the war to end all war', which tragically was to prove to be only an interlude between world wars. He wished his pontificate to be a time of renewal, renewal in the individual, in the Church and in civil society. His motto was *Redintegrare omnia in Christo*, 'to renew all things in Christ'. His first encyclical was on the peace of Christ in the Kingdom of Christ, published in December 1922. He devoted much time to the normalisation of relations between the Holy See and Italy through the Lateran Treaty, which renounced the Pope's rights to the former Papal States and established instead the independence of the Vatican City State. This put an end in principle to the reality and the mystique of the Pope as 'the Prisoner of the Vatican', and secured for the Holy See the internationally recognised autonomy which has since served as a legal basis for its supranational activities. The concordats which he signed with Italy and Germany were intended to guarantee freedom for the Church's works and mission in these countries; but, faced with the ruthlessness of the Nazi and Fascist regimes, they largely failed to achieve their aims.

Pope Pius XI actively promoted lay involvement in the mission and work of the Church, mainly through organisations known collectively as Catholic Action, which collaborated closely with the bishops and clergy in the life and work of the Church. This inevitably met with opposition from totalitarian regimes. The encyclical, *Non Abbiamo Bisogno* (We Have No Need), written, unusually, in Italian, and issued on 29 June 1931, protested vigorously against the disbandment of Catholic associations and the suppression of Catholic Action by the increasingly anti-Christian Fascist regime in Italy. The encyclical had to be delivered personally to the nuncios in Germany and in France, lest it be confiscated by the Fascists. A young Monsignor, G. B. Montini, the future Pope Paul VI, travelling in civilian clothes, delivered the document in Berlin, and Monsignor Spellman, later Cardinal Archbishop of New York, delivered it in Paris.

The Nazi regime in Germany was brutal and barbaric in its suppression of human and religious freedom and its destruction of human life, on a scale without precedent in human history. In March 1937 Pius XI wrote his strongest encyclical ever, in protest against this evil regime. It was written in German, with the title, *Mit Brennender Sorge* (With Burning Anxiety). Copies of it had to be smuggled into Germany in order to avoid its confiscation and destruction by the Nazis; it was distributed secretly by the bishops and read from the pulpits of Catholic churches throughout Germany. This document was an indignant protest against lying propaganda, destruction of truth, of human dignity, of Christian faith and of morality, by the Nazi regime, and of multiple violations by the Nazis of the Concordat. The Pope appealed particularly to youth not to be seduced by the appeal of the false gods of race and blood and nation. There have been reports of a still stronger condemnation of Nazism which was in preparation when Pius XI died, but which was overtaken by the outbreak of the Second World War and was never published.

Pius XI is perhaps best known for his encyclical on social justice, *Quadragesimo anno*, which was issued in 1931, on the fortieth anniversary of what it refers to as Pope Leo XIII's 'peerless encyclical', *Rerum novarum*. This document was eagerly studied by seminarians of my generation in Maynooth and by Catholic lay associations and study circles all over Ireland. It provided part of the motivation for the foundation of the Christus Rex Society, about which I have written in an earlier chapter. It dealt with the rights and responsibilities of capital and of labour, the right to a just wage, related to the individual and family responsibilities and burdens of workers; it dealt with the individual and social aspects of work. Addressing the need for reconstruction of the whole social order, the encyclical stressed the need for 'subordinate bodies' between the State and the individual, 'in observance of the principles of subsidiary function'. This is the first mention in papal social teaching of what we now know as the principle of 'subsidiarity'. It is interesting that this term has now passed into the secular and political vocabulary of modern society. This encyclical explores the possibility of a 'middle course' between radical capitalism, on the one hand, and dogmatic socialism on the other. With a courage remarkable for its time, the encyclical points to an evolution within socialism, 'to the point that imperceptibly these ideas of the more moderate socialism will no longer differ from the desires and demands of those who are striving to remould human society on the basis of Christian principles'.

Unfortunately, this 'middle ground' position was falsely interpreted in some quarters, notably in Salazar's Portugal, as a blueprint for a so-called 'corporatist' society, and led to an expansion rather than a reduction in State power. This was a complete misinterpretation of *Quadragesimo anno*. In Ireland, the encyclical was partly responsible for the setting up of a commission aimed at a decentralisation of State power through the setting up of vocational bodies. This Commission on Vocational Organisations was chaired by Bishop Michael Browne of Galway. Its report went the way of many reports from Government commissions everywhere; it was received, noted, filed and forgotten.

Pius XII

Pius XI died in February 1939. The ranting voice of Adolf Hitler was repeating more and more stridently, 'Danzig will and shall return to the Reich'. The next Pope would once more be called to speak peace amid the bedlam of war. After a Conclave of one day and three ballots Eugenio Pacelli was elected and took the name of Pius XII. A member of a patrician Roman family, Papa Pacelli had spent his life in the diplomatic service of the Holy See. He had served as Nuncio in Germany and had then been Secretary of State to Pius XI for the ten years preceding his election. His motto was 'Opus Justitiae Pax', 'Peace, the Work of Justice'. In August, a few weeks before the invasion of Poland, the new Pope issued a dramatic eleventh-hour appeal for peace. He said:

> Standing above all public disputes and passions, I speak to all of you, leaders of nations, in the name of God…. Nothing is lost by peace; everything may be lost by war….

His first encyclical, *Summi Pontificatus*, published in October 1939, was given the English title *Darkness over the Earth*, a title which well expresses the doom-laden atmosphere of that terrible year, and which recalls the words of Our Lord, quoted in the encyclical: 'This is your hour; this is the reign of darkness' (cf. Luke 22: 53). The Pope diagnosed the cause of this new war as a 'deep spiritual crisis, which has overthrown the sound principles of private and public morality'. He denounced racism and the deification of the State. He declared:

> Today all men and women are looking in terror into the abyss to which they have been brought…. Gone are the proud illusions of limitless progress. To hope for a decisive change exclusively from the shock of war and its final issue is idle, as experience shows.

He spoke of the suffering so unjustly inflicted on 'our dear Poland', and looked forward to the restoration of its freedom in harmony with the principles of justice and peace.

The theme of peace naturally dominated the first half of Pius XII's nineteen-year pontificate. Through encyclicals, radio messages, exchange of letters with President Roosevelt and diplomatic contacts with other world leaders, the Pope continued to work for peace; and, in his defence of human rights and social justice, he kept insisting that peace and justice are inseparable.

Pius XII was a great teacher and spiritual guide. His June 1943 encyclical, *Mystici Corporis*, on the Mystical Body of Christ which is the Church, made a significant contribution to ecclesiology; as did his encyclical, *Divino afflante Spiritu*, of September 1943, to the progress of Catholic biblical studies. Indeed, this latter encyclical stands to this day as a landmark document in this regard; it is, for example, the first authoritative document of the Catholic Church which recognises the importance of the diversity of 'literary genres' in the Bible for the interpretation of biblical texts. With the encyclicals *Mediator Dei,* of 1947, and *Musicae sacrae,* of 1955, on the sacred liturgy, Pius XII provided important resources for the overall renewal of the liturgy by Vatican II. During his own pontificate, Pius XII introduced a very successful revision of the liturgy of the Holy Week triduum, which made this liturgy, even though still celebrated in Latin, much more meaningful for both priests and people, and made what had earlier been, especially for the Mass of Chrism and the Easter Vigil, a clerical preserve, into an occasion for strong popular participation, as was fitting for the apex of the whole year's liturgy. *Evangelii praecones* of 1951 was an important contribution both to the theology of missions and to the renewal of missionary effort. *Fidei donum* of 1957, on the present state of Catholic missions, did the same with particular reference to Africa.

Pope Pius XII also made important contributions to moral theology, particularly in the domain of medical ethics. He also kept in touch with developments in modern science and technology; he confronted in a faith context the problems posed to Christians of today by advances in science, medicine, etc., and made frequent pronouncements on these subjects. Well before the Council, therefore, he had begun that 'dialogue with the modern world' which was so well addressed by Vatican II. No name is more frequently cited in the Council's documents than that of Pope Pius XII.

Pope Pius XII had his critics, however, in his own time and since. His encyclical, *Humani generis,* while stating many valid and necessary criticisms of some theological trends, also had the effect of retarding progress in theology for a time. This was chiefly because its condemnations were sometimes too generalised and unspecific, and because it was misused by some zealots, not as a 'hammer of heretics', but as a hammer of good and loyal theologians, who would later be pillars of Vatican II, and two of whom, unintentionally rendered suspect by the encyclical, namely de Lubac and Congar, would later be named Cardinals.

I met Pius XII only once; that was on the occasion of a congress of Catholic social teaching which I attended in Rome during the Holy Year, 1950. Each participant was introduced to the Pope in turn, even if only for a brief moment. He was tall, thin, somewhat hieratic and detached, almost other-worldly. Picture cards of this Pope, in white cassock, with arms extended in the shape of a cross, with the title, 'Pastor Angelicus', were common at the time. This made all the more striking the pictures of his visit to devastated areas of the city following a war-time bombing raid on Rome: the flecks of blood and dust on his immaculate white cassock brought vividly home the horror and the evil of war. His radio broadcasts, especially each Christmas and Easter, made Pius XII the first Pope to use the mass communications media, and thus establish direct contact with people all over the world.

Pius XII was, therefore, a great and modernising and reforming Pope, a Pope of justice, of compassion, of peace. But it has become almost an automatic reflex, in some quarters nowadays, to criticise him. When he spoke, in his first encyclical, about the failure of his efforts to avert the outbreak of war, he said:

> While still some hope remained, we left nothing undone to avert the horrors of a world conflict … even at the risk of having our intentions and our aims misunderstood.

His intentions and his aims were indeed respected by many at the time, even if his efforts were not successful. At his death, fulsome tributes were paid to his heroic work during the war for the relief of distress, the harbouring of refugees, the comforting of all who suffered from the ravages of war. During my year in Paris, seven years after the end of the war, I heard numerous stories of the chains of monasteries and religious houses in which refugees, fleeing from the Gestapo, and especially Jews fleeing from the Holocaust, were sheltered and through which they passed, from one religious house to another, and were conducted along mountain paths over the Pyrenees into Spain and safety, or by other unfrequented routes to ports and to freedom. All of this was done through the auspices of the Church and the Holy Father. There is no counting the numbers of Jews whose lives were thus spared: some estimate a figure of 700,000. Even though those saved were only a pitifully small proportion of those callously massacred in the Holocaust, many Jewish voices after the war and at the time of his death were raised in praise of Pius XII and in gratitude for his wartime role. Among them were the Prime Minister of Israel, Golda Meier, and two successive Chief Rabbis of Rome, one of whom, Israel Zolli, became a Catholic, partly under the influence of Pius XII, and took the name Eugenio as his baptismal name. Yet the Pope's alleged silence, if not indeed complicity, with regard to the Holocaust, has now become conventional wisdom in some journalistic circles. One Irish newspaper even had the grotesque headline: 'Why did the Pope not stop the Holocaust?' Kenneth Woodward, religious affairs correspondent for *Newsweek*, in the issue of 30 March 1998, quotes the editorials in the *New York Times* of December 1941 and March 1998 respectively. The 1941 editorial called Pius XII 'about the only ruler left on the Continent of Europe, who dares to raise his voice at all'. The 1998 editorial of the same newspaper declaims against 'the Vatican's failure to stand squarely against the evil that swept across Europe'. Woodward's headline speaks of 'a neat bit of revisionist history' in respect of Pope Pius XII, and concludes, 'It is time to lay off this Pope'.

There is no space here to discuss the whole question of the Pope and the Holocaust, but I can only state my conviction that future historical research will fully vindicate the wisdom, as well as the courage and the compassion of this great Pope.

After a long illness, Papa Pacelli died on 9 October 1958, at 3.52 a.m. He was aged eighty-two.

John XXIII

After a Conclave lasting one week, the celebrated white smoke heralded a result, but it was a result which few expected. Angelo Giuseppe Roncalli, Patriarch of Venice, had been elected Pope. He took the name John XXIII. The choice of the cardinals was a surprise to all, a cause of astonishment to many, and of dismay to some. This was particularly so in France, where Roncalli had been Nuncio. During my stay in Paris I had often heard jokes about Archbishop Roncalli; he was generally regarded as an 'amiable old buffer' (the words are Peter Hebblethwaite's), who was certainly good and kind and holy, but by no means *papabile*. His French was approximative and heavily accented, and there were many tales of his gaffes in speaking French. Nevertheless, the French liked him and were pleased when he chose the name John, saying that part of his reason was that the last Pope John had been a Frenchman. The French priests and faithful later, of course, became the greatest admirers of 'Jean Vingt-Trois'. At best, people thought, Papa Roncalli would be a 'Pope of transition'. Some spoke of him as someone who would 'keep the seat warm' for a 'real Pope' to follow. More maliciously, it was rumoured that some cardinals voted for the Patriarch of Venice in order to keep out Archbishop Montini, who had some opponents in the Curia. It is possible, of course, that John also saw himself as a stop-gap Pope. I have remarked earlier that Nuncio Roncalli, at the dedication of the monastic church of the Benedictine Sisters in Vanves, Paris, said, pointing to his rotund figure, that he was good at filling gaps! He may well have felt that he was intended to 'keep the seat warm' for a certain G. B. Montini, then Archbishop of Milan. Some indication of this may be found in his naming of Archbishop Montini as Cardinal in his first consistory in November 1958. The received wisdom in Rome is that a new Pope's naming of his first Cardinal is an indication of the policy of his pontificate. Pope Leo XIII in fact said that the policy of his pontificate would be made known by his first nomination; and this turned out to be the nomination of Father John Henry Newman.

In 1961, for the seventieth anniversary of *Rerum novarum*, the new Pope published the encyclical *Mater et magistra* on the social questions of the day. It had the particularity of being one of the few papal encyclicals to treat of the situation of small farmers and agricultural workers as a depressed sector in modern economies. Pope John had not forgotten his small farm roots in Sotto il Monte, ten miles from Bergamo in Lombardy.

The 'amiable old buffer' had a greater surprise for everyone when, on 25 January 1959, he announced the convocation of an ecumenical council, which came to be called the Second Vatican Council. As Cardinal Suenens so aptly said, John XXIII proved to be one of the greatest of the 'surprises' of the Holy Spirit.

Already in 1923, Pius XI had expressed an interest in calling a Council, and asked to see the files of Vatican I. But he first wished to settle the 'Roman question' by negotiating the Lateran Treaty, and he never returned to the idea. Pope Pius XII also considered a Council, but set the idea aside, allegedly because of the enormous practical difficulties of bringing so many bishops together and organising the necessary accommodation and facilities for their meetings. As often happens, we can see, in retrospect, that God's time had not yet come.

Pope John XXIII seems to have decided on a Council early in his pontificate. Those with whom he discussed the idea gave it guarded support, but mainly because it would be an occasion for a condemnation of theological errors. Pope John's idea was quite different. He wanted something much more positive: a Church-wide return to the Gospel of Jesus Christ, a renewal of holiness among all members of the Church, a reinforcement of unity within the Church, a search for unity with other Christian Churches. Peter Hebblethwaite, in his splendid book, *John XXIII, Pope of the Council*, records how John spoke to Monsignor Capovilla, his secretary, the day before his announcement of the Council, saying:

> Christ has been there on the Cross, with his arms outstretched, for two thousand years. Where have we got to in proclaiming his Good News? How can we present his authentic doctrine to our contemporaries?

On the next day, 25 January 1959, the concluding day of the Week of Prayer for Christian Unity, he invited the Cardinals of the Curia to join him for a Service of Prayer in the Basilica of St Paul's-Outside-the-Walls. After the ceremony, they repaired to the chapter-room of the Basilica, and there Pope John made his historic announcement of an 'ecumenical Council for the universal

Church'. ('Ecumenical' is used here in its original sense of 'world-wide'.) He asked for prayers for 'a good start, a successful implementation and a happy outcome', for the project would involve hard work 'for the enlightenment, the edification and the joy of the Christian people, and a friendly and renewed invitation to our brethren of the separated Christian Churches to share with us in this banquet of grace and brotherhood'.

Perhaps a Pope with wider culture, a keener sense of organisational problems, a more penetrating grasp of theological obstacles to unity, would have hesitated, especially at seventy-eight years of age, to embark on such a mammoth undertaking. All these qualities were subordinated in John XXIII to an intense faith in God, an absolute and total trust in the Holy Spirit. He may have had naive ideas about a Council; it was certainly naive to think that it would be completed in one session, or that it would be content to adopt and to issue previously prepared documents. As we have seen in the last chapter, it became clear, early in the course of the Council, that Pope John had no 'pre-established plan', no overall method of procedure, for the Council. But John knew with total conviction that the Holy Spirit would be there, and that all would be well.

The Council, with its crises, its occasional panic and with the cauldron of rumour, speculation, gossip, intrigue, which burbled and simmered away in the pressure-cookers of journalists and assorted clergy at its periphery, was a demonstration of how God brings order out of human disorder, peace out of human dissension, light out of manmade dust; and how his presence in the Church prevails over all the all-too-human limitations and failings of the Church's members and hierarchy. The Council was for me the clearest proof of how God 'reaches from end to end mightily and orders all things sweetly' (cf. Wisdom 8:1). Perhaps only Pope John could have convened the Council. Only God could give success to the work of its hands. An atheistic communist, in an outburst of temper against Pope John and his influence, is reported to have said, 'That man is dangerous, he *believes* in God.'

Pope John is the Pope of the Council. But the Council was not his only achievement. His contribution to ecumenism is a matter of history. It was one of his priorities as Pope and one of the first issues to engage his attention. In 1962 he set up the Secretariat (now Pontifical Council) for Christian Unity, with Father Bea, just appointed a Cardinal, at its head. Cardinal Bea and the Secretariat were to play a crucial role in the coming Council.

There has been, of course, a certain 'mythologisation' of the Good Pope John, as if he was not concerned about dogma or about theology, or about Church tradition or discipline, but only about dogma-free love. In theology he was actually 'conservative', in spirituality and piety he was thoroughly 'traditional'. He was by no means a 'progressive' in the contemporary sense of that term. The conduct and conclusions of the Roman Synod reflect his 'conservative' ideas. The Synod for the diocese of Rome was announced in the same address to the Curial Cardinals in which the Pope announced the Council. The decrees of the Synod were definitely 'pre-conciliar', reflecting a 'clerical' and 'juridical' phase of the Church rather than a conciliar and post-conciliar one. Peter Hebblethwaite quotes Pope Paul VI's remark to Jean Guitton about his predecessor: 'Pope John was much more conservative than I, much more traditional'.

In the six months of life still left to him when the Council ended, Pope John XXIII finalised his great encyclical on peace, *Pacem in terris*. Significantly, he deputed Cardinal Suenens to deliver it in his name to a meeting of the United Nations Assembly in New York. His commitment to peace on earth was not a matter of words only. Peter Hebblethwaite tells us of the important role he had played in the Cuban missile crisis in October 1962, when he sent a special message to Krushchev and addressed a radio message to the statesmen of the world, in which he said, 'We beg all rulers not to be deaf to the cry of humanity.' Hebblethwaite quotes Krushchev as saying, 'What the Pope has done for peace will go down in history'. He tells us that the genesis of *Pacem in terris* was in fact the Cuban missile crisis, and that this great encyclical was Pope John's 'last will and testament'. It was completed in Holy Week 1963.

On the evening of 3 June following, as Mass was being celebrated for him in the Square below, when the celebrant had just dismissed the faithful with the words 'Ite missa est', Pope John died. The last words he spoke were 'Lord, you know that I love you', and he repeated the words twice. He was aged eighty-one years, and had been Pope for less than five years. They were years which changed the Church and which had an unprecedented impact on the world. The flag over Belfast's City Hall was lowered to half mast: an eloquent sign of how much respect and love the 'good Pope John' had evoked in the most unexpected places.

Paul VI

There have been a number of good and full biographies of Pope Paul VI. Peter Hebblethwaite's, *Paul VI: The First Modern Pope*, is comprehensive and detailed and indispensable, even if it does reflect many of the author's own preferences, which some might call his partisanship. I am indebted to this book, as to his biography of Pope John XXIII; but I have no intention of trying to compete with them or other biographies. I am concerned primarily with my own experience of Paul VI, whose fifteen years as Pope coincided with nine of my fifteen years as Bishop of Ardagh and Clonmacnois.

Few were surprised when the Cardinal Archbishop of Milan, Giovanni Battista Montini, was elected Pope on 21 June 1963, on the second day of the conclave and on the sixth ballot. He accepted the result of the voting by replying, 'Ita, in nomine Domini', 'Yes, in the name of the Lord'. In this, he was adding to the required 'Yes' the words of his own episcopal motto. His long experience in the Vatican's Secretariat of State and his closeness to both Pius XII and John XXIII, as well as his own deep spirituality, left him no illusions about the burdens and the sufferings which go with the Papal office; so, to the words of acceptance, he further added, 'Adsum. Crucifixus cum Christo', 'Here I am, crucified with Christ'. Hebblethwaite reminds us that on 29 June the London *Tablet* published a letter from Cardinal Montini on 'Pius XII and the Jews'. It was a vigorous defence of Pius XII's war-time record. Hebblethwaite remarks: 'Pius XII was his model of how to be Pope, not John XXIII'.

My first meeting with the new Pope came four years later, when I came to Rome for my retreat in preparation for my ordination as Bishop of Ardagh and Clonmacnois on 16 July 1967. My audience was fixed for 8 June, the last day of my stay in Rome. The Pope received me in his study, and he was working at his desk as I entered. He rose to greet me and offered me a chair at the side of his desk. Here is how I described my impressions at the time:

> The Pope was very gracious, very simple and humble. He asked me for details about my new diocese. When I remarked that I had been a university teacher and had no parish pastoral experience, he said, 'Don't be afraid; Irish priests have pastoral instincts in their blood.' He assured me that my priests, brothers, nuns and active Christian laity would all help me. He sent his kind greetings to Cardinal Conway and to President De Valera. I mentioned my mother, and immediately he opened a drawer of his desk to find a beautiful rosary for her, saying, 'Ask her to pray for me.' As I left, he gave me his blessing, which he said he was extending also to my new diocese and especially to its faithful laity, as well as to all my own dear ones. He gave me rosaries, prayer-books and picture-cards for my family and friends. He embraced me as he took leave of me.

My first impressions were confirmed by all my subsequent contacts. Pope Paul had the rare quality of making a person feel in his presence that he or she was the most important person in the world for him, that he had all the time in the world for the person now before him. He never seemed to be in a hurry to see his visitor leave, never gave the impression that he had more important, more urgent or more interesting things to do. One journalist wrote of him:

> He had the enviable but potentially inconvenient gift of making each visitor feel that he or she was a person Montini had been waiting all his life to talk to (cited by Peter Hebblethwaite, op. cit.).

Pope Paul seemed totally unconscious of his own dignity or importance. For me, all these qualities are the hallmark of a truly great man. I have found exactly the same qualities in Pope John Paul II.

Paul VI was certainly quiet, reserved, somewhat shy. He lacked the outgoing, demonstrative and even ebullient qualities of Pope John XXIII. In this respect, he had certain disadvantages in comparison with his predecessor. Cardinal Casaroli, who, as Secretary of State, worked very closely with him, paid a moving tribute to Paul VI in September 1997, at a commemorative ceremony to mark the centenary of his birth. He said that, in the beginning of his pontificate, coming, as he did, immediately after John XXIII, people generally felt a certain twinge of what might be called emotional disappointment with Paul VI. It was enough, Casaroli remarked, for Pope John to appear with that kind and smiling face of his, and immediately he conquered all hearts. Cardinal Casaroli concludes:

> Nevertheless it would be difficult to find a person more warm-hearted, even if in a controlled way, and more kind and more sensitive than Paul VI.

He was criticised for being indecisive, hesitant, slow to take decisions. He was assumed to see both sides of every question and to require a long time to make up his mind. The long interval between the report of the Commission on birth control and the publication of *Humanae vitae* was cited as evidence of this indecisiveness. This led to his being frequently called 'Hamlet-like'. He was well aware of this description himself. With rare humility and candour, he left a private note, written in 1975, when he was seventy-eight, asking:

> What is my state of mind? Am I Hamlet? Or Don Quixote? On the left? On the right? I don't think I have been properly understood.

He gives another indication of his personality in a reflection written in 1930, during a retreat on the tenth anniversary of his priestly ordination:

> To choose the humblest offices in the Church, because they are closer to the Kingdom. Not to have a career; to prefer the apostle to the canon lawyer, the parish priest to the cathedral canon or religious; the missionary to the bureaucrat; the teacher to the scholar.

In 1922, when Benedict XV was dying, Paul, as a young priest, had reflected on the sort of Pope who was needed in today's world. Always a 'man of the pen', he could clarify his thoughts best by putting them on paper. Here is what he wrote; it is a portrait which has in it elements of both the great Popes of his own lifetime, Pius XII and John XXIII; and it also indicates the kind of Pope that he himself would later try to be:

> The Church is about to be embodied in a man who after twenty centuries should represent not only the powerful Christ but the Christ who is evangelical, peace-loving, holy and poor. Let us pray that we may merit a pope who is very like Jesus; and for that he would have to be crucified by the world which hates what is not its own; its salvation demands as much. (citations from Peter Hebblethwaite, op. cit.)

Paul always had frail health, and in fact he had to be dispensed by his bishop from residence in the diocesan seminary; he was allowed to live at home and be a 'daytime' seminarian. This makes it all the more remarkable that he lived so long, accomplished so much, and undertook such arduous journeys. Ireland was among the countries that he visited, together with England and Scotland; this was in the year 1934, when he was a Monsignor in the diplomatic service of the Holy See. He spent four days in the Nunciature in Dublin. Monsignor Riberi was the counsellor at the Nunciature at the time, and he himself later became Apostolic

Nuncio to Ireland. Monsignor Montini visited Armagh and called on Cardinal MacRory. He often spoke about this Irish visit afterwards.

I was often struck by his particularly affectionate attitude towards Ireland and his enquiries about its welfare, and, from the onset of the 'Troubles' onwards, his repeated assurances of his prayers for peace in Ireland. Cardinal Conway told me of how Pope Paul had said to him that every night, before going to bed, he turned in the direction of Ireland and gave it his blessing. Until I read Peter Hebblethwaite's book, I did not know that this interest in Ireland was inherited from his father, Giorgio. Giorgio was editor of the local Catholic newspaper in Brescia, *Il Cittadino*, 'The Citizen'. He was politically active in the spirit of what later became the Christian Democrat party. The Irish struggle for independence was strongly supported by progressive Catholic political activists and their journals in Europe in the 1920s, and they received regular information about Irish affairs from Monsignor John Hagan, Rector of the Irish College, Rome. Peter Hebblethwaite tells us that Alcide de Gasperi, later leader of the Christian Democrats, gave a lecture on Ireland in Brescia in 1921, and Giovanni Battista's elder brother was in the chair. So Paul VI's affection for Ireland went back to his boyhood. It is interesting to note that Pope John Paul II's Drogheda appeal to the IRA, 'On my knees I beg you to turn away from the path of violence', was inspired by Pope Paul's dramatic appeal in 1978 to the Red Brigade to release Aldo Moro, leader of the Christian Democrats, whom they had kidnapped. Pope John Paul II in Drogheda said that he 'joined his voice to that of Paul VI', his revered predecessor, in calling for an end to violence and a search for political solutions. In the course of those years, Paul VI sent several messages to Cardinal Conway, pledging his prayers, condemning all violence, and calling for a just settlement by peaceful methods.

Pope Paul, as we have noted, aspired to be a teacher rather than a scholar, a missionary rather than a bureaucrat. He was a superb teacher and an indefatigable missionary. Writing always in a classical style of logical order and clarity of language and often lapidary phrase, he vastly enriched the Church's theology, especially in the area of eucharistic theology (*Mysterium Fidei*, 1965), priesthood and, particularly, celibacy (*Sacerdotalis coelibatus*, 1967) and marriage (*Humanae vitae*, 1968). He always kept in mind the need for dialogue between the Church and the modern world, in the spirit of the Vatican Council's *Gaudium et spes*. Indeed, his first encyclical, *Ecclesiam Suam* (1964), was devoted to the theme of dialogue; it is a masterly study of the nature of dialogue, the spirit and attitudes which it requires, the methodology it should follow. Politicians and media people, as well as bishops and priests and lay Christians, could well learn from it. In a sense this document is an expression of Pope Paul's own personality and papal style.

Pope Paul had a lifelong interest in religious art and encouraged the work of contemporary artists in the religious field. Many of these donated works to the collection of contemporary sacred art which the Pope set up in the Vatican. Although I shared his enthusiasm for the great sculptor, Giacomo Manzu, I regret that my tastes and preferences in sacred art often differed from his; but happily infallibility does not extend to this domain!

Pope Paul was ardently committed to justice in society and in the world. His exhortation, *Populorum progressio*, issued in 1967, is as vibrant and as relevant today as when it was issued. *Octogesima adveniens*, published in 1971 for the eightieth anniversary of *Rerum novarum*, further developed papal teaching on justice and human rights.

Both the desire for dialogue and the commitment to justice and concern for suppression of religious freedom and of human rights in communist-controlled Eastern Europe were the motivation for what became known as his Ostpolitik, which he conducted with the help of his devoted Secretary of State, Cardinal Casaroli. His patient and persistent efforts in this connection were met with criticism from some political regimes and from some circles within the Church as a form of 'appeasement'; but it prepared the ground for the *glasnost* and *perestroika* which followed later. Paul's successive visits to the United Nations in New York and in Geneva, and his many discourses and addresses on peace and human rights, brought his message to the United Nations and to the world.

Paul's missionary journeys to India and other Asian countries, to Africa and to Latin America, opened a new chapter in the papal ministry and were part of his qualification to be called 'the first modern Pope'. His exhortation, *Evangelii nuntiandi*, which was his concluding statement of the conclusions of the Synod of Bishops in 1974, has retained its freshness and its inspiration ever since its publication in 1975.

Alongside these great teaching documents, Pope Paul continued to pursue untiringly his huge task of implementing the decisions of Vatican II and pushing forward its wide-ranging programme of renewal across the world-wide Catholic Church. A series of norms for the implementation of the Council's decrees made Paul VI's a great reforming pontificate. From the beginning of my own ministry as bishop, I felt privileged to have his teaching and his directives, together with those of the Vatican Council, as the basis for my efforts at diocesan pastoral planning and as guidelines for my approach to my episcopal ministry.

Over-arching all his concerns was the solicitude for fidelity in faith and for growth in holiness. He proclaimed a Year of Faith for 1967/8, which was brought to a close by his own statement of faith, the *Credo of the People of God*, published in 1968. This was, of all his papal documents, probably the one which gave him the most satisfaction. He referred to it near the end of his life, in an 'examination of conscience' on his pontificate.

He also planned and carried through a radical reform of the liturgy, as postulated by the Council, while all the time taking care that liturgy should enhance, rather than diminish, the sense of mystery and reverence which make it divine service rather than human performance. Sadly, this reform was distorted by some, who interpreted it as permitting all kinds of liturgical experimentation, and by others who refused altogether to countenance change. This was one of Paul's great sufferings, particularly when it was pushed to the point of defiance and eventually schism by Archbishop Lefèbvre.

One of the most significant, and at the same time, most delicate projects of reform undertaken by Paul VI was the reform of the

Roman Curia. There were many voices raised during the Council calling for this reform, and a petition to this end was signed by more than a hundred bishops and sent to the Pope. Paul himself shared the sense of the need for change. The proceedings of the Council itself showed that most of the senior Curial Cardinals and many of its senior personnel were not attuned to the mind of the majority of the bishops at the Council. Pope Paul was well placed to address the problem, having himself served in the Curia for thirty years. He began preparing for it very soon after his election. In September 1963, before the opening of the Second Session of the Council, he called a meeting of the Roman Curia and addressed them in what Peter Hebblethwaite calls the 'speech of his life'. He put plainly before the Curia his own thinking about its functioning, hinting at its shortcomings and stating the ideals which it should aim to serve. He said:

> People everywhere are watching Catholic Rome, the Roman Pontificate, the Roman Curia. The duty of being authentically Christian is especially binding here.... Everything in Rome teaches, the letter and the spirit, the way we think, study, speak, feel, act, suffer, pray, serve, love.... [Everything we do] can be beneficial if we are what Christ wants from us, or harmful if we are unfaithful.

The reform, when it came, was chiefly aimed at internationalising the Curia, and thereby making it more representative of the universal Church. This development had begun, if more modestly, under Pius XII. The members of the Curia had traditionally been predominantly Italian and virtually all the heads of congregations were Italian. With Paul VI's reform, other countries and continents began to be represented. Dioceses across the world were asked to release priests for service in Curial offices. Procedures were updated. Comprehensive changes were introduced, with the aim of bringing the Curia more into line with the mind of the Council and the needs of the post-conciliar Church. This was one of Pope Paul's major reform achievements.

The Synod of Bishops, directly intended by Paul to be an instrument of episcopal collegiality, was set up in 1966, and held its first General Assembly in 1967. An indication of Paul's esteem for Cardinal Conway is that he asked the Irish Cardinal to be one of the two co-presidents of this first Synod. Its agenda centred on 'the current crisis concerning Catholic faith and doctrine'. It commissioned a report, which was drawn up by its special Synod Commission and approved by the Synod and then submitted to the Pope. This Synod also called for a revision of the Code of Canon Law, and it updated procedures relating to mixed marriages.

An extraordinary General Assembly was called in 1969, with the purpose of exploring ways of giving practical effect to the collegiality of bishops with the Pope. A further ordinary meeting was held in 1971, with two themes: the ministerial priesthood and justice in the world. This Synod published a trenchant document on 'Justice in the World', which still provides inspiration in the struggle for justice. The third General Assembly was on the theme of 'Evangelization in the Modern World'; this led to the document *Evangelii nuntiandi*, to which I have already referred.

The last meeting of the Synod in Pope Paul's time was the General Assembly of 1977. Its theme was 'Catechetics in our Time'. The Synod opened on 30 September, and Sunday 2 October was the date fixed for the ordination of Monsignor Tomás Ó Fiaich as Archbishop of Armagh in succession to Cardinal Conway. I flew back to Ireland in order to be present for the ordination in Armagh, and returned to Rome the next day. I was one of the two delegates from Ireland at this Synod, although I was there as substitute for Cardinal Conway who had died in April and whose successor had not yet been ordained when it opened. I accompanied Archbishop Dermot Ryan of Dublin on this occasion. I found the Synod a wonderful human and spiritual experience of episcopal collegiality, and a welcome opportunity of seeing how the Synod works. Furthermore, the topic of catechetics was always of interest to me; I was at the time President of the Irish Bishops' Commission on Catechetics and as such had an involvement with the new catechetical programmes and materials which we were introducing at that time. Indeed, I felt proud to see our Irish catechetical books and materials displayed alongside those from other countries represented at the Synod, and felt that the Irish materials were in many ways superior to those from any other country, both in terms of content and in terms of presentation and methodology. Archbishop Bernardin, of Chicago, soon to be become Cardinal, was Chairman of the discussion group of which I was a member, and I admired the firm but gentle way in which he directed the discussion. A group of members of the Irish Commission on Catechetics came to Rome for an experience of the Synod; it is interesting to note that these included two priests who are now bishops, Donal Murray of Limerick and Bill Murphy of Kerry, together with Father Des Forristal and Sister Kathleen Glennon. They will doubtless remember an animated discussion on catechetics which we had with Archbishop Dermot Ryan of Dublin, later to be Prefect of the Congregation on the Evangelisation of Peoples.

Pope Paul's eightieth birthday was celebrated during the Synod. He was already infirm at that time and suffering from severe arthritis. He was able, therefore, to attend only some of the sessions; but he took a very close interest in the speeches which were made and was obviously following the progress of the Synod very closely. This was to be Pope Paul's last Synod. We had a special audience with him at the end; he greeted each person warmly, and had a personal word for each. In my case, he renewed his expression of affection for Ireland and assured me once more of his prayers for peace in our country. As we were leaving, he looked alone and lonely, and no one had any doubt but that we were seeing him for the last time.

In addition to the Synod, Pope Paul also encouraged meetings of bishops at continental level. CCEE (Council of European Episcopal Conferences) was set up in 1971, and CELAM (Episcopal Conferences of Latin America) was set up in 1955. Cardinal Conway of Armagh and Cardinal Höffner of Cologne were asked by Pope Paul to draft statutes for CCEE. Monsignor Etchegaray, now Archbishop of Marseilles, was elected its first President. It held periodic symposia on current Church concerns, in several of which I participated. In collaboration with KEK, the Council of European Churches grouping the Protestant and the Orthodox Churches, it organised several ecumenical meetings, including one at Chantilly near Paris in 1970, and one at Logumkloster in Denmark in 1981. I attended both of these, and, in the course of them, was invited to address the symposiasts on the situation in Northern Ireland. I shared this experience in each case with a Presbyterian minister, Very Reverend Dr Jack Weir. In each case, without previous consultation with one another, we both spoke from a common Christian perspective. I refer to this again in chapter ten.

Pope Paul was deeply committed to the search for Christian unity. In the course of his life, he made many Anglican friends. He entertained a party of Anglican clergy in Milan when he was Archbishop there. His friendship with Archbishop Ramsey is part of ecumenical history, as are his meetings with the Patriarch of Athenagoras. He admired the Protestant theologian Oscar Cullmann. He met annually with Brother Roger Schutz of Taizé. The setting up of the Anglican Roman Catholic International Commission (ARCIC), and the visits to Rome of Archbishops Fisher and Coggan, raised hopes of reunion with the Anglican Communion. If the hopes are as yet unrealised, the relations between Anglicans and Roman Catholics were, and remain, nevertheless, transformed.

The Anglican decision to ordain women to the priesthood was a grave setback. Pope Paul wrote to Archbishop Coggan in 1976 expressing his sadness at this 'new obstacle on the path to reconciliation'. In the same year, the papal document, *Inter insigniores*, was published, declaring that the Catholic Church 'does not believe itself authorised' to ordain women to the priesthood. The Lambeth Conference of 1978, held at Canterbury, debated the issue, although more from the point of view of intra-Anglican communion than from the point of view of the theology or the ecumenical implications of the ordination of women. I was asked to attend this Conference as an observer, representing the Holy See's Secretariat for Christian Unity. I was deeply impressed by the spirit of fellowship with which I was received and by the spiritual and prayerful atmosphere in which the Conference was conducted. Each day began with a spiritual reflection, led, in the first fortnight, by the great Orthodox spiritual writer and lecturer, Archbishop Anthony Bloom, and, in the second fortnight, by the Archbishop of York, Stuart Blanch. The Eucharist was celebrated daily in one or other of the rites currently in use in the Anglican Communion. There was one 'quiet day' set aside for prayer and reflection. A great spirit of charity and fellowship prevailed, and I felt myself included in that. I was touched also by the cordiality extended to me by the Church of Ireland bishops, led by the great and saintly Archbishop George Otto Simms. Indeed someone remarked that I seemed to have been 'co-opted' to the Bench of Bishops of the Church of Ireland! This was also my first occasion for meeting with Bishop Robin Eames, later to become Lord Archbishop of Armagh, with whom I worked closely during my ministry in Armagh. Archbishop Coggan and the Conference graciously allowed me to address the assembly on behalf of the Secretariat and the Holy See, on the question of women's ordination, calling attention again to the serious difficulties which it posed for future ecumenical progress. I recall that the observer from the Orthodox Church, speaking as representative of the Orthodox Ecumenical Patriarch, Dimitrios I of Constantinople, was very much more vehement than I had been in pointing to the difficulties this matter posed for Church unity. I have spoken above, when treating of Paul VI, about his grave concerns in this regard.

Pope Paul died while the Lambeth Conference was in session. I received many expressions of deeply-felt sympathy on his passing. Obviously Paul had touched many hearts in the Anglican Communion. In an act of extraordinary ecumenical sensitivity, the Conference gave permission for the celebration, in the main assembly hall of the Conference, of a Requiem Mass for the soul of Pope Paul. Archbishop Simms read one of the lessons. I was privileged to be chief celebrant and homilist at the Mass. The Mass in this setting, with the presence of many Anglican bishops, was a wonderful tribute to the Pope who, as he said in the Common

Declaration signed with Archbishop Ramsey, wished to entrust to the God of mercy 'all that in the past has been contrary to the precept of charity'.

A more light-hearted memory of Lambeth for me is of Desmond Tutu, the irrepressible young bishop, who was coordinator of discussion groups at one session. He briefed the group of which I was a member, and then, sending us off to our meeting room, said, 'So off you go now, and work like niggers'! It takes a really great man to speak like that.

Now I return to Paul VI. He had two great loves in his life, an intense love for the Church, and a love for the modern world. He often spoke with enthusiasm of the world of our day. At the press conference to launch his first encyclical, *Ecclesiam Suam*, he spoke of dialogue as the word which describes 'the art or style that must inspire the Church's ministry to the dissonant, voluble, complex concert that is the contemporary world'. In a private memo, reflecting objectively on the contrasts which many made between himself and Pope John XXIII, he wrote:

> In the field of work, of culture, of human and diplomatic relations, perhaps our life is characterised more clearly than anything else by the love of our own time and our own world.

In 1977, when death was clearly near, he wrote 'Thoughts on Death'. He said:

> Now that the day draws to its close, and I must leave this wonderful and turbulent world, I thank you Lord, and I call yet again for your divine blessing to descend upon it.

His intense love for the Church is revealed in this same text. He wrote:

> I pray to the Lord that I may offer my coming death for the Church, which I have always loved.

These two loves were together in his thoughts on death. He said that he believed that he had lived for the Church, and that he wished to tell the Church about that love, but that it was only at the last moment of his life that he had the courage to say this. That love extended to all humankind. He wrote:

> Men and women, understand me, I love you all in the grace of the Holy Spirit.... This is how I look upon you, this is how I greet you, this is how I bless you, all of you.

He shared this deep love of the Church with Saint Thérèse of Lisieux, and this was presumably one of the reasons why he so greatly loved and admired that young saint, who died in the same year in which he was born. She had written: 'In the heart of the Church, my mother, I will be love'.

In his 'Thoughts on Death', his 'last testament', he also said:

> I want my funeral to be as simple as possible, and I want neither tomb nor special monument. Prayers only and good works.

If it took Pope John to call the Council, it took Pope Paul to complete it and carry through its programme of renewal of the Church, bringing the whole Church, with few exceptions, with him. His alleged indecisiveness was the fruit of charity, patience, and sensitivity to the feelings of others. Peter Hebblethwaite sums it up well:

> He managed to complete the Council without dividing the Church. He reformed the Roman Curia without alienating it. He introduced collegiality without ever letting it undermine his papal office. He practised ecumenism without impairing Catholic identity. He had an ostpolitik that involved neither surrender nor bouncing aggressiveness. He was 'open to the world' without ever being its dupe. He pulled off the most difficult trick of all: combining openness with fidelity.

Pope Paul suffered for the Church, and suffered from people within the Church. He suffered physically, particularly in his last years, from severe arthritis. But above all he suffered spiritually. The departure of priests from the sacred ministry pained him deeply. He said that he agonised over each single dispensation that he granted. It was his crown of thorns. He suffered deeply from dissension within the Church, from dissent by some theologians from the Church's teaching; he suffered from betrayals, both from the 'left' and from the 'right', of the clear meaning and authentic spirit of the Council. We get a glimpse of his distress when we find this man, normally so calm and moderate in language, speaking in 1973 of the 'smoke of Satan', which had penetrated a corner of the Church. But then others too were dismayed by some post-conciliar aberrations. Cardinal Suenens tells how Cardinal Doepfner, his fellow-moderator and leading 'progressive' at the Council, had remarked to him in 1968:

> 'Prophets' today are not what they used to be. In the old days they had a deep sense of the Church and a deeply rooted faith.

Yet none of this personal anguish disturbed Paul's inner peace and joy. In 1975, which he had proclaimed as a Year of Reconciliation, he wrote a moving exhortation on joy as the mark of Christians. He entitled it, in the words of St Paul, *Gaudete in Domino*, 'Rejoice in the Lord'. He spoke of the deep and overflowing joy which he felt in the midst of all the problems.

It was appropriate that he should die on the feast of the Transfiguration, 6 August 1978. His two secretaries, Monsignor Pasquale Macchi and Monsignor John Magee, later Bishop of Cloyne, were with him constantly during his last days and hours. He kept asking them to pray for the Church. He followed Mass offered by Monsignor Macchi on the morning of the feast, and he pressed Monsignor Magee's hand tightly at the words of the Creed, 'I believe in one, holy, catholic and apostolic Church', repeating these words in a strong voice together with the celebrant. His life was truly lived for and given for the Church and its Lord. On the previous 29 June, feast of Saints Peter and Paul, he had said:

> My duty was to be faithful. I have been faithful. Now I have done all I can. I have finished.

Like his Lord, he had finished the work the Father gave him to do. It was appropriate that he should die on the feast of the Transfiguration. Now, faithful servant, he would enter fully into the joy of his Lord. Now he would be crushed, not any longer by problems and anxieties, but by the weight of glory.

John Paul I

The conclave to elect Paul VI's successor was held on 26 August 1978. On the third ballot, Cardinal Albino Luciani, Patriarch of Venice, emerged as the choice of the Cardinals. He took the name John Paul I, thereby indicating that his intention was to continue the work of both his predecessors. He had not been much in the public eye before, but immediately he won all hearts by his loving smile and his kind and gentle manner. Sadly, his pontificate was to be the shortest in history; as Cardinal Marty of Paris said, 'only the time of a smile'. He died of a heart attack just five weeks after his election, on 29 September. Early in the morning of that day, his body was discovered by Monsignor Magee; he had been propped up in bed studying his papers. Continuing the work of John and of Paul was now left for other hands to do.

John Paul II

The next conclave began on Sunday, 15 October, and resulted on the following day with the election of 'a man from a far country', the first non-Italian in five centuries, the Polish Karol Wojtyla, Archbishop of Krakow. I was in Paris when the news came. I immediately thought of Father de Lubac's prescience of thirteen years earlier, and I was not too surprised at the conclave's choice. One was struck immediately by the new Pope's youthful appearance, his physical vigour and his strong voice and brisk manner. I visited the Irish College, Paris, which had been leased by the Irish bishops to the Polish hierarchy for use as a secondary school and seminary, mainly for Poles of the post-war diaspora in Western Europe. The Polish priests teaching there were obviously delighted, although, if triumphalist, as they had every right to be, they showed no sign of this. Their own contemporary experience in Poland under the iron hand of the Soviets did not encourage triumphalism! They spoke with enthusiasm about the new Pope as a man of learning, kindness, accessibility and prayerfulness, with powers of enormous concentration. The present pontificate is, of course, so much a matter of public knowledge that I shall write only of aspects of it which intersect with my personal experience.

The new Pope took the name John Paul II, another tribute to his two predecessors and a commitment to continue their work. From the outset, it was obvious that the second John Paul would be a man for all countries, an indefatigable traveller for Christ, and not just a Pope for Poland. His first visit, naturally, was to his native Poland, then celebrating its 'millennium of faith'. This visit was the beginning of a thaw in the black ice gripping all of Soviet-controlled Eastern Europe, a thaw which would in time melt away the Soviet system itself. His second visit was to Ireland.

The possibility of an Irish visit was explored from July 1979 onward. The Pope was due to visit the United Nations in October of that year, and the two visits could obviously be included in the one travelling schedule. The new Archbishop of Armagh, Tomás Ó Fiaich, after two years in office, was appointed Cardinal at the consistory on 30 June, and he immediately instituted enquiries about the possibility of a papal visit to Ireland. The visit was officially announced on 21 July, and the dates were fixed as being from 29 September to 1 October. Preparations were immediately begun by the Irish bishops and occupied all our energies for the next two months. The itinerary of the three-day visit was mapped out, and intensive preparations began in Dublin, Knock, Galway, Limerick and Maynooth for liturgies or other encounters with the Pope. A spiritual programme of prayerful preparation for the visit was drawn up and implemented across the country.

Great co-operation was received from the media, both electronic and print, from the Garda and CIE and Ulsterbus, from PR specialists, from many other agencies, and from the laity of the Church, co-operating enthusiastically with their priests and bishops. The television and radio coverage of the visit can still be claimed as perhaps RTE's finest hour.

Cardinal Ó Fiaich was very anxious that the Holy Father should visit the North, and this proposal was meeting with a favourable reaction from Rome. Then came the murder of Lord Mountbatten on 27 August, and, on the same day, the killing of fifteen paratroopers at Narrow Water near Warrenpoint. These events obviously made the whole atmosphere in Northern Ireland so polarised that a visit by the Pope could not be contemplated. With great sadness, both for the Pope and for the Cardinal and the Irish bishops and people, particularly in the Northern dioceses, the proposal had to be abandoned. Cardinal Ó Fiaich remained, to the end of his days, convinced that the visit to Northern Ireland would have taken place but for the murder of Lord Mountbatten and the killings in County Down. Drogheda was selected as the alternative site for the Pope's meeting with Catholics from Northern Ireland and the border counties. It was also the venue at which the Pope would address most directly the conflict situation in the North in all its aspects.

I was asked to work with a team from the Vatican Secretariat of State in doing some preparatory work for the Holy Father's addresses in Ireland. This work went on intensively all through September. The group included Monsignor Coppa, Monsignor Justin Rigali (now Archbishop of St Louis) and Father Jan Schotte (now Cardinal Secretary of the Synod of Bishops). The first meeting, on 5 September, was presided over by Cardinal Casaroli, recently appointed by Pope John Paul II as Cardinal Secretary of State. Here we were briefed about the Pope's own thoughts and wishes in respect of the various themes to be addressed in Ireland.

There were twenty-two addresses in all to be delivered in Ireland. The other members of the team were to work also on some thirty addresses for the visit to the United States, which also had to be prepared during that September. I was amazed at the capacity for hard work, day after day and night after night, all through those weeks, of the staff members of the Secretariat of State. There clearly was no question of 'office hours' in their life of service to the Holy See and the Church. The technological back-up, the typing services, etc, were also of the highest efficiency.

I was to spend most of the month of September in Rome, flying home at weekends in order to keep in touch with preparations in the diocese of Ardagh and Clonmacnois, as well as nationally, for the visit. The Pope expressed his wish to visit an ancient monastic site in Ireland, and, to my delight, Clonmacnois was placed on the itinerary. An energetic committee was formed in the diocese to prepare for this, and my secretary, Father Sean Casey, liaised most efficiently between the committee and myself.

On 11 September, I had the first of several 'working meals' with the Holy Father and other members of the group. These 'working meals' were to become a regular feature of the life of the new Pope. We were far away indeed from the older mystique of a Pope who, by immemorial tradition, always dined alone. John Paul seems never to dine alone, and never to dine in such a way as to interrupt his work. I was impressed above all by his relaxed manner, his friendliness, the total absence of protocol or pomp, the simplicity of the whole setting. There was no question of feeling inhibited in his presence or hesitant about expressing one's opinion. Pope John Paul is a marvellous listener, patient, attentive, interested in hearing the opinions of others. He has an extraordinary interest in people, and an amazing ability to remember their names and recall when he had met them before. He gives complete freedom to everyone to express their views. He had obviously studied the tentative preliminary drafts very carefully, and his comments were penetrating. It was clear from the outset that the Pope had no time for platitudes or generalisations or for vagueness. He believes in direct language, calling things by their names, as we were to see again recently in Cuba, in presence of Fidel Castro, and in Nigeria, in presence of General Abacha.

So far as the conflict in the North was concerned, he was determined to place everyone squarely before their responsibilities. In respect of armed violence and the security response to it, he confronted the men of violence, the security forces, the governments, the politicians, the prison authorities, the general public. He stressed the primacy of justice and of human rights, the role of deprivation and alienation and unemployment and poverty in creating conditions conducive to violence. His Drogheda address, the one primarily concerned with our Northern problems, has often been cited subsequently as one of the Pope's most comprehensive analyses of political violence, its moral evil, its counter-productive character, its causes, its remedies, the need to respond to it by political measures. He pointed out, in the clearest terms, the fact that violence is often the result of the failure of governments and politicians to create justice and fairness and equality of opportunity in society. In the Irish situation, he stressed the particular importance of good ecumenical relations between Catholics and Protestants. All of these elements in this most carefully constructed address were evident in such passages as these:

> If politicians do not decide and act for just change, then the field is left open to the men of violence. Violence thrives best when there is a political vacuum and a refusal of political movement.... May no Irish Protestant think that the Pope is an enemy or a danger or a threat. My desire is that instead Protestants would see in me a friend and a brother in Christ.

I believe that Pope John Paul II's Drogheda speech marks the beginning in Ireland of a reflection, a debate and a process which had their culmination in the Belfast Agreement of Good Friday 1998.

There has been speculation about 'speech writers' for the Pope's addresses, in Ireland or elsewhere. But Pope John Paul's speeches are his own; from the first outline to the final text, it is his thinking, his style, his priorities and emphases, which predominate. The whole experience of working with that team gave me a privileged insight into how Pope John Paul II works, how he relates to his collaborators, his extraordinary powers of concentration, linked with a wonderful personal simplicity. The very fact that, from the beginning of his pontificate, he used the simple term 'I', rather than the more formal 'We', which even Paul VI had used, was significant.

At the end of the month, I returned to Ireland on the eve of the Mass in the Phoenix Park, exhausted but elated, in time to see the immense crowds moving towards the Park, in readiness for the largest gathering of people ever to assemble in Ireland (estimated at one and a quarter million), at the beginning of three days which brought out the best in Ireland and saw Ireland at its best.

Of the other events of these days, I refer only to Clonmacnois. History was made in the diocese of Ardagh and Clonmacnois when the Pope visited this ancient monastic site on the banks of the Shannon, on the morning of 30 September 1979. Clonmacnois had been one of the great monastic centres of Europe for a thousand years, from the sixth to the sixteenth century, when its final destruction was ordered by Cromwell. It was a centre of liturgy and contemplation, of learning and teaching, of missionary outreach, of art, of hospitality and care for the poor. Pope John Paul, with his great sense of history, and fresh from the celebration of the millennium of the faith in Poland, reflected that monks from Clonmacnois might well have come as missionaries to Krakow, as they had certainly evangelised parts of Poland, and travelled much further east, as far as Kiev. As he remarked afterwards, he felt that he was linking hands with them in communion of faith across the centuries.

As we waited for the Pope's red helicopter on that foggy morning, we listened to recordings of early medieval chants, sung by the monks of Glenstal Abbey and Nóirín Ní Riain, which might well have been the very chants used by the Celtic monks of old. These were interspersed by readings from a concise history of Clonmacnois, prepared for the occasion by the late Father John Corkery, and written out by his own hand in beautiful script, which was later presented to the Holy Father as a souvenir of the visit.

For the occasion, we had brought to Clonmacnois the tenth-century crozier, attributed to St Mel, younger contemporary of St Patrick and first bishop of Ardagh. I shall never forget the scene of the Pope's kneeling in prayer before the altar in the new sanctuary in Clonmacnois, and the symbolism of his holding in his hand that thousand-year-old crozier of one of what the old annals call 'the first order of Catholic saints ... in the time of Patrick, and they were all bishops'. When the Pope began to walk around the monastic enclosure of Clonmacnois, the crowd surged forward to be closer to him and, momentarily, the stewards lost control. Archbishop Marcinkus, who was responsible for keeping the Pope's itinerary on schedule, was worried; but Pope John Paul, with people pressing all around him, was undisturbed, indeed he seemed to be in his element. At one point he stopped, pointed to a mother some rows back, who was holding up her baby, and said, 'Please bring that lady over to me.' He waited until she made her way through, took the baby in his arms, kissed it on the forehead, blessed it and gave it back to the mother, who was too emotional to speak. Afterwards, Archbishop Marcinkus remarked, 'Your police were wonderful; a pity at one moment they were so keen to be near the Pope themselves that they seemed to forget that they were there to keep the people back!' Seriously, however, he did say that the Gardaí, in Clonmacnois and at all the other venues, were magnificent, and that, all through the visit, the Irish security operation around the Pope had been flawless.

When Pope John Paul returned to Rome from his visits to Ireland and United States, he addressed the crowd gathered to welcome him in St Peter's Square. Speaking of Clonmacnois, which obviously had been for him one of the highlights of the two visits, he said:

> Those ruins are still charged with a great mission. They still constitute a challenge. They still speak of that fullness of life to which Christ has called us. It is difficult for a pilgrim to arrive at those places without those traces of the apparently dead past revealing to him or her a permanent and everlasting dimension of life.... Here is Ireland.

The Pope's visit was the highlight of Cardinal Ó Fiaich's primacy and undoubtedly the highlight of the Catholic Church in Ireland in the past thirty years. The visit gave us all a new sense of pride in our past and confidence in our future. The spiritual preparations for the visit, and the charisma and the words of the Pope, were an occasion of profound spiritual renewal in the lives of many. Seldom indeed had a whole people been so united in their concentration on one man of God and on his message. Almost every sector of life in Ireland was somehow involved. A group of poets came together and published a small collection of poems written in his honour. They printed as frontispiece: 'Salute to a visiting artist'. They knew that Karol Wojtyla was himself a poet; a collection of his poems was published in English translation in that same year, 1979, with the title *Easter Vigil*. Several works by modern Irish artists were commissioned by the bishops for presentation to the Holy Father, including an impressive piece of sculpture, 'Saint Francis and the birds', by John Behan. A small but very beautiful stained glass window by Evie Hone was among the pieces of art presented to the Pope by the bishops as a souvenir of his visit.

The scandals and troubles which were to afflict the Church in Ireland ten years later could not have been foreseen at that time. They have given to all of us a new awareness that the way of the Church is a pilgrim way, and that we all, the pilgrims who constitute the Church, are sinners, penitents always needing forgiveness, converts all our lives long, always in process of striving for fuller conversion. We are an *ecclesia semper purificanda*, a Church always in need of conversion and renewal. But we are pilgrims who can always recall that, in the words of the Council's *Constitution on the Church, Lumen gentium*:

> By the power of the risen Lord, [the Church] is given strength to overcome patiently and lovingly the afflictions and hardships which assail her from within and from without, and to show forth in the world the mystery of the Lord in a faithful although shadowed way, until at last [that mystery] will be revealed in total splendour. (8)

In spite of scandals and disgrace, weakness and failings, we still remember the splendour of the Church which was revealed to us by Pope John Paul's visit, determined, in Coventry Patmore's words, 'not to forget in the darkness what we have seen in the light'.

Pope John Paul II is frequently criticised, and some of the criticisms have become clichés in some contemporary writing, repeated, parrot-like, by journalists and others, inside the Church as well as outside it. Peter Hebblethwaite is a respected biographer and writer on religious affairs; yet even he, in his otherwise admirable biography of Paul VI, speaks disparagingly of John Paul II. He regards this pontificate as 'a repudiation of the policies of Paul VI', a 'dismantling of the heritage of Paul VI'. I have to confess that I simply cannot understand this kind of remark or recognise in it the Pope John Paul II whom I feel I can say that I know. Hebblethwaite tells us that Paul VI was 'the most naturally talented man to become Pope in this century'. Great though my esteem for Pope Paul, my choice for this description would have been John Paul II.

In John Paul II we have the only Pope ever who has been a manual labourer in war-time, an amateur actor and a playwright, a poet, a philosopher in the phenomenological tradition and a friend of philosophers and intellectuals, a theologian, a mountain-climber, a skier, and also a contemplative, a man of action and a man of prayer, a specialist in the philosophy and theology of anthropology, of human dignity and of human rights. We have a Pope who has had two attempts made on his life and who bears bullet marks on his body. We have a Pope who each summer invites scholars from different disciplines to Castelgandolfo for an *ad hoc* seminar on a prearranged topic in the physical or human or social sciences; in short, a fully 'modern Pope', one, indeed, whom his most recent biographer, Jonathan Kwitny, calls 'Man of the Century' (in the book of that title, published by Little, Brown and Co., London, 1997).

He is called 'hard-line', whereas the principles he enunciates and the values he defends are identical with those of John XXIII and those of Paul VI, who is, be it recalled, the author of *Humanae vitae*, condemning artificial birth control, and of *Sacerdotalis coelibatus*, reiterating and strongly defending the tradition of priestly celibacy in the Latin Church, and of *Inter insigniores*, affirming the inability of the Catholic Church to ordain women to the priesthood. Pope John Paul is said to be autocratic, authoritarian, one who does not consult and does not listen. I have already commented on his exceptional capacity for listening and his openness to new learning. Probably no Pope has ever had such a breadth and depth of personal knowledge of the state of the Church throughout the world, acquired through his unprecedented and extended papal journeys, his reform of the style of episcopal visits *ad limina*, through his personal contacts with bishops, and through the Synods of Bishops, which he has convened with great frequency.

Evolution of the Synod of Bishops

I wish to refer particularly to the special style and stamp which John Paul has placed upon the Synod. Eleven Synods have been held in Pope John Paul's time. The year 1980 saw a special Synodal Assembly for Holland, and also an Ordinary General Assembly on 'the Christian Family'. The next Ordinary General Assembly was held in 1983, on 'Penance and Reconciliation in the Mission of the Church'. An Extraordinary General Assembly of the Synod was called for the year 1985, to mark the twentieth anniversary of the conclusion of the Second Vatican Council. I personally participated in the four subsequent Synods, the Ordinary General Assemblies on the laity (1987), on the formation of priests (1990), the Special Assembly for Europe (1991) and the Assembly on consecrated life (1994). I had earlier participated in the 1977 Assembly on catechetics, in the time of Paul VI. Intimations of episcopal mortality come to my mind as I recall that, for my first three Synods, I attended as a 'substitute'; substituting for the late Cardinal William Conway in 1977, for Archbishop Kevin MacNamara in 1987, and for Cardinal Tomás Ó Fiaich in 1990, each of these having just recently died at the time. I attended the Synods of 1991 and 1994 'in my own name'. There have also been special Synods for Africa (1994), for Lebanon (1995) and for America (1997). A Synod for Asia has just concluded (1998). Further Synods are in preparation for Oceania, and, for the second time, on Europe. These 'continental' Synods are intended as part of the Catholic Church's preparation for the Great Jubilee of the year 2000.

Each of these synodal assemblies has, in my experience, seen the Synod, while remaining what, by definition, it is, namely a Synod of Bishops, become at the same time the occasion for a listening and learning and sharing experience between the Pope and the bishops and between them and priests, religious men and women, lay men and women and young people. Lay people, including women, addressed the Synod for the first time in 1987. In 1987, these interventions were formal affairs in sessions called 'hearings' or 'listenings' (*auditiones*). In 1994 women were invited to address the Synod in an ordinary session. Women, religious and lay, have regularly participated in discussion groups (or *circuli minores*), which have had a part in formulating 'propositions' to the Pope as an aid for the drafting of the post-synodal document. All the religious women to whom I spoke at the end of the 1994 Synod on consecrated life agreed that the suggestions they had put forward in discussion groups had found their way into the final 'propositions'. There was one exception: their wish to have an input into the eventual drafting of the post-synodal document was not included. At the concluding luncheon, the Pope announced that he would find ways to ensure that this would indeed happen. Many women religious, including several who participated in this Synod, have expressed their satisfaction with the document ensuing from the Synod, *Vita consecreta* (1996), and have found that it corresponds faithfully with the Synod discussion and fulfils many of their hopes and wishes in regard to it. So far as the Synods I have personally attended are concerned, I have always found the concluding Apostolic Exhortation to be a faithful reflection of the discussions at the Synod and to follow closely the synodal 'propositions'.

At the end of each Synod, Pope John Paul invites all Synod participants, bishops, clergy, religious, lay men and women, to a luncheon which he hosts personally. At this concluding 'agape', he delivers a short and informal and unscripted address; it is often one of the best contributions to the Synod. At the end of the meal, as he takes leave of each participant individually, there is a feeling that it is a parting of friends and that the Pope is sad to see the participants leave. During the Synod he will have attended every general session, except that on Wednesday morning, the time for his weekly General Audience, listening attentively and taking notes; he will have had each single participant share in a small group at a working breakfast following his Mass, or at a working lunch or a working supper. The meal is a relaxed affair, but has always a purpose in enabling the Pope to listen to first-hand accounts of the state of the Church in different countries and continents. Those present are invariably impressed by the knowledge he displays of their different situations and by the pertinent questions he asks. The time which John Paul makes available for the Synod in his punishing schedule never ceases to amaze.

Indeed, some of the important initiatives of Pope John Paul II were taken in response to proposals made at one or other Synod of Bishops. For example, the revision of the Code of Canon Law was requested by the Synod of 1967 and the new Code was published in 1983; the *Charter of the Rights of the Family* (1983) by the Synod of 1980; the *Catechism of the Catholic Church* (1994) by the Synod of 1985. The Encyclical *Evangelium vitae* or *The Gospel of Life* (1995) was proposed by the special Consistory of Cardinals in 1991, and was preceded by a personal letter from the Pope to each bishop in the world, asking them, in 'a spirit of collegiality', to offer him 'their co-operation' in drawing up the document. Other initiatives, such as the programme for the celebration of the Great Jubilee of the year 2000, were the fruit of discussion at a specially convened Consistory of Cardinals and of widespread consultation across the Church.

There certainly could be improvement in some of the procedures of the Synod. Many bishops are dissatisfied with the first part of the session's proceedings, during which each bishop has the right to speak for the allotted eight minutes, and can speak on any topic related to the Synod's theme. This results in a series of speeches on disparate aspects of the theme, following one another in no logical order, and sometimes repetitive. There is no opportunity of following a particular theme through, or of responding to the speaker who has just spoken. There can be a loss of sense of direction (and sometimes of concentration!). The procedure has, however, the merit of allowing everyone to participate, and of preventing the Synod from being monopolised by a few more powerful personalities. It might not be too easy to find an alternative, without excluding some synodal members who have ideas which they wish to share. The group discussions, arranged by language groups, are generally regarded as the more effective part of the synodal programme. The last week of the session is extremely crowded, with little time to translate the 'propositions' formulated by the various discussion groups into a single list, which is voted upon and which then forms the basis for the eventual published conclusions of the Synod. It would probably help if time could sometime be set aside for a review of the present procedures of the Synod.

It is, I believe, demonstrably untrue that 'Rome' tries to 'control' the agenda or to 'impose' its own agenda on the Synod. The *Lineamenta* or Outline Document for the recent Synod for Asia, for example, was not drawn up unilaterally by 'Rome', as has been suggested. In fact, the Pope set up a pre-Synodal Council, composed of Asian bishops, aided by Asian theologians, to work with the Synod Secretariat in preparing for this Synod. It is this Council, jointly with the Secretariat, which drew up the *Lineamenta* and circulated them to the bishops of the Asian continent. They in turn prepared the *Instrumentum laboris*, or Working Document, which is offered as a reference point for the debates at the Synod Assembly. It is a regrettable tunnel vision which causes some journalists routinely to present the Synod as a struggle between the Pope and the bishops, rather than as an exercise in collegiality.

Nor can I agree with suggestions that the bishops are not allowed to select their own themes. Suggestions for future synodal themes are invited at the end of each Synod; and, in addition, the episcopal conferences of the world are regularly invited to submit themes, in order of their preference, for consideration by the Synodal Council which is elected by the Synod itself. It is from these lists that the Pope selects the theme for the next Synod. Nor can I accept suggestions that the bishops do not feel free to express their views openly at the Synod. My experience of the Synod, despite occasional misgivings about the effectiveness of some of its procedures, has been entirely positive. I believe that it is fulfilling the desires expressed by the Vatican Council and has proved its value as a genuine instrument of collegiality.

Another forum for dialogue between Pope and bishops has been overhauled and updated by Pope John Paul, and deserves also to be called an instrument of collegiality; I speak of the *ad limina* visits of bishops to Rome. Following a long tradition, Catholic bishops come to 'the shrines of the apostles' once every five years. In my first ten years as bishop, these visits were made individually and were largely a formality. One paid a visit to the Basilicas of St Peter and of St Paul-Outside-the-Walls, signed the appropriate registers and received certificates to that effect, and paid a courtesy visit to the Cardinal Prefect of the Congregation of Bishops. In 1972, when Cardinal Confalonieri was Prefect of the Congregation, I called on him and had a brief and friendly conversation. It was after Pope Paul's reforms of the Curia. There was now an age limit of eighty on Curial Cardinals for continuing in their posts and on all Cardinals for voting in conclaves. When I rose to leave, the Cardinal moved to help me to put on my overcoat. I demurred, but he replied, with a twinkle in his eye, 'I insist. This is almost the only privilege now left to the Cardinals of the Holy Roman Curia!'

During the present pontificate, the procedures have become much more meaningful and more pastorally effective. Bishops now come in groups, either nationally (as in Ireland) or by province or by apostolic region. They meet with the Pope for a thorough review of the pastoral situation in the country or region. They systematically visit the various dicasteries or Curial departments, having previously indicated the topics which they wish to raise. This provides valuable opportunities for greater understanding and sharing and collaboration between the Pope and bishops and between the Curia and the bishops of the world. This is one more of the innovative ways in which Pope John Paul has striven to increase both 'affective' and 'effective' collegiality between himself and the bishops of the Universal Church.

Criticism of the Roman Curia

There has also been criticism of the Roman Curia under Pope John Paul, and this is nothing new. The Vatican Council itself called for reform of the Curia. Pope Paul VI lost no time responding to this call. Paul knew the Curia intimately. He appreciated its great strengths, he knew its weaknesses, he knew the need for reform. Pope Paul, as I wrote earlier in this chapter, carried through a radical reform of the Curia, and made it a very different entity than it had formerly been, while reinforcing the strengths it had always had. Some of today's critics seem to forget that that reform happened and that it met the demands formulated by the Council itself.

The Curia is a necessary instrument at the service of the Pope's God-given ministry of doctrinal and pastoral oversight of the universal Church. It is more than a civil service or a bureaucracy, because it shares closely in the Pope's own sacred mission. So closely is it related to the Pope that criticism of it is sometimes a 'code' for criticism of the Pope himself. However, criticisms of the Curia are commonplace. There are claims that it acts as if it were a body superior to the bishops, fails to trust bishops, seeks to invigilate their activities, sometimes judges them on the basis of complaints from suspect groups or individuals. In my experience, the practice of the Curia has usually been to refer complaints about matters arising within a diocese to the bishop concerned and to ask him to deal prudently with the matter of the complaint. No one could object to that. However, it is easy to see that there are some types of complaint for which this procedure would not be appropriate. If, for example, there were complaints about the bishop himself, the practice generally followed in the Curia, so far as I am aware, would also be to refer complaints to the bishop concerned so that he would have the opportunity to respond.

Obviously, there can be cases where confidentiality must be respected and where serious issues are at stake. Difficulties which bishops might experience in this area can and should be brought up at some of the many opportunities bishops can have of meeting with whatever Curial dicastery may be in question. It would not be good that suspicions between Curia and bishops would be allowed to grow on the basis of unidentified reports and unknown complainants. The more open and frank and trusting the exchanges between bishops and Curial officers can be, the better for all.

Cardinal Danneels has spoken about an undue proliferation of paper, a profusion of documents and brochures which busy bishops do not have time to read. The Curia has not escaped the paper explosion, which eats up time as well as depleting the world's forests!

As against all this, I have to say that, in my thirty years as bishop, no intervention or comment or criticism was ever made by the Holy See about any one of the many pastoral letters and statements or other documents which were issued by the Irish Episcopal Conference. Other episcopal conferences can doubtless say the same thing. Nobody could say that the bishops' right to teach is impeded or superseded by the Curia or by the Holy See. Indeed, in all my time as bishop in three dioceses, the Curia has never intervened in any way whatever in any of my diocesan activities or responsibilities.

Equally, surely, nobody could claim that situations can never arise when a bishop might express opinions contrary to authentic Catholic doctrine, or conflicting with authoritative norms of Catholic pastoral practice. If a bishop were found to speak or act in such a way, the Pope, successor of Peter, who inherits Peter's mandate to confirm his brothers in the faith, must have a right to point this out and to use his agencies in the Curia to do so. In such a case, the Pope would be acting collegially, since he is the ultimate guarantor of the collegial unity of the episcopate; and, furthermore, the bishop would be himself offending against the collegiality of bishops with one another, as well as against the spirit of collegiality between bishops and the head of the episcopal College. Again, there are, sadly, some episcopal conferences, albeit a very small number, where there seem to be serious divisions between bishops themselves in respect of their oversight of both pastoral and sacramental practice, and, perhaps, also their oversight of doctrine, or at least of matters touching on doctrine. Sometimes these divisions can be resolved only by the action of the Holy See. To present the argument as if bishops were necessarily and always right, and the Curia necessarily and always wrong, is not to be objective.

The Curia is accused of unjust treatment of theologians. This did happen in the 1950s, when, as I have said earlier, some outstandingly orthodox theologians were censured and deprived for a time of their right to teach and write. The Vatican Council and the post-conciliar Popes reversed these injustices. The Holy Office has been transformed into the Congregation for the Doctrine of the Faith, and has as its Prefect a distinguished theologian. Its procedures have been significantly reformed, most recently in 1997, with a view to providing greater safeguards for the rights of theologians to a fair hearing. Many complaints about theologians have been satisfactorily clarified and many disputes resolved through dialogue, whether at diocesan or Curial level. The Pope, however, has ultimate and supreme responsibility for unity of faith and orthodoxy of doctrine in the universal Church. If all the resources of dialogue prove ineffective, the Pope and the Holy See must have the right to declare that certain writings or propositions are not in harmony with the Church's teaching. As an Instruction of the Congregation of the Doctrine of the Faith on 'The Ecclesial Vocation of the Theologian', published in 1990, put it:

> When it acts in such ways, the Magisterium seeks to be faithful to its mission of defending the right of the people of God to receive the message of the Church in its purity and integrity....

It is worth recalling what Pope Paul VI said to the French bishops in 1963, namely that, if due vigilance and oversight in respect of orthodoxy in doctrine and practice are exercised by bishops at local level, there will be less need for recourse to the offices of the Holy See or for intervention by the Curia. I believe, for example, that if we bishops had been more courageous in proclaiming unpopular truths in doctrine or in morality, some of the pronouncements of both Paul VI and John Paul II and of departments of the Curia would have been less necessary. If each of these Popes has at times been made to seem isolated in their teaching on, for example, questions of sexual morality, or has been falsely perceived as being too preoccupied with these issues, this was in great part because we bishops were too often silent. I include myself fully in that confession of fault.

Nominations of bishops
Procedures for the nominations of bishops and appointments of particular candidates or types of candidate have also become matters for criticism. For objective discussion of this question some facts need to be recalled. Although, as a bishop, I can be accused of *parti pris*, I submit that a great majority of appointments made under the present systems are successful, are well received by priests and people, and indeed are very often the appointments desired by both priests and people. Indeed, it should be acknowledged that the so-called 'progressive' bishops, who constituted the large majority at the Second Vatican Council, were appointed largely under the same systems as those of today, and, I make bold to say, reflected credit on the Roman Curia of that day. It should also be remembered that under an earlier system in Ireland, whereby voting by clergy on episcopal candidates was more open and the results of the voting were known, with candidates being ranked in order of preference as 'dignus, dignior, dignissimus', 'suitable, more suitable, most suitable', dioceses sometimes became deeply divided and the 'splits' among clergy and people sometimes took a long time to heal. It is true that, in a small number of cases, episcopal appointments under the present system have also proved to be divisive, and divisions have not yet been healed. These, however, were exceptional and many occurred in dioceses and countries where there had been serious problems, and

sometimes real irregularities and deviations, and exceptional measures were necessary.

There is already considerable place for consultation under the present system. In Ireland, the bishops of each diocese conduct a consultation every three years among their priests, diocesan and religious. This consultation is conducted under conditions of strict confidentiality. Confidentiality is less easily accepted in modern culture – and, sadly, is less observed; but it is not part of a clerical 'culture of secrecy'; it is designed rather to respect the privacy of candidates and lessen the dangers accruing from 'campaigns' for individual candidates which might be conducted, with the divisiveness which can result therefrom. The results of the diocesan consultation are brought by each bishop to a provincial meeting of bishops, held once every three years. The bishops discuss each name on the total list and vote by secret ballot on their adjudged suitability. The results of this whole process are sent to the Apostolic Nuncio and are sent by him to the Congregation of Bishops. There is, therefore, a standing list of eligible candidates, which is regularly updated, and forms a 'pool' of potential candidates in advance of any vacancy. When a vacancy arises in the diocese, the Nuncio conducts a further consultation of clergy and of a number of lay persons in the diocese in question. The result of the whole process is the submission by the Nuncio to the Congregation of Bishops of three names of candidates, and it is from these that the Pope normally makes his final choice. The system is, therefore, far from arbitrary. There is widespread consultation of the clergy, and there is scope within the system for wider consultation among the laity. But undue concentration on a very small number of contested appointments distorts the whole discussion, and can lead to unjustified criticism of a system, which, while not perfect, is almost certainly better than the suggested alternatives.

In concluding this discussion of the Curia, I have to say that, for many of the shortcomings of the Curia as perceived by bishops, the responsibility is shared by us bishops ourselves and the remedies are sometimes in our own hands. Those who work in the Curia are not some distinct species of *homo ecclesiasticus*. Most of the heads of Curial congregations or dicasteries are former diocesan bishops. The officials of the Curia are drawn predominantly from the diocesan clergy everywhere or from the religious clergy. They are released and recommended for service in the Curia by bishops or by religious superiors. For every bishop who finds a Curial official 'difficult', there is usually another bishop somewhere who has recommended or released that official for Curial service. The Curia has great difficulty in recruiting personnel, especially in countries where there is a shortage of priests. Bishops do find it very difficult to release the kind of priest who is competent and suitable for this very special ministry. I confess that I have myself on occasion thought it impossible to release people when requests for personnel were circulated. I now realise that, despite the enormous difficulties, it is vitally important that, on occasion, dioceses be prepared to make the sacrifice of releasing what may be one or other of their best priests for Curial service.

It is unfortunate that some of the highly publicised criticisms of the Curia have been one-sided and have given insufficient attention both to the positive qualities of the Curia and to the difficulties with which it has to contend. My own experience over thirty years of dealing with the personnel of the various dicasteries of the Curia has been overwhelmingly positive. I have encountered nothing but courtesy, understanding and helpfulness. I have some experience, as I have remarked earlier, of their extraordinary work-rate. In terms purely of output and service per unit of staff, the Curia, in my view, scores far more highly than any comparable organisation anywhere. Their hours and quality of work put many of their critics to shame. Their stipend is incredibly modest. In addition to their office duties, they often have other ministries or charitable works to which they devote their care in non-office hours. I have found them to be men of God, men of prayer, people with a deep love of the Church. I believe that they welcome criticism, provided it is fair, balanced and constructive. I believe that they subscribe to Pope Paul's words, addressed to the Curia in September 1963:

We should accept criticism with humility, reflection, and even gratitude. Rome has no need to defend itself by turning a deaf ear to suggestions made to it, when they come from critics who are fair-minded, particularly when they are friendly and fraternal.... The Curia itself [is] in the forefront of the continuous reform which the Church itself needs, insofar as it is a human and earthly institution.

Pope Paul declared on that occasion that he would personally hope for 'a more effective and responsible collaboration with his own beloved brothers in the episcopate'. Collegiality works both ways; it calls for open but fraternal and friendly dialogue between bishops and Curia in the spirit of communion which is the Church. As St Paul tells us, by speaking and by doing the truth in love we shall all grow in all ways into Christ, and the body of the Church will grow until it has built itself up in love (cf. Ephesians 4: 15-16).

Pope John Paul's papal ministry

Pope John Paul's papal ministry has been so wide-ranging and his achievements so vast as to fill volumes. I shall briefly indicate only a few aspects of his pontificate. His contribution to theology has been immense. His great trinitarian trilogy: *Dives in misericordia* (1980) on God the Father; *Redemptor hominis* (1979), which was his first encyclical, on God the Son; and *Dominum et vivificantem* (1986), on the Holy Spirit, constitute an enrichment of trinitarian theology and spirituality. His encyclicals on moral issues, *Veritatis splendor* (1993) and *Evangelium vitae* (1995), are a timely and much needed reaffirmation and development of basic principles in Catholic moral teaching. His writings on the Blessed Virgin Mary, particularly the encyclical *Redemptoris Mater* (1987), are a major contribution to mariology and to a renewal of Marian devotion. Pope John Paul's contribution to ecumenism has been immense. He has described the search for Christian unity as 'one of the pastoral priorities' of his pontificate. His encyclical *Ut Unum Sint* (1995), and his Apostolic Letter *Orientale lumen* (1995), are an expression of his deep commitment to this cause. His social encyclicals,

Laborem exercens (1981), on work, its human and social significance, and the rights and responsibilities to which it gives rise, *Sollicitudo rei socialis* (1987), written to mark the twentieth anniversary of Pope Paul's *Populorum progressio*, and *Centesimus annus* (1991), published to mark the centenary of *Rerum novarum*, make an important contribution to the debate on justice and human rights, and offer a profound analysis of 'liberal capitalism' and the 'free market' in a post-communist world. Indeed, few people have contributed more than Pope John Paul to both the theology and philosophy of justice and of human rights and to the prophetic call for their practical implementation in both democratic and authoritarian societies. As Mikhail Gorbachev acknowledged, Pope John Paul has contributed more than any other person to the process which led to the collapse of the Soviet communist system from Poland to the Urals. He has been the first Pope ever to devote an extensive document to the dignity and vocation of women (*Mulieris dignitatem*, 1988) and to write a *Letter to Women*, greeting them 'most warmly', on the eve of the Fourth World Conference of Women, which took place in Beijing in September 1995. No Pope has ever given such special recognition to the role and place of women in the Church as has Pope John Paul. To present him as a misogynist is ludicrous.

Pope John Paul has taken bold initiatives for the sake of truth and reconciliation, even in matters controversial for the Church, for example: by his rehabilitation of Galileo; by allowing access to the Vatican archives relating to the Inquisition for historical study; by his asking forgiveness from the Jewish people for sins of anti-semitism among some Catholics, his historic visit to the Rome synagogue, and his patient pursuit of good relations between the Catholic Church and the Jews; by his untiring efforts and pleading and prayer for peace and justice in the world; by his persevering efforts for reconciliation and unity with the Orthodox Church; by his unprecedented invitation to Protestant and Orthodox Church leaders and theologians to engage in 'a patient and fraternal dialogue' with him on the exercise of the Petrine Primacy; by his repeated calls for forgiveness of sins committed by Catholics against unity.

Yet this man of dynamic action, of physically exhausting pastoral journeys across the world, of prophetic speech and of exceptional moral and physical courage, is also a contemplative. It is necessary to have been close to Pope John Paul II when he celebrates Mass to appreciate fully how contemplative a person he is. His utter absorption in the mystery he is celebrating and his obliviousness of all else, his concentration, his reverence, his sense of the sacred, are deeply impressive. The same spirit is evident in his writing, where his scripture-filled meditations and theology, and his philosophical thinking, find a harmony and a unity which can only be described as contemplative. It is not for nothing that he chose St John of the Cross for his doctrinal research in theology, or that one of his favourite theologians is Hans Urs von Balthasar.

André Frossard has written extensively about his conversations with Pope John Paul II. The following anecdotes illustrate both the self-deprecating humour of this Pope and the deep reverence and humility before God which mark his life. On one occasion, he retailed to Frossard a current Roman joke, to the effect that the Pope asked God in prayer whether Poland would regain its full freedom some day, and God replied, 'Yes, but not in your lifetime.' The Pope then asked God, 'When I am gone, will there be another Polish Pope?' God replied, 'Not in my lifetime.' On another occasion, a Polish visitor, concerned about the Pope's safety, pleaded with him always to use the 'popemobile' at general audiences. She added: 'We can't help being worried about Your Holiness.' The Pope replied, 'I'm worried about my holiness too!' The flippancy here conceals a deep seriousness which is revealed in the third anecdote. The Pope is speaking about man or woman on the threshold of judgment. He says:

> [Judgment] is to be understood as a need to see where [one] stands when finally confronted by absolute and universal truth.

I have myself always found the Truth which God is to be an awesome thought. It cuts through all my hypocrisies and self-justifications, my deceptions and self-deceptions. It cuts to the bone and it hurts. But it also heals. I am consoled by remembering St Thérèse of Lisieux; she saw that God's justice is also his love and mercy. God's truth is also his merciful love; and on that mercy and love we can confidently place all our trust.

Criticisms of Pope John Paul II unfortunately sometimes, it seems to me, spring from a manifest prejudice, personal or ideological, against the present Pope. They are eagerly relayed by a world media committed to the 'liberal consensus', and apparently seeing in John Paul II the chief and sometimes only obstacle to the 'liberal agenda'. More worryingly, there are traces in some sectors within the Church of what Hans Urs von Balthasar called an 'anti-Roman complex'. It is important that this be challenged and theologically resisted. It is irreconcilable with Vatican II. Indeed, at times the very nature of the Roman Catholic Church is at issue. The debates about the nature of the Church at Vatican II were concerned with expressing the proper balance between papal primacy and collegiality. These do not conflict with or contradict one another. Both are essential constitutive elements of the Church as Catholic teaching understands it. A major preoccupation with some theologians nowadays seems to be to resist 'papal centralism'. They should pay heed to Cardinal Danneels' warning against 'national Churches' in dissent from the Church, one and universal.

Pope John Paul towers intellectually and, above all, spiritually above all the criticisms. The last word about him must be one of prayer: in the words of a familiar prayer for the Pope, 'Dominus conservet eum et vivificet eum', 'May the Lord preserve him and give him long life'. He has called the Great Jubilee of the year 2000 the 'hermeneutical key' to his whole pontificate; may his great dream for that Jubilee be realised for him and may his hopes for it be fulfilled. By the power of the Holy Spirit and with the maternal intercession of Mary, Mother of the Lord, may he lead 'the men and women of the millennium towards the One who is the true light that enlightens every person coming into this world' (cf. John 1: 9).

CHAPTER NINE

FIFTY YEARS A PRIEST: REFLECTIONS

I celebrated the fiftieth anniversary of my ordination as priest on 22 June 1991. It was an occasion for recollection and for reflection, as well as for thanksgiving and for repentance. In Part Two of this book, I give the text of my homily at Mass on the occasion of my first visit to Loughguile as Cardinal, in July 1991, and there I record my recollections of my ordination and first Mass. I recall that, soon after ordination, I spent some weeks as temporary curate, supplying for the parish priest during his vacation. This was in the Parish of Lower Mourne, at the foothills of the lovely Mountains of Mourne. These were weeks filled with the joy and enthusiasm of a novice priest. Father Ned Smith, on his return from vacation, was a genial host and an entertaining raconteur, full of clerical lore, who relished an audience and found a certain pleasure in 'shocking' the innocent which I was. He foresaw that I would be sent for postgraduate study, and somewhat chillingly reminded me that the letters 'DD' would not occupy much space on my tombstone! He probably discerned my tendency to be too serious and to work too hard at my studies.

In the summer of 1942 I 'supplied' in Cushendun for Father Padraig Murphy, who had volunteered to serve as chaplain to the 'Gilbraltarians', who had been evacuated to various locations in Northern Ireland because of wartime conditions. I covered much of the parish on my bicycle, growing in my love of the Glens and the

Glens people. One cycling exploit of which I was proud was to ride to say Mass in Culraney, a lovely little chapel on the coastal road to Murlough Bay and Ballycastle. This meant a heavy push-and-shove up the formidable 'Dan Nancy's Brae', and that in the days before it was tarmacadamed and when it was barely passable by motor car. The going up was strenuous and exhausting, the free-wheeling back down was exhilarating. After Mass, the whole little community gathered in a neighbour's house for a lovely breakfast.

For several subsequent summers in succession, I 'supplied' in Carnlough, to let the parish priest, Father Terry Toal, have his annual two or three weeks holiday. Again, the bicycle trips and walks up and down the Glens and along the lovely Coast Road have left me memories of a natural beauty few Irish counties can rival and of a people with a beauty of spirit and heart that seemed to blend naturally with their physical environment. The remaining weeks of those summers were spent visiting the homes of Loughguile and Magherahoney, having a taste of the joy and fulfilment of the pastoral ministry of a priest.

At night in Father Toal's house, alone save for his faithful housekeeper, Maggie, I began to develop my love for poetry and for the serious novel – Irish, English, American, French and Russian (in translation) – a love which I never lost. Apart from the delights of sharing the minds and experience of great novelists and short story writers, I have derived valuable insights into human nature from their works. Second only to experience of life and of people, I believe great writers, as much as, and perhaps even more than philosophers, can help us to understand something of the reply to the Socratic question: 'But who are we?'

I have always found it interesting that the writers who have given me the greatest insights into human nature and the heights and depths of human and specifically of man-woman relationships, were the writers who predated the sexual explicitness which is now accepted as permissible – if not mandatory – for writers.

The Maynooth post-graduate centre, the Dunboyne Establishment, was to be my next destination. I entered there at the end of the summer vacation of 1941. I had little difficulty in choosing my doctoral thesis theme, resuming my study of Tertullian. Now I selected for research Tertullian's theology of penance and of baptism, linking this with the theology of St Cyprian. Professor R. M. Henry had in fact very wisely provided in advance for such a development in my studies, by introducing me, five years earlier, to Tertullian, a writer of difficult and sometimes tortuous but stylistically highly original and often brilliant Latin, and a most fascinating figure of the early Church. My first postgraduate year, leading to the Licentiate in Theology, was devoted to reading the basic patristic texts, as well as to further study of theology in general. In spite of my familiarity with Latin and my earlier exposure to Tertullian, the Latin of Tertullian was quite a challenge, even when I became familiar with his original style and idiom.

I overworked all through that year and had a breakdown in health in June 1942 after the Licentiate examination, in spite of the efforts which the Sisters in the College Infirmary had made during the year to keep me fit. (I had been their 'Infirmarian' during the previous year.) I developed pleurisy with suspected tuberculosis and spent some time in the Infirmary. While there, I had a visit from the College President, Dr John D'Alton, who had just been appointed Coadjutor Bishop of Meath and who in due course was to become Cardinal Archbishop of Armagh. Later, I spent some weeks in hospital. On discharge, I needed nearly six months' convalescence, which I spent in Loughguile with my mother, only slowly regaining my vitality. During this time, I became overweight, but this was on the advice of my doctor, who seemed to believe that one could eat one's way out of the danger of TB! I was able to return to Maynooth and resume my studies only in April 1943. Consequently, I needed three years to complete my doctoral research instead of the usual two.

I completed my thesis on 'Tertullian the Puritan and His Influence' in May 1944 and sat for my defence of it in June. There were no resources for publication in the College at that time, and it was not until 1993, nearly fifty years later, that the thesis was published.

In my final years in Maynooth I was told confidentially that Monsignor Kissane, now become President and having vacated his Chair of Sacred Scripture, with some other members of the Faculty, wished me to go to Rome for further biblical studies, with a view to appointment to a post in Sacred Scripture in Maynooth. Nothing came of this; and, though I have always loved Scripture and biblical science, I had no regrets that this idea was not followed up.

In September 1944, I was appointed teacher in St Malachy's College, where I taught Latin and Greek, as well as religion. Some fourteen months later I was appointed lecturer in the Department of Scholastic Philosophy in Queen's University, Belfast, as assistant to Monsignor Arthur H. Ryan. I had not formally specialised in philosophy during my own undergraduate years, though I took the full 'Pass' courses in the subject, which were obligatory for seminarians, and I had already developed a great interest in philosophy. I enthusiastically welcomed the challenge of this appointment as opening up a whole new field of interest and I prepared to throw myself into it with all my energies.

Bishop Mageean relieved me of duties in St Malachy's College from Christmas 1945, leaving me free to take some courses in University College, Dublin, and to do some reading in philosophy during the months from January to May. In UCD, I followed courses in metaphysics with Monsignor John D. Horgan, in ethics with Father Denis O'Keefe, in logic with Father John Shine. On arrival in UCD, I was 'put in the charge' of a Dublin seminarian, Desmond Connell, later to be Professor of Metaphysics in that University, and later still to be Archbishop of Dublin. I had lodgings in Sandymount, along the sea front. I read voraciously in philosophy, having much ground to make up in that field, before beginning to lecture in Queen's at the end of the summer.

In September 1946, I took up duty as lecturer in Queen's University, where I was most warmly received and initiated into academic life by the Head of Department, Monsignor Arthur Ryan. I was long to enjoy his friendship and later I was particularly privileged in having his company and his brilliant conversation in the Irish College, Rome, during the years of the Vatican Council, when he was theological adviser to Bishop William Philbin. In my first year at Queen's I lived in digs in South Parade, off the Ormeau Road in Belfast, and then, in 1947/8, rented a flat in Derryvolgie Avenue, which I shared with some other members of my family. In 1948 we acquired a house in Fitzwilliam Avenue, from which we moved in 1961 to Rosetta Avenue, further up the Ormeau Road. Over the years, my mother spent more and more of her time in Belfast and less of it in Loughguile, although, as I have said already, Loughguile was for ever 'home'.

My summers were, for many of those early years, spent in Tully, where I helped the parish priest and curate with daily and Sunday Masses. I cycled round Loughguile, Corkey and Magherahoney, visiting the homes, blessing the houses, listening to people's stories. As a student, I had helped my father in the years before his death, taking classes for him, especially religion and pre-confirmation classes. Hence, I acquired a good knowledge of all age-groups in the parish. I had, then and always, a great love of preaching, and regarded sharing the Word of God as one of the first duties and greatest joys of a priest's life. I also obtained a great love for the pastoral life of a priest, which offered me much satisfaction in itself, as well as enriching the academic and intellectual life, to which I was to devote most of my time and energies during my tenure in the Department of Scholastic Philosophy in Queen's University from 1946 to 1967. This university period of my life was a very happy and fruitful time for me, as I point out elsewhere in this book.

My golden jubilee of priesthood was also a time for reflection on the changes in religious practice and on the new challenges facing priests in Ireland today, as compared to fifty years ago. I turn to these changes and challenges now.

Resources of faith in Ireland

We priests of 1941 were little different from most ordination classes in taking it for granted that we were going to change the world and that the Church was waiting for us. There was not much questioning or awareness of a need to question the traditional pastoral methods of the Irish clergy. Religious practice in Ireland was quasi-universal. Irish pastoral methods had manifestly 'worked' and were still working well. Perhaps the first experience that somewhat dented our self-confidence was that of the mass emigration of the war years and later of the 1950s and the 1960s. It became clear that, while many of the Irish emigrants continued to be strongly committed to their faith and to the Church, there was nevertheless a significant number who abandoned religious practice almost as soon as they disembarked from the cross-channel boat. Clearly, the religious practice of some was superficial and was much too dependent on routine and conformity. The lesson was quickly taken to heart by many priests and by the Irish bishops, who responded magnificently to the challenge of providing pastoral preparation for our emigrants before their departure and pastoral care for them in their new home in Britain, through the Irish Emigrant Chaplaincy, still vigorously active.

If complacency and even a certain triumphalism were temptations for the Irish Church in the past, the risk of the present is as likely to be unjustified pessimism There are grounds for concern. There is no room for complacency. But equally, there is no ground for pessimism, much less for defeatism, so far as the state of the faith in Ireland today is concerned. The condition of the Church in Ireland is still healthy, the potential for the future is great.

The quality of religious faith cannot be mathematically measured. Spiritual growth or decline are not quantifiable. There are, however, certain manifestations of faith which can be measured and which are of their nature correlated with faith itself. Religious practice in terms of attendance at Sunday Mass and frequenting of the sacraments can be measured, and measurements can be repeated at intervals. Variations over time in the results can provide some benchmarks by which we can indirectly discern trends of decline, stability, or growth, in matters appertaining to religious faith. In 1974 the Council for Research and Development of the Irish Episcopal Conference conducted a first scientific survey of 'Religious Practice, Beliefs and Moral Attitudes', the results of which were published in 1975. (The survey did not include Northern Ireland, where it was felt that, in the circumstances at the time, it would not be prudent to put questions to people concerning religious affiliation and practice.) A follow-up survey, using the same criteria, was carried out by the same unit in 1984, the results being published in 1985. Meanwhile, Father Michael MacGreil conducted a survey of 'Church Attendance and Religious Practice among Dublin Adults – Roman Catholics, 1972-3', the findings of which provide interesting parallels to the Research and Development survey. The year 1984 also saw the publication of the Irish Report of the European Value Systems (EVS) Study, conducted in 1981 and entitled *Irish Values and Attitudes*. These studies too refer to the Republic of Ireland only. Finally, in 1992, we have preliminary figures from a follow-up EVS Study of 1990; this particular study covered Northern Ireland also and provides further indication of trends in respect of religious and moral values and practice in both parts of Ireland.

Religion in Ireland, therefore, has been subjected to careful scientific scrutiny. We are not just guessing about religious practice and attitudes, but have objective evidence to back up our statements. Although there are trends that cause serious concern, nevertheless, it must be said that the overall picture is more positive than is sometimes allowed.

To refer to weekly Mass attendance only, the 1974 survey showed a weekly Mass attendance of 91%. Ten years later, in 1984, this figure had fallen to 87%. There was, therefore, a decline of 4%. The European study of 1981 (published in 1984) found 86% 'going to church weekly or oftener'. A second survey by Father MacGreil in 1989 showed a further drop of 5%. This indicates that the figure for weekly Mass attendance was then falling at a slightly accelerating rate: the 4% fall over a ten-year period had later become a 5% fall over a five-year period. The fall was notably more marked among the younger age groups than among those over thirty-five; the fall was more significant in the greater urban areas than in rural areas, where, for the most part, religious practice continued to be virtually universal; also unemployed groups were

Mother (about 1912)   Father (about 1937)

BA Graduation, 1937

Queen's University Lecturer, 1950

With mother in Tully, 1945

With mother, 1959

*With Pope Paul VI at time of appointment
as Bishop of Ardagh and Clonmacnois, July 1967.*

Episcopal Ordination in St Mel's Cathedral, Longford,
16 July 1967.

In Ara Coeli, Armagh, 1991
Photographs in background show Cardinal Conway with Pope Paul VI
and Bishop Daly as Bishop of Down & Connor with Cardinal Ó Fiaich.

Synod of Bishops, 1990

Synod of Bishops, 1994

Pope John Paul's arrival at Dublin Airport,
September 1979.

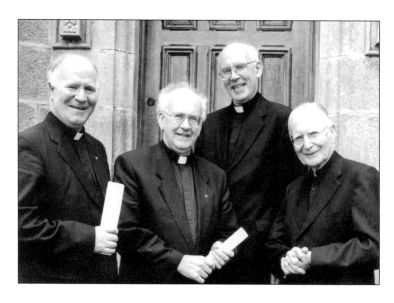

Conferral of Honour of Monsignor, July 1995
L to r: Mgr Denis Faul, Mgr Raymond Murray, Dr Seán Brady
Coadjutor Archbishop of Armagh, Cardinal Cahal Daly.

found to be markedly more irregular in church attendance than others. It was worrying also that, as the EVS reports show and as pastoral experience confirms, there is developing a degree of confusion in the minds of many about matters of doctrine and about moral beliefs and practice.

Nevertheless, the figures in the 1984 European study led Professor Michael Fogarty to remark that 'Ireland remains an outstandingly religious country'. In a comment on the same survey, Professor Liam Ryan of Maynooth's sociology department said:

> By any standards, Ireland is still a pre-eminently religious country. More people attend Church once a week in Ireland than in any other country in the world. Asked how important God was in their lives, the Irish were far ahead of any nation in Europe. When it comes to belief in the soul, in life after death, in heaven, and in prayer, the Irish are so far ahead of the rest of the Western world that any comparisons are totally irrelevant.

The 1990 EVS report, published in 1994, showed Mass attendance weekly or more often in Northern Ireland at 85%, almost identical with that for the Republic. All the other indicators for religious practice and attitudes in both parts of Ireland were also virtually identical. Later reports for the Republic showed weekly Mass attendance at 78% (John Weafer, 1992); and 77% (Lansdowne Market Research, 1994).

In 1998, however, the Market Research Bureau of Ireland (MRBI), for RTÉ's *Prime Time*, showed 60% weekly Mass attendance in the Republic. An Irish Marketing Surveys (IMS) survey in 1997 showed 65%; but the variation in the two latter figures would be in line with standard estimates of possible error in survey findings. For the 15-34 age-group, however, only 50% attend weekly Mass. There are no comparable published figures for Northern Ireland since 1990. It seems probable, however, that the figures here do not differ significantly from those in the Republic. I shall return to this point later.

There are, however, positive findings also in the more recent surveys. The 1997 IMS survey found that more Catholics receive Holy Communion weekly today than in 1974. The 1998 MRBI survey found that 82% of Irish Catholics consider religion very important or important in their lives; while, even for the 18-24 age group, the spiritual dimension of life is still important in their lives. Even so far as Mass attendance is concerned, over and above the 60% of regular attenders, there are a further 5% who attend fortnightly, 6% who attend every three to four weeks, 5% every two to three months, 6% less often than that. There are only 18% who rarely or never attend Mass. In European and, indeed, in world terms, these are exceptionally positive findings. Ireland is very far from being a 'post-Catholic' country or a country where, as one columnist put it recently, 'modern Irish society has walked away from religion'.

Nevertheless there has been a continuing downward trend, and the slippage since 1990 has been major. It is a slippage which it would be foolish to ignore or to minimise. In some parishes, especially in cities, the fall in Sunday Mass attendance is visible in empty pews. We have the evidence of our eyes also for the smaller numbers attending Mass from the younger section of the population. The decline in practice has been most marked in respect of the sacrament of Penance; the decline here has been universal throughout Ireland and across all age groups. These are certainly extremely disturbing phenomena.

Much has been written about the causes and the consequences of this decline. Media lay much stress on scandals in the Church as the main cause of alienation from the Church and from churchgoing. I am far indeed from denying or minimising the impact of this factor. I express elsewhere in this book my deep sense of concern, and indeed anguish, at these scandals. I want to suggest, however, that it is more scientific and more objective to set this Irish decline in the context of what has been happening in Europe and in comparable countries elsewhere. If decline in religious practice has been a universal phenomenon in other countries, it is proper to look at the common factors operative in all these countries, and to assume that these are important causative factors in the religious sphere as well. Such factors are greater economic prosperity, industrialisation, increased mobility of population, rural depopulation, growth in material comforts and consequently in this-worldly attitudes and in materialism and consumerism; there has been increased marriage and family instability, and serious breakdown in sexual and in public morality, with considerable moral confusion; there has been the spread of relativism in relation to all truths and values, especially religious truths and values; there has been greater economic independence for young people, and increased exploitation of the teenage market; there is the pervading cultural bias against authority in all its forms and against institutions of all kinds; there has been the growing influence of media and the growth within media of secular ideology. In other words there has been in the past decade social and cultural change of a scale, intensity and rapidity never experienced in any period of the same length in Ireland before. Here as elsewhere, the advance of these factors has been correlated with decline in religious practice, and must be seen as having a causal effect thereon.

When we look at the Irish decline in that context, we must be struck by the fact that the decline in religious practice in Ireland has been notably less drastic and less rapid than in any comparable country. Comparison with countries or regions historically, culturally and religiously similar to Ireland, bears this out still more clearly. The decline in religious practice in French Canada, Holland, Brittany and Flanders has been much greater and faster than in Ireland. In spite of everything, Michael Fogarty's remark is still true: 'Ireland remains an outstandingly religious country'.

The decline in Ireland began many decades ago. Early in my years as bishop, I was already saying to the priests of Ardagh and Clonmacnois that the 1970s could well be the last decade of near-universal religious practice in Ireland. In the 1970s I was already worried about the decline in priestly and religious vocations. In the 1990s we are not being faced with a sudden crisis, but rather with an accelerating build-up of factors negatively influencing religious faith. We do not need to panic. We do need calm and clear-headed planning of many-sided pastoral strategies to confront these factors in the power of the Gospel of Jesus Christ, to find new opportunities of outreach to non-practising or intermittently practising Catholics, and to promote, in small but cumulative ways, the re-evangelisation of the public culture.

The factors I have mentioned are present in the North also; but there are counter-factors at work here, many of them connected with 'the Troubles'. Faced with the tragedy of 'the Troubles', people feel their need of God and turn more fervently to prayer. Because of the absence of normal social life over much of the past quarter century, communities have been thrown more closely together with those of 'their own kind' and have developed a stronger sense of solidarity, a stronger community identity, a sense of need to support one another. This can lead to 'ghettoisation', and the sense of identity can take on a sectarian tinge. But Church community and human community can reinforce one another. Community, indeed, is part of any definition of Church. This, it seems to me, is part at least of what has helped in the North to counter-balance the forces influencing the decline in religious practice.

Many people feel that, at present, the Republic is, at least in its public and official face, a more secular society than Northern Ireland. Northern society, however, almost certainly will change when, as we fervently hope, peace and normality become consolidated. Secularisation and even secularism will probably increase in Northern Ireland too, with the new challenges which this will pose for the Catholic Church, and indeed for all the Churches. We must be aware of this possibility and do all in our power to respond positively to a changing situation. The Churches can learn from one another, and in many cases co-operate with one another, in meeting the new challenges.

Meanwhile, the recent statistics of religious practice in both parts of Ireland have positive elements as well as negative ones. The degree of intermittent or irregular attendance at Mass and other sacramental occasions is still high. The phenomenon of irregular or intermittent Mass attendance is new in the Irish Catholic situation.

It is regrettable, but it can be turned to advantage. It gives us more opportunities for evangelisation than are to be found in any other comparable country. I shall argue in the final chapter that we must make the most of these evangelising moments. I believe that coming decades will show a slowing up, and indeed the beginning of a reversal, of the downward trends in religious practice which we have been witnessing. I am quite convinced that the quality of religious commitment is often better today, because it is more personal, more convinced, more intellectually active and more freely chosen than it might have been in what older people sometimes call 'the good old days'.

There are surely solid grounds for confidence in the strength and the future of the faith in Ireland. There are surely grounds also for confidence in the pastoral methods of Irish priests. Such a degree of persistence in religious practice is certainly a tribute to the witness and the ministry of the bishops and the priests who preceded us in our various dioceses and parishes, as well, of course, as a tribute to the prayerful and apostolic lives of religious men and women, a tribute to the work of Catholic teachers, a tribute to the faith of our lay people and to their active involvement in the life and mission of the Church. Past generations of priests, religious and lay people are those who have laboured, and we today are harvesting the fruit of their labours. There must be something precious to conserve in the pastoral methods of the past. They need to be renewed and updated, they should not be uncritically rejected. *Vetera noviter*, old things in new ways, must accompany the *novum novale*, the new furrows of which Isaiah speaks. If we in Ireland have very largely managed to retain fellowship, solidarity and communication between older and younger clergy and between both of these and most sections of the laity, and between so-called 'liberal' and 'conservative' groups, this is a tribute to both age-groups and to both mind-sets. Perhaps it can be fairly claimed to be a tribute in a special way to the senior clergy, who have shown themselves to be on the whole open to new ideas and new ways and committed to brotherhood among clergy of all ages and mentalities. It is essential that this be maintained. It is essential that younger and older priests and bishops, 'liberal' and 'conservative' priests and bishops, be open to one another, really listen to one another and be ready to learn from one another. The scribe of the New Law brings forth from his treasury new things as well as old. The Spirit blows where it will and we cannot always immediately discern from where its breath comes and to where it points.

It is to God, therefore, that we entrust the future of the faith and of the Church in Ireland. We do so with a confidence born of the experience we have had of the powerful workings of his grace in the souls of the people entrusted to our pastoral care. We do so with confidence founded on solid evidence of the continuing loyalty to the Church and fidelity in religious practice of a large majority of our people. The MRBI/RTÉ survey of 1998 found that 72% of Catholics rate as 'good' ('very', 36%; 'fairly', 36%) the general quality of the spiritual and community work done by the priests of their parish; while 63% state that the Church scandals have not affected their confidence in their priests or their bishops. However, we know also that there is no room for complacency. We remember the words Pope John Paul spoke to priests and religious in Maynooth on 1 October 1979:

> The degree of religious practice in Ireland is high. For this we must be constantly thanking God. But will this high level of religious practice continue? Will the next generation of young Irish men and Irish women still be as faithful as their fathers were? After my two days in Ireland, after my meeting with Ireland's youth in Galway, I am confident that they will. But this will require both unremitting work and untiring prayer on your part. You must work for the Lord with a sense of urgency. You must work with conviction that this generation, this decade of the 1980s which we are about to enter, could be crucial and decisive for the future of the faith in Ireland. Let there be no complacency.

I can find no words more fitting than these to conclude my recollections and reflections on fifty years of priesthood. Courage and confidence, but not complacency, should mark those who now face the next fifty years. Indeed, today's young priests can feel that they are special, in being called to face a new challenge which none of their predecessors ever faced, that of a new evangelisation of a new kind of Ireland, more critical, more questioning, more demanding, but still searching, still open to listening to the reasons for the hope which, in Christ Jesus, we offer to them. There will be more Seán Dunnes in the future. Seán, a typical young Irish person of our time, was a journalist with the *Examiner* in Cork. He left the Church at the age of sixteen, disillusioned, angry, wanting to escape from boring sermons and from the 'suffocating pressure' of a Catholicism which he experienced as 'narrow, intolerant and regressive'. He continued to search for a meaning and purpose in life. After many a false turning, he came back to the Church, but found in it now 'signs of tremendous tenderness, excitement and promise', the best of them beginning in an 'interior space shaped by silence and prayer'. He would by no means give up his 'innumerable arguments with Catholicism', but, he wrote, 'now I will argue with love from within and not with hatred from without'. He was to die soon afterwards, in his early forties, but not before describing his journey in *The Road to Silence*, published in 1994. I believe that many who now seem to have left us, will come back to that road.

CHAPTER TEN

THIRTY YEARS A BISHOP
1967-1997

What follows is by no means a history of my thirty years as bishop; it is only a series of snapshots of events which stand out in my memory of life in three dioceses. They are not necessarily depicted in chronological order. I marked the silver jubilee of my ordination as bishop by celebrating a Mass of Thanksgiving in St Patrick's Cathedral, Armagh, on 1 July 1992, with my Auxiliary, Bishop Gerard Clifford, and the priests of the archdiocese. Bishop Clifford celebrated in the same year the silver jubilee of his ordination as priest. It is interesting that he was ordained priest in the year in which I was ordained bishop: an apt illustration of the way in which the faith is handed on and, in our case, the apostolic succession of bishops prolonged, in an unbroken line across the generations.

ARDAGH AND CLONMACNOIS

Having been one of the first post-Vatican II bishops ordained in Ireland, I feel that there was some significance in the fact that the first and only time when I wore the white gloves formerly used by bishops at a Solemn Mass, was on the day of my consecration as bishop in St Mel's Cathedral, Longford. This was perhaps in its small way symbolic of the passing of a pre-conciliar era and the opening of a new post-Council era in the life of the Church. There were other changes in episcopal garments and general episcopal protocol in subsequent years, none of them of great importance in themselves, but all of them pointing to the call for a new style of episcopal leadership in the wake of the Council. I was content from the very outset to have the Council documents as guide and inspiration for my new life as bishop, and felt happy that, if I were called by God to this ministry, then it was good that it was in this exciting new period of the Church's life that the call came.

Having assisted at all four sessions of Vatican II, I had found the Council an exhilarating experience and was conscious that the Holy Spirit was indeed renewing the face and the heart of the Church as by a new Pentecost. It was a great time to be alive, to be a Catholic and to be a priest. It was even a good time to be a bishop, if this was indeed God's will and plan. Cardinal Suhard declared his belief that it is a mortal sin to want to be a bishop. Yet, when accepting, in strict obedience to the Holy Father, his appointment as Archbishop of Paris, Suhard immediately formulated a resolution to strive earnestly to be a saint in order that he might be a good Archbishop of Paris. I contented myself with at least aiming to be a good bishop once it became clear that this was what God was asking of me.

The story began for me on 30 May 1967 when, in my study in Belfast, preparing a philosophical lecture, I had a telephone call from the Apostolic Nunciature inviting me to come and talk with the Nuncio about 'an urgent matter' on the following day. I had no clear idea as to what lay ahead, and had much apprehension and little sleep that night. On the next day, the Nuncio, Archbishop Sensi, informed me that it was the Holy Father's will that I should become Bishop of Ardagh and Clonmacnois. I knew virtually nothing about this diocese, except that it was my late father's home before he left County Roscommon for County Antrim, at the turn of the century. I also knew one convent in the diocese, Our Lady's Bower, Athlone. A Christus Rex Congress had been held there in 1954 and I had visited there from time to time when passing through Athlone. As a young priest in the 1940s, I had twice visited my father's home in Keadue, and this had been almost my only contact with the diocese. I protested to the Nuncio about my lack of pastoral experience, my lack of knowledge of the diocese to which I was being designated, my anxiety about my suitability for the task. The Nuncio assured me that everything had been considered and that it was the Holy Father's will that I should accept. One could not but say yes to the will of God, as expressed through the Supreme Pastor of his Church.

Archbishop Sensi was most encouraging. He stressed the importance of teaching in the role of a bishop, particularly at a time of transition and change, as he saw the present period in Irish history to be. He particularly emphasised the need for doctrinal instruction and spiritual leadership in our changing society, and laid special stress on teaching about problems of justice and on the proclamation and application of the social teaching of the Church. Archbishop Sensi was shortly to leave Ireland to be Nuncio in Lisbon and, thereafter, Cardinal. He is now retired and, at ninety-one years of age, is in failing health, and has virtually lost his eyesight. He attended the Consistory in June 1991 when I was made Cardinal, and there we met again, twenty-four years after he had called me to the Nunciature in 1967. I have never forgotten his words to me on that 31 May and I came to realise as the years passed how accurate was his sense even then of the needs of the Irish Church in the last quarter of the century.

It was on Friday, 2 June, the Feast of the Sacred Heart of Jesus and the First Friday of the month, that my nomination as Bishop of Ardagh and Clonmacnois was announced. President De Valera was the first to telephone me, a few minutes after the nomination was officially announced. Shortly afterwards, Mr Jack Lynch, the Taoiseach, telephoned. On the next day I visited Ara Coeli, Armagh, to discuss with Cardinal Conway arrangements for the ordination and to talk about the future generally. The date of 16 July was fixed for my ordination. I preferred it because it was the feast of Our Lady of Mount Carmel and the date of the last apparition of Our Lady to Bernadette at Lourdes. Within the week, I visited what was to be my new diocese and saw the beautiful Cathedral of St Mel in Longford, which was for fifteen years to be my cathedral. One of the highlights of my later life as bishop was the renewal of the sanctuary in that cathedral – a work in which to this day I never cease to find joy and inspiration.

Early in July, I went to Rome for a week's pre-ordination retreat, which I spent at Vicarello, near Bracciano, in the hills north of Rome. Here was a convent of German Sisters, linked with the German College in Rome. In this beautiful setting, where the cicadas chanted their evening prayer and their night hours in the trees, I read the Gospels, particularly the chapters on the calling and the sending of the Apostles; I read the Acts of the Apostles, the Pastoral Letters of St Paul, and the Letter to the Hebrews, with special attention to chapters 11, 12 and 13, from which I took my episcopal motto: *'Jesus Christus heri et hodie'*, 'Jesus Christ is the same today as he was yesterday, and as he will be forever' (Hb 13:8). I read the letters of two great bishops of the early Church, St Clement of Rome and St Ignatius of Antioch. I read again the documents of the Second Vatican Council, with special attention to *Lumen gentium*, the *Constitution on the Church*, and to the *Decrees on the Pastoral Office of Bishops* and *on the Ministry and Life of Priests*. I read *Gaudium et spes*, the *Constitution on the Church in the Modern World*, as well as various modern studies on the role of the bishop in the Church. I read some books on Celtic Christian spirituality, with special reference to the monastic period and to Clonmacnois.

The episcopal ordination took place in St Mel's Cathedral. The ordaining prelate was Cardinal Conway himself, who had come to Longford on the preceding night. His encouragement and friendship were an immense support to me at that anxious time. The 'co-consecrators', as they were then called, were Archbishop Sensi and Bishop Neil Farren of Derry, who was then the Senior Suffragan in the Province of Armagh.

First impressions
Episcopal ordination was then called 'consecration'. A little niece of mine kept telling her classmates that she was going to Longford for 'the consternation of my Uncle Cahal'. This was truer than she knew. It was indeed a new journey for me through uncharted land,

a real 'journey without maps'. Parting with my mother and family, with whom I had lived in Belfast for most of the previous twenty-five years, was painful and brought its own great loneliness. Leaving the world of books and teaching was also difficult, for I had found academic life and philosophical research immensely satisfying, and contact with young people at university was always stimulating. As bishop, I quickly learned, however, that wisdom and knowledge are by no means confined to academic seminars and senior common rooms. In the academic world, it is possible to have the illusion of being in contact with the whole range of intelligent opinion about most of the important issues in contemporary debate; forgetting that in fact these opinions are often variations on a common mind-set, which can be out of touch with important areas of reality. In pastoral contacts with people, I quickly discovered that there is among what are wrongly called 'ordinary' people a great fund of wisdom, garnered from life experience, and rarely reflected in books and libraries. It is in people's capacity to respond to the great crises of life – illness, death, bereavement, sorrow, family and marriage and personal problems – that true wisdom is found. I have constantly derived immense inspiration and enrichment from contact with people who humble me by their capacity to respond in faith to the great crises of life, and to the recurring problems and stresses of daily living. I have learned more in pastoral ministry than I learned from books, though both are important.

In the days following ordination, I found my way to the village of Ardagh and to the ruins of the first cathedral, sited there in the fifth century by St Mel, a young disciple of St Patrick, who first proclaimed the Gospel to the people of that midlands region. Liam de Paor and his wife Máire conducted archaeological investigations there in the early 1970s, and found evidence of a series of church buildings on the site, the earliest of them constructed of wood and bearing signs of destruction by fire. They dated the oldest of these buildings to Patrician times and found Roman objects in the ruins. I then visited Clonmacnois with my sisters, Sheila and Rosaleen. Clonmacnois is, of course, the great monastery founded by St

Ciaran in the sixth century, a monastery which was to survive for one thousand years, through repeated wars and vandalism, both native and foreign, until it was finally destroyed by Cromwell's soldiers in the sixteenth century. I felt the need of the prayers of St Mel and St Ciaran, the diocesan patrons of Ardagh and of Clonmacnois, at that time.

I normally keep a daily diary, in which I try to enter a brief note of the events of the day. My entries for the rest of that year 1967 are extremely scanty, with many pages left completely blank, and my memories of those months are very sketchy. This reflects the kind of time through which I was then living, in a kind of prolonged daze, in totally new surroundings, meeting new people and trying to remember new faces, and daily encountering new problems totally outside my previous experience. My earlier training had given me little preparation for the responsibilities I now had to carry. The welcome of the people and the support of the priests and the religious and the kindness which surrounded me on all sides in my new diocese were, however, an immense support, and soon I found myself completely at home there. The priests of Ardagh and Clonmacnois were extremely kind in their welcome to me, as also were the Sisters. Canon William Quinn, Parish Priest of Lanesboro, came in almost weekly, just to make sure I was not feeling lonely or lost in my new home. Many other priests were equally solicitous.

It was a great help to me that this was in fact the diocese where my father had had his home and which he left in the first years of the century to come to County Antrim, which was to be his home until his death in 1939. The parish of Keadue, County Roscommon, was his native parish, and was to become my native parish of adoption during my years in Ardagh, as indeed it remains to this day. The renovation and reordering of the parish church in Keadue, dedicated to the Nativity of Our Lady, gave me great satisfaction. Containing some of the best work of Ray Carroll, it is a church of rare beauty, liturgical rightness and prayerfulness. The sanctuary lamp of the pre-renovation church was given to me by the parish priest and parishioners as a present when I was leaving the diocese; it still hangs in the oratory in Ara Coeli, Armagh. An iron cross from the gate which my father would have entered on the way to Mass is now at Ard Mhacha in Belfast.

The village of Keadue has been transformed over recent years and can now claim to be a model village. Twice winner of the Tidy Towns Competition, its aspect reflects immense credit on the local development committee and on the whole community. The annual O'Carolan Harp Festival has made it widely known as a centre of revival of traditional Irish music and crafts, art and culture. I have several times had the honour of being invited to declare the Festival open, and these visits to Keadue have been real homecomings for me.

In October 1967, three months after leaving Belfast, I received the worrying news that my mother had suffered a heart attack. I hurried back to Belfast to see her. She was sitting up in bed and held out her arms to me. She said, 'You know, of course, why I got this. It was because you had to leave.' Happily, she recovered and lived for another seven years.

Shrines and pilgrimages
One of my early tasks was to provide a fitting and secure emplacement for one of the diocese's and, indeed, Ireland's great treasures, the shrine of St Manchan, in County Offaly. Concern about its safety had been made known to Cardinal Conway during the vacancy in the diocese. The Cardinal came to the diocese for the inauguration of the new shrine in September 1970. Another task was the provision of a sanctuary space in Clonmacnois for the celebration of Mass in the open air for pilgrims to this ancient pilgrimage site. With the help of the Board of Works and its architect, Percy Le Clerc, a man with a wonderful feeling for the spirit of Clonmacnois, a canopy with four stone pillars was erected, covering a granite altar by Ray Carroll. The ensemble blends appropriately with the ancient ruins. The dedication, again attended by Cardinal Conway, who preached, was in July 1969.

There is a traditional pilgrimage to Clonmacnois on the Sunday prior to the feast of St Ciaran, 9 September. The custom seems never to have lapsed, even in penal times, of observing the 'pattern' of St Ciaran, when pilgrims drank water from St Ciaran's Well and then proceeded to the monastic site to do the round of its ancient crosses, praying. The pilgrimage was made more of a diocesan event and brought a larger congregation, who gathered in a natural amphitheatre, facing the Shannon, as priests concelebrated Mass before them in the new sanctuary. Later, youth pilgrimages to Clonmacnois were organised annually; and it was striking to witness the young people's empathy for the fields and stones of Clonmacnois. The principal of the local school, situated beside the monastic enclosure, had a great interest in our Celtic Christian heritage, which he transmitted to his pupils. He told me that once, while digging in a field near the school to put up goalposts, he discovered Danish coins contemporary with the Battle of Clontarf, which are now in the National Museum in Dublin. The highlight of Clonmacnois in my time was, of course, the visit of Pope John Paul II. I write about it elsewhere in this book. It is commemorated by a bronze plaque at the shrine, the work of Ray Carroll. Many churches in the diocese were built or refurbished in those years. I refer to the refurbishment of St Mel's Cathedral at a later point in this chapter. During the Holy Year, 1975, we organised pilgrimages to other ancient sites, including the Abbey at Fenagh, the medieval Franciscan Friary at Creevelea and at Jamestown, County Leitrim, and again, at Clonmacnois. It was a moving experience to celebrate Mass in these ancient sites, hallowed by the prayers and chant of the monks and friars of so many centuries ago.

The 1970s were also years of unprecedented expansion of educational facilities in the Republic. Free second-level education for all and free school transport caused an urgent need for increased school space. I marvelled at how expeditiously the teaching sisters, brothers and priests coped with vastly increased numbers, providing, often at their own expense, additional accommodation and facilities. It was a further example of the immense but too often unacknowledged contribution which Church personnel have made to education in Ireland. Many new primary schools were being built, replacing superannuated buildings. As far as possible, the Department of Education ensured that the link between school and parish, and therefore between school and local community, was maintained. At second level, community schools were proposed as a model for the merging in certain areas of secondary and vocational schools. With exemplary unselfishness, the Principal of the diocesan secondary school in Moyne, County Longford, Father James Faughnan, supported the merger of his diocesan school, the celebrated 'Latin School', with the local vocational school, in a new entity, Moyne Community School. He was convinced that this would ensure a better quality of education for all the children of the area. I am happy to say that this was one of the first, if not indeed the first, community school in the country.

Formation for religious women
When I came to Ardagh, I found in the diocese ten novitiates for young women preparing to enter religious life. In one of these years, there were nearly fifty novices in all in the diocese, though not all were for diocesan congregations. It seemed important to establish for them a common diocesan formation programme to supplement their individual programmes. This flourished for many years, with visiting lecturers providing input in scripture, theology, liturgy and spirituality.

Ongoing formation for Sisters was not well developed at the time, and it seemed important that Sisters be encouraged to pursue further studies in theology. The Sisters of Mercy released two Sisters for study in the Regina Mundi Institute in Rome. These later became, in succession, Superior General of the amalgamated Ardagh and Clonmacnois Union of the Sisters of Mercy. The preparation for and setting up of that Union is another happy memory of those years. In the same connection, renewal courses for Sisters in scripture, theology, liturgy and spirituality were organised and were eagerly availed of by the Sisters of the diocese. Two seminars for religious were organised, in 1972 and 1977, with wide participation from all over the country. Distinguished lecturers provided input. Both were held in Our Lady's Bower in Athlone and included an open-air Mass in Clonmacnois.

I always found confirmations a very happy experience. Meeting with children, parents, teachers and parishioners in the various parishes was a joy. The meal and opportunity of relaxed socialising with priests and teachers after the ceremony was enjoyable and important. I always regarded catechesis as a fundamental duty of a bishop; and in Ardagh and Clonmacnois I arranged, a week in advance of each parish confirmation, a meeting with children and parents for catechetical preparation for the sacrament. The schools of the parish were also visited on these occasions. The secondary schools were visited separately each year. As President for many years of the Episcopal Commission for Catechetics, I was able to keep in touch with progress in catechetical methods. As liaison person for the bishops with the writing teams for the new catechetical programmes, I was able to appreciate the dedication and professionalism, the faith and orthodoxy of these teams.

A brush with Northern violence

During my time in Ardagh and Clonmacnois I had one personal close encounter with the Northern violence. In the early 1970s I was being driven by road from Longford to Belfast via Cavan and Monaghan. I habitually used the car as a travelling 'study' and was busy with my work in the back seat and paying no attention to the road, when I heard a 'rat-tat-tat' sound like that of a stone hitting the side of the car. My driver braked sharply and the car stopped suddenly by the roadside. I looked up to see three or four young men (they seemed to be in their late teens) jumping out of the long grass beside the road, wearing balaclavas and carrying rifles. Two of them were running across the road, signalling to my driver to stop. One ordered the driver out and another opened my door and ordered me to 'get out and stand there'. I did not know at that moment whether we were in County Fermanagh or County Monaghan. My first thought was that this might be a loyalist assassination 'operation', since these were not uncommon at the time. I certainly felt that death was near, and I tried to prepare myself for death by repentance and prayer. The feeling I recall from these moments was that, while it was not for me to choose the time to die, I would still have liked to have more time to complete many things that I had planned to do, and had some regret that death should come so soon!

Suddenly, the young man near me ordered me back into the car and told me to stay there. His words to me were the only words spoken during the episode. He and the other man rushed back across the road to where a third had held up a southward bound car. The occupants were ordered out and the young men piled into their car with their guns, and drove down the road past us. I still thought that they intended to turn and to shoot us on the way back. However, they turned off into a side road and did not return.

We continued our journey to Belfast and reported the matter to the Garda on our way. The story emerged only some days later. Apparently the young men were members of the IRA. They had sent a bogus message to the RUC about a suspect car on a bridge which we had just passed. Their intention was to open fire on the RUC car as it came down the road in response to the message. Only days after the incident did I recall that a car passed us just before the men with the guns appeared, and I seemed to have brief sight of the driver drawing his hand across his brow and of the passenger holding on to the car door, which seemed to be opening while the car was in motion. The RUC men were not in uniform. In fact, the 'rat-tat-tat' I had heard had been rifle fire, and a bullet had grazed the brow of the RUC driver, while other bullets shattered the passenger door. The injuries had, thank God, proved not to be serious.

The object of the men with guns in holding up our car was apparently to hijack it so as to make their escape. When another car going southward came along, they seemed to have changed their minds and hijacked it instead. The whole matter probably took only a few minutes, but for me it was an experience outside time, and filled with an extraordinary clarity and calm as I waited for what I thought would be death. I can only ascribe that clarity and calm to the grace of God. Compared with what so many others have endured, my experience was trivial, and I was immensely relieved that no life had been lost and no serious injuries caused to others. But this was some small indication for me of the reality of what we euphemistically call 'the Troubles'.

Ecumenical activity

Ecumenical activity was a feature of my life during virtually all my years of active episcopal ministry. I was involved in the first ever Catholic-Protestant Church Meeting in Ireland, held in Ballymascanlon in 1973. We are celebrating its silver jubilee this year. It was not the first, nor was it to be the last, ecumenical occasion to be honoured by a Paisleyite protest. 'Ballymascanlon', as such meetings came to be called, evolved gradually into the Irish Inter-Church Committee, which meets on average bi-monthly and is a valuable instrument for inter-Church dialogue. I was its co-chairman as Archbishop of Armagh. It has two main departments, one on social questions, the other on theological questions. Each has produced a series of valuable reports on issues of interest to all the Churches in Ireland.

I was privileged to co-chair with Reverend Dr Eric Gallagher, formerly President of the Methodist Conference in Ireland, an inter-Church working party which met regularly over two years and produced in 1976 a report entitled *Violence in Ireland*. Its conclusions and recommendations retain much validity more than twenty years later. Bi-monthly meetings of the 'Four Church Leaders' became a feature of my life when I became Archbishop of Armagh. All these meetings enriched my life and my faith through deeper understanding of the Christian insights of other Churches and through many cherished friendships. In Ireland too, Church people of all the mainline churches have become, 'not strangers but pilgrims'.

I was further privileged to share in ecumenical activity at European level through participation, as delegate of the Irish Episcopal Conference, in ecumenical encounters, jointly organised by CCEE (Council of Episcopal Conferences of Europe) and KEK (Council of European Churches), at Chantilly, Paris, in 1978, and in Lögumkloster, Denmark, in 1981. At both of these, I was accompanied by Reverend Dr Jack Weir, formerly Clerk of the General Assembly and formerly Moderator of the General Assembly of the Presbyterian Church in Ireland. Jack and I were asked to make presentations on the Northern Ireland situation at

239

Lögumkloster. We did not have time to prepare or compare our presentations together; nevertheless, there was a remarkable degree of convergence in our analysis of the situation. I think that this, more than anything that we said, was what impressed our audience, many of whom had shared the widespread impression that the conflict in Northern Ireland was a 'religious war', and that Catholic and Protestant clergy here would not even be on speaking terms. I had a similar experience, with similar reactions, at an inter-faith conference in Louvain, in 1976, when my partner in the presentation on the Northern Ireland situation was a Presbyterian, Reverend Dr Victor Lynas.

The importance of dialogue with the modern world and with contemporary culture was stressed by the Second Vatican Council and by Pope Paul VI, and is a constant theme of Pope John Paul II. I feel it to be an important part of a bishop's life. In Longford, I had several interesting conversations with John Broderick, novelist of Athlone. I shared with him his love of Paris, which he often visited. He was a friend of the Franco-English novelist, Julien Green. I corresponded with Francis Stuart and once shared with him a radio discussion on the respective roles of theologian and novelist. I corresponded also with Bernard Mac Laverty. All of those brought me insights valuable to a theologian or to a pastor.

The years when I was bishop in Ardagh and Clonmacnois were extremely happy years for me. The challenge of spreading the spirit of the Second Vatican Council and implementing its decrees, at national and diocesan level, was exciting. The Church in Ireland faced up to the task confidently but prudently, under the guidance of Cardinal William Conway. He was always concerned about finding the right pace of change, and about bringing the people forward, on what he liked to call 'a broad front', with their priests and their bishops, in introducing the necessary changes. In retrospect, I believe that he did succeed in finding the right pace of change, with the consequence that the Church in Ireland escaped much of the deviation, dissension and polarisation which damaged the Church in many other countries in the period of post-conciliar renewal.

Cardinal Conway died at the early age of sixty-four, on 17 April 1977. It was the Sunday after Easter, Low Sunday. Cardinal Tomás Ó Fiaich was appointed his successor on 2 October 1977, the first priest of the Archdiocese of Armagh for many decades and, as he was proud to point out, the first and only native of County Armagh since St Malachy to be so appointed. I write more extensively in later chapters about both of my predecessors as Cardinal Archbishop of Armagh.

DOWN AND CONNOR

Meanwhile, I was myself to receive a sharp reminder of mortality and of the feeble hold we have on God's gift of life. I had a heart attack during the night of 3/4 February 1982. I was not particularly worried at its first onset, since the symptoms seemed to be those of indigestion. Only in St Vincent's Hospital, Dublin, where I arrived in the afternoon of 4 February, did I fully realise that it was indeed a coronary attack. The journey to Dublin was the 'longest day' and most anxious journey of my life as the symptoms worsened and the malaise increased with every mile. It was an immense relief to reach the entrance doors of the hospital. There had been some vague rumours in circulation earlier to the effect that I was to be asked to go to Down and Connor as bishop, but this heart attack seemed to be God's way of scotching any such rumours! I was heavily sedated during the first day of my stay in hospital, and it was only on the second day that I could think clearly. My first clear thought on the morning of 6 February was: 'This heart attack puts an end forever to all talk about me for Down and Connor, thank God'. This thought came to me with exceptional clarity and brought a great feeling of relief.

That particular sense of relief and joy was not to last long. The Apostolic Nuncio came to see me in hospital a few days later, by which time I had been pronounced 'stable and recovering well'. He said that it had indeed been intended that I should go to Down and Connor and that this was still the Holy Father's wish. Anxiety quickly replaced relief. After three months' convalescence, spent with my sister Sheila in Belfast, I was able to return to Longford, though still greatly shaken and weakened by my illness. On the evening of Monday, 16 August, I was called to the Nunciature for the next morning. When I arrived, I was told by Archbishop Alibrandi that it was still the Holy Father's firm wish and decision that I should be Bishop of Down and Connor. Again, the time had come to say, 'God's will be done'. It was a moment for remembering that, when Christ calls and one puts one's hand to the plough, one must not look back.

The days that followed, however, were days of anxiety and apprehension. My health and energies were still far from being restored. I now looked on Longford as my home and had had no desire or intention of ever leaving it. Indeed, I had already begun to think in terms of where I would like to have a house for retirement, should I live that long, and a burying place near St Mel's Cathedral when the time came. After fifteen years, I had grown away from Down and Connor and felt that I was out of touch with its situation and its problems, compounded by more than a decade of violence, during all of which I had been absent. However, I looked for consolation to words such as those of St Augustine, to the effect that God does not command the impossible; whatever he commands, he gives the grace to make it possible.

The announcement of my appointment was made on 8 September 1982. I had just returned to Longford after the Ardagh and Clonmacnois Annual Pilgrimage to Knock. I was happy that the announcement was made on another feast-day of Our Lady, the feast of her birthday. The date was important to me also because it was the anniversary of the death of my sister Margaret in 1961. The installation in Belfast was fixed for Sunday, 17 October.

I went to Rome at the end of September for my pre-installation retreat, which I spent in the Rome Cenacle Convent. My reading and prayer were largely a re-living of the Vicarello retreat experience of fifteen years earlier – but now with the benefit of lived experience of episcopal ministry behind me, helping both to increase my humility in respect of many failures and to make my resolutions for the future more realistic. Retreats are often associated with a particular thought or phrase or prayer. The Rome

Cenacle retreat for me remains associated with the prayer ascribed in Irish tradition to St Brendan, the seafaring saint, who is special to me, since Brendan is my second name. The prayer runs:

> Lord, have pity on me.
> My boat is so tiny
> And your ocean is so vast.

It exactly described my feelings at that time of launching out into unknown waters. On reflection, however, I remembered that God is himself described by the medieval mystical writer, Denis, as 'an infinite ocean of substance', and that God's name is Love. Wherever I travelled across God's vast ocean and however lost I might feel, I was always going to be surrounded by and borne up by God's love and pity which know no bounds or limits. I was helped also by the words of St Thérèse of Lisieux: 'Anything you ask, Lord; but do have pity on me'.

The installaton in St Peter's Cathedral on 17 October 1982 was a moving event. There was a huge congregation, with a strong presence of people from St Peter's Parish and with representatives drawn from every parish in the diocese. The Falls Road had for more than a decade become associated with bombs, bullets and riots. Now in St Peter's we had a strikingly different scene. I remember remarking in my homily, 'This is the real Falls.' One of my happy experiences as bishop was to see St Peter's formally declared a cathedral church.

From the installation onward the welcome I received from the priests and people of my native diocese of Down and Connor was an immense encouragement, at a time when both my health and my spirits were frankly quite low, for I was still convalescing from my coronary attack. Belfast wit showed itself when a graffito was seen near St Peter's Cathedral after my installation with the words 'ET is back' – an allusion to a character in a film of that time, a gaunt figure with some resemblance to my then emaciated profile.

It was, of course, a great help that Down and Connor was my home diocese and that I had known a great many of the priests already. The scene had greatly changed since I left, but it was possible to pick up the threads again relatively quickly. It was also a consolation to feel, as I then did, that this at least was to be the last lap of my pilgrim journey as priest and as bishop.

Ministering in the midst of conflict

Belfast in particular had changed drastically from the city I had known fifteen years earlier. Between bomb damage and 'peace-lines' and demolition for urban redevelopment, the street map of the city had altered almost beyond my recognition. Urban blight and community deprivation, with massive unemployment, had become much more visible than before. The high-rise housing, hailed in the 1960s as the progressive modern answer to inner-city rehousing, had come to be seen as another of the mirages of that brittle decade. It rapidly became a symbol of urban blight rather than of urban renewal.

On visits to the Falls Road and outer West Belfast and Ardoyne and New Lodge and the Markets and the Short Strand, I realised more clearly than ever something that I had long believed, namely that there is a close correlation between violence and urban deprivation. If one were to place side by side maps illustrating the various indicators of deprivation and poverty, on the one hand, and the incidence of acts of political violence and politically motivated street rioting and disorder, on the other, the degree of correspondence between the two would be glaringly evident. It was beyond doubt that no political or security measures to overcome violence could have a hope of succeeding without an attack on the social injustices and inequalities which produced an environment conducive to violence. It is when politics fails to promote justice and equality of opportunity that violence steps in to fill the vacuum.

The violence itself, however, although originally motivated in part by a desire to end injustice, merely aggravates the injustice, by increasing the deprivation, the poverty and the urban decay, lowering the quality of life and undermining the morale of whole communities. Violence in itself becomes a new and potent source of injustice. Furthermore, violence in Northern Ireland, whatever its original motivation or political purpose, could not and cannot but become sectarian in perception and often in fact. If there ever were a situation where political violence is of its nature self-defeating and counter-productive, it is that of Northern Ireland.

Violence was a problem which the Church had to confront, both as a moral evil in itself, and as a source of spiritual and moral decay in individuals and in communities. Condemnation of the moral evil of violence is a duty of conscience which the Christian pastor cannot shirk and concerning which he must never equivocate. Yet it was and is very clear that moral condemnation alone is not enough. There also has to be action to remedy the multiple social injustices which give political violence its pretext and which create the environment in which violence can find some degree of community sympathy and support. This is a requirement of social justice, and an integral part of the proclamation of the Gospel of the Kingdom of God, as well as a necessary accompaniment of the condemnation of violence.

My early assessment of the situation also made it clear that a potent factor in perpetuating violence was the massive and sometimes intimidating presence and the often oppressive character of security force operations in these same deprived areas, coupled with the perception in nationalist communities of political or religious partisanship on the part of some army or police personnel. This was particularly evident in the case of elements in the UDR and the RUC. Abuses and excesses on the part of the security forces called for continuous pastoral vigilance and often for pastoral intervention.

Finally, the large number of prisoners indicted for paramilitary offences, a majority of whom came from the kind of alienated and deprived communities which I have mentioned, were an important factor in sustaining the climate of political violence. For each prisoner in jail, one could count on average at least thirty or forty people in the extended family or in the wider community who were closely affected by that person's imprisonment. Conditions for prisoners, prison discipline, the behaviour of prison officers, the arrangements, or lack of them, for family and marital visits, the granting or refusal of compassionate parole, release dates for life-sentence prisoners, all of these had direct impact on the extended family outside, and often on whole communities. This was an obvious area calling for pastoral concern.

Religious war?
It was always a source of vexation to hear the conflict in Northern Ireland described as a 'religious war'. This description is simplistic and gravely misleading. Undoubtedly, there is a religious or pseudo-religious overlay to the basically national, political, cultural, social and socio-economic dimensions of the conflict. To ignore that overlay would be equally simplistic, and I have more than once said that a politician should be the last person to deny the non-religious dimension and a Churchman should be the last to deny the religious dimension. Even a preliminary assessment made it obvious that ecumenical outreach and the pursuit of mutual understanding and respect between the religious denominations were an inescapable duty for a bishop ministering in a divided and conflict-ridden city and diocese.

It is true that there is a baleful tradition of sectarianism and religious bigotry in Northern Ireland. This is still fomented by a small but virulent group of politico-religious demagogues, who continue to pour out from church pulpit and from political platform, as well as by pamphlet and tract, the most vile and black propaganda against the Catholic Church and against ecumenically-minded Protestant clergy.

An Inter-Church Report published in 1975 called on the Churches for a campaign to combat sectarianism. The mainstream Churches have accepted this challenge. A great step forward was the Inter-Church Report on Sectarianism, commissioned by the Irish Inter-Church Committee and published in 1993. It was studied at a very productive inter-Church seminar in 1993 and is now before the individual Churches for study and action. Much still remains for the Churches individually and collectively to do to eradicate this pernicious evil from our society.

It was always essential to proclaim publicly the responsibility of governments and of politicians to demonstrate actively and effectively that politics can and does promote justice, redress grievances, eliminate inequalities and unfairness in employment, in housing, and in everything that touches on human rights and on the dignity of human beings and of human communities. Politics must be shown to provide the way forward to a just society. To proclaim this is not to interfere in politics; it is part of the proclamation of the Gospel of Jesus Christ.

The Church's response to conflict

On analysis of the Northern Ireland problem, the above seemed to me and to priests and lay men and women whom I consulted to be the factors which were most relevant to the devising of a comprehensive pastoral strategy for responding effectively to the total situation. Indeed, from the beginning of 'the Troubles' in 1969-70, I had the conviction that the credibility and the relevance of the Church in Ireland in our time would be judged by many on the basis of the Church's response to the Northern conflict, as well as by its response to the problem of social injustice in Ireland as a whole. Although I was then Bishop of Ardagh and Clonmacnois and had no direct pastoral involvement with the North, I was convinced that the Northern problem was a matter of concern for the Church in Ireland as a whole, and that I could not refrain from commenting on it. On numerous occasions, particularly on successive World Days of Peace on each New Year's Day, I gave homilies or addresses on the topic. An edited version of some of these addresses was published in a book called *Violence in Ireland and Christian Conscience,* published by Veritas in 1970, and later in *The Work of Justice*, published by Veritas in 1979. A third book, *The Price of Peace,* published by Blackstaff Press, was to follow in 1992, when I was Archbishop of Armagh. A smaller publication, *Northern Ireland: Peace: Now is the Time*, also published by Veritas, appeared in 1993.

My views on the situation have not changed, but they were naturally given a sharper focus by my appointment as Bishop of

Down and Connor and by my ministry there from 1982 to 1990. My first priority when I came back to Belfast was to make frequent visits to the parishes most affected by violence, to listen to the experience of the priests 'in the front line', and to meet with and listen to the people there in their own environment. Anyone visiting these areas is struck above all by the cheerfulness of the people, their resilience, their community spirit and neighbourliness, the quickness of their wit and repartee. Special admiration is due to the women of Belfast and the North, who, through these bitter years, have endured so much. They have been at the 'cutting edge' of unemployment, imprisonment of family members, bereavement due to violence, worry about the risk of their children becoming involved in paramilitary organisations, or about the effects on their teenage children of constant harassment by the security forces. Tribute also is due to the grannies and grandads, who share in the rearing of the children and who hand on the faith, the traditions and the values which have held communities together and helped them to survive in bad times and in good.

For the priests who have ministered to the spiritual and temporal needs of their people through the years of violence, one could not sufficiently express one's admiration. They have patiently and courageously preached the gospel of truth and of love and of peace, they have worked for justice, they have administered the last rites to people dying of bomb or gun-shot wounds. Two priests of Down and Connor, Fathers Hugh Mullan and Noel Fitzpatrick, were shot dead in the early 1970s while ministering to the dying amid hails of bullets. They surely merit a place among the martyrs of our time. Priests have worked with young people, trying to guide them into constructive activity. They have joined with lay people in working to resolve social problems like alcoholism, substance abuse and joy-riding. They have laboured to create community and to promote economic development in new estates and in deprived areas. They have promoted job-training and job-creation. They and their counterparts among the Protestant clergy have played a major role in maintaining hope and community spirit and stability in communities which could without them have slipped into mere anarchy. Irish priests have never seen their role as confining them to sacristy or sanctuary or pulpit. The gospel which they preach constrains them to work for justice, for human rights and for the safeguarding of human dignity. It required from them and from their people a struggle against injustice, poverty and unemployment and sometimes harassment of their people by security forces as well as by the IRA. A real and effective 'liberation theology' has been preached and lived by the priests in the north over this past quarter-century of conflict.

Rehabilitation in deprived communities

The same concerns had to characterise the ministry of a bishop. It was vital to allocate resources for this non-violent struggle for justice. For this purpose a campaign called Catholics Caring was instituted in 1984, with a view to providing financial resources and identifying personnel for social rehabilitation and community development in poorer areas. An annual collection in the parishes of the diocese provided resources for this purpose. Additional contributions to this fund were made by the Catholic bishops of Germany. An invitation was issued to people with relevant training and skills or business experience who would volunteer to work in setting up work schemes, small enterprise units and job training and job search programmes in areas of high unemployment. An appeal was made at the same time to the more prosperous parishes to come to the help, in personnel and in resources, of more deprived parishes. A 'twinning' system was set up whereby several parishes in South or outer West Belfast were brought into regular contact with parishes in inner West and North and East Belfast, to the mutual benefit of both.

As bishop, I derived great satisfaction from this work of rehabilitation in deprived communities, long denied their rights and their fair opportunities in education and unemployment. These projects were primarily lay-directed and lay-managed. Non-profit-making companies were set up, controlled by lay boards, to serve as legal instruments for the processing of projects and the management of funds. They were not 'clerically organised job creation schemes'. Business people set up these companies and made their services available to them without payment or profit or personal gain or interest of any kind. Anything these men and women have done was to help in promoting works of real community self-development. Government grants and funding from other sources were hard-won and were awarded strictly on the merit of their project research, their planning and their performance.

Work for improved housing was another priority. West Belfast, with its notorious Divis Flats, needed prime attention. The decision to demolish the Flats was eventually taken; it was the culmination of much lobbying, many public statements and appeals and prolonged correspondence. The decision was an enlightened one on the part of the Housing Executive and brought great satisfaction to me and to the clergy of West Belfast.

I found it most unjust and personally hurtful when these overdue measures of community development were criticised by people of one tendency as connivance in some British government plan of 'counter-insurgency', or as some Catholic Church strategy to 'control government funding' in West Belfast; or were represented by people of an opposite tendency as discrimination in favour of Catholics, 'riding on the backs of the IRA'. It was both hurtful and ludicrous to dub such operations 'networks of Church control'. Also hurtful were allegations that I had gone to the United States on several occasions, under the auspices of the British government, to lobby and to campaign against the Mac Bride Principles on fair employment. These allegations were false and absurd. I always thought that the British government was foolish to campaign against the Mac Bride Principles. I never had or took any position on the Principles, but always urged that they should be linked with efforts to secure more investment for the creation of new jobs.

An important initiative, developed jointly by the United States Conference of Bishops and the Presbyterian Church, USA, in association with the Churches in Ireland, was the joint Call for

Investment and Fair Employment in Northern Ireland. Launched publicly in 1994, this call was promoted by Reverend Dr John Dunlop, former Irish Moderator, and myself, in a joint visit which we made to the United States in 1995. It led to our being invited to participate in President Clinton's White House Conference on Trade and Investment in Northern Ireland and the Border Counties in 1995. I must add here that in all that I tried to do in promoting sound development and economic justice in the North and in the long pursuit of peace, I received constant and crucial help from the American cardinals, and particularly from Cardinal O'Connor of New York, Cardinal Law of Boston, Cardinal Hickey of Washington and Cardinal Bevilacqua of Philadelphia, and also from the extremely efficient, well-informed and hard-working staff of the US Conference of Bishops' Department of Social Development and World Peace, and particularly from John Carr and Gerry Powers.

I am happy to say that, wherever it was possible, the projects of which I speak were developed along the 'peace-lines', so as to draw in workers from Protestant communities as well as from Catholic ones; and these were organised, wherever possible, in collaboration with Protestant clergy and Protestant community workers. This gave a most valuable dimension of cross-community reconciliation to the work of development. Demanding justice from the State in no way places the Church in a situation of 'dependency' on the State. The passion for social justice shown by priests in West Belfast and similar areas would be lauded in Latin America as preferential option for the poor and as putting 'liberation theology' into practice. It is sad indeed when similar social involvement in Northern Ireland is represented as a programme of 'social control' by bishops and clergy and as somehow making the Church subservient to British government policy. When the State in Northern Ireland, even when this is in response to urgings from Churchmen, allocates grants to projects in Catholic areas, it is not, as has been claimed, 'providing very great benefits for the Church'; it is giving some belated measure of justice and equality to a long discriminated-against community of citizens.

It was always emphasised, however, that these parish-community-based undertakings were not in conflict or in competition with any other groups or activities working or desirous of working in the field of redevelopment. It was also emphasised that these undertakings in no way absolved government or statutory bodies from their primary public responsibilities for the rehabilitation of deprived areas and the redressing of social injustice.

Prisoners

Work for the needs and rights of prisoners and for the welfare of prisoners' families is also a clear command of the Lord in the Gospels. I have spoken above of the importance of prisoners in the whole field of pastoral care for the wider community. Visits to the wings of the Maze and Maghaberry and Crumlin Road prisons revealed again and again the close connection between social deprivation and law-breaking. So far as republican prisoners are concerned, these visits left no doubt but that very few indeed of these prisoners would ever have been involved in criminal activity or would ever have seen the inside of a prison, had it not been for the circumstances in which they grew up. This does not condone their crimes, but it does point to the wrongness of calling them 'criminal types' or 'thugs' or people who choose 'mindless violence' or who opt for violence for violence's sake. I visited loyalist prisoners also, and in conversation with them, learned how similar their social background and history were to those of republican prisoners.

It was clear also that the essential and sufficient element of punishment for prisoners is the loss of freedom; and that prisoners should not be further unnecessarily punished while in prison. Furthermore, normal relations between prison officers and prisoners are in the best interest of both. Humane treatment of prisoners is required, not only by considerations of justice but even in the interest of enlightened and effective security policy. Unrest in prison inevitably provokes unrest in the community from which paramilitary prisoners come; and it merely complicates the problems of the security forces.

There have been deplorable miscarriages of justice in Northern Ireland, leaving numbers of people in prison for many years for crimes which they did not commit. Several visits of mine to the Birmingham Six and the Guildford Four in different prisons in England, and my meetings with Mrs Sarah Conlon, Gerry Conlon's mother, and my knowledge of the Maguire family, left me in no shadow of doubt about these prisoners' innocence of any crime. These miscarriages of justice raised most serious questions about the impartiality of the British judicial system. However, justice was eventually, albeit belatedly, done. For this result, Cardinal Basil Hume deserves a large share in the credit, as do Monsignors Denis Faul and Raymond Murray. Cardinal Hume's personal involvement was highly impressive and was crucial. It must be admitted that a judicial system which can find within itself the honesty and the courage to recognise its own unjust decisions and the machinery with which to correct them is not corrupt as a system. It did, however, require a radical review of its own processes, and particularly of its appeal procedures.

During my visits to the prisons I could see how intensely republican prisoners studied and debated political issues. In many ways politics was their whole reading, their conversation, indeed their life. Someone called the prisons in Northern Ireland 'universities of terrorism'. The fact is that they were 'universities of politics'. The same was true on the loyalist wings, as is amply demonstrated by the political articulateness, sophistication and maturity of the leaders of the smaller loyalist political parties. I frequently had vigorous debates with republican prisoners, in which, while utterly condemning violence, I also urged the greater strength of the political process for the advancement of legitimate political causes. I stressed that the British presence in Ireland is really the unionist presence, and that it was unionists with whom republicans had to dialogue and eventually to share this land. I pressed upon them the moral power which they could mobilise by renouncing violence and by standing alongside peaceful and democratic nationalists in Ireland and in the United States, in the democratic pursuit of their nationalist aims, with full recognition of the equal rights of unionists. We did not arrive at agreement, but it was good to see serious debate going on among them.

Over recent years, there has been satisfaction in seeing a more humane prison policy being evolved and gradually pursued. This, I am convinced, had positive results, in terms both of security within the prisons themselves and security in the wider community. The Good Friday Agreement requires the release of prisoners. This will be an extremely painful matter for families and friends of victims. All effort must be made to recognise and try to heal their pain. We must pray that the achievement of permanent peace after a quarter-century of conflict will be the first consequence of the Agreement and that this will bring comfort and a beginning of healing to all who have lost loved ones.

Sectarian murders

The most sinister manifestation of the religious or pseudo-religious dimension of the conflict was the campaign of loyalist assassinations of innocent Catholics, which always ran in parallel with the republican campaign of violence. The loyalist murder campaign against the Catholic and nationalist community was historically always proactive as well as reactive, and has itself been a potent causative factor both in the origination and in the continuation of the IRA campaign.

By far the most stressful and distressing experiences I have had in ministering in a situation of conflict have been when visiting the homes of families bereaved by sectarian violence, and assisting and preaching at the funerals of victims of violence. During my eight years as Bishop of Down and Connor, I assisted at the funerals of more than forty innocent Catholics murdered by loyalist gunmen. I never became used to the encounter with grief. Each grief following a death through violence is unique and different from any other. I never preached at such funerals without first visiting the home and meeting with the family, for only thus could I speak out of their grief and to their heartbreak.

Most of these visits were to the homes of parents or of young widows whose sons or whose young husbands had been murdered by loyalists. I visited also the homes of parents and widows of RUC officers murdered by the IRA. I recall being very touched by the remark of the father, himself an RUC officer, of one young constable. He said to me, 'Pray for us Catholic police officers. We are very much alone.' I have visited, having first made sure that a visit from me would be welcome, the homes of Protestants murdered by the IRA, whether as members of the security forces or under one or other of the variety of categories of people dubbed at various times by the IRA as 'legitimate targets'. I visited the homes of IRA members who had been killed, when I could first make sure that there was no paramilitary display and when my visit could be clearly seen as a purely pastoral one. Each grief, I have said, is particular and unique. Yet there is a common human heartbreak, there are universal human tears, in all these tragedies; and they have no political or religious colouring. Protestant tears and Catholic tears have the same colour; nationalist tears and loyalist tears are indistinguishable. When I visited these homes, there was nothing I felt able to say, there was nothing that I really wanted to say. All that I could do or that I felt like doing was just to pray with them, to share their grief, to be with them and often weep with them the tears that well up spontaneously from the heart of human tragedy, more particularly when this tragedy itself is due to human sin.

I visited many scores of homes of violent death, both in Down and Connor and later in Armagh. In almost every case, it was the bodies of young men which lay in those open coffins. Whatever their political affiliation – and sometimes the dead men were victims of each other's paramilitary organisations – they were young people who had the same interest in sport, in music, who shared similar interests and hobbies, used the same teenage argot, were often fans of the same football teams or rock stars, with the same pin-ups and posters in their rooms. I often found myself thinking that if the killers had to visit the grieving homes and see the misery, the broken hearts and the shattered lives which they had caused, they could never continue with their evil deeds. But the training and the brainwashing of a killer has to aim at dehumanising the victim, reducing him or her from person to object, a 'legitimate target', 'unavoidable casualty of war', a 'Brit', 'Fenian scum', or 'Taig' or whatever, instead of being some girl's young husband or boyfriend, some children's daddy, some parents' son.

Yet everywhere, with no exception in my whole experience, I found an absence of all bitterness, a spirit of forgiveness. Often I heard a grieving wife or mother say that it would have been worse to have a dear one who was a killer than to have one who was an innocent victim. I can only marvel at what faith and the grace of God can do in cases where forgiveness seems humanly impossible.

A great sadness shared by all the bereaved, however, was the feeling that their grief would be forgotten by the public when another atrocity hit the headlines and their own dear one would become for most people only another digit in the statistics of death. The tragedy is that, for years afterwards, the grief will be as agonising, the loneliness as overpowering, as the day the murder happened. The children will still be receiving therapy. The fear will still haunt the parents that their children could be permanently scarred, or that their young ones might grow up to learn to hate, and that other wives and mothers may have to go through the same vale of sorrow in future generations. There is no way of computing the quantum of grief and misery which has been caused by the violence of the past twenty-five years. Nothing in the past has justified it, nothing that may happen in future years will validate it. It is of the very nature of the Northern Ireland conflict that there will be no returning heroes.

That last sentence was written in September 1993. I revised it in September 1994, when the IRA declared a cessation of hostilities. I revised it once more at Easter 1998, after the Good Friday Agreement. There will be returning heroes. They will be the people who worked for peace, dialogued for peace, endured savage criticism, took personal risks for peace. Some of them were leaders of constitutional parties, some of them were leaders of Sinn Féin, or leaders of loyalist political parties, former supporters of violence. I have strongly criticised and condemned paramilitaries and supporters of violence. I now pay tribute to the work of those among them who have laboured for peace during recent years and who are now actively endeavouring to persuade their comrades to commit themselves definitively to the democratic process of peace. I have said many times that I longed to see peace permanently established in our land before the end of my earthly pilgrimage. That, by God's grace, may now be possible.

Lay partnership

It gave me great satisfaction during my years as bishop in Down and Connor, as in my other two dioceses, that partnership in diocese and in parish between bishops, priests and lay people has, however slowly, become more of a reality. There is much work still to be done, but real progress has been made. Since the beginning, I made it a rule that at least half of all members of parish pastoral councils and of the diocesan pastoral council, as well as of all diocesan commissions open to lay people, should be women. Women have always had an equal voice in all their deliberations. It has always been a fundamental principle also that the setting up of a parish or diocesan pastoral council should be preceded by a prolonged programme of spiritual and theological formation. This programme is, as far as possible, shared by priests and lay people together, and the aim is that priests and lay members of the pastoral council should share a common vision of Church and of the respective and complementary vocations, responsibilities and charisms of priests, religious and lay people in the Church. Unless the laity have a good formation in the theology of the Church and in its self-understanding and its teaching, they will not be properly equipped to put their spiritual and human gifts at the service of the Church, side by side with priests and religious. This formation cannot be a 'one-off' thing; it must be ongoing. The new Catechism of the Catholic Church will be a powerful aid in this formation.

Lay people thus formed will not be a threat to priests but instead a great support to them. They will not find priests 'superfluous' except as 'functionaries' with certain sacramental services to perform; instead, lay people will need and will want their priests, more than ever, as evangelisers, teachers of faith for youth and adults, leaders in prayer, spiritual directors, builders of communities of faith. Indeed, such lay people will increasingly release priests for these duties, which are, after all, the fundamental duties of the priesthood, freeing them from more secular office and organisational and administrative tasks.

Ongoing formation of priests and lay people in this new Vatican II vision of the Church is essential. I took particular satisfaction from residential two-week renewal courses for priests in St Mary's College, Belfast, with input from the staff of the Religious Studies Department of the College. I was also happy in the setting up of a Diocesan Pastoral Council, with priests, religious and lay people sharing in a comprehensive formation programme in preparation for making the vision a reality at parish as well as at diocesan level. It was hard to walk away from all this when the next step in my pilgrim journey had to be taken.

ARMAGH

I referred above to the consolation I derived, on coming back to Down and Connor, from knowing that this was to be my last appointment before death or retirement. So, at least, I confidently thought at the time. Too soon, however, was to come the dreadful shock of the unexpected death of Cardinal Tomás Ó Fiaich. Death came to him with a suddenness which stunned everyone, on 8 May 1990, while he was leading the Armagh Diocesan Pilgrimage to Lourdes. The news reached me in Glasgow, where I had gone for an ecumenical meeting. I found it impossible to take in what I heard when called to the telephone to receive the news from my sister Sheila.

When people were recovering from the shock of Cardinal Tomás' death, the inevitable speculation began about a successor. Any rumours concerning myself never troubled my peace of mind. I was serenely confident that my age (I was then seventy-three), not to speak of my health, ruled me immediately out of any possible consideration. There was much which I had helped to begin and hoped to see through to completion in Down and Connor.

I went to Rome in October 1990, acting as substitute for the late

Cardinal at the Synod on Europe. On Sunday, 21 October, Cardinal Gantin invited me to his home, to celebrate Mass with him in his Oratory. Even though he is Cardinal Prefect of the Sacred Congregation of Bishops, which recommends episcopal appointments to the Holy Father, I was undisturbed in mind; for I had known Cardinal Gantin in the past, and knew of his admiration for Ireland's missionary history; and it was natural and nice that he should invite me to concelebrate Mass with him on that Sunday, which was Mission Sunday. However, after the Mass and a pleasant chat over breakfast, the Cardinal suddenly became more serious and told me that he had an important message for me from the Holy Father; it was that he, the Pope, wished me to be the new Archbishop of Armagh. I was shocked by the news, I pleaded my age and my health, but the Cardinal replied that all this had been taken into full consideration and that the Holy Father's wish and decision were clear; I should, he said gently, see this as a manifest indication of the will of God. He told me not to be afraid, to put my full trust in God. It was Dr Seán Brady, now my successor, who took me in his car that day. Returning to the Irish College, I spent the rest of the day in the College Oratory, trying to come to terms before God with this unexpected challenge at this late hour of my life.

Two days later, I had a private audience with the Holy Father. He too affirmed that this was God's will for me. He assured me of his prayers. I still treasure his words: 'I prayed much for Armagh. I pray much for Ireland'. He has often said to me since then that he prays every single day for Ireland. Once, to my great consolation, he added, 'and for its Primate'.

The date for the announcement of my appointment was arranged to take place after my return to Ireland, for 6 November 1990, the Feast of All Saints of Ireland. The installation in Armagh was fixed for 30 November. Again there began the huge task of transporting books and personal chattels – for the third time – to a new residence. At the same time, there were the Masses of leavetaking and the sad and lonely partings from priests, Sisters, laity, young people, my devoted staff in Lisbreen and many personal friends. There was again, especially, my pre-installation retreat, this time spent in the solitude of the little 'poustinia' in the grounds of the Siena Convent in Drogheda, where the contemplative Dominican Sisters supported me by their prayers and hospitality. Memories of Vicarello in 1967 and of the Rome Cenacle in 1982 were made vivid again and my reading and reflection returned to the same texts and the same themes. During this retreat, as before, I was spiritually sustained by the prayers of Charles de Foucauld, Thomas Merton and Rupert Meyer, which are printed in an appendix.

Only after her death was I to know how utterly devastated my sister Sheila was on my appointment to Armagh. She feared for my health, she felt her own aloneness in Belfast. In this sadness, as in her own increasing health problems, she suffered silently and kept it all to herself, so as not to cause worry to me.

I took 'canonical possession' in the Archdiocese on 30 November, presenting my 'bulla' of appointment from the Holy Father to the Dean and the chapter. Dean Francis MacLarnon welcomed me in the name of the chapter. Frank was a friend from student days in Maynooth onward and we shared many memories and had many interests in common. He had for many years been Armagh representative in the Christus Rex Society. He left me in no doubt about the sincerity and warmth of the welcome extended to me in Armagh. He has been a tower of strength to me ever since. The members of the chapter were equally generous in their welcome. From then on I took up residence in my new home, Ara Coeli, which took its name from the church of the same name in Rome on the Palatine. This was assigned to Cardinal Logue as his titular church in Rome and he conferred the name on his residence in Armagh. In spite of my first misgivings and anxieties I was able to feel completely at home in Armagh in the short space of just over six years which I spent here. I could not sufficiently express my gratitude to the priests, the religious and the people of the archdiocese for the welcome they have given me and the friendship and support they have shown towards me. I ask God to reward them all for the wonderful kindness, generosity and loyalty, and patience with my shortcomings, which they have extended to me ever since I came among them.

On 28 June 1991 the Holy Father gave to me and to Armagh the great honour of making me a Cardinal. The Consistory was followed next day by a Mass in St Peter's Square, in which I received the pallium. On the next day, 30 June, I said Mass in the church assigned to me as Cardinal, St Patrick's Church in Rome, the Irish Augustinian Church, which had been the titular church of my two predecessors, Cardinal Ó Fiaich and Cardinal Conway.

I shall never forget the welcome I received from the people of the archdiocese when I returned from Rome after the Consistory. From the moment I crossed the Boyne at Drogheda, it was incredible. In Drogheda itself, in Dundalk, in Faughart, at the Border, in Newtownhamilton and in Keady, the warmth of the welcome was wonderful. Here in Armagh itself, it was overwhelming. If I ever could have had the slightest doubt of it, now I knew for certain that I was 'at home' in Armagh, and here I shall be happy to find my last resting place when the time comes for the Master to call.

My six years in Armagh coincided with the traumatic years of scandals in the Church, and these were exceedingly trying times. They were also years of republican violence and loyalist sectarian murders; they were the years of the hard struggle for peace. Drumcree and the marching season brought us near to despair year after weary year. Nevertheless, the tasks of spiritual and pastoral renewal remained the priority on the diocesan agenda. Cardinal Ó Fiaich had commissioned a survey of the priests of the diocese, conducted by a team of Jesuits, who interviewed each priest individually to ascertain their views on a pastoral programme for the archdiocese as it faced towards the end of the millennium. The final report, endorsed by the priests at general assemblies of the clergy in 1989, provided the elements of 'a pastoral plan' which I was happy to adopt as a guideline for my own ministry in Armagh. An interim Diocesan Pastoral Council was set up with representation from every parish in the diocese, bringing together priests and religious and lay men and women to share their hopes and their talents and gifts for the future of the Church in the archdiocese. A programme of formation for foundation members of parish pastoral councils was set up at parish level. Some parishes adopted the Renew programme. This latter programme has now become official diocesan policy under Archbishop Brady, and it is hoped that the millennium will see this programme fully consolidated.

The Irish Episcopal Conference
The Archbishop of Armagh is traditionally also President of the Episcopal Conference and as such chairs its meetings. It is a weighty responsibility, particularly at this time. It is, however, an opportunity to form an overview of the Conference, its functioning and its personnel. The Conference has evolved greatly over the thirty years since I became a bishop. Like other episcopal conferences, we have always to be reviewing the effectiveness of our procedures and trying to improve them.

Bishops must constantly be seeking ways of presenting our message more effectively to and through the media. There are no easy answers, and the Church must avoid anything which might look like a 'packaging' or 'image-making' or 'spin-doctoring' of the message of Christ. That message is often unpalatable to a secular world, and if we suffer for proclaiming it, we should rejoice, for so also, but infinitely more, did our Divine Master. Cardinal Newman once remarked that if the Church is not being criticised, it is because she is not proclaiming the Gospel of Jesus Christ. Nevertheless, the advice of professionals must be sought, in this as in other fields, and can certainly help to make bishops and priests more credible heralds of the Good News, 'workmen who need not be ashamed' before the Lord. I will refer later to the urgent need for a greatly increased involvement of lay men and women in the exposition and defence of Catholic teaching.

No single media programme ever brought me so much mail as the *Late Late Show* with Gay Byrne on 3 November 1995. Reactions to the programme varied from outrage at the audience for giving me such a 'rough ride' (and these were in the majority), to outrage at me for the positions I defended and outrage at the Church for holding those positions. Some held that I was ill-advised to appear on the programme at all. I cannot agree with this view. I believe that Church people have to be prepared to state and defend their convictions, even and perhaps particularly against opposition. I actually enjoyed the programme. From my university years I retained a love of vigorous debate. As a bishop I could not but be happy to see religious topics debated with passion, provided people are prepared to listen to the views of others, and the listening must be mutual. People in that audience were angry; but anger is much to be preferred to apathy. St Paul got a 'rough ride' when he addressed his Greek audience in the Areopagus in Athens. But he continued to proclaim the Good News of Jesus Christ, and not only to God-fearing people of faith in the synagogues, but also 'every day in the market place ... to anyone who would face him', including Stoic and Epicurean philosophers (cf. Acts 17:17). His 'rough ride' in the Areopagus did not deter him from 'proclaiming the message and, welcome or unwelcome, insisting on it' (cf. 2 Timothy 4:1). Television, radio, the internet, the newspapers, are the Areopaguses of today. Whatever the difficulties and the opposition of our times, we must get in there with Christ's message.

My admiration for the personnel of the Episcopal Conference, if I may modestly say so, has only grown over the years. The Irish bishops are a very hard-working and dedicated body of men. There must be few diocesan bishops anywhere who accomplish so much on such modest budgets and with such small secretarial staffs. I hasten to add that the dedication of the staffs of diocesan offices matches that of their bishops! The Irish bishops have always had a horror of large curial departments and have a strong resistance to clerical bureaucracy or to large episcopal or diocesan budgets. No item on an episcopal conference agenda receives closer scrutiny than the budget. Keeping it cut to the feasible minimum is a priority. The bishops are always conscious that our budget is funded entirely from the donations of the lay faithful, and that these are already hard pressed by various demands and often by straitened circumstances. Priests share with their bishops a great reluctance towards imposing more financial pressures on their parishioners or introducing new collections.

One image of the Bishops' Conference frequently entertained is that they are 'out of touch', 'live in an ivory tower', do not consult, do not listen. We must certainly not dismiss these impressions out of hand. They should be taken seriously to heart. However, from my personal experience I can say that my fellow bishops make it a priority to keep in close pastoral contact with their priests, religious men and women and lay groups and individuals. They try to be accessible with the minimum of formality. They do consult and they do listen. They try above all to be pastors, close to their people and sensitive to their needs and their feelings. The episcopal 'style' has changed radically and for the better since Vatican II, and face-to-face contact between bishops and people is now sought by bishops as much as it is needed and wanted by people.

One remark often made about bishops is that they are never told 'the real truth'. From personal experience I can emphatically deny that. Since becoming a bishop, I have been told, face to face as well as by letter, more of the brutal truth about myself that I would ever have otherwise been told; most certainly I have been the recipient of more frank speaking about myself than I would ever have used in talking to a priest about himself, or to anyone else, for that matter. I have at times not liked it, thought it unfair, but on reflection I have often found in the criticism a truth about myself which I was refusing to face. There may be an immediate sense of hurt and injustice, but on reflection, I have come to see myself a little more clearly when seeing myself through the eyes of others. The truth can hurt; but it always sets us free.

When I think of the priests who have most inspired me and helped me and who have been trusted advisers in my episcopal life, I judge their distinctive quality to have been that they were free men and women. I think of Dean Hendley, to whom I have already referred. I think of the late Monsignor James Faughnan, my Vicar General in Ardagh and Clonmacnois. I think of the late Dean Montague, my Vicar General in Down and Connor. I think of the late Canon Walter Larkin, a parish priest of Down and Connor, a classmate and dear and valued lifelong friend (and I name only those no longer with us). I think of Father John Green, a parish priest of Clonbroney, County Longford, who came in to me one day to give me a good 'dressing down' for preaching too long, keeping people too long at Mass, and 'driving people away from religion'! With very different personalities, these men had this in common: they were not afraid of truth; they were not afraid to tell it, they were not afraid to hear it. When asked for their opinion or advice, they gave it honestly, never concerned as to whether it would please me or not, never caring about whether it might make them popular or not. They were uniquely free men, untrammelled by ambition, unencumbered by desire for 'promotion'. They were free because they were devoid of self-importance, having nothing to lose, wanting nothing to gain. They enjoyed what the Imitation of Christ calls 'a certain prerogative of a free mind, not cleaving with an inordinate affection to anything created'. A bishop is blessed indeed to have friends and advisers like these.

To return to the question of consultation of priests, religious and people by the bishops, it must be granted that more structured and organised forms of meeting and of listening are needed now, as society at all levels becomes more complex and more sophisticated. It is true that committees and councils, etc. can themselves get out of touch with the memberships whom they represent and officers at their desks can develop their own separate agendas. Nevertheless, these committees and councils and their 'desks' and offices exist and they fulfil an undeniable need in the complex and changing world of today. Contacts with unorganised people at local level is precious and must be preserved. Contact and dialogue at organisational level, however, is also needed, and must be planned for.

In particular, contact and mutual listening between bishops and religious, at both local and national level, are greatly needed. A spirit of trusting partnership and 'collaborative ministry' between bishops and religious congregations of men and women is essential and special efforts are needed from both sides to make it effective. The 1994 Synod on Consecrated Life returned often to this theme and should make an important contribution into episcopal policy and practice in this regard.

The bishops and national problems

I think it must be said that we bishops are happiest dealing with questions arising at diocesan level. The late Speaker of the US House of Representatives, Tipp O'Neill, coined the famous remark, 'all politics is local'. Bishops are happier when acting with the belief that 'all pastoral planning is local'. We have, however, constantly been trying to develop better strategies and more effective Episcopal Conference structures for debating in depth broad religious and pastoral issues of national significance, together with national strategies in response to them. The diocesan and local focus of bishops has, of course, much in its favour. Reform and renewal of the Church happen at diocesan level and parish level or they do not happen at all. But no parish and no diocese is an island, insulated from change originating elsewhere. Ireland itself is no longer a cultural or religious island; changes, including changes affecting religious beliefs, attitudes and values within Ireland, come to our shores from Great Britain, from the European Union, from North America, indeed from the wider world; and the cultural influences which help to shape people's attitudes to religion and morality are not confined to any one diocese or indeed to Ireland. In today's jargon, we pastors must 'think globally' and 'act locally'.

To return to the personnel of the Episcopal Conference, my overall impression after thirty years is of the great pastoral wisdom and the immense personal and pastoral charity of the Irish bishops, collectively and individually. Discussions at the Conference always reveal a great fund of wisdom derived from pastoral experience and pastoral contact at diocesan level, strengthened by the inherited wisdom of priests and people transmitted by diocesan tradition in the different dioceses, and always tempered by charity. When we decide to issue collective statements or joint pastoral letters, much time is given and enormous care taken to secure a full consensus, with which everyone is in agreement. Full and universal and free expression of opinion is encouraged and the debates impressively cover every aspect of the question at issue. Firmness of doctrine will never be compromised; and this not because of any alleged 'fear of Rome' but out of deep personal and collective conviction; for the truth which we teach we have received from Christ and it is a sacred deposit which we must faithfully guard, with the help of the Holy Spirit. But that truth the bishops will always be careful to speak in love. Any word that is harsh or hurtful or extreme will always be avoided.

The joint pastoral letters produced over the quarter century will, I believe, vindicate the claim that the Irish Episcopal Conference works hard to 'proclaim the message' of Christ, but to do it always in love and 'with patience and with the intention of teaching'. (cf. 2 Timothy 4: 1-2). The list of the major joint pastoral letters is as follows: *Christian Marriage* (1969); *Change in the Church* (1972); *Development* (1973), (this was the pastoral letter which launched the Catholic Bishops' overseas development agency, Trócaire); *Prayer in the Home* (1973); *Human Life is Sacred* (1975); *The Work of Justice* (1977); *Ireland Awaits Pope John Paul II* (1979); (The above documents were collected in a single volume, with the title *Justice, Love and Peace,* published by Veritas in 1979.); *Love is for Life* (1984); *Work is the Key* (1993); *Conscience* (1998). There was also a series of joint statements on Northern Ireland, extending through the whole period of the Troubles. There were also several special statements about social and economic justice.

Special meetings of bishops

Special meetings of the Episcopal Conference designed for the study of the challenges facing the Church in a changing Ireland were initiated by Cardinal Conway and continued by Cardinal Ó Fiaich. We met at Maynooth in 1969 and at Mulrany in 1974. I deal briefly with these two meetings in my chapter on Cardinal Conway, later in this book. We met for a scripture-based reflection and retreat directed by the late Father Barnabas Ahern CP at Dalgan Park in 1977. The Pope's visit in 1979 was a great spur to renewal of Church life. The Pope had called us to work with a sense of urgency. We bishops were determined to keep up the spiritual momentum generated by the visit and to respond to Pope John Paul's challenge to Ireland for the coming decade, which, he declared, could be crucial and decisive for the future of the faith in Ireland. We held a special post-papal-visit meeting of the bishops in Killeshandra in December 1979. We tried to keep alive this sense of pastoral urgency, as was shown by the decision to convene another special meeting of the bishops in Emmaus Retreat Centre during a full week of September in 1986. This meeting was intended to review the situation since our special meeting in Mulrany twelve years earlier. To a greater extent than on previous occasions, Emmaus had a strong participation in several sessions of priests, religious and lay men and women. One day was largely given over to open-ended discussion with young people. During my time in Armagh, another special meeting of the bishops was held in Dundrum, County Tipperary, in 1996. These meetings have become an important instrument of episcopal collegiality in Ireland. Free of routine items of administrative agenda, they enable bishops to look at the broader picture of Church and society in Ireland. They also enable them to share with one another, in a more informal setting, the experiences they have gained in their own dioceses, and to deepen the spirit of friendship and brotherhood which are such a source of strength in the pressurised life of a bishop today.

These meetings were, each in its way and time, an important contribution to the life of the Church in Ireland. The conclusions and resolutions of these meetings were admirable. Many of them have entered into the mainstream of the life of the Church in this country. It is, however, humbling and salutary to reflect on the fact that it is one thing to draw up stirring statements, to formulate far-reaching plans and to draft fine-sounding resolutions; it is something else and something more difficult to put them patiently and persistently into practice and to monitor progress in their implementation. The documents which emanated from these various meetings are indeed excellent; they could still stand as a blueprint for renewal of the Church and of a diocese. But there is a massive programme of unfinished follow-up work still awaiting us.

Collectively, the conclusions and recommendations of these special meetings constitute the equivalent of a pastoral plan for Ireland for the 1980s and 1990s. It is salutary for us bishops now to refer to these recommendations and check over subsequent success or lack of it in implementing them at diocesan or parish level. Progress has undoubtedly been made, but it is still too spasmodic and too uneven. We must work with greater urgency, but still without pessimism or defeatism. It is the Lord's work which we share and its marks must be confidence and 'joy and peace in the Holy Spirit'.

Heavenly patrons

On the occasion of my silver jubilee as bishop in 1992, I found it good to recall the names and seek the intercession of the three diocesan patrons of Armagh, St Patrick, St Malachy and St Oliver Plunkett.

Here I shall recall only the words of St Oliver. I recall them for my own benefit first of all. He wrote:

> God knows that neither by day or night have I given thought to anything but the service of souls and my duties to the Holy See.

One year after he became Archbishop, Oliver wrote this:

> I will not fail to work with the pen, with the tongue, with my slender energies, and this for three motives; (1) to serve the Divine Majesty; (2) through gratitude and the reverence which I own to the Apostolic See ...; (3) because God commands me to obey and serve the Holy See and its service is inseparable from that of Christ.

I wish and I pray that I could make those words my own and could live them to the full for whatever years may now remain to me.

Lights and shadows

I have not attempted to write a detailed account of my pastorate as bishop in three dioceses. Anyhow, I could scarcely see it objectively enough to be a dependable historian. I have contented myself with recollections of a few lights and shades.

I have been blessed in all three dioceses with superb household and diocesan office staffs, priests and lay persons, men and women, all outstanding in efficiency and above all in generosity, dedication and loyalty. Leaving them has in each case been painful. My faithful helper, James Donnelly, has stayed with me during all the changes. I think that they know of my gratitude to them all.

I have been blessed with very precious friendships, with men and with women, which have sustained me all through my life as priest and bishop. It is thanks in great measure to them and to the brotherhood of my fellow priests and bishops that my life has never been a lonely one. I thank God that celibacy has always been for me a joy and a blessing. It has brought an ease and a freedom to my relationships and my friendships, particularly with women, which otherwise would have been missing from my life.

I have been blessed in the priests, religious, lay people and young people with whom and for whom I have prayed, planned and worked in each of the dioceses where I served. I am perhaps unique as bishop in having three successors in my own lifetime. In Bishop Colm O'Reilly, Bishop Patrick Walsh and Archbishop Seán Brady I have the great satisfaction of knowing that the three dioceses to which I was so closely attached are in excellent pastoral care. I have had the joy of being involved in the building or reconstruction of many churches, both in Ardagh and Clonmacnois and in Down and Connor and more recently in Armagh. In the majority of these, the late Ray Carroll worked as liturgical designer and artist, helped by the bishops' hard-working Sacred Art and Architecture Advisory Committee. A highlight of them all is St Mel's Cathedral in Longford, reordered in 1977. There were difficult moments of misunderstanding and hurt when the changes to that sanctuary were being planned, but the final result met with virtually universal satisfaction and indeed admiration. The architects were Richard Hurley and, at a later date, Wilfrid Cantwell. The success of this renovation is due outstandingly to Ray Carroll's magnificent tapestry of the Second Coming and to his design of altar, ambo, chair and many other features of the sanctuary space and of the Blessed Sacrament Chapel, with his splendid Emmaus mural. Much of Ray's best work is found in these dioceses and includes, I believe, some of the best works of sacred art carried out in this country in the post-conciliar period.

I have had great satisfaction from working with lay people in parish and diocesan pastoral councils and encountering at first hand the depths of prayer and faith and love of the Church to be found among them, as well as becoming more aware of their talent and expertise and their readiness to be invited to contribute these to the work of the Church. More and more I have been convinced that this is the future path for the Church and that the Christian resources of lay people are particularly rich in Ireland and willing and waiting for the invitation to be developed.

Experiences of praying and working with young people, first as a university teacher and then as a bishop, give me great hope for the future of the Church. Recollections of annual diocesan youth pilgrimages to Lourdes are particularly happy ones for me. My experience of the Youth Days in Denver, Colorado, in August 1993, and of the Youth Days in Paris in 1997, was truly inspiring.

Praying and working with religious women has been a great joy and privilege for me all through my life as priest and bishop. To be associated with people who had consecrated their lives completely to God and to the Church, people for whom Christ and the Church were their daily love and care and life, people for whom to live was Christ and who thought and felt with and for the Church, made these women natural 'partners in ministry' with priest and bishop. I think of the Dominican Friar, Blessed Jordan of Saxony, addressing his friend the Dominican Sister, Blessed Diana of Andalo, as his 'co-partner in religious life'. This is what the Sisters of Ardagh and Clonmacnois, Down and Connor and Armagh have been to me. I have expressed my thanks to them elsewhere in this book. The Seminars for Religious held in Ardagh and Clonmacnois in 1972 and 1977 and in Down and Connor in 1984 are for me particularly happy memories.

It has been a sacrifice in my life as bishop never to have had time for the sustained reading and intellectual research which I found so stimulating as an academic. The few but welcome opportunities I have had since my university days of being with academics and very occasionally addressing university audiences have brought home to me again the importance for the Church of the work of the intellect and the need for and value of dialogue between Church and university. I have bequeathed my books to Queen's University in gratitude for what I owe to that University. Since my old University established its new outreach campus in Armagh, I have the great satisfaction of knowing that my books will soon be relocated and kept intact in Queen's University at Armagh. I trust that, together with the Cardinal Ó Fiaich Memorial Library, they will provide a valuable resource for religious studies at Armagh.

Decline in vocations

There have been lights and shadows in my life as bishop. The decline in vocations to the priesthood and to religious life has brought me great sadness. The shortage of personnel in future will call for much sacrifice and much pastoral readjustment. It will also have positive side effects in the greater involvement of laity in parish life and in Church life generally. However, it is not only shortage of personnel which causes concern; it is also the change in the quality of faith among the public which underlies this shortage. Even committed Catholics are becoming more this-world-centred, less concerned about what St Paul calls 'the things that are above, where Christ is'.

I believe that the decline in vocations for religious women is, in this sense, just as serious for the Church and just as worrying in terms of the quality of faith. The most effective sign of the presence of the real and living Lord Jesus Christ in our world is the presence of men and women who have chosen to give up everything and live for him and him only all their lives long. Religious women have long been that effective and visible sign in our midst. Their declining numbers represent a great impoverishment, a great weakness in the life of the Church. This decline has been one of the great sadnesses of my life. I firmly believe, however, that the tide will turn, though vocations in later and more mature years may become more the norm.

Scandals in the Church

There have been dark shadows as well as lights in my life as bishop. Many would find it unrealistic on my part, if not dishonest, if I were not to mention, among the 'shadows' of my twenty-seven years in active ministry as bishop, the sad matter of Bishop Eamonn Casey. The news which broke in May 1992 was certainly a great shock and a huge blow. My very first knowledge of it had come only two days before the public announcement. I was making my retreat with my priests in Dromantine College, Newry, when a telephone call alerted me that news was about to break. The news was all the more of a personal shock because I had known Bishop Casey over many years and had admired his work, not only as bishop but long before he became bishop, through his involvement with Christus Rex, many of whose annual congresses he attended and at several of which he gave addresses, and then through his work in the Irish Emigrant Chaplaincy and in Shelter in England. All this was foretaste of the great work he was later to do in Trócaire and in the Irish Episcopal Commission for Emigrants.

Nothing had prepared me or any other bishop for the news of May 1992. I shared in the general sense of bewilderment when I first learned of it. True to his nature, however, Bishop Casey immediately and publicly admitted that he had sinned grievously and he begged forgiveness from God and from his priests and people, as well as from all those whom he had harmed. No brother-bishop could or did make light of his sin. No brother-bishop could or did refuse the forgiveness for which he pleaded. It was entirely of his own volition that Bishop Casey left the country at the time.

When I and other bishops asked that he be given space and silence to make his peace with God, this was out of genuine feeling for himself and worry for his welfare. Silence had nothing to do with any attempt to minimise the wrong or to control the damage.

I believe that most people now feel that enough has been said and enough has been written about the affair. But the silence which people now want is not indifference, it is not forgetfulness; nor is it a blotting out of painful memories. It expresses a desire to leave with God that of which only God can be the judge, namely sin and repentance, atonement and new beginning. Meanwhile, Bishop Casey's work remains. He himself remains in our thoughts and our prayers.

Child sexual abuse

The other great 'wound' of the Church in my time as bishop and the other deep sorrow to myself personally has been the occurrence of sexual abuse of children, particularly when perpetrated by priests or by religious brothers. Whoever the abuser, the crime is a particularly detestable one. The damage inflicted on the young person can be grievous and the consequence for his or her family anguishing. When the abuser is a priest or consecrated religious person, there is the added outrage of the violation of a sacred trust, and a despicable abuse of the friendship, confidence and respect, or sometimes even veneration, in which the priest or religious was held by the family and by the child.

Society has come, gradually and painfully, to realise that child sexual abuse is not confined to any particular group in the community; it has been found in all social classes and in virtually all professions and walks of life; it occurs in families and within extended families; married people as well as single people can be abusers. Understanding of the nature of child sexual abuse and of its impact on victims has developed over recent years and is still developing. In the 1960s and into the 1970s even professionals in the field had an inadequate understanding of the specific nature of child sex abuse and of its effects; there also was an inadequate understanding of the psychology of abusers and of their propensity to reoffend. Knowledge of child psychology and provision of child-care generally were not as developed as they have now become. In the past, complaints of sex abuse made by children were commonly disbelieved almost on principle; and this was true especially when the named abuser was a priest or religious brother or some person held in respect and esteem in the community. Children feared that their complaints would be ignored and that they might be chastised for making them. In any case, children did not have the language for communicating their experience.

Now that we are more aware of the nature and the extent of the problem of child sex abuse, society needs to develop a range of strategies for the prevention of sex abuse of children. More research is needed in the areas of therapy for abusers and healing for victims. Better public understanding is needed of the problem of child sexual abuse and of how to respond to allegations of abuse.

The Church, like society in general, has had to learn from very painful experience about the nature and gravity of this problem. In the past, there was inadequate knowledge and imperfect understanding in the Church, as in society, of the specific nature of child sexual abuse, as distinct from other forms of sexual offence, and of the kind of response which it demands in respect both of the abuser and of the victim. The first reports of child sexual abuse by priests or religious caused extreme shock and scandal in society and brought distress at all levels in the Church. The bishops' collective response was to set up an Advisory Committee, composed predominantly of lay men and women, specialists in all the relevant fields, to explore the problem in all its aspects. After much study and wide consultation, the committee produced a document, *Child Sexual Abuse: Framework for a Church Response*. Published by the Episcopal Conference in 1996, the document sets out a code of practice to which all bishops and religious superiors are committed, and which is being implemented in co-operation with the health authorities and the police in both jurisdictions in Ireland. The structures recommended in this document are in place in every diocese. The appropriate personnel have received the training needed for their role and their mode of operation is regularly reviewed. Programmes of seminary formation have been reviewed, especially in the light of the document, *Pastores dabo vobis*, issued as a result of the 1990 Synod of Bishops on the formation of future priests. There is more emphasis now on the human and emotional and affective development of seminarians and on appropriate processes of discernment to assess the suitability of candidates for the life of priestly celibacy. All this is a gauge of the Church's commitment to this problem, giving paramount attention to the protection and the rights of the child, without violating the principle that a priest, like any citizen, has the right not to be presumed guilty in advance of proof.

Our procedures can never hope to measure up perfectly to the heinousness of the crime. But the effort will go on to make them as perfect as possible, in respect of the victims, the abusers and the scandalised faithful. Christ's own love and care for little children, his stern warnings to those who would scandalise his 'little ones', demand no less than our maximum efforts in the protection of children from abuse and in their healing when abused.

The Father Brendan Smyth case

In September 1994, media coverage in Ireland about the Father Brendan Smyth abuse case reached a climax. I was then Archbishop of Armagh and was attending a Synod of Bishops in Rome. It clearly was necessary for me to make a statement about the case, since some of the abuses occurred in Belfast when I was bishop there. This, however, needed careful checking of all facts and dates, and had to await my return home. On 5 December 1994 I issued a statement which was published in full in many newspapers. I took care to make no statement of fact or date which was not verified by independent witnesses. My statement is in the public domain and there is no need to reproduce it here.

My statement made clear that, as soon as I was informed by a parent that some of her children had been abused by Father Smyth, I immediately contacted his Abbot, first by telephone and then in a personal meeting. The Abbot accepted full responsibility for Father Smyth and undertook to take prompt and immediate steps to deal with the matter. In February 1990, the parent approached my diocesan agency for family welfare and counselling, the Down and Connor Catholic Family Welfare Society. The social worker, with my approval, advised that the RUC should be informed, and she subsequently reported the allegations to the RUC. The same social worker also informed the Health and Social Services authorities. On 7 March 1990, a formal statement of complaint was made by a member of the family to the RUC, and further statements were made to the police by other members of the family within the next two or three weeks thereafter. In December 1990, I became Archbishop of Armagh. In March 1991, Father Smyth presented himself for interview to the RUC and made an admission of wrongdoing. At no time was I aware, nor was I made aware, of Father Smyth's long previous history of paedophile crimes. I came to know of that sordid history only through the media coverage in 1994. I was profoundly shocked and distressed to learn of this appalling saga; but my thought was and is primarily of the pain of Father Smyth's victims. It should not be necessary to add that I had no involvement of any kind with the matter concerning extradition proceedings in relation to Father Smyth.

So far as these scandals in the Church are concerned, we can only say in conclusion that sin has been committed, scandal has been given, grievous harm has been done to people and much damage has been done to the Church. But the Church is placed by God in the world to proclaim the reality of sin, still more to proclaim the power of God's grace and forgiveness. The first announcement of the Good News by Jesus Christ himself was the proclamation of repentance for the forgiveness of sins. The Church will always have to live with the reality of sin within her own members, clerical as well as lay; but the Church will never cease to proclaim the still more powerful reality of God's forgiveness. The death which Christ on the Cross, in his infinite love for us, offered up to God in atonement for the sins of the world far outweighs the whole mass of human evil. That atoning death is our assurance that God's infinite love and God's redeeming grace triumph over all human perversity, and that, as St Paul puts it, 'where sin abounded grace abounded even more' (Rm 5:21). The Second Vatican Council reminds us of 'how great a distance lies between the message [the Church] offers and the human failings of those to whom the gospel is entrusted' (*Gaudium et spes* 43). The great Constitution on the Church declares:

> The Church, embracing sinners in her bosom, is at the same time holy and always in need of being purified, and unceasingly pursues the path of penance and renewal. (*Lumen gentium* 8)

Pursuing that path of humility, penitence and conversion, the Church will, more strongly than ever, show forth in the world, 'in a faithful though shadowed way, the mystery of the Lord, until in the end this mystery is revealed in all its splendour' (*Lumen gentium* 8).

Auschwitz

The triumph of grace is often difficult to discern. Evil can be so obvious and so overwhelming, even in our supposedly enlightened century. In May 1998, I visited Auschwitz, for a conference of Christians and Jews. A tour of Auschwitz and nearby Birkenau is a journey in the valley of the shadow of death, cruel death, obscenely, insanely and evilly inflicted death, a moral cesspit. I felt the evil of the ideology which could drive human beings to do this to one another, but also the evil of the human beings who could be so driven to do it. I felt shame at what evil human beings are capable of, and therefore at what I as a human being, a member of the same species, am capable of. I felt fear for the future of the human race, with its proven capacity for evil now reinforced by modern technology and facilitated by modern methods of moulding and manipulating public opinion.

'How can one believe in God after Auschwitz?' some have asked. But surely the deeper question is, 'How can God continue to love a humanity so flawed as ours in its capacity to abuse God's great gift of freedom, made for choosing good, made for choosing love?' Why did God send his Son to save such a race, to be 'made sin' for such a race, to die on the Cross for such a race? That is the mystery – God's respect for our freedom and his patience with our abuse of that freedom, his mercy for our moral misery. After Auschwitz, how can we live without God? How can we go on hoping without God? There was grace even in Auschwitz, and its triumph is shown in the lives and in the deaths of the Maximilian Kolbes and the Edith Steins and the countless other saints and martyrs, Jewish as well as Christian, who died in Auschwitz and Birkenau and who taught us, in the midst of evil, how to believe and how to hope.

Personal struggles of faith

My life, like the life of many, if not most, Christians, has often been a struggle for faith. My cry to the Lord has often been the cry we find in the Gospel: 'Lord, I believe, but help the little faith I have'. Ours is an age when faith is under challenge on every side – from the sciences, from new biblical research, from scandals in the Church, from anti-clericalism, from increasing indifference in some sectors to religious practice and to the Church's teaching, from the pervading secular culture, from what Cardinal Suhard called the 'untroubled irreligion', in which many, particularly intellectuals and writers, seem to settle down. One is forced to ask questions about one's own faith. My own faith has been tested. Has it failed or wavered in the test?

My own struggles of faith have not tended to be on the intellectual plane. In so far as the 'God of the Philosophers' is concerned, I can honestly say that I have never doubted the existence of God at the level of philosophy and of reason. The reasons pointing to his existence seem to me to be so many, so converging, so mutually reinforcing, so much in conformity with human experience, that I confess I would find it irrational to deny the existence of God. I do not feel in any way superior, however, to those who do deny him; rather I feel grateful for the privilege of knowing that God exists and that I am loved by him. I feel that the difficulties often lie in the narrowing and restricting which has happened in our culture of the concept of reason, of rationality, even of the meaning of the word 'rational'. Science, or rather a reductionist approach to science, philosophy, or rather an unargued positivist approach to philosophy, have narrowed these disciplines down to the empirically verifiable or the experimentally demonstrable, to the point where the very concept of God and his existence are almost defined out of the sphere of reason or rationality or truth. One of the most important tasks of philosophy at the present time, it seems to me, is to enlarge our concept of reason and of rationality, and indeed of truth, and thereby to break free of the stranglehold of positivism and from the wasteland of relativism.

Nor is it only reasoning which leads me to God; it is also nature, literature, art, music. The view of Niagara or the Victoria Falls, Mont Blanc seen from an aircraft or a train, a sunset over Lake Constance, the quiet peace of Clonmacnois or Glendalough or Mellifont or Monasterboice, all these are pointers to the 'grandeur of God' (Hopkins). The extraordinary power of the Christian religion to attract writers and artists of genius in every age, the contribution made by Christianity down the ages to architecture, painting, sculpture, poetry and music, its impact on African and Asian art today, all speak of God who 'fathers forth' all this human creativity, and whose 'beauty is past change' (Hopkins).

The really important thing, however, is not to prove the existence of God but rather to know and experience God as a person, to know him as lovable and to love him. The God of reason must become also the God of the heart. God is not just a 'problem' to be solved, or a God to be rationally demonstrated, reasoned about or even believed about (the language is that of Gabriel Marcel), but a 'mystery', a mystery of love to be experienced and to be explored. God is not an object to be found (or not found) somewhere 'out there' in or above the universe. He is not something abstract and impersonal which 'lies behind' the visible world, but Someone who made the world out of love; someone who is constantly at work within the world and within each one's heart, creating a 'civilisation of love' and preparing for the coming of a Kingdom of love. Above all, he is someone who loves and cares about me and about each and every human being, calling each one by her or his name, individually, personally.

Any weakening of my faith in that personal God, the true God revealed to us in Jesus Christ, has come about when I neglected talking to God in order to make more time for writing or talking about God. It has come about when I preferred reading books about prayer – or day-dreaming about writing a book about prayer! – to actually praying. It is, I fear, a special temptation of the preacher or of the writer about religion, that words or phrases are heard or read as suitable for use in writing or talking about God to the neglect of using them to speak to God, or to the neglect of simply putting words aside, just to be with God and to be in love with God. One can read passages of Scripture in order to use them in addressing others rather than as God's message to my own self. These have been the times when I personally had most reason to fear for the weakness of my faith. St Paul prayed 'lest, having preached to others, he himself become a castaway'. This is why I have so often prayed, 'Keep me faithful to your teaching and never, never, let me be separated from you.'

Faith lost, or thought to be lost, is often refound by once beginning to pray again. This is why occasions which lead people to feel a need for God – occasions like sickness, death, a funeral, a wedding, a baptism, the loss of an unborn child – can often be occasions for return to faith, when a priest or a believing and praying friend can lead the person through that experience of pain and loss to the awareness of the presence of a loving God. It must be remembered also that what sometimes seems to us to be loss of faith is really an invitation to move to a deeper level of faith, putting aside, as St Paul would put it, the things of a child and the thoughts of a child in one's relationships with God or one's prayer to God, and entering, or letting oneself be drawn by the Holy Spirit to enter, a more adult level of faith and prayer. Faith can never remain static: it either grows or it withers and dies. Christ's call to become like little children is not a call to what psychologists might term a regression to infantilism. Instead it is a call to maturity in loving, spontaneity and sincerity in using the language of trust, abandonment and love in our relationship with God. Our Lord says significantly, 'You must change and become like little children.' His own characteristic use of the term 'Abba' for God is at once the clearest self-revelation of his own divine Sonship and the norm for all Christian prayer. Tertullian called the Our Father the 'compendium' of all Christian faith.

Apart from the pain of the scandals and the deaths of my mother and my sister Sheila, the greatest personal sadness I have had in the past thirty years of my episcopate has been the continuance of the violence in Northern Ireland and its prolonged resistance to all efforts to bring it to an end. Assistance at so many funerals of victims, whether of republican or loyalist gunmen, closeness to so many broken hearts of the bereaved, experience of all the spiritual and moral, physical and mental suffering inflicted, have brought home to me abundantly the evil and the futility of war and violence. We have seen for ourselves in our own situation that, in the words spoken some years ago by Andrea Riccardi, the founder of the Community of San Egidio, 'There is no such thing as a holy war; there is only a holy peace'. It is still my fervent prayer and hope to see at last before I die an Ireland of peace and justice, reconciled within its own communities and reconciled with its nearest neighbour, Great Britain, and with North and South actively co-operating with one another in the interests and for the welfare of both, and fully participating in the European Union. That prayer and hope seem nearer to fulfilment as I write these lines than at any time in my lifetime. May God make all of us ready for the changes of heart and mind and attitudes and structures which are the preconditions for a lasting peace.

Retrospect

Looking back, I am able to see a unity and a coherence between different periods of my life. The unity and coherence are given to us by Christ, who, in the words of St Paul, 'holds all things together in unity' (Col 3:17).

All the various fields of learning and of literature and of art, of study and of teaching, of language and culture, philosophy and theology, of personal and pastoral experience, to which I have been exposed, have, by God's grace, strengthened my conviction about the truths of our faith and intensified my desire to make that faith known and loved and lived. I venture briefly to summarise some of the variety of studies and experiences through which I have lived. My first areas of post-primary study were, as I have said, what used to be known as the Ancient Classics, Greek and Latin language and literature. Again and again in reading the classics of this literature, I was able to find in these pre-Christian writings seeds and anticipations of the Gospel which was to come. I could understand why St Augustine felt that already the philosopher Plato was a divine preparation or propaedeutic for Christian teaching. G. K. Chesterton, an English Catholic writer of the early part of this century, spoke of 'soils for the seeds of [Catholic] doctrine'. This was my experience of those early years of my study and reading.

I have already referred to my Master's Degree study of Christianity in North Africa in the time of Tertullian. Tertullian was an early Christian writer at the end of the first century and first half of the second, who, after writing outstanding works in exposition and defence of the Christian faith, moved steadily in the direction of rigorism and puritanism, broke with the Catholic Church, and joined the puritan sect of 'the pure' called Montanists, and apparently later broke with them and led a sect of his own. His writings provide marvellous insight into the life of the young and flourishing Church of North Africa in the early Christian centuries. Studying Tertullian, I was constantly struck by the continuity between the Church of Tertullian's time and the Church of today, nineteen centuries later. Despite the historical and cultural changes which have transformed and occasionally convulsed humanity and the Church since then, I still knew that the faith which I believed and which I tried to live was the same faith which the Catholic Tertullian had lived and defended 1,900 years earlier.

That reading of Tertullian was continued in my post-graduate studies in theology. Researching Tertullian's theology of baptism and of penance, I once more experienced the extraordinary continuity of the Church's teaching across the centuries, and the fundamental identity of the faith of the Church today with the faith of the Church of the earliest centuries. There had been development, of course, but not any change of substance. Christ was faithful to his promise: the Holy Spirit of Truth was indeed guiding the Church into deeper and deeper understanding of the faith once revealed to the Apostles and transmitted faithfully by them and their successors across the centuries. I was able to appreciate, through my own reading of the early Christian writers, or Fathers of the Church, how it was that Cardinal Newman came to the Catholic faith through his discovery of the Catholic Church of today in the early Fathers of the Church.

Following my studies in theology, I returned to the study and teaching of philosophy. This entailed reading and research in Greek philosophy, in medieval philosophy, especially that of St Thomas Aquinas, and in modern philosophy. I specialised in the study of the philosophy of theism and of moral philosophy, with special reference to moral philosophers in the British and American traditions, and in modern French philosophy, particularly in the existentialist tradition. Here again, my conviction was strengthened that all the things which I found true and valuable in these various systems of philosophy found their proper place and fulfilment, and indeed their real home, in the wholeness of the Catholic faith. So far from being a threat to that Catholic faith, these various expressions of truth were for me a reinforcement of that faith. I had something of the experience of G.K. Chesterton. Before becoming a Catholic Christian, Chesterton had developed a 'personal philosophy or natural religion', which he thought was his own unaided discovery. Then, he writes:

> I made the startling discovery that the whole thing had been discovered before. It had been discovered by Christianity.

I could modestly say with Chesterton:

> A man is not really convinced of a philosophical theory when he finds that something proves it. He is only

convinced when he finds that everything proves it.
(*Orthodoxy*, John Lane)

I can firmly declare, however, that I have learned more about faith and prayer and Christian living, and indeed about the human condition, from what are wrongly called 'ordinary' men and women, or 'simple' Christians in the world, than I have from books.

I never cease to marvel at how Christian and Catholic faith can be lived to the full, and give meaning and purpose to life and enlarge the mind and fire the imagination of men and women in all centuries and continents, be they intellectual giants or very ordinary persons, be they artists, poets, writers, philosophers or theologians or plain Everyman or Everywoman. I have found men and women raised to the heights of contemplative prayer and even mysticism through constant unsophisticated repetition of the Rosary. I have also found intellectual giants with a faith as simple and profound as that of my mother; she who never had second-level education, but had a relationship with God which could be the envy of any theologian, and was certainly my envy and my admiration.

I thank God for that faith and for the Church through which it has been transmitted. I thank God for the faith I have been given. I thank God for the faith of others which has nourished and strengthened my own. I take my confidence for the future, Christ's future, from the words from which I took my episcopal motto:

> Jesus Christ is the same today as he was yesterday and as he will be forever. (Hb 13:14)

PART TWO

STEPS ALONG THE ROAD

CHAPTER ELEVEN

START OFF NOW

Jesus said to them: Start off now ...
Whatever house you go into, let your first words be,
'Peace to this house!'
(Lk 10:1-9)

ARDAGH AND CLONMACNOIS
1967-82

(a) Arrival in Ardagh and Clonmacnois
(i) Statement at press conference
2 June 1967
(in Belfast on the day of the announcement
of my nomination as bishop)

The news that the Holy Father has decided to appoint me as Bishop of Ardagh and Clonmacnois has left me in a state of confusion since I first heard it confidentially from the Apostolic Nuncio a week ago.

The appointment calls me to a diocese I scarcely know, and yet to a diocese with which I have felt close ties since my boyhood, because it is the diocese from which my father came at the beginning of the century to take up his first post as a newly qualified teacher in Corkey, in the parish of Loughguile. As a boy, I learned from him the names of several of its parishes, especially

Kilronan or Keadue, his parish of birth, with Arigna and Ballyfarnon, also Drumshanbo and Carrick-on-Shannon. I learned the names of some of its mountains, such as Slieve an Iaran, and Shelton Hill, its lakes, especially Lough Allen and the lovely lakes of Leitrim; its rivers, especially the lordly Shannon. I learned from my father to sing some of the songs of his native western province of Connacht. He would have been happy that I am going back as bishop to his home and among his people.

The nomination calls me away from the diocese of Down and Connor which formed me and which I love, away from where I have lived these twenty years in Belfast, away from Loughguile, which will always be 'home', away from my dear mother and family, away from many greatly loved friends.

It calls me away from the academic work which I love and from Queen's University, where I have been happy as student and as teacher and where academic colleagues and students both have given me so much.

I leave all this with sadness. I leave it also with apprehension, for the future is for me an uncharted sea, a journey without maps. I shall miss the world of books and of study which have filled most of my life until now. Even transporting the books to Longford will be a great upheaval in every sense. Little as I know about the life of a bishop, I know enough to be aware that it leaves little time for sustained reading, much less for philosophical or theological research.

Yet I also love pastoral ministry. I found great fulfilment in such 'holiday supply' opportunities as I had during my university years and welcomed the weekend assistance I was able to give in parishes. I drew great spiritual satisfaction and benefit from the visitation of homes, particularly homes of the sick, in Loughguile during holidays. I look forward to a more pastorally-oriented life as bishop, and I am confident that there, among people of faith, I shall find affirmation in my own faith and wisdom of the kind which is not found in libraries or in academic common-rooms. And now, to adapt words of St Paul: I commend myself to God and to the word of his Grace (Ac 20:32).

(ii) Episcopal Ordination:
St Mel's Cathedral, Longford
16 July 1992
Feast of Our Lady of Mount Carmel

Address to Priests

It is a very moving moment in my life when, on the evening of this day of my ordination as bishop, I meet for the first time in a body the priests of the Diocese of Ardagh and Clonmacnois, the diocese in which, as faith assures me, the Holy Spirit has placed me as bishop to rule the Church of God. But I am consoled and reassured by what the same Holy Spirit, speaking through the voice of the Second Vatican Council, tells us about the manner of that rule. For the documents of the Council repeat again and again that it is a rule based upon dialogue, discussion, co-operation between bishop and priests, with fatherliness and service on one side, frankness and sincerity and loyalty on the other, and, in and above all things and on both sides, love.

The very definition of a diocese in the *Decree on The Pastoral Office of Bishops in the Church* is as follows:

> A diocese is that portion of God's People which is entrusted to a bishop to be shepherded by him with the cooperation of the presbytery. (*Christus Dominus* 11)

Co-operation between the bishop and the whole body of his priests is thus part of the essence of the episcopal office.

The nature of this co-operation is spelled out unforgettably in later paragraphs of the same document. We read, for example:

> To accomplish these things effectively, a bishop ... should arrange his life is such a way as to accommodate it to the need of the time. A bishop should always welcome priests with a special love, since they assume in part the bishop's duties and cares and carry the weight of them day by day so

zealously. He should regard his priests as sons and friends. Thus by his readiness to listen to them and his trusting familiarity, a bishop can work to promote the whole pastoral work of the entire diocese.... The relationships between the bishop and his diocesan priests should rest above all on the bonds of supernatural charity so that the harmony of the will of the priests and that of their bishop will render their pastoral activity more fruitful. Hence, for the sake of greater service to souls, let the bishop engage in discussion with the priests, even collectively, especially about pastoral maters. This he should do not only occasionally but, as far as possible, at fixed intervals. (*Christus Dominus* 16)

Similarly, in the *Decree on The Ministry and Life of Priests*, we read:

Therefore, on account of his communion in the same priesthood and ministry, the bishop should regard priests as his brother and friends. As far as in him lies, he should have at heart the material and especially the spiritual welfare of his priests.... He should gladly listen to them, indeed consult them, and have discussions with them about those matters which concern the necessities of pastoral work and the welfare of the diocese. (*Presbyterorum ordinis* 7)

A new note in the definition of priestly obedience is sounded in the same Decree when it declares:

At the same time, obedience demands that priests confidently propose their plans and urgently expose the needs of the flock committed to them, while remaining ready to submit to the judgment of those who exercise the chief responsibility for governing the Church of God. (*Presbyterorum ordinis* 15)

I refer to these texts because I quite firmly and unreservedly want the entire teaching of the Second Vatican Council to be the basis of my whole approach to the episcopate and the whole of my dealings with you. And this is no virtue on my part but my plain and simple duty, at this time when the universal Church is called by God to renewal in the light of Christ. For my part, I am immensely grateful to God that, if I have to be a bishop, it should be now, in the springtime of conciliar renewal, with the Vatican Council's splendid picture of the bishop's office to guide and inspire one, that I should be called to assume this office.

But all this will evaporate in fine words and pious intentions unless you, my brother priests, can help me by your co-operation, your disinterested and sincere advice, and by your prayers. I shall never forget the kindness, the sincerity, and the welcome which the priests of Ardagh and Clonmacnois have already extended to me at this anxious time in my life. God grant that I may prove not to be totally unworthy of it. Returning, as I now do, to the diocese from which my father came to the North at the turn of the century, I would anyhow have felt that I was not coming among strangers. But you have made sure that I should feel that I am indeed coming home.

Like Saint Cronan of Roscrea, I should like my house to be a place where 'priests and people can find me readily'. And in that place, God willing and God helping me, and with your co-operation, I shall try, as St Cronan said, 'To serve my Lord, Christ, the King of Kings'.

Address to Laity

It is a moment full of emotion for me to meet for the first time the public representatives, the lay organisations, and the faithful and apostolic laity of the Diocese of Ardagh and Clonmacnois, and to be assured by you formally of the welcome which you have already made me feel since I was named as your new bishop. I am deeply moved by your words, of such generous warmth and such clear sincerity.

Last Saturday, when I had the privilege and joy of being received by Pope Paul in private audience, His Holiness asked me in a very particular way to convey his special blessing to the active apostolic laity of the diocese. 'They', said Pope Paul, 'will be a great strength to you and a great force for the Church in these dramatic times.' I am proud to be able to convey that message and that blessing to you today. Saint Francis de Sales, one of the great bishops of all time, advised a fellow bishop as follows:

> You should devote particular care to two categories of persons, because they are the heads of the people, namely the parish priests and the parents. It is from these two groups that all the good you hope to see realised in your parishes or in your homes will proceed.

Above all, the Second Vatican Council, as you know, speaks eloquently and often of the calling of lay men and women in the Church. The Council spells out memorably the relationships between bishops, priests and laity in the Christian life of a diocese. If we all let ourselves be inspired and guided by the teaching of the Council, then we can hope not to fail Our Lord at this point of history where he has placed us. We can hope to do something great for God in the diocese where God has placed us, a diocese blessed by God in the past and in the present by so many saints, missionaries, priests, religious and lay apostles.

Among the relevant paragraphs of the Council is one which it is appropriate to quote in the presence of so many public representatives of national and local government.

> Assuredly, while sacred pastors devote themselves to the spiritual care of their flock, they are also in fact having regard for social and civil progress and prosperity. According to the nature of their office and as behoves bishops, they collaborate actively with public officials for this purpose, and advocate obedience to just laws and reverence for legitimately constituted authorities. (*Christus Dominus* 19)

In the presence of so many whose apostolic work is directed

towards the poor, the old and the suffering, it is appropriate to recall the Council's words:

> With a special concern bishops should attend upon the poor and the deprived classes to whom the Lord sent them to preach the Gospel. (*loc. cit.*)

For the bishop himself it is salutary to remember the words of the same Council:

> Finally, let bishops have the kind of dwelling which will appear closed to no one and which no one will fear to visit, even the humblest. (*loc. cit.*)

It is not only faith that will move me and help me to love the Church of Christ, established in Ardagh and Clonmacnois; it is also the goodness and sincerity and kindness I have already experienced among priests, the generosity and loyalty of its people, the hallowed and venerable past of it and its fervent and faithful present. It is the diocese of my father and of my forebears. I have already, in the past six weeks since my nomination, been made to feel that I am coming home. For having by your message made me feel that, for making me feel it even more intensely now by words of welcome, I thank you and I ask God to bless you.

(b) Departure from Ardagh and Clonmacnois
September 1982

(i) Farewell Mass with the priests of the diocese
in St Mel's Cathedral, Longford
Thursday, 23 September 1982

My dear brother priests, it is most fitting that it is in the setting of the Eucharist that I make my farewells with the priests of Ardagh and Clonmacnois. It was in the setting of the first Eucharist that Our Lord gave his farewell discourse to his disciples. He is in our midst this afternoon as we gather round this altar.

There is pain in my parting from you; for it is, I fondly believe, a parting of friends. The French say, 'to leave is to die a little'. We are reminded by partings that 'all things pass; only God does not change'. Only in him do our friendships find the eternity which all our real friendships seek; and only that search for eternity in human friendships brings peace and fulfilment to the heart. 'Only God is enough' (St Teresa).

I came to Ardagh and Clonmacnois with a feeling of lostness; alone in an unfamiliar and unknown territory, among priests and people who were almost entirely strangers. The welcome of the priests of the diocese quickly assured me that I was received as 'one of your own', one of yourselves. I said in my first address to you, and repeated often in the early years:

> I shall never forget the kindness, the sincerity and the welcome the priests of Ardagh and Clonmacnois have extended to me at this anxious time in my life.

I prayed then that God might grant that I might prove not to be totally unworthy of that kindness and that welcome. That first feeling deepened, that first prayer became more urgent, as the years passed.

That early welcome was no conventional courtesy. It was followed, over fifteen years, by the most loyal co-operation which a bishop could ever hope to receive from his priests. Above all, it was followed by what I have always felt to be a sincere personal friendship between me and each of my priests. You have made me feel this diocese to be my home in a way that lies deep, beyond words. There has been talk of my 'returning home' in going back to the diocese of Down and Connor where I was born, where I lived for fifty years, and where I spent twenty-six years of my priesthood. But after my fifteen happy years in Ardagh and Clonmacnois, it will take me a long time in Down and Connor before I feel as much at home in my native diocese as I have come to feel in Ardagh and Clonmacnois. For having made it be like that, I thank you all, priests and people, with deep sincerity.

I have often said about you in your absence, and I now say it to you in your presence: There is no finer body of priests in Ireland than the priests of Ardagh and Clonmacnois. May the Lord complete the good work which he has begun in each of you, until the day when he comes to take each of us home for good (cf. Philippians 1:6).

When the Lord calls

My leaving Ardagh and Clonmacnois is not the result of any human choice. In the aftermath of my heart attack last February it even might seem to run counter to human prudence and calculation. My leaving occurs only as a response to that call which has brought you, as it has brought me, down all the years to where we are now, namely the call: 'Follow me'. That call, I have always believed, never sounds so clear nor is so unambiguous as when it is expressed through the decision of our superiors in the Lord and in his Church. Before I was ordained (or, in the language of that time, 'consecrated') Bishop of this diocese, I first took a solemn oath of obedience. I said in the language of the rite of episcopal ordination of that time:

> I will now and at all times be loyal and obedient to Saint Peter, to the Holy Roman Catholic and Apostolic Church, to our Leader, Pope Paul VI, and to his lawfully elected successors.

During the ordination liturgy, several questions were put to me by the ordaining prelate, the late Cardinal Conway. One of the questions was:

> Are you willing in all things to be loyal, submissive and obedient, in accordance with the Church's laws, to the holy Apostle, Peter, to whom is given the power to bind and to loose, and to his Vicar, our Holy Father, Pope Paul VI, and his successors, the Bishops of Rome?

I answered:

> 'I am.'

In the present call to leave this diocese, the Lord has seen fit to put the sincerity of that answer to the test.

The Lord is faithful to his promises
We follow a God of fidelity, whose name is 'Amen'; as though to say 'I give you my Word, and you can depend upon it'. 'He is the faithful God, who is true to his graciousness for a thousand generations' (Dt 7:9).

Our recognition of him as our God, our acceptance of him as Lord of our lives, requires an answering fidelity on our part. I have been looking back on my fifteen years among you, examining myself on my fidelity to the promises I made on 16 July 1967. In addition to the question which I quoted earlier, the following questions were put to me by the ordaining prelate:

> Are you willing to teach, by word and example, what you learn from the divinely inspired Scriptures to the people for whom you are to be consecrated?

I answered then: 'I am'. Today, I sincerely hope that, relying on God's forgiveness for the failures, I can say that at least I tried.
I was asked:

Are you willing to receive reverently, teach and observe the traditions of the Fathers of the Church and the decisions of the Holy and Apostolic See?

I answered then: 'I am'. It is my wish today that, relying on God's mercy for the omissions, I might be able to say that at least I tried.
I was asked:

Are you willing to shun evil conduct and, by God's grace, so far as you can, to seek only what is good?

I answered: 'I am'.
I was asked:

Are you willing, with God's help, to practise and teach chastity and moderation?

I answered: 'I am'.
I was asked:

Are you willing at all times, as far as human frailty permits, to give yourself to spiritual things, and not occupy yourself in worldly affairs or in the pursuit of material gain?

I answered: 'I am'.
I was asked:

Are you willing yourself to practise humility and patience and teach these virtues to others?

I answered, fifteen years ago: 'I am'.
Looking back over those fifteen years, and examining them in the light of those questions, I can only invoke the Holy Spirit, sent among us for the forgiveness of sins, and address to him the words of that wonderful prayer, *Veni Sancte Spiritus:*

Wash clean what is unclean in us;
water what is dried up in us;
heal what is broken in us;
soften what is hard in us;
warm what is cold in us;
make straight what is twisted in us.

I was asked finally:

Are you willing to show gentleness and tenderness for the
sake of Christ, Our Lord, to the poor, to strangers and to all
needy persons?

I answered: 'I am'.

Today I am very conscious of what was sinful in those years, in
things that I did and in things that I failed to do, and I simply join
with all of you in saying, 'O God, be merciful to me, a sinner'.

In this, our last Mass together, you are yourselves about to renew
your own priestly commitment, and I join with you in doing so.
May God grant us forgiveness for the past and grace and strength
and courage for the beginning in the future to which he calls us.

A personal commitment

In addition to looking up again the questions put to me at my
consecration, I have also for today read again my first address to the
priests of Ardagh and Clonmacnois, given in the evening of the day
of my episcopal ordination. May I be permitted to recall some of
those words now.

I said that I wanted 'the entire teaching of the Second Vatican
Council to be the basis of my whole of my dealings with you'. I
noted, however, that all this would 'evaporate in fine words and
pious intentions' on my part, unless you, the priests, helped me 'by
your co-operation, your disinterested and sincere advice, and your
prayers'. That co-operation, that disinterested and sincere advice,
and those prayers, have never been lacking on your part. I thank
you for this.

As I now leave my home in Ardagh and Clonmacnois for my old and new home in Down and Connor, I hope and believe that your friendship will accompany me and your prayers will follow me and continue to support me in the daunting future I face. In our prayer before the Lord, distance is obliterated and we remain together in his love. Can I refer to my first address again, when I quoted words from St Cronan of Roscrea, and said, 'I should like my house to be a place where priests and people can find me readily.' That will still be true of my house in Down and Connor for priests and people of Ardagh and Clonmacnois. You will find me readily there; and the door will always be open to you.

I leave to God's forgiveness and to yours the ways and the times in which I have misunderstood or misjudged one or other of you, wronged or hurt this one or that one among you. In this Mass, in every Mass, is abounding forgiveness and reconciliation. We shall look, not to the past with its failings, but to the future with its hopes, a future bright with God's promises. Saint Paul says:

> I forget the past and I strain ahead for what is still to come. I am racing for the finish, for the prize which God calls us upwards to receive in Christ Jesus (Ph 3:13-14).

I think of Saint Paul's farewell to the presbyters of Miletus:

> And now I commend you to God, and to the word of his grace that has power to build you up and to give you your inheritance among all the sanctified (Ac 20:31-32).

In the words of Dag Hammarskjöld:

> For all that has been, Lord, thanks.
> To all that will be, Lord, Yes.
>
> May the grace of Our Lord Jesus Christ be with you all (2 Th 3:18).

(ii) Farewell Mass with the religious Sisters of the Diocese in Our Lady's Bower Convent, Athlone
Sunday, 26 September 1982

My dear Sisters in Jesus Christ, it is most fitting that is in the setting of the Eucharist that I make my farewell with the Sisters of Ardagh and Clonmacnois. He is in our midst this afternoon, as we gather round his altar. In the great Constitution on the Church, *Lumen gentium*, we read:

> In any community existing around an altar, under the sacred ministry of the bishop, there is manifested a symbol of that charity and 'unity of the Mystical Body, without which there can be no salvation'. (*Lumen gentium* 26; the quotation is from St Thomas Aquinas)

There is, therefore, a very special depth and power in our prayers for one another in this, our last eucharistic gathering together.

There is for me loneliness and sadness and pain, deep pain, in my parting from you; for it is a parting of friends. It is from God, 'the Father of all light' (Jm 1:17), from whom all good things come, that has come all the enrichment that our years together in his love and service have brought to me and, I hope, also to you. Anything that we have given, everything that we have received, has come to us from him; to him be the thanks, the praise and the glory. Our friendship in Christ will endure. I like the words about this kind of friendship, spoken by a French scripture scholar, Beda Rigaux:

> We are truly friends only when we share together that which is the deepest concern of our lives, namely the love of Jesus Christ, which leads us to the Father. When people place their friendship on this level... they are standing together on the rock on which their very existence rests. Nothing can ever break the ties that bind them. They have placed a foot in eternity. God is in them, God is between them. Their friendship becomes a sacred thing, because each day they

bring it before God in Holy Communion and they never feel more present to one another than when they receive the Saviour who is himself their bond of friendship.
(*Paroles d'Évangile,* Duculot Gemblaux, 1947, p.72)

Such my dear Sisters, is our friendship for one another, and it is not affected by time or distance.

I came to Ardagh and Clonmacnois with a feeling of lostness; alone in unfamiliar and unknown territory, among priests, nuns and people who were almost entirely strangers. The welcome of the Sisters of the diocese, the warmth of the reception I found in all the religious communities of the diocese, quickly assured me that among you I had found, not lost, my home. I wanted, from the very beginning, to be your father and brother in Christ. You have never failed to be true sisters in Christ to me. I trust that in God's sight I may not have proved too unworthy of your loyalty and love and trust.

I have often said about you, and I recall saying it in these very precincts, during one of our so memorable Seminars for Religious in Athlone in 1972 and 1977, and now I say it again: 'I am very proud of my Sisters in Ardagh and Clonmacnois. There are no more devoted, no more faithful consecrated women in any diocese in Ireland.' To quote St Paul, with only slight adaptations, you have been 'my joy and my crown' (Ph 4:1).

I [shall] thank my God whenever I think of you; and every time I pray for all of you, I [shall] pray with joy; remembering how you helped to spread the Good News from the day [I first arrived among you]... it is only natural that I should feel like this towards you all, since you have shared the privileges which have been mine... my work defending and establishing the Gospel. You have a permanent place in my heart, and God knows how much I [shall] miss you all, loving you as Christ Jesus loves you (cf. Philippians 1:3-8).

When the Lord calls

There has been talk of my 'returning home' in going back to the diocese of Down and Connor, where I was born; where is my beloved native parish of Loughguile; where my father and my mother await the resurrection; the diocese where I lived for fifty years and where I spent twenty-six years of my priesthood. But the grace of God's calling of me to come here as bishop, and God's gift to me of all the friendship and affection I have found here, have made Ardagh and Clonmacnois my home. Ever since I came, I have wanted no other home. Here is where I wanted to stay for all the years that remained to me; here I wanted to retire, if I lived long enough, and here I wanted to die. Here I planned for my mortal remains to be laid, by the side of my predecessors in the shadow of our great Cathedral. But such was not God's will; and only in his will is our peace.

My leaving Ardagh and Clonmacnois is not the result of any human choice. In the light of my recent illness, it might seem unwise; but it takes its meaning from Christ's call, 'Follow me'.

When I was being ordained Bishop of this diocese, I first took a solemn oath of obedience 'to the Holy Roman Catholic and Apostolic Church, to Our Lord, Pope Paul VI, and to his lawfully elected successors...'. Nothing was further from my thoughts at that time than going back to Down and Connor as bishop, and yet, in God's providence, it was an unknown part of the obedience I was promising on that day.

With no presumptuous intention of comparing myself with St Paul I think of his farewell to the presbyters at Miletus. (My adaptations of the words are very slight):

> I am on my way to [Belfast], but have no idea what will happen to me there....

The account in Acts tells us that 'when he had finished speaking [Paul] knelt down with them all and prayed' (Ac 20:36). That is what we are doing today. St Francis de Sales, a model bishop, wrote:

Union of our will with God's will is the greatest thing one can do for the Church and for God's glory and for our own sanctification.

We pray for that grace in today's Eucharist.

A bishop's responsibilities to his religious

From the day of my nomination as bishop – it was 2 June 1967, a First Friday and the Feast of the Sacred Heart – I had a clear conviction that one of a bishop's pressing duties is to be at the service of religious in their search for holiness and for true renewal. I wished to do everything possible to see that religious women might more and more take their full place and play their full role in the Church. I had been myself so much helped in my own priestly life by religious women, whose holiness inspired me and whose kindness and friendship and love supported me, that I felt an obligation as bishop to use every opportunity of manifesting the Church's esteem for the religious life of consecrated women. It had sometimes seemed to me that religious women were too often taken for granted; or were treated as persons with services – albeit much appreciated services – to render, but too rarely as persons with valuable ideas and insights to contribute. I felt that, at best, religious women were often appreciated more for what they did than for what they are, as women and as religious.

During my pre-ordination retreat at Vicarello, near Rome, in early July 1967, I read again more carefully some of the conciliar documents about the Church, about the pastoral office of bishops, and about religious life; and my convictions about the obligations of a bishop in respect of religious women were deepened. How could I, as bishop-elect, preparing for my episcopal ordination and the beginning of my episcopal ministry, fail to be moved by the Council's description of the religious state as a state which

> reveals in a unique way that the Kingdom of God and its overmastering necessities are superior to all earthly considerations. (*Lumen gentium* 44)

During that pre-ordination retreat, I reflected, as bishop-elect, that I was being mysteriously called by Christ and was about to be set apart by the Holy Spirit to be 'listed' among the successors of the Twelve Apostles (cf. Acts 1:26). I was being sent by God to reveal Christ to the world through the Church. How could I forget that, as the Council says:

> [It is through religious that] to believers and non-believers alike, the Church truly wishes to give an increasingly clearer revelation of Christ. Through them Christ should be shown contemplating on the mountain, announcing God's kingdom to the multitude, healing the sick and the maimed, turning sinners to wholesome fruit, blessing children, doing good to all, and always obeying the will of the Father who sent him. (*Lumen gentium* 46)

During the ordination liturgy, I was asked:

> Are you willing to teach, by word and example, what you learn from the divinely inspired Scriptures to the people for whom you are consecrated?

I answered:

> 'I am.'

I could not forget that the opening paragraph of the *Decree on the Appropriate Renewal of the Religious Life* says that religious institutes take their origin from

> the teaching and example of the Divine Master, [who] laid the foundation for a pursuit of perfect charity through the exercise of the evangelical counsels; and... such a pursuit serves as a blazing emblem of the heavenly kingdom. (*Perfectae caritatis* 1)

It follows that the vocation of a bishop and the vocation of a religious are closely linked; and in the course of my episcopal ministry I have come to realise more and more clearly that, in God's plan, each is called to support and encourage and inspire the other in our common following of the Lord.

The sense of my responsibility towards religious has been deepened by subsequent insights into the theology of the Church and of religious life, particularly as these are authoritatively expounded in documents from the Holy See. I shall refer in particular to the 1978 document, Mutuae relationes: *Directives for the Mutual Relations between Bishops and Religious in the Church.*

Here we read:

> The Bishop, by virtue of his very ministry, is held to account for the growth in holiness of all his faithful. (7)

How much more exacting that account must be in the case of religious, 'inasmuch as they are called to be, as it were, specialists in prayer' (16). The document goes on:

> In the vast pastoral field of the Church, a new and very important place has been accorded to women. Once zealous helpers of the Apostles (cf. Acts 18, 26; Romans 16:1ff.), women should contribute their apostolic activity today in the ecclesial community, realising faithfully the mystery of their created and revealed identity, and taking notice of their growing influence in civil society.
>
> Bishops should, therefore, in view not only of the number of religious women, but especially of their importance in the life of the Church, do their utmost to see that the principle of their greater ecclesial promotion be put into effect, lest the people of God remain deprived of that special assistance, which they alone, by virtue of the gifts conferred on them by God in their quality of women, can offer. (49-50)

Begging mercy for my failings

As I look back over the past fifteen years, and examine myself in the light of these and so many other responsibilities of a bishop, I am very conscious of much that was sinful in those years, in things that I did and in things that I failed to do. I simply ask all of you to pray for me to the Lord our God.

In this, our last Mass together, you are yourselves about to renew your religious commitment and, as you do, I shall be renewing my own commitment as priest and bishop. May God, the source of all holiness, he who alone is holy, he who takes away the sins of the world, grant us forgiveness for the past and grace and strength and courage for a new beginning in the future to which he calls us.

As I now leave my home in Ardagh and Clonmacnois for my old and new home in Down and Connor, I hope and I believe that your friendship and affection will accompany me and that your prayers will follow me and continue to support me in the future. Our brotherhood and sisterhood in Christ is not affected by distance. When we pray before the Lord we shall remain together, you and I, inseparable in his love.

The prayers of Mary, the Mother of Jesus, will be with us. It was at her prayer that Jesus' first miracle was wrought at Cana. Through her intercession, and through your prayers united with hers, may Jesus bring about the great miracle of peace and reconciliation in the North, so that his glory may be seen and his disciples may believe in him.

I know that there have been occasions when I have misunderstood or wronged or hurt or been insensitive towards the needs or feelings of this one or that one among you. In this Mass, in every Mass, we receive and we exchange forgiveness and reconciliation.

I have been re-reading in its context in the Letter to the Hebrews the words of my episcopal motto: *Jesus Christus, heri et hodie.* From there I quote:

> We too should... keep running steadily in the race we have

started. Let us not lose sight of Jesus; ... and then you will not give up for want of courage.... We have been given possession of an unshakeable kingdom. Let us therefore hold on to the grace we have been given.... Jesus Christ is the same today as he was yesterday and as he will be forever. (Hb 12:1-4; 13:8)

Nothing can separate us from the love of Christ, or separate us from one another in his love and service; and so:

> May the God of hope bring you [and me] such joy and peace in [our] faith that the power of the Holy Spirit will remove all bounds to hope. (cf. Romans 15:13)

My concluding wish for you today and my continuing prayer in the future is this:

> May the God of peace make you perfect and holy; and may you all be kept safe and blameless, spirit, soul and body, for the coming of our Lord, Jesus Christ. God has called you, and he will not fail you. (1 Th 5:23)

> The grace of the Lord Jesus be with you. My love is with you all in Christ Jesus. (1 Co 16:23-24)

CHAPTER TWELVE

NO LASTING CITY

There is no lasting city for us in this life but we look for
one in the life to come.
(Hb 13:14)

DOWN AND CONNOR
1982-90

(a) Arrival in Down and Connor
(i) Statement at Press Conference
8 September 1982
(in Dublin on the day of the announcement
of my nomination as Bishop of Down and Connor)

Priorities of a bishop
During the past fifteen years of my life as bishop in Ardagh and
Clonmacnois, I have had some opportunity to define certain
priorities for a bishop at this time in the history of the Church in
Ireland and in the world. The documents of the Second Vatican
Council and my participation as adviser to Bishop William Philbin
and then to Cardinal William Conway during the four sessions of
the Council from 1962 to 1965, and my co-operation in at least the
outer fringes of some of the preparation of conciliar documents,
especially on priestly ministry (*Presbyterorum ordinis*) and on the

Church in the modern world (*Gaudium et spes*), helped to form a new vision of the role of a bishop at this time, both in its exciting challenge and in its formidable complexity.

I list some priorities here, realising that I am describing ideals, and that it is extremely difficult to combine them with one another and to try to achieve them amidst the multifarious matters to which a bishop finds himself called day by day to attend.

1. A bishop must be a man of prayer; whatever and however many and urgent be the other demands upon his time, he must at all costs make time for prayer. The Vatican Council reminds him that, before all else, the bishop is 'a sanctifier of his priests, religious and people, a leader in prayer, an animator of the life of the spirit'.

2. A bishop must be a teacher of the faith. He must be ready to give doctrinal and moral guidance to his priests and people in the many and complex problems confronting Christians in today's world, at personal, family, professional, social and, in the non-party political sense of the term, at political levels with a moral dimension. He must try to keep in touch with theological development in the Church as a whole and with intellectual trends in contemporary culture. For this purpose, he must try to find time for serious reading and must seek discussion and dialogue with people competent in the various theological, scientific and cultural disciplines. He must acquire familiarity with the use of the mass media, which play such an enormous role in contemporary culture. As far as is in his power, the bishop must try to use every available medium for proclaiming the Good News of Jesus Christ and for endeavouring to 'capture every thought into obedience' to the truth of Jesus Christ (cf. 2 Corinthians 10:5).

3. At the same time, the bishop must try to be constantly available for meeting with his priests, respecting confidentiality but making time for relaxed, friendly, unhurried and informal relationships

with them. He must have a special care for priests who are ill or infirm or retired or under stress or in any kind of difficulty.

4. The bishop must take a special interest in the welfare of religious communities of men and women. He must try to visit them regularly and give them any support which he can in living their consecrated lives, appreciating not only their incalculable contribution to education, healthcare and social welfare and charitable works, but also and especially their witness to God and his Kingdom by their lives of prayer and pursuit of holiness. He must have a particular care for contemplative religious communities and for persons in the world consecrated to contemplative life. He must try to ensure in particular that religious women are allowed to make their full contribution to the life of the Church and are given every encouragement and facility for spiritual growth and for ongoing scriptural, theological and liturgical education.

5. The bishop must also make time for personal contact with lay people, making himself accessible to them and available for meeting with them with as little formality as is possible. Person-to-person and face-to-face contact have become more important than ever in our age. The bishop has to try to be 'the Church with a human face'. Barriers and distances of misplaced awe which may still persist have gradually to be eliminated.

6. The bishop must have special care for the aged and the sick, visiting hospitals and senior citizen's homes. He must have a preferential love for the poor.

7. The bishop must aim at being an efficient administrator, and, if he has not himself the gifts or the training for efficient administration, he must seek the help of people, including lay people, with those gifts and that training, and must provide the technical and technological resources for efficient administration. It is true that the bishop must be much more

than a good administrator; but administrative efficiency is an important part of the pastoral service of people. It matters to priests that their material conditions of living are attended to, that sickness benefit and retirement and pension schemes are adequate. It matters to priests and to people that their letters be answered and their business attended to. It matters to priests and to people that careful planning be devoted to the building, renovation and maintenance of churches and schools, and that church buildings are designed or re-designed in keeping with the new insights into liturgy and sacred art brought to us by the Second Vatican Council.

8. The bishop must have a special care for youth. New forms of ministry to youth have to be explored. Young people are living through a period of great change, both in the Church and in society, and the pace and quality of change are likely to increase in the coming decades. Catechetical methods and programmes must be adapted to their new needs and adequate to help them to find answers to their questioning in a world that is going to be very different from that of their parents and indeed from that of their bishops. Ongoing post-school formation in faith programmes for young people is essential. Opportunities for listening to young people and for dialogue between the bishop and young people are essential.

9. The bishop must have a constant concern for social justice. Familiarity with the social teaching of the Church, as outlined in the great social encyclicals of the Popes, must be part of the theological formation of priests and must be brought to the knowledge of the people. The work long carried on by the Christus Rex Society, founded by the Maynooth ordination class of 1941, for the study and implementation of the Church's social teaching, is as relevant as ever in this generation. The bishop is one who is sent to continue in our time the mission of the Lord Jesus Christ who, in his first sermon in his native village of Nazareth, announced that he was sent in the Spirit of the Lord

'to bring the good news to the poor, to proclaim liberty to captives ... to set the downtrodden free' (cf. Luke 4:18). The themes of human dignity, human rights and social and international justice are an inseparable part of the proclamation of the Gospel. The search for peace and justice and the cessation of all violence in the Northern part of our country is one of the tests of relevance for the Church in Ireland at this time.

10. For all this, and in addition to friendly and informal contact with his priests, the bishop must seek more formal dialogue and consultation with the priests of his diocese and with lay people in planning ways of working together in a purposive way for addressing the pastoral needs and the social problems of the people of the diocese. Collaborative ministry between bishop, priests and lay people is one of the great needs and the great resources of the Church in our time. The bishop must also make his contribution to the work of the bishops of the country as a whole in their task of spreading the message of the Second Vatican Council and implementing its directives at national level.

11. A bishop must enter wholeheartedly, both doctrinally and practically, into the work of ecumenism, sharing fully in the new understanding of the search for Christian unity which has been one of the fruits of the Second Vatican Council. The pursuit of ecumenical dialogue and the furtherance of mutual understanding between the religious communities in Northern Ireland are a Christian priority at this time.

12. Responsive to 'the signs of the times', the bishop must be attentive to the insights of women and ensure that their gifts are fully utilised in the life and mission of the Church. The development of an authentic Christian feminism, enriched by the figure of Mary, the Mother of the Redeemer, and by the documents of the Second Vatican Council developed subsequently by the insights of Pope Paul VI and Pope John Paul II, must be an important concern for a bishop in our time.

(ii) Installation Homily
in St Peter's Cathedral, Belfast
Sunday, 17 October 1982

As I look down on this packed church, filled to overflowing with
people representing every parish in Down and Connor and
particularly representing this parish of St Peter's, my first thought
is: 'This is the real Falls'. The Falls Road has received such a bad
press over recent years, it has for many such a negative image; but
today we see its true face. Thank God for it.

Conflicting emotions
It is with mixed feelings and conflicting emotions that I speak for
the first time as Bishop of Down and Connor. My first feeling as I
stand here is, I gladly confess, a feeling of contentment at being
once more among the priests of Down and Connor, with whom I
shared the best years of my priesthood, with whom I prayed and
worked, debated and laughed, for twenty-six years as priest. It is
good too to be back among the people 'I was reared with', and with
whom I formed strong friendships which were never lost but were
in some sense suspended fifteen years ago. The roots put down in
boyhood and young manhood are very deep. The memories and
the emotions associated with the word 'home' are never obliterated.
Home in the deepest sense for me had always to be Loughguile and
the Diocese of Down and Connor, St Malachy's College, the
Department of Scholastic Philosophy in Queen's University. These
formed me and made me. How could I not be glad to be coming
back home?

Yet there is great and deep sadness too at leaving Ardagh and
Clonmacnois, which has been my home for the past fifteen years:
and I use the word 'home' without any qualification or reservation.
I took that diocese to my heart, and I hope that this was reciprocal.
That diocese formed me and made me as a bishop. It will always be
part of what I am. Ardagh and Clonmacnois is a great diocese. I
have always been proud that it was my father's diocese. I shall
always be proud to have been its bishop for fifteen years. Leaving

Ardagh and Clonmacnois was a second 'leaving home' in my life, and was an experience of real loneliness and pain.

Yet consolation comes again in experiencing the warmth and sincerity of the welcome which has been extended to me by the clergy and the people of Down and Connor and which is so evident today in St Peter's Parish. This leaves no possible doubt in me that I am welcome back among you as your bishop. This gives solid substance to my hope that much can be done for Christ in the years ahead with the co-operation and the support of priests, religious and lay men and women of the whole diocese. The work is Christ's and he is working with us as we set to our task.

I confess also on this occasion to a feeling of prideful humility at becoming bishop of this great diocese of Down and Connor. All its priests and people are proud to belong to Down and Connor. I am proud to have been called to be its bishop. Proud: but also humble at the sense of my own inadequacy, my deep sense of physical and especially spiritual inadequacy at joining in the distinguished succession of bishops of Down and Connor. Only the knowledge that I am sent could give me courage to accept the responsibilities of this ministry.

The problems ahead

Finally, apprehension seizes me on this day; for the past fifteen years have changed so much in the life of society and of the Church in our diocese and in our city and a host of new problems has arisen. The implanting of violence in our midst has brought a harvest of bitter grapes, grapes of wrath, grapes of sorrow. Violence is the greatest evil in our midst. Violence is a primary malignancy, with secondary growths eating into the healthy tissues of whole communities. We must, by every means in our power, shun violence, reject violence. We must never do anything which would, directly or indirectly, give or seem to give support and encouragement to violence. To end violence in a just and reconciled society is our most urgent task.

Clustering around this, in part caused by it and certainly immensely accelerated by it, is a multitude of religious, spiritual and moral problems, whose litany is familar and need not today be repeated. Most of our problems are seriously aggravated by the effects of economic depression. In times of economic growth those who are already privileged become more so. In times of depression, it is the unprivileged who suffer the most. Always the gap between richer and poorer widens. This is not only an economic but also a spiritual problem. Unemployment, bad housing and badly planned housing, lack of basic amenities and of a decent human environment, lessen people's self-respect and deprive them of the respect due to them by virtue of their human dignity. They are conditions which make the struggle for virtue more difficult. They are conditions which help to foster violence. They stand condemned by the Gospel. A society which tolerates them is not truly Christian.

Furthermore, socio-economic change has direct effects upon religious allegiance and upon spiritual and moral values. It is certain that we are now in a new chapter in the history of the Church in Ireland. We are in a phase of evangelisation and re-evangelisation, in a decade where cessation of religious practice and secularisation are spreading, here in Ireland, to an extent and with a rapidity which few would have thought possible only twenty or even ten years ago. This is the problem which will dominate our thinking, praying and acting as pastors in the future. Our problems will be spiritually to feed those who hunger, because they think they have lost God and now do not know what it is they are hungering for; our problems will be to make the weak in faith strong; to bandage the bruises of the sick at heart and the discouraged; to heal the hurt and the rejected, especially those who feel hurt and rejected by the Church; to bring together again the scattered and divided; to go in search for the strays, to bring back the lost (cf. Ezekiel 34:2-5) – these are the problems which we face together as co-workers with Christ at this point in our history; these must be the basis of our pastoral planning for the future.

A bishop is one sent
The problems are enormous, intimidating. But the ultimate and the

sufficient consolation of the bishop is that he bears the mitre of teacher and sanctifier, and carries the crozier of the shepherd among his people because he was sent to them – sent to them by the Father to preach to them Christ's Good News from God; sent to act in the person and the power of Christ among them; indeed sent to strive to be Christ for them.

Bishop Philbin came here because he was similarly sent twenty years ago. He was my teacher of theology in Maynooth, and his learning inspired me, his research stimulated me, as student and as postgraduate. His friendship and his encouragement accompanied me in the years that followed. His episcopal leadership in Clonfert and throughout Ireland continued to be an inspiration. He was my bishop for five years in Down and Connor.

Bishop Philbin came here in 1962, the year in which the Second Vatican Council opened. He did me the great privilege of inviting me to be a theological adviser at the first session of the Council. For twenty years, he has not spared himself in the work of the Lord in some of the most terrible years of conflict and turmoil ever seen in the history of the diocese. Today, he could truly say, in the words of St Paul's farewell address at Miletus:

> My conscience is clear as far as all of you are concerned, for I have without faltering put before you the whole of God's purpose (Ac 20:26-27).

May 'the word of Christ's grace', which he has preached and which he has sacramentally administered, with such courage and such energy, bring him peace and joy in the rest which he has so well earned. May the Christ in whom he placed his trust, as his episcopal motto, *Scio cui credidi,* attests, be his reward.

Today a new bishop is sent. The meaning of a bishop's ordination or, in this case, his installation, is to be found only in the mystery of Christ's being sent by his Father and, in turn, choosing, forming and sending his Twelve Apostles to continue his mission in the world. Between today's bishops and the Twelve, and between them and Christ, the link is historical, extending across the centuries and the decades; the link is at the same time vertical, a link with the Christ of Glory, the *Pantocrator*, sitting as Lord at the right hand of the Father, but working with the bishops of his Church now, and through them continuing his mission in the world until he comes again.

The guarantee of this twofold link between your new bishop and the Twelve is his communion with the College of Bishops who hold succession from the Twelve Apostles. This communion is guaranteed by communion with the Head of the Episcopal College, the present successor of Peter, the first of the Apostles. The reading of the Apostolic Letter in which Pope John Paul II announces his nomination of the new Bishop of Down and Connor and sends him to this See, is the guarantee to all of you that the mission of Christ, the mission of the Apostles, continues without interruption among you; and that, through your Bishop and the priests whom he ordains and calls to share his work, Christ's word is being truly proclaimed, Christ's sacraments validly celebrated, Christ himself truly present among you, with power coming out from him through his ministers to heal and strengthen you. It is the guarantee that Christ's Spirit is guiding and empowering his Church for your salvation. I repeat to you today words spoken by St Augustine:

> Believe in that Church.
> Live in that Church.
> Be that Church.

In the power of the Spirit

The Church of today is the same as the Church whose faith and life are described in the Acts of the Apostles. Two things in the Book of the Acts are very striking: first, how the ministry of the disciples is shown to be a continuation of the public ministry of Jesus Christ; second, how the ministry of the disciples, like Christ's own ministry, is shown as being carried on in the power of the Spirit of Jesus. Jesus began his work of preaching in Galilee, St Luke tells us, 'with the power of the Spirit in him' (Lk 4:14). So must your new bishop know that he begins his ministry today in the power of that same Spirit. The Church of Acts was certain that the Spirit of Jesus empowered and guided and controlled its work; but the Church of the Acts had no greater and no other reason to believe that the Spirit of Jesus worked with it and through it than we ourselves have today for believing that the same Spirit of Jesus works with us and through us in our time. For your part, just as St Peter said in the first of all Christian sermons on the day of Pentecost, 'what you are seeing and hearing today is the outpouring of that Holy Spirit' (cf. Acts 2:33).

Therefore, as a further decade begins in the life of the Church of Down and Connor, we should be 'aglow with the Spirit' (Rm 12:11). We can pray with confidence and with great fervour the prayer of Pope John Paul II:

> Let your Spirit come down.
> Let your Spirit come down
> and renew the face of the earth,
> and renew the face of the Church,
> renew the face of our land.

The spirit of forgiveness, love and peace
What the Spirit brings is detailed by St Paul. His list is sometimes called 'the fruits of the Spirit'. They are:

> love, joy, peace, patience, kindness, goodness, trustfulness, gentleness and self-control. (Ga 5:22)

What is often all too evident in our society is not this, but the works of the 'Anti-Spirit', or what St Paul calls 'the flesh', opposed to the work of the Spirit. St Paul enumerates these:

> feuds and wrangling: jealousy, bad temper and quarrels; disagreements, factions, envy.... (Ga 5:19-20)

Between our two divided communities here in the North there is a sad lack of trustfulness. There is too much readiness to impute ulterior motives, even sinister intentions, each to the others. There is a marked tendency to hold whole communities guilty of the crimes of a few. The mutual imputation of collective or community guilt is one great manifestation of mentalities that have not yet been really converted to Christ and pervaded by his Spirit.

There is too much mistrust, suspicion, fear; stemming often from sheer prejudice, misinformation and misrepresentation. There are some in our society who foment bigotry, who promote prejudice, who exploit suspicion and fear. This, surely, is not the way of the Kingdom of God. Commitment to ecumenism is a clear and urgent Christian duty. Without an ecumenical spirit, it is not possible to be a good Christian, to be a good Catholic. The Vatican Council leaves no room for doubt about this.

An essential condition of the trustfulness which the Spirit brings is that each community be ready to accept the other as the other sees and knows itself. Some in each community desire to impose on the other their own conception of what the other community should be. Some insist on laying down their own terms and conditions as the only terms and conditions on which they will accept the other. Instead, each community must come to accept the other, not as we want them to be, not on condition that they accept our definition of their identity, but as they define and identify themselves. We are all called at this time to a common Christian task, to work for mutual recognition in each community of the complete legitimacy and legality, the equal dignity and rights, of the other community, with its own self-defined identity, its own sense of loyalty, its own political aspirations, so long as these are peacefully held and peacefully promoted. To work for this is a true work of reconciliation, a beginning of forgiveness, a hope for a new future.

Until the wrongs of the past are forgiven, there can be no endurable future. The duty of a Christian bishop is to practise and to promote forgiveness and to proclaim reconciliation. St Paul says:

> It is all God's work. It was God who reconciled us to himself through Christ and gave us the work of handing on this

reconciliation.... God ... has entrusted to us the news that [people] are reconciled. So we are ambassadors for Christ; it is as though God were appealing through us, and the appeal that we make in Christ's name is: Be reconciled to God. (2 Co 5:18-20)

The work of reconciliation will also be a work of liberation. We are prisoners of our fears, our suspicions and our hates. Only Christ can set us free. 'Where the Spirit of the Lord is, there is freedom' (2 Co 3:18).

There is only Christ

Since my appointment and at my arrival, some have been asking: 'What solutions have you to propose? What have you to offer?' To such questions the only reply I can give or want to give is this: 'I have no solutions – except Jesus Christ. I have nothing to offer – except Jesus Christ and his Gospel.' As Pope John Paul said in his first address as Pope, as he began his papal ministry:

> The greatest service which the Church can give to the cause of justice and of peace is to open the hearts of men to Jesus Christ; to open doors for Jesus Christ.

The deepest conviction of my life is that Jesus Christ and he alone is the ultimate solution to all human problems. I would have no business being a bishop unless I could say: 'Life to me, of course, is Christ' (Ph 1:21). 'There is only Christ; he is everything and he is in everything' (Col 3:11).

Therefore I make no apologies for having nothing to preach but the Gospel of Jesus Christ. As St Paul said:

> I am not ashamed of the Good News: It is the power of God saving all who have faith. (Rm 1:16)

Mary, our hope and our youth

Faith in the Gospel of Jesus Christ is inseparable from hope. Difficulties, setbacks, failures, years of fruitless effort, must not and cannot dim the hope of the Christian.

> Sufferings bring patience ... and patience brings perseverance, and perseverance brings hope, and this hope is not deceptive, because the love of God has been poured into our hearts by the Holy Spirit which has been given us. (Rm 5:4-5)

Situations become hopeless only when Christians abandon hope; but then, whether they realise it or not, they would be abandoning the Gospel of Christ. The Gospel does not allow a Christian to abandon hope. The ministry of a bishop must be a ministry of hope. His prayer and his message must be those of St Paul:

> May the God of hope bring you such joy and peace in your faith that the power of the Holy Spirit will remove all bounds to hope. (Rm 15:13)

Hope is a distinctive quality of youth. Not only must we mobilise the Christian hope of our young people; we ourselves must try, with them, to remain young in the enthusiasm with which we set to work for Christ.

Mary, the Mother of the Lord, she of whom our Irish ancestors spoke as 'the flowery, chalk-white virgin', she 'who brings flowers upon the earth again', she will keep us close to the springs of our youth. When my mother died, Monsignor Arthur Ryan – that great adornment of our diocese whose presence we miss – wrote to me. He said: 'As long as a man's mother is alive, there is still someone for whom he is always young'. May Mary, Mother of the Lord and Mother of us disciples of the Lord, keep us young in our love and service of her Son, the Eternal Youth, who is constantly 'making all things new' (Rv 21:5).

When life's race is run
Because of all this, and with God's help,

> there will be no weakening on our part ... none of the
> reticence of those who are ashamed, no deceitfulness or
> watering down the word of God; but the way we commend
> ourselves to every human being with a conscience is by
> stating the truth openly in the sight of God ... for it is not
> ourselves that we are preaching but Christ Jesus as the Lord,
> and ourselves as your servants for Jesus' sake. (2 Co 4:2, 4-
> 5)

When I finish my episcopal ministry in Down and Connor, when
my life's race, be it long or be it short, is run, may God in his mercy
grant to me to be able to say what St Paul said in that farewell
address at Miletus:

> Life to me is not a thing to waste words on, provided that
> when I finish my race, I have carried out the mission the
> Lord Jesus gave me – and that was to bear witness to the
> Good News of God's grace. (Ac 20:24)

(iii) Address to the Priests of Down and Connor in St Malachy's College, Belfast
26 October 1982

My dear brother priests, it is good to be back home.

It is good to be with the priests of Down and Connor among whom I worked for twenty-six years, until 1967; including the priests I studied with and was ordained with, those I did my annual retreats with, those with whom and among whom I worked. These have always remained my friends; I hope as bishop to work in continuing friendship with them.

It is good to be among the priests who were my former students. They have learned much since they sat in front of me in scholastic philosophy classrooms. Their teacher has, I hope, learnt some things too. I tried, though with many lapses, to be their friend as well as their teacher. I hope that the feeling was reciprocated – or the lapses forgiven; and that our future work together will be in friendship.

It is good also to be among the priests I have not yet personally met, whether young priests whom I did not have as students, or priests who have come to help us in the acute shortage of priests which the diocese experienced in some recent years. They are welcome amongst us and their help is greatly valued. I hope that they feel happy in our midst.

It is good also to be working with the religious priests, who have given and continue to give the diocese such indispensable services, spiritual and pastoral, and with whom I hope to work in harmonious and mutually beneficial partnership.

It is good, finally, to have in the diocese our contemplative brothers, the Trappists in Portglenone, and our contemplative sisters, the Poor Clares and the Adoration Sisters. Without their prayer 'on the mountain', we should not have the strength or courage to battle on the pastoral plain.

Authority and responsible obedience
St Paul said to Timothy: 'To want to be a presiding elder is to want

to do a noble work' (1 Tm 3:1). *Bonum opus desiderat.* We used cynically to translate this: 'Is looking for a good job'! But the office of bishop is one whose goodness comes only from the Lord. The joy and consolation it brings come from knowing that one is working for the Lord in shepherding and 'overseeing' his Church in a diocese. The ministry of a bishop makes no sense and gives no joy or life unless it is seen and lived within the mystery of the Lord and his mission of salvation, and within the mystery of his Church.

Yet if, or since, one is called to be bishop, there is no better time to be one than in the present period in the life of the Church. Now, thanks to the Second Vatican Council, we know that authority has to find new expressions and has to be exercised in new ways. It has to be exercised in dialogue, in listening, in partnership, in brotherhood and in friendship. It has to be exercised in service.

I am deeply convinced that authority is not eliminated or diminished thereby. On the contrary, I believe that it is strengthened. It is strengthened because then it can be willingly accepted; it can evoke responsible obedience. Authority deferred to in unconvinced conformity, or accepted in unwilling and perhaps resentful submission, can hardly be either the authority or the obedience postulated by the Gospel. Authority and obedience in the context of the relations between a bishop and his priests (or a bishop and his people – and the same can be said of a priest and his people) can be understood and can be lived only in the context of the Gospel. They are a necessary condition of fidelity to the Gospel and of the following of Christ and the carrying on of Christ's work in the work through the Church. We are not coerced into following Christ. He says: 'If anyone wants to be a follower of mine...' (Mt 16:24). But because, as priests, we do want to follow Christ, then, as a condition and a consequence, we must follow those whom he has appointed to 'be on guard ... for all the flock of which the Holy Spirit has made [them] the overseers, to feed the Church of God' (Ac 20:28). The bishop at his ordination makes a promise of obedience to the Pope, successor of Peter and Head of the Episcopal College, just as a priest, at his ordination, makes a promise of obedience to his bishop. This promise could entail hard consequences for the priest; it can entail hard sacrifices for the bishop too. The sentence from St Matthew which I began reads in full:

> If anyone wants to be a follower of mine, let him renounce himself and take up his cross and follow me. (Mt 16:24-25)

Friend and brother

The office of a bishop is enriched nowadays by the inspiring doctrine of the Church and of the ministry of a bishop given to us by the Vatican Council. It is good for a bishop now to have the model of a bishop set before him by the Council. It is good for a priest now to have the model of priestly ministry spelled out inspiringly for him by the Council. We must consciously work together to base all our future relationships on the models of bishop and priest given us by the Vatican Council.

So far as a bishop is concerned, we must turn especially to the document *Christus Dominus,* the Decree on the Bishop's Pastoral Office in the Church. This tells the bishop that he

> should always welcome priests with a special love ... he should regard his priests as sons and friends.... (16)

> Hence, for the sake of greater service to souls, let the bishop engage in discussion with his priests, even collectively, especially about pastoral matters. This he should do not only occasionally but, as far as possible, at fixed intervals. (28)

Fraternal co-operation of priests

If as bishop I were to make this my constant aim, it would not be any act of virtue on my part. It would simply be my plain duty. I have no business being a bishop or doing the work of a bishop unless this is how I try to be and to do.

But all this will remain mere pious talk unless you work with me to make it reality. For myself, I wish, not just to talk, but also to listen; and there is no use in my listening if I am not to be told the truth, or if I am to be told only the things I like to hear, the things perhaps that flatter me and persuade me that all is well. The work that you and I are put here by the Lord to do is far too serious and far too urgent for that kind of nonsense. It is just waste of time, waste of the Lord's time, the time he gave us to work for his Kingdom. A bishop is called to be a friend to his priests. If a person is to be your friend only when you flatter him, then his friendship is doing no good either to you or to him. We can do Christ's work only when we are together seeking the truth.

Sometimes I won't like the truth. My first reaction could well be one of pain and hurt, or of disbelief. But it will be a healing hurt. If I am told things that I dislike hearing, I make you a promise that I won't dislike the person telling them to me. On the contrary, I shall consider him or her a valued adviser; it is from such as he or she that come those who 'do the truth in love' (cf. Ephesians 4:15).

As I would hope to seek my guidelines for how to be a bishop in the documents of the Council, so you priests must seek your directives for your priestly ministry from the same source, and particularly from the Decree on the Ministry and Life of Priests, *Presbyterorum ordinis*. In reference to your relationship with your bishop, you will read this:

> This union of priests with their bishop is all the more necessary today, since in our present age, for various reasons, apostolic activities are required not only to take on many forms, but to extend beyond the boundaries of one parish or diocese. Hence no priest can in isolation or singlehandedly accomplish his mission in a satisfactory way. He can do so only by joining forces with other priests under the direction of Church authorities. (*Presbyterorum ordinis* 7)

Brotherhood among priests

The Council urges upon priests the need to exercise their pastoral ministry in brotherly co-operation with their fellow priests.

Established in the priestly order by ordination, all priests are united among themselves in an intimate sacramental brotherhood. In a special way, they form one presbytery in a diocese to whose service they are committed under their own bishop.... Hence it is very important that all priests, whether diocesan or religious, always help one another to be fellow-workers on behalf of truth. Each one therefore is united by special bonds of apostolic charity, ministry and brotherhood with the other members of the presbytery....

Each and every priest, therefore, is joined to his brother priests by a bond of charity, prayer and every kind of co-operation....

Consequently, older priests should receive younger priests as true brothers and give them a hand with their first undertakings and assignments in the ministry. They should likewise try to understand the mentality of younger priests, even though it be different from their own, and should follow their projects with good will. For his part, a young priest should respect the age and experience of his seniors. He should discuss plans with them, and willingly co-operate with them in matters which pertain to the care of souls.

Inspired by a fraternal spirit, priests will not neglect hospitality, but cultivate kindliness.... They will be particularly solicitous for priests who are sick, afflicted, overburdened with work, lonely.... (*Presbyterorum ordinis* 8)

Men of prayer

I have left the most important thing to the last. We must, before all else, be men of prayer. We must, like brothers, help one another to be men of prayer. Our greatest service to our people is to be men of prayer. It is not for nothing that traditional names for the liturgy and especially the breviary or Liturgy of the Hours are 'divine service' or 'divine office'. We pray and worship God, publicly and privately, on behalf of our people. This is a service we perform for our people, a duty we discharge towards them. The time we spend on our knees is time that our people have a right to expect from us. If we neglect it, we are failing in our duty to them as well as in our duty to God.

We must try to be holy to save our own souls, and to give God due worship and to follow Christ. We must try to be holy also in order to give our people the priestly service which is their due. We are doing as much for our people, maybe more, when we are praying as when we are out among them administering the sacraments or on pastoral visitation, or meeting them in reception rooms, or attending parish pastoral meetings, or organising parish functions or lobbying for their rights. For the pastoral priest (or for the bishop) it is not a question of praying or working, not even quite praying and working; it is a question of praying as and because one is a busy pastor, of working and preaching and serving as and because one is a man of prayer. All that I have said applies to me as much as, or even more than, it does to you.

Our model in this is the great High Priest himself, Jesus Christ. Amidst the most pressing pastoral activities and demands, Christ always was 'the Man for the Father', the man of prayer. Even when multitudes crowded round the door, when the sick crushed in to be near him, when problems cried out for his attention, when people kept calling out in their need for him, he always made a time and found a place to pray. St Luke tells us:

> His reputation continued to grow, and large crowds gathered to hear him and have their sickness cured; but he would always go off to some place where he could be alone and pray. (Lk 5:15-16)

Unless we are men of prayer, we cannot be truly priests of Jesus Christ, priests like Jesus Christ. Unless we pray, we will not be acting meaningfully in the person of Christ when we preach his Gospel and celebrate his sacraments. Our preaching may make headlines; but it will not move souls or change lives. We want to be, as priests we must be, ways to Christ and ways through Christ to the Father. But, as Father Henri Nouwen has said, 'Unless we are the way, we are in the way.'

Fathers and brothers, unless we pray, we will not be good pastoral priests, the sort of priests the Church wants and the world needs today. Unless we pray we will not even survive as priests in today's world. It is hard for the busy priest to pray. It is hard for the busy bishop to pray. The only way to find time to pray is to pray; and there is no other way. We shall only be trying to learn how to pray every day as long as we live. Only by prayer and nowise without prayer can we build up a deep personal relationship with Jesus Christ; and without that our priesthood will lose its whole meaning for ourselves and for our people.

Mary in the life of a priest

Inseparable from this relationship with Christ is a faith-based and Christ-centred, and also warm and confident, relationship with Mary, the Mother of the Lord. I think we had perhaps in recent years been allowing devotion to Mary to recede somewhat into the background of our public and private prayer. We may have spoken about Mary; but we spoke too little to her. When we spoke about her it was often theologically, intellectually, defensively, almost apologetically. One of Pope John Paul's great contributions to the Church is that he has taught us again not to be afraid of having and of showing a spontaneous and affectionate devotion to Mary.

This devotion stands on solid biblical ground and on sound theological foundations. Let us not think that there is very little about Mary in the Gospels – just peripheral accounts of events she participated in, passing references to her, scant words spoken by her. There is, in fact, a whole rich theology of Mary in the Gospels. It takes on a different colouring in each evangelist, but the four Gospels together provide a real Gospel Mariology. When the Beloved Disciple is referred to in St John, he is meant to be taken as the type and model of all discipleship. He is the disciple, the model of the disciple; and therefore eminently of the priest. On Calvary, the disciple is given Mary by the Lord as his Mother; and with him all disciples, all believers, all Christians, are given Mary as their Mother. This applies particularly to priests. When St John says, 'From that day the disciple made a place for [Mary] in his home' (19:27), we priests must take this as being directed also and paramountly to us. We too must make a place for Mary in our hearts and in our homes.

Mary is called 'full of grace' by the whole Church, following the angel's greeting. Old Gaelic spirituality called her 'Mary of the Graces'. I end with the words which Douglas Hyde wrote as the last paragraph of his book *The Religious Songs of Connaught*:

> They shall go, they shall all go, men and their glory, the writers and the books, the fame of those who have gone, the renown of those who shall come; there is only one thing … that shall be lasting in this world – the grace of God.

May Mary's prayers obtain that grace for us, 'now and at the hour of our death'.

(b) Departure from Down and Connor
November 1990
(i) Farewell Mass with Laity
in St Peter's Cathedral, Belfast
Sunday, 18 November 1990

It is eight years and one month precisely since I first celebrated Mass and preached in this Cathedral at my installation as Bishop of Down and Connor, on 17 October 1982.

On that occasion, I expressed my happiness and contentment at 'being back home' in Down and Connor, my home diocese; a happiness and contentment tinged with sadness at leaving my first diocese of Ardagh and Clonmacnois, where I had spent fifteen extremely happy years. I gave the name *Coming Back Home* to my first pastoral letter, for Lent 1983. I felt then that I was 'home for good' and that I would end my days here, be they short or longer.

God had different plans. Eight years later, I am called to another task in God's vineyard, and am given another place to be my home in these closing years of my life. It is with deep sadness that I leave Down and Connor. There is much apprehension in my heart as I undertake another journey for Christ. I can face it at all only because of my certain knowledge that it is God's will that I go, and that it is a journey to which Christ is calling me. The Holy Father has assured me that he took my age, my health and all the other factors into full consideration. He assured me that he had reflected and prayed much about the appointment to Armagh and that it was his firm decision that I should be appointed Archbishop of that great See. He asked me to see it as God's will and to go forward with courage and in faith. The appointment was something which I never wanted or sought or expected. But one could have no clearer or more direct indication of God's will than the decision of the successor of Peter, to whom Jesus Christ himself said:

> I will give you the keys of the Kingdom of heaven. (Mt 16:19)

> I have prayed for you, Simon, that your faith may not fail, and ... you in your turn must strengthen your brothers. (Lk 22:32)

> Feed my lambs.... Look after my sheep.... Feed my sheep. (Jn 21:16-17)

God's will

It is this which gives me the certainty that God now prepares a new home for me. The true home for the Christian is where God is and waits, where God the Father dwells and calls, where Christ invites us, leaving all things behind, to follow him and be with him, where the Spirit hovers over our troubled thoughts and confused emotions to create light and life. For us there can be no true home except where we make a place for Mary the Mother of Jesus and the Mother of all disciples, and where she makes a place for us. For us there can be no home except where the Church, our Mother, whom St John calls 'the Beloved', the 'Chosen One', 'the Bride of the Lamb', is present in faith and in love.

For us Christians, home is being in God the Father's house, seeking his will and being about his business, as Jesus was (cf. Luke 2:49). Jesus asked us to be ready to 'leave house, brothers, sisters, lands' for his sake and 'for the sake of the Gospel'. If we do this, he promises us reward 'a hundred times over', even 'in this present time' and 'in the world to come, eternal life' (Mk 10:30).

It is because of Christ's call, and putting all my trust in his promise, that I try to go to Armagh with confidence and in peace and hope and even joy, for one's 'Yes' to God must never be a 'Yes, if...', or 'Yes, but...', but a wholehearted and unconditional 'Yes'. As I try to follow Christ's call, I know that God will be there and that Christ will walk by my side, as he walked beside the two disciples on the way to Emmaus, when it was 'nearly evening and the day was almost over' (cf. Luke 24:29), as it must be in my life at my present age. For the Christian there are always two certainties, first the certainty of one's own helplessness without God; and secondly the certainty about our power to do anything or to accept anything with the help of his grace. Jesus said:

Without me you can do nothing. (Jn 15:5)

He also said:

Nothing is impossible for God. (Mt 19:26)

Things that are impossible for men and women are possible for God. (Lk 18:27)

He gave St Paul the unshakeable confidence with which he could say:

There is nothing I cannot master with the help of the One who gives me strength. (Ph 4:13)

The words would be arrogant but for Paul's total conviction that the power and the achievement do not come from himself but from Christ:

I have worked ... yet not I, but the grace of God within me. (1 Co 15:10)

Workers together for the Kingdom

I welcome this meeting with representatives of the laity of the diocese in the communion of the Eucharist, because it gives me the opportunity of thanking you and through you all the lay faithful of Down and Connor for all the support and co-operation, all the loyalty and affirmation and encouragement, all the love and the affection which you have given to me over the past eight years, as together we tried to be more and more fully and actively the Church in Down and Connor. Lay people sometimes do not realise the extent to which bishops and priests need the affirmation and encouragement and support, and above all the prayers, of their lay people. At the recent Synod of Bishops in Rome, on the theme of the formation of priests, many bishops spoke of this need, on their own behalf and on behalf of their priests. That support and encouragement and those prayers have always been given to me by the people of Down and Connor, and have been for me an immense comfort and strength. They have brought me hope in moments of discouragement, consolation in days of sorrow and new energy in days of weariness. This is what makes the Church a communion of faith and love.

There have been times in the past when the word 'Church' was used as though it meant the hierarchy or the clergy, or as though the laity were something distinct from 'the Church', or at least as though the laity were passive members of the Church, not full and active participants in the Church's life and mission. This was never true. Any appearance of truth which it might ever have had has been taken away by the Second Vatican Council and by the renewal of the Church since then. In the words of *Christifideles laici*, the conclusive document following the 1987 Synod of Bishops on the Laity, we know that we all, bishops, priests, religious and laity together, are called to be fellow-workers, labouring side by side in the vineyard of the Lord. *Christifideles laici* reflects on the words of Christ in the parable of the vineyard:

> You go into my vineyard too. (Mt 20:7)

The document goes on:

> *You go too.* The call is a concern not only of pastors, clergy, and men and women religious. The call is addressed to everyone: lay people as well are personally called by the Lord, from whom they receive a mission on behalf of the Church and the world. (*Christifideles laici* 2)

It then quotes the Vatican Council, especially its *Decree on the Apostolate of Lay People*:

> The Council makes an earnest plea in the Lord's name that all lay people give a glad, generous and prompt response to the impulse of the Holy Spirit and to the voice of Christ,

who is giving them an especially urgent invitation at this moment. The Lord himself renews his invitation to all the lay faithful to come closer to him every day.... They ought to associate themselves with him in his saving mission. Once again he sends them into every town and place where he himself is to come. (*Christifideles laici* 2)

Social justice

When I was ordained Bishop of Ardagh and Clonmacnois in 1967, and when I was installed as Bishop of Down and Connor in 1982, I outlined some priorities as I saw them for a bishop at this time in the history of the Church: among them were to work for renewal in every area of the Church's life, in fidelity to the Second Vatican Council; and to work for social justice as an integral part of the proclamation and the living of the Gospel of Jesus Christ.

The Holy Spirit has led the Church to see that renewal in all its aspects is closely linked with the calling of the lay faithful to their full and proper place in the life and mission of the Church. This in turn is closely connected with the promotion of social justice and with the struggle to transform society into greater harmony with the Gospel. *Christifideles laici* calls attention to two temptations to which committed lay people can be exposed: one is to become so involved in what may be called purely internal Church tasks (what some would call 'churchy concerns') that they neglect 'their responsibilities in the professional, social, cultural and political world', and the other is to allow a gap to develop in their day-to-day existence between their faith and prayer, on the one hand, and on the other their lifestyle and patterns of behaviour (*Christifideles laici* 2). The Gospel is for living and nor merely for speaking about, and even not solely for praying. The Irish bishops, in their pastoral letter *The Work of Justice* (1977), said:

> One of the urgent needs in the Church today is to remove the partitions separating religion from life and tending to keep religion confined to Sundays and to churches. We must bring the faith into everyday life. We must take

religion out into the streets, the factories, the offices and the farms.

In the area of social justice, I wish to salute and to thank those many lay men and women, professional people, business people, management and marketing specialists, who have responded to the call of Catholics Caring and have worked so effectively over recent years in many job creation and enterprise development projects for the benefit of deprived areas. This is true Christian lay involvement. This is genuine application of the Gospel to society. Their time and work, voluntarily given, their skills and experience offered without any personal profit or gain or selfish advantage, have already put several hundreds of people in real jobs and carry promise of more jobs to come, and this in areas of intolerable levels of unemployment.

I applaud what has been accomplished in the field of employment and small enterprise through the work of the West Belfast Enterprise Board and in Kennedy Way, in Glenwood Enterprises, in Colin Glen and in many other local enterprise centres, and I applaud the new North Howard Street Development, launched the other day. I welcome what is being done in the Ashton Development in North Belfast and what is currently being planned in St Matthew's Parish, Ballymacarret, in East Belfast.

We need much more industrial development in the unemployment blackspots like West and North Belfast and parts of East Belfast. The will to work is there; the 'trainability' and skill potential of the available workforce are very high. These areas need jobs. They want jobs and they deserve jobs. I hope government and statutory agencies and voluntary enterprise boards and development groups will work still more closely and effectively together for the good of communities neglected for far too long. There is scarcely any more important precondition of peace in Northern Ireland than this.

Housing
I welcome the completion of the first phase of new housing to

replace demolished blocks of flats in Divis. I welcome the long overdue beginning of the demolition scheme for Unity Flats. I congratulate the Housing Executive on the high quality of replacement housing which is being provided in these areas. This will correspond with the rights and entitlement of a people who have preserved their dignity in spite of all the difficulties created for them by decades of living in a degrading environment. I hope that the demolition and replacement will not be too long dragged out because of budget cuts.

A living Church

Christ came 'that we might have life and might have it to the full'. We are all called to live that life as individuals and as communities, and to share it with others. We are called to be active members of a living Church, in the diocese, in the parish, in the neighbourhood and in the home. It was for this purpose that in 1987, on the occasion of the Synod on the Laity, we set up the first Diocesan Pastoral Council. That is now a well-established part of the life of the Church in Down and Connor. It aims to reach out into each part of the diocese, and, in collaboration with local priests and lay men and women, to help each parish of the diocese to become a living parish. This is only a beginning in the implementation of *Christifideles laici*, which called for 'a more convinced, extensive and decided appreciation for Parish Pastoral Councils' (*Christifideles laici* 27).

Apostolic groups

But lay involvement in the life of the Church did not begin with the setting up of our Diocesan Pastoral Council or with the publication of *Christifideles laici*; far from it. Many lay associations have been active in the apostolate in the diocese for many decades. The St Vincent de Paul Society, the Legion of Mary, CMAC, CURA and other bodies working in the area of family and marriage ministry, the CYMS, the Pioneers, the Apostolic Work, the Catholic Scouts and Guides, the Catholic Youth Service, the Down and Connor Catholic Family Welfare Society, and many others, all have a long history of dedicated service to the Lord and his Church. I thank God for them all. I offer this Mass for all lay people in the diocese, that they, together with the religious, priests and myself, may live our Christian lives to the full.

Catholic teachers

A special and indeed unique place in the apostolate of lay people is that of Catholic teachers. They share directly with priests and bishops in what is the primary and defining mission of the Church, namely to proclaim the Good News of Jesus Christ and to hand on the faith to the next generation of believers. *Christifideles laici* has some beautiful paragraphs on the special place of children in the life of the Church and on the blessing and example which they bring to the Church, reminding us of the nature of God's Kingdom and of the qualities required of those who are to enter the Kingdom. The Kingdom of God is surely very near in our children. Those who teach them are brought close to the Kingdom and will share abundantly in its blessings. In my own name and in the name of parents and of the whole Christian community in Down and Connor, my dear teachers, I thank you and ask God to bless you.

Call to holiness

All fruitfulness and apostolic work come from Christ. The beautiful image of the vine and the branches brings this out vividly. *Christifideles laici* develops this image, giving to one of its chapters the title, 'All Branches of a Single Vine'. The words of Jesus need to be prayerfully pondered and kept in mind every time we set about planning or doing his work in the world:

> As a branch cannot bear fruit all by itself
> but must remain part of the vine,
> so neither can you, unless you remain in me.
> I am the Vine,
> you are the branches.
> Whoever remains in me, with me in him or her
> bears fruit in plenty,

for cut off from me you can do nothing....
Anyone who does not remain in me
is like a branch that has been thrown away
– he or she withers....
Remain in my love.
(Jn 4-9)

We remain in God's love by our prayer and by our seeking and our doing of God's will and by keeping his commandments. This is how we draw continuously from Christ the life and the sap, the energy and the enthusiasm, which we bring to Christ's work. If we keep this link of prayer with God in Jesus Christ, then everything we do is done for his glory and everything we do builds up his Church. St Paul says:

> Whether you eat or drink or whatever else you do at all, do it for the glory of God. (1 Co 10:11)

Without this constant return to union with God in Christ, then all that we do may well build up our ego, but it will not build the Kingdom; it may make some noise in the media, but it will be the noise of 'the gong booming or the cymbal clashing', not the authentic sound of God's truth working through love (cf. 1 Corinthians 13:1).

The fundamental vocation of the Christian is the call to holiness; and this means the call to live the Christ-life, to become the Christ-person, which baptism calls us and empowers us to do and to be. That is not left to our own human efforts to achieve, for it lies far beyond our human powers. It is God's work in us. We have only to let God do and complete his work in us, the work which he began at our baptism and will complete only when we die in Christ, to rise with him in Glory.

In conclusion, I make the words of St Paul my own for you:

> I never stop thanking God for all the graces you have received through Jesus Christ. I thank him that you have

been enriched in so many ways, especially in your teachers and preachers; the witness to Christ has indeed been strong among you, so that you will not be without any of the gifts of the Spirit while you are waiting for our Lord Jesus Christ to be revealed; and he will keep you steady and without blame until the last day, the day of our Lord Jesus Christ, because God by calling you has joined you to his Son, Jesus Christ; and God is faithful. (1 Co 1:4-9)

Glory be to him whose power, working in us, can do infinitely more than we can ask or imagine; glory be to him from generation to generation in the Church and in Christ Jesus for ever and ever. Amen. (Ep 3:20-21)

In giving glory to God we are joining with Mary, Mother of the Lord, whose whole being was a song of praise to the glory of the grace with whose fullness God has graced her. May God's Holy Spirit be in us, as it was in her, that we may sing with her:

My soul glorifies the Lord,
My spirit exults in God my Saviour.

(ii) Farewell Mass with Young People
in St Peter's Cathedral, Belfast
23 November 1990

It is with great sadness and loneliness that I leave Down and Connor. I go because I have the personal assurance of our Holy Father the Pope that this is God's will for me. I am very conscious of the great honour which the Pope confers upon me by appointing me Archbishop of Armagh, Ireland's Primatial See. But my ties with Down and Connor are anchored deep within my heart, and breaking them pulls at the heart. My contacts with young people are among the most precious of those ties and my memories of Down and Connor youth shall remain among my fondest memories.

I recall my annual visits to the Down and Connor Folk Group Seminars and the Masses celebrated so joyfully at them. I recall the Masses for young people celebrated in Belfast, Downpatrick and Ballymena in 1986. I recall with special happiness our annual pilgrimages to Lourdes, when Down and Connor youth brought such a dimension of joy and enthusiasm to our diocesan pilgrims. There are few things I shall miss more than those marvellous days spent each year at Lourdes. I shall feel lonely not to be with you there in future, although I shall also enjoy being with Armagh pilgrims and young people at Lourdes.

My dear young people, thank you for all that you have given to me and all that you have been for me during my eight years as your bishop. Please continue to pray for me after I leave. Although I shall no longer be 'Cahal your bishop', I hope I can have a tiny whispered place in your prayers after your new bishop is appointed and is mentioned during Mass at the place where I used to be mentioned at each Mass celebrated in Down and Connor over the past eight years.

The joy of youth
One of the Psalms speaks of 'the joy of our youth' (Ps 42:4). The joy which you are bringing to this Mass is the joy which should mark every celebration of Mass. Joy and youth and newness go

together. The Gospel of Christ is Good News; it is all about joy and about newness; a New Testament, a New Covenant, a New Law, a New Creation, a New Heaven and a New Earth, a New Song. All things are made new in Christ. Christ is always new and always young. Christ has only one time dimension: with Christ it is always 'today'. In Christ's time-scale, the time is always 'now'.

You will be living much of your lives in the twenty-first century. A baby born today will have his or her twentieth birthday on 23 November in the year 2010, the tenth year of the twenty-first century and of the third millennium. Some of us won't be around then. It will be your century. What will you be making of it? Will you be making it Christ's century? It will be Christ's century anyhow: 'All time is his and all the ages', as we say during the Easter Vigil. But will it feel Christ's presence through you? Will it reflect Christ's countenance through you?

Christ asked once: 'When the Son of Man comes, will he find any faith upon the earth? (Lk 18:8). Only you can answer that for the twenty-first century. We of the older generation can't. But if the faith is not strong and deep in you in twenty years' time, we who have tried to form Christ in you will have failed you. We will have failed Christ. The author of one of the Psalms prayed to God 'not to let his old grey head go down to the grave in sorrow'. That would have to be our prayer if we were to fail you and to fail Christ.

But I am confident that faith will be strong and deep in you, in your century and your Ireland and in the last two decades of the twentieth century and into the twenty-first. I have personally no anticipation of having to lay down my 'old grey head in the grave' in sorrow and sadness on your account. It is with joyful hope that I look forward to the future, your future.

The Church needs you

I have said that otherwise we would have failed you and failed Christ. But you too would have failed Christ yourselves. I sometimes ask young people: 'Does the Church do enough for young people today?' I've taken some valuable lessons from your replies. But to be honest I should have to go on and ask: 'Are young people doing enough for the Church?' The Church isn't the bishop, the priests, the brothers, the nuns or your parents or your teachers. You are the Church. The Church needs you. Christ needs you. He depends on you. Christ is always young. He needs you to show his youth to the world. He can be seen as young only in your faces, in your lives. You can show Christ in your own lives in such a way that, as Gerard Manley Hopkins said:

> Christ plays in ten thousand places.
> Lovely in limbs, and lovely in eyes not his
> To the Father through the features of men's faces.
> ('As Kingfishers catch Fire')

The Church is always young. She can be seen as young only through the commitment of your young lives, your youthful energies, your new skills and talents. You are the Church's youth. The Church needs you. But you will find yourselves and fulfil yourselves only in Christ and in the Church.

Pope John Paul has told you that he needs you. I tell you now that the bishop needs you. I like to try to make as many opportunities as I can to talk with and listen to young people. It is vital to me in my work for Christ to try to understand the world of youth. A person of my generation was brought up in a world different in many respects from yours. I have no right to impose the mentality and the prejudices of my time and world on you. I have to distinguish in my own thinking between what comes from the culture of my generation, and is therefore relative and changeable, and what comes from Christ and is absolute and eternal. I have a duty to propose Christ's truth to you. Christ said:

> Heaven and earth shall pass away but my words will never pass away. (Lk 21:33)

But I have no right to propose my own personal likes and dislikes to you, much less impose them upon you. I need your help to know the difference. You must help me to appreciate the true values of your culture. You must help me to understand 'where it's at' in your world. It is in that culture of yours that I must try to insert the Good News of Jesus Christ. But I can do this only with you. Priests, brothers and sisters can do this only with you. Together, but only together, we can bring the young world to the young Christ.

Christ in the Gospel looked on a young man and, as we read in the Gospel, 'loved him'. He said to that young man: 'Go, sell all that you own and give it to the poor, and come, follow me'. But we read on: 'That young man went away sad, because he had great possessions' (Mt 19:16-22). Dear young people, don't you go away from Christ sad because you have too much to lose. Come to Christ joyful and generous because you have so much to give.

Give yourselves

In life, don't ever be afraid to give. It is in giving that you will receive. It is in losing yourself that you will find yourself. Jesus has said:

> Anyone who wants to save his or her life will lose it; but anyone who loses his or her life for my sake will save it. (Mt 16:25)

Remember these words, particularly in respect of your choice of your vocation in life. Each one has a vocation from God: each one has a special work, a special career, a special profession or life-task to fill with Christ's presence and his love. Don't be too afraid of risk in life's choices. Risk is justified when it is made in trusting love. Don't look for too many precautions, too many safeguards, too many guarantees. You could bankrupt yourself by taking on too many self-insurance premiums. You don't need to fill in a coupon for an all-risks insurance policy every time you cross the road or go out in the car.

If, for example, you feel within you what you think may be the stirrings of a vocation to the priesthood or to the religious life, don't take half a lifetime to hesitate and calculate. Don't be afraid to give yourself. When is it reasonable to take the risk of giving? You will take the risk rightly and gladly in trust, when there is someone whom you love enough to know that you can trust that person and that nothing else is as important to you as to face the risks of life together with that person whom you love.

A boy or girl who feels the stirrings of a religious vocation feels just that way about Christ. Christ is one that you can come to know and love so much that nothing seems to matter except to share his life, whatever the risks; because you know that without him you could not find yourself or be yourself.

I want to say to you young people very seriously that your generation will have failed Christ and failed the Church and failed your century if there are not sufficient priestly and religious vocations from among your age-group to ensure that Christ is proclaimed by your generation to a world that is waiting for him.

I have said, and I repeat: don't be afraid to give yourselves. Eric Gill has said:

> The sign of the Cross is against the sky.
> It is painted, carved on the face of heaven.
> It is on the very door of Eternal life.
> 'He that loses his life shall save it.'
> All things are a sacrifice – everything is sacrificial.
> Nothing, nothing, nothing can be won,
> except by the giving of oneself.
> Against the sky it is written.
> (*Social Justice and the Stations of the Cross*, James, London, 1939, p. 18)

Lay vocation

Vocations in the Church, of course, are not confined to priestly and religious vocations. Every woman and every man, every young person, has a special vocation from God. We should not ask young people, 'Have you considered whether you may have a vocation?' but rather, 'Have you thought seriously about what your vocation in life is?' Each one has a special calling from God, a calling to do something special with his or her life, something which no one else can do.

If there is someone whom we greatly love and to whom we want to give a present, we take great care to select something that that person would like, particularly something special which no one else has thought of and no one else will give. This is how it should be between us and God. That something special which you can give to God is your own self. No one else can give that. You are special in God's eyes, you are unique. In God's eyes, there is literally nobody else on earth like you. There is nobody who can take your place in God's heart. Nobody can give to God that special thing which you can give, or can be that special person which you can be. God says:

> Do not be afraid, for I have redeemed you.
> I have called you by your name, you are mine...
> You are precious in my eyes.
> You are honoured and I love you...
> Look, I have, branded you on the palms of my hands.
> (Is 43:1-4; 49:16)

The 1987 Synod of Bishops had for its theme 'the Vocation and Mission of the Laity in the Church and in the World'. Its conclusions are contained in the document on the lay faithful, *Christifideles laici*. This document addresses a special appeal to young people. It says:

> The Church sees her path towards the future in the youth.... Youth must not simply be considered as an object of pastoral concern for the Church: in fact young people [ought to be] ... leading actors in evangelisation and active participants in the renewal of society.

The document notes particularly young people's sensitivity to 'the values of justice, non-violence and peace', their capacity for 'fellowship, friendship and solidarity', their concern about 'the quality of life and the conservation of nature'. The document declares:

348

The Church has so much to talk about with youth and youth
have so much to share with the Church.
(*Christifideles laici* 46)

Pope John Paul has always shown a great confidence in young
people. He has a unique charism for rapport with youth in all
continents and cultures and languages. He wrote a special message
to young people in 1985, the year set apart as International Youth
Year. He called young people 'the hope of the Church'. He recalled
how often he had himself benefited from accompanying young
people in their journey of faith and in their discovery of love,
including the love of boy and girl for one another, in which they
can together find new insight into the love which is God; for, as St
John says:

> God is love
> and anyone who lives in love lives in God
> and God lives in him.
> (1 Jn 4:16)

Facing the future
Some people fear for the future of our own country, the future of
humanity in the nuclear age, the future of planet earth. My dear
young people, do not be afraid of the future. The future is in God's
hands, and these are loving hands. The future is in Christ's hands,
and these are the hands which bear the marks of the nails with
which they were pierced for love of you. Christ is the Lord of all the
future time there will ever be. During the Paschal Vigil, we mark
the Paschal candle with the digits of the year, and say 'All time
belongs to him and all the ages'. There is nothing repeated more
often in the Bible than the words of God:

> Do not be afraid:
> I am with you.
> (Is 41:10, 43:5, etc.)

I am with you always
to the end of time.
(Mt 27:20)

You will come to receive Holy Communion with hands held out to receive the Body of the Lord. Christ says to you, 'I have work to be done: I need hands to do it', and you will be saying to him, 'Amen. Yes, Lord, here are my hands, I will do your work.' 'Amen' means 'Yes'. St Bernadette, when in great pain towards the end of her life (she was only thirty-five when she died), said:

In any physical or mental pain, we must say Yes to God, without any 'ifs' and without any 'buts'.

'Amen' means 'Yes'. We end all our prayers with 'Amen'. St Paul said:

Do you think I say 'Yes, yes' and 'No, no' at the same time? (2 Co 1:17)

Jesus himself said: All you need to say is 'Yes' if you mean 'Yes' (Mt 5:37). Let our 'Yes' to Jesus mean 'Yes' — not 'Yes, if…', or 'Yes, on condition that…', or 'Yes, some other time…', but simply 'Yes'.

Nietzsche said that Christians are 'No-sayers'. How wrong he was. Christians are the great 'Yes-sayers', saying Yes to God and thereby saying Yes to truth, to life and to love. Mary is the first and greatest Christian 'Yes-sayer'. She became Mother of Jesus when she said to God 'Fiat'; 'Yes', 'Let it be done to me according to your word'. This Mass is the Yes to God of our hearts and our lives. With words adapted from Dag Hammarskjöld, you and I are saying in this Mass:

For all that has been, Lord, thanks.
To all that will be, Lord, Yes.

(iii) Farewell Mass with Religious Communities in the Church of the Good Shepherd, Belfast
24 November 1990

'To depart', the French say, 'is always to die a little'. 'Parting' and 'departing' go together; and it is hard to part from dear friends and familiar faces and places and their happy associations and their cherished memories. It is especially hard to leave home; Down and Connor was the place of my first home; it is for me and always will be home in a unique way. It is hard to leave one's family; and I am leaving two families – first, the human family where I first learned love and have known its maturing and its deepening and its faithfulness all through life, and where I first came to know the God of love through parents, brothers and sisters; and then the Church family where I was helped to grow in faith and love as boy and student, seminarian and priest, and to which I came back eight years ago to be your father and brother in Christ, a bishop for you and a Christian with you.

It is hard for a father to part from his family. And you have been the family over whom and among whom the Holy Spirit appointed me Father in God, Pastor, Shepherd, Brother, Faith-Friend, Soul-Friend, 'Anamchara', for these eight wonderful years. I shall always thank God for those years. I shall thank God also for all of you. As St Paul said to his spiritual family in Philippi:

> I thank my God whenever I think of you; and every time I pray for all of you, I pray with joy, remembering how you have helped to spread the Good News from the day you first heard it right up to the present.... It is only natural that I should feel like this towards you all, since you have shared the privileges that have been mine: both my chains and my work defending and establishing the Gospel. You have a permanent place in my heart, and God knows how much I [shall] miss you all, loving you as Christ Jesus loves you. (Ph 1:3-8)

The bond between a bishop and his diocese is a very close one, rooted both in a human heart and in a mystery, the mystery which is the Church. The ties that bind me to Down and Connor are lodged deep in the heart, and breaking them tugs quite liberally at the heart-strings. It is with deep sadness and loneliness that I leave the diocese. I do so only because I have the personal assurance of the Holy Father that this is God's will for me. The whole meaning of the Christian life, and especially the whole meaning of religious life, is the seeking and the doing of the will of the Father. It is not always that one has the blessing of knowing for certain without any possibility of doubt that something one is called to is indeed the will of God. One could have no greater certitude than that which is given by the successor of Peter, the one whom Catherine of Siena called 'the sweet Christ on earth', our Holy Father, the Pope. When I saw him in private audience, he assured me that he had prayed and reflected much upon my appointment to Armagh. He asked me to accept his decision with faith and courage.

There was no way in which I could say anything but 'Yes', putting my trust in God for the grace and the strength to make that 'Yes' unconditional and to put into it all my effort of will and energy and, indeed, enthusiasm. I remembered Our Lord's own words:

All you need to say is 'Yes' if you mean yes.... (Mt 5:37)

I remembered St Paul saying:

Do you really think... that I say 'Yes, yes' and 'No, no' at the same time? I swear by God's truth there is no Yes and No about what we say to you. The Son of God, the Christ Jesus... was never 'Yes and no'; with him it was always 'Yes'. (2 Co 1:17-19)

For the Christian, and above all for the bishop, the priest and the religious, home is where God wishes one to be; home is being with Jesus Christ, seeking and doing the will of the Father; and being with Jesus means 'being in the Father's house', being 'about the Father's business' (cf. Luke 2:49).

Being about the Father's business for the bishop is identifying oneself completely with 'the joys and the hopes, the griefs and the anxieties' of the Church of his diocese and the Church universal. The bond uniting bishop and Church is a sharing in the bond of unconditional love, covenant love, which binds Christ to his Bride, the Church. This is the central symbolism of the bishop's ring, a sign of his spiritual marriage with his Church, his sharing in Christ's covenant of love with his Beloved, his Elect, his Chosen One, his Bride, the Church, the covenant which Christ sealed with his blood upon the Cross. The bishop has to feel for his Church something of what St Paul felt and expressed so often of solicitude, concern, anxiety, but also confidence and trust and hope and joy and pride in his Church. All of these I have felt and feel for Down and Connor.

But all of these I felt also for the first diocese which the Lord assigned to my pastoral care, the Diocese of Ardagh and Clonmacnois. To begin with, that diocese was almost totally unknown to me. But I came to know it and love it. I came to be proud of it, and I still am. It became my human home, because first it had been the home which the Lord had prepared for me and where his grace awaited me. I have confidence that the same will happen in the new Church of Armagh, to which God now calls me and where his grace now awaits me, and where, in his mysterious design, he waits to pass his grace through my unworthy hands to those who are now given to me by God to be my new spiritual family.

Bishop and religious

Religious are bound to the Church by a similar bond. Indeed, religious are the Church; they live its mystery in a special way. In truth, they embody its reality in themselves and their communities in virtue of their ecclesial consecration to a life of fidelity to the Gospel and to the spirit of the Beatitudes. Many religious women wear a ring as a sign of the spousal relationship with Christ, which they share in and with the Church of Christ. The bishop, therefore, has a special relationship of communion in Christ's love with religious men and women. Repeatedly in the documents of the Second Vatican Council and in subsequent documents emanating from the Holy Father and the Holy See, bishops are reminded of their special relationship with religious and their special responsibilities in their regard. Religious, for their part, are reminded in these same documents of their special relationship with the bishop, a relationship which is not merely juridical but is above all rooted in the mystery, communion and mission which make and mark the Church, and rooted also in the nature of religious consecration itself.

Personally, if I may say so, I have always welcomed these reminders given by the Council and the Holy See, because they correspond totally with my own life experience. As student, as priest and as bishop, I have always enjoyed the friendship and love and the human and spiritual support of religious women and men whom I have been privileged to count among my very special friends. I have been inspired by their witness to the Gospel, challenged by their earnestness in pursuit of holiness, edified by their spirit of prayer, supported and carried by their prayers for me. I have always felt it a privilege to serve in any way in which I could the ongoing formation, the renewal and the fidelity of religious.

I have always been aware that the holiness and the vitality of the Church are closely linked with the holiness of religious women and men and with the apostolic vitality of religious communities. Along with the priests of the diocese, the most immediate collaborators with the bishop in the work of the Kingdom are religious priests, brothers and sisters. The holiness and apostolic creativity of the diocesan Church depends in great measure, under God, on the closeness and the authenticity of that relationship of bishop and religious and on the openness of bishop, priests and religious men and women to partnership in Christ with lay women and men as workers in the vineyard. This is how the Church is built up in love towards full maturity in Christ. Thus does the Church become in lived reality the communion which it is by definition in God's call and plan. As Pope John Paul has said, in words which are quoted in *Christifideles laici*:

> The Spirit of the Lord gives a vast variety of charisms, inviting people to assume different ministries and forms of service and reminding them, as he reminds all people in their relationship in the Church, that what distinguishes persons is not an increase in dignity, but a special and complementary capacity for service....
>
> Thus, the charisms, the ministries, the different forms of service exercised by the lay faithful exist in communion and on behalf of communion. They are treasures that complement one another for the good of all and are under the wise guidance of their Pastor. (Pope John Paul's homily during the Mass for the close of the 1987 Synod of Bishops on the Laity, quoted in *Christifideles laici* 20)

Present difficulties in religious life

Undoubtedly, religious life is at present passing through a difficult and for many a painful period. The difficulties are not likely to lessen as the decade advances. Even if, as we hope and pray, vocations begin again to increase, the overall numbers of religious will inevitably continue to decline, the average age of religious will rise, the number of retired religious will increase and the number of aged and infirm religious will grow and the services of care and support which they need will be more demanding. In faith, we must try to see all of this as part of God's mysterious plan. At the time of your profession or consecration, you placed your hands in the hands of God, you entrusted your life to his loving care, and from that moment on he has accepted special responsibility for you and he has undertaken to care for you until the end. He says to you, in the wonderful words of Isaiah:

> It is you, my servant,
> [who are the one] whom I have chosen,
> descendant of Abraham my friend.

You whom I brought from the confines of the earth
and called from the ends of the world;
you to whom I said, 'You are my servant,
I have chosen you, not rejected you'.

Do not be afraid, for I am with you;
stop being anxious and watchful, for I am your God.
I give you strength, I bring you help,
I uphold you with my victorious right hand....

For I, the Lord, your God, I am holding you by the right
hand;
I tell you, 'do not be afraid,
I will help you'.

Do not be afraid, poor little thing,
Israel, tiny little one.
I will help you – it is the Lord who speaks –
the Holy One of Israel is your redeemer.
(Is 41:8-14)

Listen to me, House of Jacob,
All you who remain of the House of Israel,
You who have been carried since your birth,
Whom I have carried since the time you were born.

In your old age I shall still be the same,
When your hair is grey I shall still support you.
I have already done so, I have carried you,
I shall still support you and deliver you.
(Is 46:3-4)

As St Thérèse of Lisieux said: 'Everything is grace'. The present
difficulties in religious life are also grace. They test your faith, they
purify it, they strengthen it. They reveal the depth and the strength
of your trust in Christ and the sincerity of your self-giving and self-

entrusting to him. These difficulties can be a sword of sorrow; but, as for Mary at the Presentation of the Lord in the Temple, they 'lay bare the secret thoughts of many' (cf. Luke 2:35). They show how deep and sincere is our faith, our prayer, our trust, how real is our consecration. In the Garden, Jesus took all your anxieties and your anguish and your fear for the future into his own heart and made them part of his own Agony and thereby part of the redemption of the world.

He asked his disciples then to watch and to pray for him. He said to them: 'pray not to be put to the test' (Lk 22:40). The 'test' is the testing of our faith. The prayer he asks us to pray is that we do not fail in that testing. The words are the same as those which Jesus taught us to pray in the Our Father: 'Lead us not into temptation', or, as it would perhaps be more accurately translated, 'Do not let us fail in the test'. With Christ, we can finally hope to live in trust and in faithfulness through that testing and never to be found failing in love. With Christ, we shall cry from the depth of our anxieties: 'Into your hands I commend my spirit … my whole self and the years that are left to me, my community, my congregation and its future, our future'. With Christ we are certain of our sharing in his resurrection and in his final victory.

The religious consecration of a Benedictine monk or nun in some congregations includes the ceremony of the novice's lying prostrate before the altar while the Litany of Saints is sung, and then rising to pronounce the vows, and afterwards singing '*Suscipe me Domine*':

> Accept me, Lord, according to your Word and I shall live, and you will never let me be disappointed in my expectation.

The funeral liturgy of a monk or nun in these same congregations includes the placing of the coffin on the very spot before the altar where the deceased once lay prostrate as a novice and the singing once more of the chant of the 'Suscipe'. At the beginning of religious life, it was a song of trust and hope. Now at its closing it is a song of joy and thanks. God has accepted his chosen one, God has been true to his word, he has not let the young novice or later the aging nun or monk be disappointed in his or her expectation. The One who called has been faithful, for he is indeed the faithful God, true to his promises and to his covenant for a thousand generations and for ever (cf. Deuteronomy 7:9).

The best assurance of the future of religious congregations is that you remain faithful in the present and leave the future trustingly to God. We are not in charge of the future. God is. We can only live in the now and be faithful in the today which God gives us; faithful to our consecration, faithful to the Church which received our consecration, faithful to the congregation which accepted us into its brotherhood or sisterhood, faithful to its constitutions (remembering always that all constitutions are ultimately rooted in the Gospels, and like all translations they must be read in the light of the original, the Gospels of Christ, and in the light of the teaching of Christ's Church), faithful to our pursuit of holiness, as individuals and as communities, faithful to our prayer and to our vows of poverty, chastity and obedience, faithful to the ministry which the Church and those entrusted with responsibility and authority in our congregation have assigned to us. If we are faithful now God will look after our future; and already with St Paul we can 'thank God for giving us the victory through our Lord Jesus Christ' (cf. 1 Corinthians 15:56).

Mary the Faithful Virgin

Let us take for our model Mary the Faithful Virgin. Religious life cannot be lived or even understood except in the context of faith. Apart from faith in Christ, religious life is simply absurd and ultimately indefensible. Our understanding of our own religious vocation will develop in exact proportion to our growth in faith. Our model and our most powerful, prayerful help in that growth in faith and in religious commitment is Mary the Virgin of faith and of faithfulness, whose life, as the Council recalls from St Ambrose, 'is a rule of life for all' (*Perfectae caritatis* 25). It is in the face of Mary that we shall see most clearly the image of Christ, which ought to be reflected in the whole manner of living of religious.

In Dante's Paradiso, Beatrice bids the poet 'look now on the face that most resembles Christ, for only its brightness can fit thee to see Christ'. But as Dante gazed upon those eyes 'beloved and reverenced by God', he found that those eyes were directed to 'the Eternal Light, into which it is not to be believed that any creature should penetrate with so clear an eye' (*Canto XXXIII*, 40-5).

Religious vocation is the call and the grace

> with unveiled faces [to reflect] like mirrors the brightness of the Lord, all growing brighter and brighter as we are turned into the image that we reflect; this is the work of the Lord who is Spirit. (2 Co 3:18)

The best way to reflect that divine brightness is for us to look on 'the face that most resembles Christ', the face of Mary, the Virgin, the model of virgins, their patroness and protector, their glory and their queen.

Invoking Mary's prayers, I pray for you all:

> May God the Father and the Lord Jesus Christ grant peace and love and faith to all the sisters and brothers. May grace and eternal life be with all who love our Lord Jesus Christ. (Ep 6:23-24)

I make St Paul's words my own in conclusion:

> The grace of the Lord Jesus be with you.
> My love is with you all in Christ Jesus.
> (1 Co 16:23-24)

(iv) Farewell Mass Concelebrated with Priests
in St Peter's Cathedral, Belfast
27 November 1990

It was on Tuesday, 26 October 1982, just over eight years ago, that I met with the priests of Down and Connor for the first time as your bishop and concelebrated Mass with you in St Malachy's College. I still have vivid memories of the scene and of the emotions which filled my heart at that Mass. I felt then that I had 'come home for good', and that my episcopate in Down and Connor would be my last ministry in life and that I would remain here until retirement, if I lived so long, and until God called me to my true and final home.

Such was not God's will and plan. There is a well-known religious poster which reads: 'God isn't finished with me yet'. The words have been proved true for me in a quite unforeseen way in these closing years of my life. A recent book has the title *The God of Surprises*. There have been many surprises in my life in God's service, but this latest appointment is the most unexpected of all.

However, the seeking and fulfilling of God's will and plan for our lives is the whole purpose of our creation. This is true of our first birth, when our parents fulfil God's plan for their own life-giving love and co-operate in God's hidden plan for their newly-born, whom he creates but calls them to share in creating, allowing them to 'pro-create' with him and for him. It is even more true of our second birth at baptism, when we begin a new existence in Christ Jesus; for baptism is a new birth, a new creation.

Michelangelo's famous painting of the creation of Adam hints at the second while depicting the first creation of mankind. During the recent Synod of Bishops, a group of us were conducted on a tour of the Sistine Chapel by a guide who is a specialist in the period of the great artists of the Cinquecento. The frescoes on the ceiling are now newly-restored and revealed in all their original and glorious colours, which had been obscured by the dust and smoke of centuries. Michelangelo's fresco of the creation of the first man, whom St Paul calls 'the first Adam', depicts God, the Creator and Father, reaching out his hand across the infinite distance dividing

God from creature and drawing the first human being out of nothingness. He is not just drawing him into existence; he is calling him across the distance and the division between man and God, inviting him into union, into closeness with himself. The hand which creates is also the hand which calls, the hand which invites. The hand which shapes human features in God's image and likeness also calls forward and upward, lifts Adam up and draws him forward towards the Father who formed him in the divine image and likeness and now desires him to share in the companionship, the joy, the love and the life of God.

The first Adam bears already the likeness of Christ, 'the Second Adam', into whose relationship with the Father the sons and daughters of Adam are admitted through their baptism in the name of the Father, the Son and the Holy Spirit. The call of their first birth now becomes explicitly a call to enter here on earth the people 'which draws its unity from the unity of the Father, the Son and the Holy Spirit' (cf. St Cyprian), which is the Church, and to enter in eternity into the life of that same Most Holy Trinity.

For priests, for bishops, this call into union with Christ assumes a new and specific form, that of being anointed by the Holy Spirit and 'so configured to Christ the Priest that they can act in the person of Christ the Head' of the Church (cf. *Presbyterorum ordinis* 2). This requires of priests and bishops a lifelong struggle to follow Christ, to imitate him, to grow in the likeness of Christ, to 'model their lives on the mystery of the Lord's Cross' (see *Rite for the Ordination of a Priest*). It entails following Christ in his obedience, his poverty, his chastity. It means being at all times ready to go wherever he calls, to accept whatever place or ministry he assigns.

This commitment is tested not by our words but by our actions and reactions in concrete situations, particularly when these are unexpected, demanding and difficult. When a man is ordained priest, he is asked by the ordaining bishop: 'Do you promise respect and obedience to your Ordinary?' The candidate answers: 'I do'.

When a priest is ordained bishop, he is asked by the ordaining bishop: 'Are you resolved to be faithful in your obedience to the successor of the Apostle Peter?' The priest answers: 'I am'.

These solemn promises, made publicly before the whole Church, are nothing other than a repetition of the 'Yes' which was our response to the call from God which we received at our baptism, repeated at our Confirmation, renewed all during our seminary formation, and made solemn and definitive at our ordination; it is our response to Christ's call, 'Follow me'. It is the response of faith to Christ's insistent question addressed personally to each of his disciples:

Do you believe this? (cf. John 11:26)

Do you love me?
Do you love me more than these others?
(cf. John 21:15-16)

Can you drink the cup that I am going to drink?
(cf. Matthew 20:22)

Obedience for the Christian lay person, the priest, the bishop, takes different forms but is always part of what St Paul called 'the obedience of faith' (cf. Romans 1:5). The word obedience, from the Latin *ob-audire,* means to listen attentively; for the Christian it means listening attentively, prayerfully, to God's Word. Only the Word of God accepted in faith makes this obedience possible, gives it meaning, makes it necessary. In faith, a priest knows that the voice of the bishop sending him to a specific parish or ministry is the voice of Christ saying to him personally: 'You go into my vineyard' (cf. Matthew 20:5). The priest can have no more definite assurance of God's will and God's word than that, and he should seek or ask no other assurance.

For a bishop, the appointment by the Holy Father to a specific diocese or ministry is the voice of God saying: 'Go now to those to whom I send you' (cf. Jeremiah 1:7). The bishop can have no more sure and certain guarantee of God's will and call than the assurance given by the Pope, the successor of Peter, to whom the Lord said:

I have prayed for you, Simon, that your faith may not fail; and once you have recovered you in your turn must strengthen your brothers. (Lk 22:32)

So when, on 21 October last, I was told by Cardinal Gantin on behalf of the Pope that it was the Holy Father's wish and decision that I was to be the next Archbishop of Armagh, and when that call was repeated by the Holy Father in person on 23 October in private audience, I had the clearest indication that any man could have of what God was asking me to do and where God was asking me to go. It was a moment of drawing back the curtain which often conceals 'the mystery of God's purpose', and giving me a privileged glimpse of what had been his 'hidden plan, so kindly made in Christ' for a period of my life when humanly it seemed that my time on earth was 'running its course to the end' (cf. Ephesians 1:9-10).

What could one say but 'Yes'? And the Yes which we say to God cannot be grudging or hedged round with reservations or preconditions. It must not be marred by reluctance or weighed down with unhappiness. Our Yes must be unhesitating and cheerful and filled with joy and hope. It is for this, after all, that we priests were born and baptised and ordained. It is only in doing God's will and fulfilling God's plan for our lives that we accomplish the purpose of our own lives and of our priestly or episcopal ordination. 'In his will alone', Dante said, 'is our peace.' I am conscious that during my time as bishop I have assigned difficult and unexpected appointments and asked big sacrifices of many priests, and always they and you have said 'Yes'. How could I fail to do myself what I have often asked others to do?

The Yes we say to God's will is only a living out of our choice to follow Christ. During those days in October I thought of St Peter walking by the side of Jesus after the resurrection, with John following behind, Peter saying to Jesus, 'What about John?', and Jesus replying:

What does it matter to you? You are to follow me. (Jn 21:22)

In these past weeks I have thought of the two disciples on the road to Emmaus, a stranger walking by their side; the stranger was Jesus, though they did not recognise him. Their hearts were downcast, their hopes lying around them in ruins, the future desolate and dark as the tomb where the dead body of Jesus had been laid. But Jesus explained the Scriptures to them, showed them that he was himself the One to whom the whole of Scripture pointed and that he was himself the hope of all our futures. They came to the inn, and he 'made as though to go on further'. It is significant to note how often in the Gospels Jesus is seen on his journey, hurrying on ahead, always in front, always inviting us to follow and always waiting for us to keep us with him as he hurries on further, intent upon the Father's business.

On the Emmaus road, 'it was towards evening, the day was far spent', just as for me at this time the evening of my life is already there. Jesus gave in to the pleas of the two disciples and went into the inn with them. There he sat down and broke bread with them; and allowed them to 'recognise him in the breaking of the bread' (cf. Luke 24:13-35). So it is with us at every stage of our life journey. Jesus walks by our side, even though we do not always recognise him or feel his presence, and he calls us to follow him. He is always our companion on the road of our mission, which is one with his own mission, the doing of the Father's will, the proclaiming of the Father's Kingdom. A 'companion' is one who shares bread with us. Jesus is our daily companion in the Eucharist, as we try to carry out our ministry in his name in whatever place he has assigned to us.

I think too of the last words the risen Lord addressed to Peter:

> When you grow old
> you will stretch out your hands
> and somebody else will put the belt around you
> and take you where you would rather not go.

After that he said, 'Follow me'. (Jn 21:18-19)

I do not wish it to be understood that I go to Armagh reluctantly or under protest. The assurance that it is God's call and God's will gives me strength and a real peace and joy in going and overrides even the deep human sadness and loneliness which I feel in leaving Down and Connor. The joy, the confidence and the enthusiasm with which one sets out when young to follow Christ must not lessen with the passing of the years or the lengthening of the shadows. Having put our hand to the plough, we must not look back (cf. Luke 9:62). Our life in Christ is always young, always new, always ready for fresh challenges and new surprises. It is today that we must listen to his voice, for with Christ it is always 'today'. I must personally try to live by my motto:

Jesus Christus Heri et Hodie
Jesus Christ is the same today as he was yesterday and as he will be for ever. (Hb 12:8)

Each day until the end of our lives we must be saying:

Yes, Lord, you know all things, you know that [today] I love you. (cf. John 21:17)

Yes, Lord, [today] I will follow you wherever you go. (cf. Luke 9:57)

My years in Down and Connor

I came to Down and Connor in 1982 with considerable apprehension and anxiety. I had been extremely happy during my fifteen years in Ardagh and Clonmacnois and I hoped and expected that Ardagh would be my permanent home. There was great sadness for me in leaving it. Furthermore, I was just recovering from my coronary attack. I seriously doubted whether I would physically and otherwise be able to face the new and heavy responsibilities of the second largest diocese in Ireland, with its difficult challenges and its complex problems posed by deprivation, discrimination, unemployment, social change, community tensions, violence.

Looking back, however, on those eight years, I can say without the slightest hesitation that for me they have been years of very great happiness and fulfilment. For this I thank God, who is ever faithful to his promise to be with his people all days, even to the end of time.

Under God, I above all thank you, my brother priests. I doubt if there is anywhere a body of priests of whom a bishop can be more proud or who make it easier or more pleasant for a bishop to serve you and to work with you. In my first address to you on 26 October 1982, I spoke of the new ways in which authority has to be understood and exercised in the Church in the light of the Vatican Council, new ways which in fact are only the ways indicated by Jesus Christ the Lord himself in his teaching and his personal example. I said:

> Authority has to be exercised in dialogue, in listening, in partnership, in brotherhood and in friendship. It has to be exercised in service.

I am very conscious, looking back, of the many ways in which I have failed to make my attitudes and my actions match my words. But I do say with total sincerity that I wanted to be a personal friend to each single one of you, my priests, and I wanted you to see me as a friend and to approach me as such. From my point of view, I felt that each of you was a personal friend. I wanted you to trust me enough to tell me the truth, not just the things I would like to hear. I wanted you to speak the truth to me in love, even when it might hurt me to hear it; and I promised never to dislike the person telling me the hurtful truth, because that would be a healing hurt.

I know how often I have failed. I know that I must have disappointed some of you, misjudged some of you, hurt some of you; that some of you may have felt unappreciated, unaffirmed, misunderstood or unfairly treated. At the penitential rite of this Mass, when asking forgiveness of God and of you, my brothers, for much that I had done and failed to do among you, I reflected on all of that, and my feeling of need for forgiveness, my asking for forgiveness, were very sincere.

I thank you for your patience with me. I thank God and I thank you for all that we lived through together in the Down and Connor vineyard, all that we tried to do together, all that we planned to do in the future in partnership with our laity, for the glory of God and the coming of his Kingdom. We pray the Lord of the harvest to grant growth and increase to the Gospel seeds he enabled us to plant. I ask your prayers as I enter this new and last chapter of my life in Armagh, be it short or be it longer. As St Augustine once said:

> It is good to have been together in the Lord's presence. It is good to have listened together to his word. Now we go away from one another, each one to his own place. But as we part from one another, we do not part from God.

In God, in prayer, though distant geographically, we can still remain close to one another and still support one another as friends and brothers in God's love and service.

When taking my leave of the priests of Ardagh and Clonmacnois, I recalled St Paul's farewell to the presbyters of Miletus. He said:

> Now I commend you to God and to the word of his grace that has power to build you up and to give you your inheritance among all the sanctified. (Ac 20:31-32)

I wish that I could truthfully say what Paul also said on that for him so sad occasion:

> I swear that my conscience is clear as far as all of you are concerned, for I have without faltering put before you the whole of God's purpose. (Ac 20:26-27)

But God's purpose is fulfilled even in spite of our shortcomings and God's power is manifested even more clearly in our weaknesses and his grace can do infinitely more than we can ask or even imagine.

So my concluding words to you are again from St Paul:

> Grace to you and peace to you from God our Father and the Lord Jesus Christ. (2 Co 1:2)

May Mary, whom the Irish called Mary of the Graces, by her example inspire you and by her prayers assist you to fan into a living flame the grace of priesthood you have received, so that you may save both yourselves and those who listen to you (cf. 1 Timothy 4:14-16; 2 Timothy 1:6).

CHAPTER THIRTEEN

REMEMBER YOUR LEADERS

Remember your leaders
who preached the word of God to you.
(Hb 13:7)

I – Cardinal William Conway

Cardinal Conway was closely associated with my life ever since my years as a boarder in St Malachy's College, which I entered in 1930. The university students/seminarians, though they lived in St Malachy's College, formed a distinct group and the boarders did not have much contact with them. However, one had to be aware of one unusually tall and well-built university student, who was already known then as an honours student of distinction (even though, it was also noticed, not equally distinguished, manly effort notwithstanding, on the sports field!). It was 'Big Bill' Conway.

In my first year in Maynooth, the newly-ordained Father Conway was a post-graduate student in the Dunboyne Establishment. One of the traditional duties of a post-graduate to his own fellow-diocesans was to give them a daily news bulletin. Students then were not allowed access to newspapers, but receiving them was one of the 'perks' of a post-graduate. Each diocese in those far-off days had a place of rendezvous or 'pos' (position) where they congregated after each meal, before dispersing to walk around the grounds or play games or whatever (or, in the case of an occasional bookworm like myself, to choose the moment to slip away as unobtrusively as possible to one's room). Father Conway prepared for these daily morning news bulletins as carefully as he would later do for every duty of his life. He had the major news items of the day arranged in his head in order of importance, and gave an outline of each in turn with the professionalism of a radio newscaster. This was the period of Hitler's relentless military annexations of alleged German lands beyond Germany's frontiers, as Europe held its breath in suspense on the verge of major war. In 1941, I myself inherited his task as 'newsreader' for Down and Connor students and tried, with less success, to emulate his methods.

Father Conway then went to Rome for post-graduate studies in Canon Law. Occasional letters to the 'Di', or diocesan student group, kept us in touch with his experiences in Rome, though wartime censorship prevented any comment on military or political matters. Those were exciting times, although in many respects, difficult and lean times in Rome. Father Conway's sense of history appreciated them better than most. The story of his return to neutral Ireland in 1940, by a chance air flight via Lisbon, was an epic one, which I often later heard him recount with zest. In later life, he used to recall that his mother had difficulty recognising the thin young man who returned to her after his years in Rome.

After a short period teaching English in St Malachy's College, Dr Conway was appointed Professor of Moral Theology and Canon Law in Maynooth; this was in June 1942. I was still a post-graduate student in Maynooth, and visited 'Bill' regularly in his rooms. From that time on, I was privileged to be numbered among his friends.

With some Down and Connor priest friends, I spent a week in Donegal with him in summer 1943. He was then as always a brilliant conversationalist, with a strong interest in people and a keen curiosity, always avid for new experiences of human nature. My intellectual interests to some extent overlapped with his and we kept each other informed about new books we had read and new places we had visited. After each holiday, particularly when continental travel became possible again after the War, he had many new stories to tell about the trips abroad, the cathedrals, the museums, the art galleries, the bookshops and his impressions of the state of the Church in the countries he had visited.

When I went to Paris in 1952, I kept a promise I had made to Dr Conway to keep him regularly informed about my experiences and impressions of life and thought in Paris. He joined me for a few days in Paris in the summer of 1953, by which time I had become quite possessive about Paris and was proud to show it off to visitors! This visit was repeated for some days in 1956, after the Maynooth Synod of that year. He was intensely interested, as was I, in the new approaches to liturgy and its pastoral application, and to pastoral methods and Church renewal generally, which were then being pioneered in France.

Contacts between us continued after he became Auxiliary Bishop of Armagh in 1958, residing in Dundalk. He enjoyed long walks and brought to them something of the competitive spirit which he brought to many of his activities, as though in a test of fitness and endurance or productivity. I remember one climb in the hills above Ravensdale, which became also the occasion for a most informative outline of the history and tradition and faith of the Cooley Peninsula, an area of which he was very proud. He had family connections in Carlingford through his mother, and later he had a summer house in Carlingford to which he occasionally escaped for the short periods of absence from Ara Coeli which he permitted himself in the later years of his primacy. I recall another day, much later, spent with him in Carlingford, which again included a long walk. This time, however, on our return to the house, I noticed a paleness and a sense of strain about his face which disturbed me. I suspected that he might not be physically as well as he usually looked. Perhaps these were early signs of future health problems.

The Second Vatican Council

In the lead-up to the Vatican Council, Bishop Conway had already been closely involved with Cardinal D'Alton in the work of the preparatory Commissions. In the First Session of the Council, as

Auxiliary, he resided with the whole Irish contingent in the Irish College. Cardinal D'Alton, with his secretary, Father Francis Lenny, was staying in the nearby complex of the Little Company of Mary Sisters (the 'Blue Nuns'). As I have mentioned elsewhere, few participants in the debates of the Council were more aware than was Bishop Conway of the historic moment through which the Church was living as the Council went through its first dramatic weeks. I recall the excitement of Dr Conway after the Council's first week, when the preparatory lists for conciliar commissions were rejected and the Fathers began their work *de novo*. He knew that he was present at a turning point in the history of the Church.

Even the theological advisers could sense from a certain distance that history was indeed being made. Even though much uncertainty still remained as to what precisely the Council was meant to achieve or could in fact accomplish, for the bishops themselves the Council was a learning experience. To spend all those months together in the Irish College was for Dr Conway a new experience of episcopal *communio*, and to spend two months each year for four years sharing views and experiences with bishops from all the continents was an experience of *oikumene* or universality, which was unprecedented. The opportunity of listening, at venues across Rome, to lectures given by the Church's leading theologians, was for the priest advisers, as well as for the bishops, a rare opportunity.

I spent the 1962 session on secondment from Queen's University as theological adviser to Bishop William Philbin. Cardinal D'Alton died on 1 February 1963. In September 1963, Dr Conway was named Archbishop of Armagh. A few days later, I received a telegram in France, where I was on vacation. It was from the new Archbishop, inviting me to come to Rome as his theological adviser for the Second Session of the Council. During this session, Father Frank Lenny resided in the Irish College, where I and the other Irish advisers or episcopal secretaries were staying. From then on, I developed a close friendship with Father Lenny, as both of us worked, in our different spheres, in the service of Cardinal Conway, for the remaining three sessions of the Council.

This friendship deepened over the years and lasted until Frank, who became Cardinal Conway's Auxiliary Bishop from 1974 onwards, died so tragically young in 1978, only a year after the death of Cardinal Conway himself, whom he so loyally and so diligently served, and less than a year after the appointment of the new Archbishop of Armagh. No one collaborated so closely with Cardinal Conway as he did, or knew the Cardinal's mind as well as he. No one was so close to the momentous changes in the life of the Irish Church in the years following the Council as he. No one was privy, as he was, to the feelings and thoughts of Cardinal Conway as he waited, in those fateful months and weeks of spring 1977, for death slowly to come. Bishop Lenny's own death, following so soon after the death of the Cardinal and so tragically soon after the appointment of Archbishop Tomás Ó Fiaich to Armagh, was a very great loss to the new Archbishop, to the Archdiocese, to the Episcopal Conference and to the Church in Ireland. His unique knowledge of many of the events of those exciting years died with him. For me, it was the end of a cherished friendship and of a link with Cardinal Conway which had marked much of my life up to that point.

I was named Bishop of Ardagh and Clonmacnois on 10 June 1967. Early that morning, Cardinal Conway telephoned me. We arranged to meet next day in Ara Coeli. He arranged to telephone my mother later in the morning, and that kind and thoughtful telephone call helped her to adjust to the shock of my appointment. On the night preceding my ordination, at which he was the chief ordaining prelate, the Cardinal came to Longford and stayed in St Michael's, the bishop's residence. He came to Ardagh and Clonmacnois twice subsequently. The first occasion was when he preached at the dedication of the new sanctuary area erected at Clonmacnois in 1969. It was here that for many years I was to celebrate Mass on the annual 'Pattern Day' of St Ciaran each September. It was always a moving experience to celebrate Mass on that site, with the Shannon behind and the walls of the twelfth-century Cathedral church of the monastery on the higher level in front, and with the congregation spread on the grass on the sloping ground, which formed a natural amphitheatre around the altar. Cardinal Conway was particularly sensitive to the setting and the occasion and to the sense of history which it evoked. The Cardinal came again in 1970, for the dedication of a special shrine in Boher, County Offaly, in honour of the local patron, St Manchan.

Chairman of the Irish Episcopal Conference

As a member of the Episcopal Conference, I came more and more to admire Cardinal Conway's superb chairing of Conference meetings, his mastery of our agendas, his utter absorption in the work of the Church, at home and universally, his readiness to break new ground with a new plough, but to plant in the furrows only the genuine seeds of the Gospel, authenticated by the tradition of *quod semper, quod ubique, quod ab omnibus*.

His leadership of the Irish Episcopal Conference during those momentous post-Council years was undoubtedly his greatest contribution to the life of the Church in Ireland. It is by this, above all, that his place in the history of the Irish Church will be measured. Much of his earlier formation and self-formation and experience can be read in retrospect as providential preparation for this concluding work of his life. His choices in reading and his interests were all of them centred, in one way or another, on the work and mission of the Church. His interests ranged widely, from contemporary literature, especially in its bearing on Christianity (it should not be forgotten that he read Honours English as his university degree course), through admiration for French Catholic culture, to a passion for romanesque, gothic and baroque religious architecture and art. He had a fascination for science, particularly in its bearing on the origin and age of the universe, and a concern for dialogue with contemporary atheism. He was fascinated by space exploration. Prominent on a wall of his study was a photograph of the first landing on the moon and beneath it a copy of the painting from the Caves of Altamira. First origins and final ends were always subjects of exploration and wonder for him, and he frequently returned to these questions in his addresses and in media interviews.

It is perhaps significant that, for someone who had long been Professor of Canon Law as well as of Moral Theology, he did not seem to me to rate Canon Law particularly high on his list of pastoral priorities in his life as bishop and as Chairman of the Conference. One had the impression that he entertained some regrets in respect of the rather literalist and legalistic way in which Canon Law had often been taught in the past. As Professor of Canon Law, as of Moral Theology, he sought in his teaching to impart a more pastoral approach to the subject.

Cardinal Conway was, however, even more interested in persons than in ideas, and more anxious to learn from people and their experiences than from books. He retained to the end of his life a young man's appetite for new experience. He was endlessly interested in learning from the experience, the reading and the wisdom of others. This was reflected in his own choices of reading. His favourite 'light' reading was the serious novel, on the one hand, and biographies on the other.

The capacity to see life through the eyes of others, thus fostered, helped to give him an unusual capacity for taking an objective view, even of situations in which he was himself involved. A close friend remarked on his lack of self-confidence, his self-doubt, his need for reassurance. I believe this was associated with the tendency to set 'targets' for himself and never feel that he fully achieved them. He certainly needed affirmation and encouragement from his close friends. He could, in conversation, be quite remarkably objective and impersonal about himself. I feel that this was a human quality on which the grace of God built to provide him with the remarkable gift of serene resignation and acceptance of God's will when the news eventually came that his days on earth were numbered. It was entirely in keeping with his life-long character that he planned, programmed and 'paced' the last months of his life with exactly the same objectivity and detachment, the same thoroughness and care for detail, with which he would have planned, for example, the business of a forthcoming meeting of the Irish Conference of Bishops.

I spoke above of his 'competitive' attitude to work and output.

He was always seeking new ways of doing more things, faster. In his first years as Professor in Maynooth, before he acquired a car, he came to Belfast and back by bus and train. He 'timed himself' from his mother's home in Norfolk Parade to his rooms in Maynooth, and kept gradually improving on his performance. He also found ways of reducing baggage to an irreducible minimum. Books, however, were exempt from his limits! After beating his own records he would often remark 'not bad'. It was entirely typical that on his deathbed he remarked to one or two of his closest friends: 'Sixty-four years; not bad'.

It was, I have said, as President of the Episcopal Conference that Cardinal Conway made his distinctive contribution to the history of the Church in Ireland. Here his rare gifts of organisation, his industry and enormous capacity and zest for work, his large vision of the Church both in Ireland and in the world, were given full challenge and scope. He brought to the chairmanship of bishops' meetings all of the determination which marked every phase of his life – whether as student, as priest, as occasional vacation-time pastoral 'supply', as professor, as Vice-President of Maynooth, as Auxiliary Bishop, as Archbishop and Cardinal – the determination to try to do with perfection whatever it was that Divine Providence assigned to him to do. From the very first meetings of the Irish bishops over which he was called to preside, those held in Rome during the second and following sessions of the Vatican Council, he set himself to master the techniques of chairmanship and to develop a more and more efficacious style for the conducting of episcopal business.

An essential key to good chairmanship is thorough homework. The late Cardinal had no rivals in this domain. At his best, he had always studied the agenda so carefully that he seemed to know more about each item of a diverse agenda than any member of the Conference. If he dominated the Conference – and he was, from sincere conviction, determined not to – it was by his sheer mastery of the business of the meetings, acquired by dint of relentless, disciplined work.

As Chairman, he attached great importance to securing the

widest possible participation by the members of the Conference in the discussion. He took great pains to outline the points at issue in respect of each topic as he introduced it. There may sometimes have been *longueurs* in these expositions, but he was convinced that the background, the pros and the cons of each item should be thoroughly expounded as a preliminary to a constructive discussion; and no one could ever find fault with the objectivity and detachment of his interpretation of the facts. When an important issue came up, he would try to have a complete *tour de table*, so that each member present would have the opportunity of making his contribution.

Leadership

Techniques of chairmanship, however, are in the end, of strictly limited value. Vision is incomparably more important than techniques or tactics – above all in the work of an Episcopal Conference. Cardinal Conway was a man of vision. Living totally for the Church and its Lord, mobilising all the energies and work potential of a disciplined life in the service of God and his Kingdom, Cardinal Conway's whole life became progressively more organised so as to serve more productively and more effectively the present and the future of the faith in Ireland. From year to year he took special pleasure and some pride in devising some new system for increasing his work output. Nearly every major initiative in Church life in Ireland in the 1970s was originated by him or at least owed its promotion to his support.

He was acutely conscious of both the opportunities and the hazards of an age of change. Equipping and guiding the Irish Church for the challenges of change was his constant concern. The problem of trying to monitor and control the pace and direction of change was a favourite theme of conversation. He liked to use the analogy of the space satellite making its hazardous re-entry into earth atmosphere, with the risk, on the one hand, of re-entering too slowly and being propelled outward again into space, or, on the other hand, coming in at too great a velocity and being burned up in its descent. The success of the re-entry operation was dependent on the angle and velocity of the descent. There were few problems to which Cardinal Conway devoted so much anxious thought as this problem of the right pace and direction of change in the Irish Church. He frequently protested against those who would suggest that the rate of change in Ireland following the Council had been too slow. He would argue that, if one could sit in an imaginary time-machine and be instantly propelled backwards in time to a date ten years earlier, one would scarcely be able to recognise the Irish Church, so great had been its transformation in the course of the ten post-conciliar years.

The Cardinal was at the height of his powers in 1969 when he set up and guided the first 'think-in' of the Irish hierarchy, a special week-long meeting in Maynooth, devoted to the theme 'Ireland in the Seventies'. Many of the structures of renewal of the Church were planned or consolidated at this meeting. The framework of the episcopal commissions, with their relevant 'infra-structures', was substantially assembled then and has functioned effectively without radical alteration since. For example, the whole programme of catechetical renewal – one of the most far-reaching programmes of conciliar renewal in this country, and one in which Ireland can rightly claim a leading place in the whole Catholic world – was initiated at this special meeting.

What has rightly been called the 'Conway period' in the Irish Church had its most productive years between this special meeting in 1969 and the second major extraordinary meeting of the bishops held at Mulrany in April 1974. The latter had many new dimensions compared with 1969. There was greater involvement of theologians, of lay consultors; there was more and better preparatory material; there was a richer liturgical life. All of these dimensions were possible because of the impetus earlier given by the first such meeting in 1969.

Mulrany also found the bishops better equipped with sociological information about the actual state of Irish Catholicism, the degree of religious practice, problem areas and age-groups, the attitudes of youth. This was due to the reports, completed or preliminary, of the Research and Development Unit, which, in turn, owed its inception in large part to the Cardinal's insatiable interest in well-researched facts, data, dossiers, projections. There was considerable difficulty in the Conference about securing approval for the budget for the first Research and Development 'Survey of Religious Practice, Attitudes and Beliefs' (1972-3), but Cardinal Conway's persistence succeeded in having it approved.

The Cardinal, as I have remarked, had a lifelong zest for new experiences and for profiting by the experience of others – all of this dominated by his passion to know the Church better so as to help the Church to serve the world more relevantly. Above all, he was interested in people, their traditions, their insights, their knowledge of the things of God, their difficulties, problems and needs. His journey to India in 1972 as Papal Legate to the celebrations in Madras of the nineteenth centenary of St Thomas, when he travelled extensively throughout the Indian sub-continent, exposed him for the first time to the overwhelming impact of the Developing World, its massive poverty and its immense human and spiritual hungers. His personal reaction took the shape of the setting up of the Catholic Bishops' Development Agency, Trócaire, which, with his persistent advocacy, was launched on 2 February 1973.

In between the special meetings in Maynooth and Mulrany, and throughout the whole fourteen years of his primacy, the initiatives of the bishops and their joint pastoral letters or organised campaigns corresponded broadly with the Cardinal's vision of the Irish Church, of its strengths which needed reinforcing, of its weaknesses which needed remedying. Such were: the campaign for prayer in the home (December 1973) – of which Pope Paul delightedly remarked to the Cardinal that 'only Ireland could have thought of it'; the campaign for sacred art in the home (October 1974); the pastoral letter on temperance (December 1974); the pastoral letters, *Christian Marriage* (Lent 1969), *Human Life is Sacred* (May 1975), the *Work of Justice* (September 1977). The system of household-by-household distribution of these pastorals and of an organised national homiletic back-up to introduce them were also largely of his initiation.

The Cardinal had a lifelong interest in the media. I spoke of his 'news bulletins' of college days in Maynooth, prepared and delivered with the professionalism of a trained broadcaster. He was a successful contributor to radio-broadcast religious services and constantly worked at mastering the techniques of radio and, later, television. It was under his impetus that the Catholic Communications Centre was set up in the 1970s for the training of religious broadcasters in radio and television and print journalism. He arranged crash courses in radio and television for bishops, and participated in them himself. He organised informal meetings between newspaper editors and bishops, between religious affairs correspondents and bishops. He gave several major newspaper interviews – notably to John Sayers of the *Belfast Telegraph* in the time immediately preceding the outbreak of the Troubles and to Vincent Browne in the *Sunday Tribune* on a favourite topic, the meaninglessness and pointlessness of human life and human history without God.

The Episcopal Conference and the Irish Church will long remain deeply marked by the stamp of Cardinal Conway's primacy and will long benefit from the impetus given by his driving energy and his prudent and enlightened leadership, his 'solicitude for all the Churches'.

Warmth of friendship

Lest the picture evoked by the above description be thought to suggest cold efficiency and impersonal concern with discharge of business, I hasten to add that what his brother bishops felt most deprived of by his passing was the warmth of his friendship and the sincerity of his personal concern for each of them. Bishops' meetings under his chairmanship were reunions of friends, as well as laborious business meetings. We knew him as a brother among brothers, as one who looked forward to being with us and was happy in our company. His personal example helped to teach us how to 'love each other as much as brothers should', his personal enthusiasm inspired us to try to 'work for the Lord with untiring effort and with great earnestness of spirit' (Rm 12:10-12). Younger bishops, especially those appointed during his time as Primate, particularly treasured his friendly welcome to the Conference, his interest and encouragement. He never failed to 'treat the younger men as brothers' (1 Tm 5:2).

He was a man of warm feeling, who felt deeply the pain of others and was sensitive to the 'tears of things' and responded compassionately to human suffering. I experienced this personally after my mother's death in Longford in January 1974. A few days after the funeral, he invited myself and my two sisters to spend the day with him in Ara Coeli. All business was set aside (and this with his crowded schedule had to be rare) and the whole day given over to helping us to rise above the loneliness and sadness of that time.

The Northern Troubles were a cause of great grief to him. I saw him wince with physical anguish from the sight of scenes of Northern violence on the television screen; indeed, on occasion, he switched off the set, unable to continue to watch. One saw him increasingly marked with the lines of care and premature ageing as year followed tragic year of violence and the conflict stubbornly resisted every effort at solution and reconciliation.

The heavy workload and the burden of responsibility which he carried inevitably took their toll. Once, while on my way back to Longford from a visit to Belfast, I called on him in Ara Coeli for a brief visit. He was, as usual, sitting at his desk in his study, surrounded by documents and papers. When I made some remark about his workload, he replied, 'Even if I knew for certain that I would have a heart attack tomorrow, I would still have to do today's work today.' I did not fully realise at the time how prophetic the words were. Even his apparently strong physique and limitless energy could not indefinitely sustain the burden of work which he imposed upon himself. We were soon to realise what a toll his work had taken. He died on 17 April, Low Sunday, in 1977. He died quietly in the evening at 10.30, as his brother Noel said the prayers for the dying and had reached the words 'Depart, O Christian soul...'.

The news caused me deep grief and sadness and a great sense of loss at the departure of a lifelong friend and a great leader of the Church in Ireland. The days and the weeks following had a sense of loss and of anxiety as we faced the future, without the leadership which we bishops had depended so much upon and had come to take for granted for the past fourteen years. We all felt poorer for his passing. Of his fourteen years as Primate and President of the Episcopal Conference, we can truly say *brevi spatio explevit tempora multa,* in a brief space, he accomplished the task of several lifetimes (cf. Wisdom 4:13).

II – Cardinal Tomás Ó Fiaich
(a) Funeral Homily for Cardinal Tomás Ó Fiaich in St Patrick's Cathedral, Armagh
15 May 1990

As the cortège of Cardinal Tomás Ó Fiaich made its sad and solemn way from Dublin northward to Armagh, I recalled another northward journey eleven years ago. Then it was a cavalcade of joy and jubilation, as the newly invested Cardinal returned from the Consistory with what is popularly called the 'Red Hat'. The date was 6 July 1979. No one could then have imagined that in just over a decade his people would be silently and sorrowfully greeting his mortal remains as they followed almost exactly the same route home to Armagh.

The people who gathered in groups all along the route of the cortège, especially the crowds which thronged the streets of Drogheda and Dundalk, who assembled in Crossmaglen and Cullyhanna, who walked in their thousands with the coffin through the streets of Armagh and who, in their tens of thousands, filed past his coffin in the Cathedral, were there to pray for his eternal rest. They were there also, not so much to pay tribute to the memory of a Prince of the Church of whom they were proud, but much more to mourn the loss of a friend whom they loved. For Tomás Ó Fiaich was very greatly and very widely loved. Few cardinals or bishops or churchmen have ever been held in such widespread personal affection as Tomás was.

This country has seldom witnessed such scenes of universal national mourning and affectionate popular tribute as Cardinal Tomás' death has evoked. For hundreds and indeed thousands of people the Cardinal was felt to be a dear personal friend. His death was experienced by us all as a death in the family. Tomás had an exceptional gift for friendship. He just loved people, took delight in being with people. So many have been saying, 'he was just one of ourselves'. He quite simply liked what we Northerners call 'a wee bit of craic', and when any party had Cardinal Tomás in their midst, 'the craic was mighty!' But with him this was not just what is sometimes cynically called the 'pressing of flesh', it was not simply gregariousness; or if it was it was in the sense of a pastor's love of being with the grex, the shepherd's instinctive need to be with the flock.

Love of people

Like the Good Shepherd himself, Tomás knew his sheep one by one and could call each by his or her own name. He knew his own and his own knew him (cf. John 10:3, 14). Tomás had indeed a unique memory for the names of those he met. He had only to meet someone once in order to be able, years afterwards, to greet that person by name as a friend. I met the other day a lady from the Moy, where Tomás was curate for a year in 1952. Thirty-five years later, she met the Cardinal again, and immediately he said to her: 'How are you, Teresa, I haven't seen you for such a long time. How is everyone belonging to you?'

His remembering of people sprang from true Christian charity and from a warmly compassionate heart, sensitive to people's suffering and always eager to speak the word of comfort. One area in which his compassion was particularly evident was in his untiring concern for prisoners. At his episcopal ordination on 2 October 1977, the Cardinal said:

> I want to be among my people in their joys and their sorrow, savouring their moments of exhilaration, sharing their burdens and their griefs, trying to heal the wounds that have been inflicted on the Northern part of the diocese in recent years.

Cardinal Tomás' charity was without distinction of social background or political opinion or religious denomination. During recent days, countless letters of sympathy have been received, many of them recalling a visit made to the home or bedside of someone ill who never expected to be even remembered by the Cardinal. I received a letter of sympathy myself from a retired Presbyterian minister, Dr Tom Patterson, a former Moderator, who had been ill, and whom the Cardinal travelled to Lisburn to visit; and this within the past few weeks, in the midst of a most gruelling schedule of diocesan and national duties and appointments.

Availability for service

Much overseas travelling was undertaken by the Cardinal in recent years in the service of his beloved Alma Mater, Ireland's national seminary of Maynooth. He visited the United States repeatedly and crossed and re-crossed that vast country from coast to coast, visiting its major cities in a great fundraising drive, designed to supplement what we were doing here at home to raise sufficient funds to refurbish the College buildings for its bicentennial in 1995 and to provide a capital endowment sufficient to sustain the College into its third century. The success of that drive owed very much to Cardinal Tomás' personal popularity and enthusiasm. It owes very much also to the great generosity of United States bishops and of many American donors, both clerical and lay, not all of them of Irish origin. The journeys were undertaken by the Cardinal gladly and with never a complaint. Undoubtedly they took their toll of his constitution.

One abiding memory I and many others shall have of him is of the little black diary coming out of his pocket when a request was made; and if the date or time was free, he would immediately say yes, however many the other commitments around that date, however long the journey or tight the schedule. We did not fully realise the burden that this punishing round of commitments was imposing upon even his apparently boundless strength and energy.

He was, we now know, already gravely ill when he set out for Lourdes on his last pilgrimage trip; but he went in order not to disappoint the pilgrims who were to accompany him, and particularly the sick, who so greatly appreciated his warm-hearted personal care of them during each annual pilgrimage.

This was typical of his life of service and availability to others. We can in sober truth say that he gave his life for God's people. In this he generously fulfilled the injunction of the First Letter of St Peter:

> Be the shepherds of the flock of God that is entrusted to you;
> watch over it, not as a duty but gladly.... (cf. 1 Peter 5:2)

Commentators use diverse criteria in presuming to measure the greatness of a prelate. The people of God all over Ireland have spoken and have resoundingly declared that Cardinal Tomás Ó Fiaich was a great Cardinal.

The scholar

Although Cardinal Ó Fiaich remained always at heart a simple man of the people, a beloved prelate and priest in the best Irish tradition of the *sagart rún,* his simplicity and humility concealed great learning and wide-ranging scholarship. He carried his learning lightly and never paraded his specialist knowledge. One could be long and often in his company without realising the extent and variety and depth of his scholarly attainment. His distinguished academic record as student in Maynooth and as postgraduate in UCD and in Louvain already showed his intellectual gifts.

Cardinal Ó Fiaich was equally at home in France, Switzerland, Germany, Austria, Belgium, Holland, Italy and Poland, and was conversant with several European languages. A fellow-cardinal remarked that difficulties of pronunciation never retarded his fluency! He invariably included among his summer commitments a trip to monastic sites and episcopal sees across Europe, which had been founded by Irish monks. On these trips he was often accompanied by members of Seanchas Ard Mhacha, the Armagh Historical Society. During the coming summer, he had planned to include Clairvaux and Cîteaux in the itinerary, since 1990 marks the ninth centenary of the birth of St Bernard at Fontaines near Dijon in 1090; and through St Malachy, Bernard has special links with Armagh and with Down and Connor. The Cardinal was himself born on the feast of St Malachy. Those who accompanied him on these trips had a privileged opportunity to appreciate his extraordinarily precise and detailed knowledge of the history of Irish monasticism, as well as his infectious enthusiasm for the European dimension of the Irish Church in one of its greatest eras.

The Cardinal's specialist fields of study were Irish language and literature and Irish history, especially Irish Church history, and in particular Celtic monasticism and its British and European missionary spread. His large personal library, however, ranged much more widely over the fields of history, biography, current affairs, theology, spirituality, the history of ideas, literature and travel.

His was no narrow or provincial nationalism. Firmly planted in his native soil of Ireland, Ulster and Armagh, he had the security to be a European man – above all because he was aware of the Christian foundations common to all European national cultures, and appreciated more than most the contribution which Ireland had made to laying those foundations. In his own book on St Columbanus, to which I refer below, the Cardinal proudly quoted the late Robert Schuman, one of the architects of the European Community, as saying that 'St Columbanus is the patron saint of those who seek to construct a united Europe'.

Bishop Joseph Duffy has produced the definitive study of Cardinal Tomás Ó Fiaich's published writings. It is a formidable list. Bishop Duffy denotes three areas of special interest to the Cardinal, in each of which he made a distinguished and original contribution to scholarship. First and predominant among his specialisms was the European outreach of Irish missionary monasticism from the sixth to the tenth centuries. His studies here culminated in his book, *Gaelscrínte i gCéin* (Irish Shrines Abroad), published in 1960. Like so much in Tomás' writings and lectures, this was no dry academic treatise; as Bishop Duffy says, it 'glows with lyrical enthusiasm for the subject'. Related to this is a shorter book, *Irish Cultural Influences in Europe (6th to 12th Century),* published in 1966 by the Cultural Relations Committee of Ireland. Here also I must include his book, *Columbanus in his own Words,* which consists of extracts from the authentic writings of St Columbanus, translated with an introduction and commentary, and published by Veritas in 1974.

A second and related area of specialisation is the study of the life and times of St Oliver Plunkett. Cardinal Ó Fiaich produced two books on St Oliver, published in connection with his canonisation in 1975. The first of these was *Oliver Plunkett, Ireland's New Saint* (1975) and the second *Oilibhéar Pluncéid* (1976). These are two distinct studies, not translations one of the other.

A third area of specialisation was the Gaelic poets of South Ulster, with special reference to the Cardinal's native Creggan. This is a little known field which the Cardinal made peculiarly his own and to which he devoted a large number of monographs extending over many years.

While Professor of Modern History in Maynooth, the Cardinal was editor for thirteen years of *Seanchas Ard Mhacha*, the Journal of the Armagh Historical Society. He not only established this as the outstanding journal of local history in Ireland, but contributed many of its most important and original articles. These ranged over many topics, such as the clergy of Armagh from the Reformation onward, a critical edition of the poems of Art MacCooey, the history of the O'Neills of the Fews.

Irish language revival
Throughout his life the late Cardinal devoted much of his great energy and enthusiasm to the Irish language and its revival. He was a long-serving President of *Cumann na Sagart*, the Association of Irish-speaking priests, and edited its journal, *An Sagart*. When the Irish government set up a special Commission on the Restoration of the Irish Language in 1959, Professor Ó Fiaich was appointed its Chairman and served in this role until the publication of the Commission's report in 1964. In the following year, he was appointed Chairman of *Comhairle na Gaeilge*, the Advisory Council set up by the government to implement the recommendations of the Report. As Primate and President of the Irish Episcopal Conference, Cardinal Ó Fiaich continued to ensure, as Cardinal Conway before him had done, that all liturgical and catechetical texts and all collective Pastoral Letters from the Irish bishops should be published in Irish as well as in English.

His passing is an immense loss to the Irish language movement. As far as the bishops are concerned, we must ensure that his solicitude for the Irish language will live on. We shall try to be faithful to his legacy, and to encourage the use of Irish in the liturgy and continue to publish important Church documents in both languages. We shall endeavour to give our people access to those peerless well-springs of spirituality which are found in the Irish speech of our forebears.

Reconciliation
A dominant preoccupation of the late Cardinal was with the imperative need for reconciliation in Ireland. On the day of his episcopal ordination in this Cathedral he said:

> I want to get to know my Protestant fellow-Ulstermen as well. They will find in me, I think, a man not too different from themselves, simple in tastes, straightforward in speech, unsophisticated in manner, hearty in laughter – one who fully appreciates the great contribution they have made to this Province, who shares with them a love of his native Ulster, who has been saddened by the terrible tragedies which many of their families have suffered in recent years, who understands their fears and apprehensions, and reaches out his hand for their friendship.

It is deeply moving to see, in these days of mourning at his passing, how many of the Cardinal's Protestant fellow-Ulstermen grasped that hand and were touched by the warmth and sincerity of the handclasp. We Catholics have been touched by the many generous tributes to the late Cardinal coming from the Protestant community and from the media.

In September 1987 the Cardinal accompanied the Reverend Dr John Thompson, former Moderator of the General Assembly, on an ecumenical trip to Hamborn in [what was then] the Federal Republic of Germany. On that occasion he said:

> There is in many Northern Ireland Protestants a deep-seated fear of Rome. We Catholics find this hard to understand, yet

we must take it seriously and try to dispel it by reaching out to Protestants in brotherhood and love. We must try to convince our Protestant brothers and sisters that we respect their faith and the spiritual riches of their Protestant tradition. We are fated to share this land with our Protestant neighbours and friends, so let us share it not in competition or rivalry, but as brothers and sisters under our common Father.

Dialogue

Dialogue is the essential key to reconciliation and peace. Words that Pope Paul VI wrote about dialogue in his first encyclical, *Ecclesiam suam,* in 1964, have striking relevance to our situation in Northern Ireland now. The Pope said:

> Our dialogue will not postpone until tomorrow what it can accomplish today. It ought to be eager for the opportune moment. It ought to sense the opportuneness of time…. [It is] we rather than those to whom our dialogue is directed who should take the initiative….

> [Dialogue] excludes the *a priori* condemnation, the offensive and time-worn polemic, the emptiness of useless conversation.

Last January Pope John Paul received the new Ambassador of Ireland to the Holy See. In his address on that occasion, the Pope said:

> We can only hope that the people of Northern Ireland themselves will urge their representatives to engage in dialogue about the situation as it really is, a dialogue without partisan constitutional or political prejudice and without exclusion. There, too, new ways of thinking are needed, more fully centred on achieving the integral well-being of all sectors of the population.

To those who are trying patiently to promote dialogue between the political parties in Northern Ireland at this time, may I be allowed to say today, 'May God grant success to the work of your hands. May you enjoy the blessing Christ promised to the peacemakers.'

Repudiation of violence

Cardinal Tomás suffered deeply from some unjust and offensive descriptions of him in some British and even some Irish media. There were nasty anti-Irish and indeed quasi-racist overtones in phrases used by some British critics, such as 'the man from Crossmaglen'. He carried no bitterness, no grudges, but the pain was keenly felt. Cardinal Ó Fiaich was totally opposed to all use of violence purporting to advance nationalist aims. At his ordination in 1977, he pledged himself to work for

> brotherly love, peace, harmony, reconciliation, mutual forgiveness, an end to past dissensions and a new beginning in the promotion of justice and charity towards all.

In Hamborn in 1987 he said:

> God has placed our two communities, Protestant and Catholic, unionist and nationalist, side by side on the island of Ireland. His intention was certainly not that we should be warring communities, but, in the words of St Paul, 'that out of the two he might make a new creation'. The validity of both identities in Ireland and the right of both to continue must be accepted as the basis for future peace.

> Our first step towards a solution of the Northern Ireland problem must therefore be to secure an end to violence on all sides. The two communities are being driven further apart by the violence. They are being made more hostile to each other, more suspicious, more fearful.

May those committed to violence listen at last in death to this plea from the heart of that great Irishman who was Cardinal Tomás Ó Fiaich.

The song of a happy man

Cardinal Ó Fiaich will be remembered as a people's prelate, a man with the common touch, a happy man who spread happiness around him, a warm-hearted man whose love was without frontiers and who was greatly loved. May this Churchman with the human face, this priest with the cheery smiling look, the man with what Barry White has called 'the mile-wide smile', gaze for ever with delight at the Face of God, whose name is Love.

We shall remember the Cardinal as a happy man, who knew how to be merry and make music with friends, a priest and bishop for whom liturgy was truly celebration. Adapting words from Psalm 41, we can say:

> These things will [we] remember....
> How [Tomás] would lead the rejoicing crowd
> into the house of God
> amid cries of gladness and thanksgiving,
> the throng wild with joy. (cf. Psalm 41:5)

When John Bunyan's Christian pilgrim neared the Celestial City, he broke into a run, and then 'he passed over and the trumpets sounded for him on the other side'. Surely when Tomás passed over the trumpets sounded for him on the other side. Tomás, like all of us who were Maynooth students, thrilled to the singing by the College choir on Ascension Day of the magnificent Beverunge arrangement of the antiphon:

> *Ascendit Deus in jubilatione,*
> *et Dominus in voce tubae.*

> God goes up with shouts of joy
> The Lord goes up with trumpet blast.
> Sing praise for God, sing praise,

Sing praise to our King, sing praise.
(Ps 46:6-7)

Tomás' voice may not blend in perfect tonal harmony with the choirs of angels in heaven, but he will rival them in volume and in enthusiasm as with them he proclaims God's glory and joins in their unending hymn of praise.

Death on pilgrimage at Lourdes

It was fitting that Cardinal Ó Fiaich should die in Toulouse while on pilgrimage to Lourdes. In the tradition of the Irish monks whose footsteps he so often traced across the continent of Europe, he was *peregrinus pro Christo,* a 'pilgrim for Christ'. He had a warm, lifelong devotion to Mary, the Mother of God. He was steeped in the Irish tradition of devotion to Mary, so lovingly and tenderly expressed in the verse of Gaelic poets and in the oral tradition of his beloved Gaeltacht. He died on a Marian feast, the feast of her whom the Irish called 'Mary of the Graces'. We pray for him, in the words transcribed from Irish by Douglas Hyde in his *Religious Songs of Connaught*:

> O holy Mary, O Mother of Our God Jesus Christ, O Queen of the heavens, O Queen of all the world, who do not forsake or despise anyone, mercifully look upon [him] with the eye of compassion and gain for [him] from your beloved Son pardon for all [his] sins ... through the grace and mercy of Our Lord, Jesus Christ, whom you have brought, O Virgin, from your womb, he who lives and reigns with the Father and the Holy Spirit, one God in a trinity most holy, for ever and ever. Amen. (Douglas Hyde, *Religious Songs of Connaught,* II, pp. 243-4)

Merrily in Heaven

Thomas More, awaiting death in his prison cell, wrote to his 'dear child Meg' and asked her to 'pray for me, as I will for thee, that we may merrily meet in heaven'. That would be Tomás' prayer too. In words from Douglas Hyde's *Religious Songs*, can we not picture him, 'where in God's garden no fear or strife is', for 'he made life fairer when here residing'? Let us not grieve, then, as St Paul says, 'like the other people who have no hope' (cf. 1 Thessalonians 4:13). Douglas Hyde's translation continues:

> No sinful mind can imagine, even,
> the joys he shall find in his home in heaven.
> There music and song and mirth surround them,
> waiting for glory with glory around them.
> (*Religious Songs of Connaught,* I, pp. 239-40)

And we pray for ourselves, that the peace and reconciliation between all the people of this island for which Cardinal Tomás prayed and worked may not be long delayed:

> Deliver us, Lord, from every evil
> and grant us peace in our day.
> In your mercy keep us free from sin
> and deliver us from all anxiety,
> as we wait in joyful hope
> for the coming of our Saviour, Jesus Christ.
>
> For the kingdom, the power and glory are yours
> now and for ever. Amen.

(b) Homily at Anniversary Requiem Mass for Cardinal Tomás Ó Fiaich, Crossmaglen, for the first anniversary of his death

It is only fourteen years since the 1977 Synod of Bishops on the theme of Catechetics. The leader of the two Irish participants was to have been Cardinal William Conway, but he had just died, after fourteen years as Archbishop of Armagh. Cardinal Ó Fiaich had been named as his successor, but was not yet ordained bishop. I was then Bishop of Ardagh and Clonmacnois and I attended the Synod as substitute, in company with the late Archbishop Dermot Ryan of Dublin. One of the reasons why I shall never forget that particular Synod is that, after going out to Rome for the opening of the Synod by Pope John Paul, I returned home to Longford the next day, in order to be present in St Patrick's Cathedral, Armagh, for the Episcopal Ordination of Monsignor Tomás Ó Fiaich. I returned to Rome again the following day. Nothing, however, would have prevented me from being present at the ordination of my good friend, later Cardinal Tomás.

The day is still in the memory of all of us, such an occasion was it of exuberant happiness and joyful celebration for the whole Archdiocese and indeed for all Ireland. Nowhere was the joy more ecstatic than here in Crossmaglen, of which Tomás was always so proud to be a parishioner, and which will always be so proud to have had Cardinal Tomás as a native son. That he, so full of life and the joy of living, would himself be dead in fourteen years, would then have seemed unthinkable. Nowhere were the shock and the grief of his death more intensely felt than here in Crossmaglen and in Cullyhanna. I myself received the news in Glasgow, where I was attending an ecumenical meeting. When I returned at night to the address at which I was staying, I was told, just as I entered the door, that I was wanted on the telephone. It was my sister, telephoning from Belfast. She began, 'Isn't this terrible news about the Cardinal?' I could only say, 'But what news?' Then she told me that he had died that day in Toulouse, while on pilgrimage to Lourdes. The news left me speechless. It seemed that there must be some mistake; it just could not be true. Someone so full of life and vitality and boundless energy, someone who simply spread joy all around him, just could not be gone from our midst without warning like this.

Yet, sadly, true it was. Only later did more detailed information about the circumstances of his fatal illness and his death begin to come through, and only later still did it begin to be grasped. For the present, there was only incredulity and bewilderment. One of the youngest of modern Archbishops of Armagh at the time of his appointment, it had seemed that he would hold the primacy for a record number of years. As it was, he was to be called to God after only fourteen years as Primate and as President of the Episcopal Conference, just the same number of years as his predecessor, Cardinal Conway. Within fifteen years, the Archdiocese had lost five bishops, Cardinal D'Alton, Cardinal Conway, Bishop Lenny, Bishop Lennon and Cardinal Ó Fiaich.

I have vivid memories also of the funeral cortège from Dublin Airport to St Patrick's Cathedral, for interment in the shadow of the Cathedral and beside his two immediate predecessors. The crowds which came to Dublin Airport and assisted at the short but moving liturgy in the airport chapel, the crowds which gathered in every town on the homeward journey, the people who lined the roads at many places *en route*, the huge numbers who gathered in Drogheda and Dundalk, all spoke of the affection in which the late Cardinal was held by people all over this country. The scenes in Crossmaglen and Cullyhanna were unforgettable in their solemnity, reverence and hushed dignity, and in the silent grief and fervent prayer of the whole people of each parish. The stewarding in each place, organised by parishioners themselves, was a model of quiet organisation, and the dignified deportment of the people was a credit to the parishes themselves and a moving tribute to a Prince of the Church, who was also one of themselves.

The current number of the Creggan Local History Society's journal, *Creggan*, is a Cardinal Tomás Ó Fiaich memorial number. It includes a series of personal reminiscences of our late Cardinal, some written in response to a touching suggestion made after his death by his sister-in-law, Mrs Deirdre Fee, that people who knew him should put on paper their thoughts about him and send the text to Dean MacLarnon. Many hundreds of responses were received and in their number and diversity they reflect the universal affection in which he was held all over Ireland and overseas, and the wide variety of persons whose lives he touched. The Creggan Local History Society has done us all a great service in recording these reminiscences. As a historian the Cardinal would have greatly appreciated them. Indeed, his sister-in-law recalled that he had once remarked that people often say interesting things about a person who has died, and that it would be still nicer if they were to put their thoughts on paper and conserve them for posterity. The publication of these reminiscences for the first anniversary of the Cardinal's death is particularly timely.

The tributes come from prelates and priests and lay persons, from fellow scholars and from former students, from fellow Cardinals and from leaders of other Churches, from lovers of the Irish language and from GAA enthusiasts, from lifelong friends and from people, both Irish and overseas, who met him only once and never forgot the meeting and who were never forgotten by the Cardinal.

The messages abound in phrases which sum up the Cardinal's many-sided gifts and talents and interests. The Cardinal is seen through the eyes of a multitude of admirers as 'a Celtic saint and pastor', 'a man of great compassion', 'the greatest Irishman I have ever met', 'the last true Prince of Ulster', 'a good priest by another name called', 'your friend, my friend, everyone's friend', 'a much-loved man', 'a man who never forgot you', 'a man whose likes we will never see again'.

Cardinal Tomás was indeed a pastor in the mould of the Good Shepherd, who knew his sheep, one by one, by name, whose voice they recognised as the voice of one of their own, one who, quite literally, 'laid down his life for his sheep'; for there is no doubt but that even his robust constitution could not any longer take the toll of the constant round of engagements which he undertook, simply to be with his people, not only in Armagh but all over Ireland and overseas as well.

The words of the Blessing of St Fursey are indeed appropriate to the man he was and the way he exercised his ministry:

> May the yoke of God's rule be on this shoulder,
> the light of the Holy Spirit on this head,
> the sign of Christ on this forehead,
> the attention of the Holy Spirit in these ears,
> the speech of Heaven in this mouth,
> the work of the Church of God in these hands,
> the good of God and of neighbour in these feet,
> may this heart be a dwelling for God,
> may this person belong entirely to God, the Father of us all.
> (From the Irish)

We offer this Mass for his eternal rest. We offer it for Cardinal Tomás, the traveller for Christ, now come to his Father's House, his eternal Ara Coeli, 'Altar of Heaven'.

Above all, we offer this Mass in memory of the Passion, Death and Resurrection of Jesus Christ, whom Tomás loved and served and helped others to love and serve. We entrust his soul now to the Lord who prayed for him and for us all in his great High Priestly Prayer:

> I pray for those you have given me,
> because they belong to you....
> Holy Father,
> keep those you have given me true to your name,
> so that they may be one like us....
> I want those you have given me
> to be with me where I am,
> so that they may always see the glory
> you have given me
> because you loved me
> before the foundation of the world.
> (Jn 17:9-10, 24)

John Ward, his faithful chauffeur and constant helper during all his years as Archbishop, has recalled how every morning when he was at home the Cardinal would enter the oratory in Ara Coeli for his morning Mass, always happy and smiling. John himself, driver and helper of four cardinals for more than fifty years, also had at all times the same happy and smiling face. So should we all, for Our Lord has said to us:

> Everybody who believes has eternal life. (Jn 6:47)

> He that eats my flesh and drinks my blood
> has eternal life
> and I will raise him up on the last day. (Jn 6:54)

The priest whose hands daily lift up the Body and Blood of Christ at the elevation of the Host and the Chalice in the Mass should have no fear of dying, because he holds up the One who said:

> If I am lifted up
> I will draw all men and women to myself. (Jn 12:32)

In every Mass, the priest prays for himself just before Communion:

> Keep me faithful to your teaching
> and never let me be separated from you.

It is a prayer filled with the unshakeable confidence of St Paul, who said:

> Nothing can come between us and the love of Christ, even if we are troubled or worried, or being persecuted, or lacking food or clothes, or being threatened or even attacked.... These are trials through which we triumph, by the power of him who loves us. For I am certain of this: neither death nor life, no angel, no prince, nothing that exists, nothing still to

come, not any power or height or depth, nor any created thing, can ever come between us and the love of God, made visible in Christ Jesus our Lord. (Rm 8:35-39)

The saintly Curé d'Ars put it very simply but very profoundly when he said:

If I thought for one moment that anything could ever separate me from him whom I hold in my hands at Mass every morning, I would never let him go out of my hands!

Mary in the garden

The Cardinal had a special devotion to Mary, the Mother of God. This is what makes it particularly fitting that he should have died while on pilgrimage to Lourdes. That pilgrimage was for the Cardinal one of the highlights of each year of his episcopate. Nothing was allowed to prevent his leading the Lourdes pilgrimage. Even the grave illness and acute distress and pain which he concealed at the time but which, as we know now, marked the days immediately preceding the Cardinal's departure on the 1990 pilgrimage, would not deter him from going to be with the pilgrims and his beloved sick.

Mary is the Mother and model of faith in Jesus Christ. When a woman in the Gospel cried out, 'Blessed is the womb that bore you and the breasts you sucked', Jesus replied, 'Rather blessed are they that hear the word of God and keep it.' Jesus was undoubtedly pointing to Mary when he spoke what has been called the 'Ninth Beatitude': 'Blessed are those that have not seen but have believed'.

May Mary, to whom the Cardinal so often prayed that she, by her intercession, would 'make us worthy of the promises of Christ', now lead Cardinal Tomás to Jesus Christ, in whom he believed with all his heart and in whom he placed all his trust.

We have the words of the Cardinal's last sermon at Lourdes. In it he said:

May someone very close to us, who stood on the rock beside

us here when the grandparents of many of us were still alive, pray for us now, as we turn to her: 'O Mary of the Graces, Mother of God, O may you protect us on the ground where you trod'.

Turning to the sick, who were always the principal object of the Cardinal's care during the annual Lourdes pilgrimage, the Cardinal said to them:

> You have given the rest of us new inspiration and hope by your courage and serenity and by your patience and resignation in the midst of your suffering.... May you feel the tenderness of Mary's love for you....

And so we in this anniversary requiem Mass turn to Mary – knowing that we are all sinners – and ask her intercession for ourselves now and when we shall most need it in the future:

> Holy Mary, Mother of God, pray for us sinners, now and at the hour of our death.

> A naomh Mhuire, a Mhathair Dé, guí orainn na peacaí anois agus ar uair ár mbáis. Amen.

CHAPTER FOURTEEN

GO NOW TO WHERE I SEND YOU

*Go now to those to whom I send you and say whatever I
command you.*
(Jn 1:7)

ARMAGH
1990-96

a) Arrival in Armagh
i) Installation homily
in St Patrick's Cathedral, Armagh
16 December 1990

I bind myself today to a strong strength,
to a calling upon the Trinity.
I believe in a Threeness with confession of a Oneness
in the Creator of the World....

In stability of earth, in steadfastness of rock,
I bind to myself today God's strength to pilot me,
God's power to uphold me,
God's wisdom to guide me.

These words from the Breastplate of St Patrick express my

prayer and my hope as I stand here today. It is only in that strong strength of God, the Rock of our faith, that I can find courage to face the daunting responsibilities which I am now called to undertake. I draw strength from Christ, who is the 'Amen, the faithful witness' (Rv 1:5), the definitive and total 'Yes' of God to all God's promises that he will be faithful to his people and his covenant 'for a thousand generations and for ever' (cf. Deuterotomy 7-9). Christ founded his Church on 'steadfastness of rock', saying to Peter:

> You are Peter, and on this rock I will build my Church.
> (Mt 16:18)

When Peter's successor, Pope John Paul, called me to be Archbishop in the See St Patrick founded, I felt that that steadfastness of rock would sustain me in this office. It is reported in the Annals of Ulster that in the year 441 'Leo was ordained forty-second Bishop of Rome and Bishop Patrick was approved in the Catholic Faith'. Patrick in the Confession called himself 'a sinner and unworthy'. Knowing myself in every respect much more truly 'a sinner and unworthy', I took heart from the feeling that I was being confirmed in the faith by Pope John Paul II in October 1990.

I recall also that Mael Meadoc Ua Morgair, or Malachy, born in Armagh, became Abbot of Bangor and was at different times Bishop of Down and of Connor and Archbishop of Armagh. I recall the links of St Oliver Plunkett, Archbishop of Armagh and Primate, with the Diocese of Down and Connor. I rely on the prayers of our three great patrons of Armagh, Patrick, Malachy and Oliver, as I face my new future in this primatial see.

Cardinal Ó Fiaich

The last time that I stood at this ambo was at the funeral Mass for the late Cardinal Tomás Ó Fiaich, on 15 May last. Nothing was further from my thoughts then than that I would be here seven months later as his successor. No one could emulate the late beloved Cardinal's unique charism for personal relationships with

people from all backgrounds and across all barriers, or his
unrivalled memory for persons and their names and life-stories. I
cannot even attempt to do so. Much less can I hope to attain to his
exceptional knowledge of the history and traditions of his native
Archdiocese and each of its parishes, or to his close and personal
familiarity with each of its priests and their families. To my loss and
to my sincere regret, I cannot emulate his unrivalled knowledge of
our Irish language and his immersion in its rich heritage of
spirituality, although I can assure all lovers of Irish, on my own
behalf and on behalf of the Episcopal Conference, that his
commitment to the Irish language will be kept up by the
Conference.

I came to Ara Coeli on 30 November, and the warmth of the
welcome I have already experienced since I came assures me that I
shall be very happy among the warm-hearted and kind and friendly
people of the Archdiocese. It is with complete trust in God's grace
that I look forward confidently and eagerly to serving you and
serving God with you in the years ahead.

I am humbly conscious of the very great honour of being called
to be Archbishop of this Primatial See of All Ireland, and it is with
joyful hope that I join with you in saying 'Yes' to God for the future
we shall share together in Armagh. So today is a day of spiritual joy.
It is with joy in our hearts today that we draw living water from the
well-springs of our salvation in this holy Eucharist (cf. Isaiah 12:3).
It is appropriate that my installation should take place on this third
Sunday of Advent. This Sunday is called in our liturgy 'Gaudete
Sunday'. It takes this name from the first word of the entrance
hymn: *'Gaudete'* – 'Rejoice'. 'Rejoice in the Lord, always', says St
Paul, 'again I say rejoice. The Lord is very near' (Ph 44:5).

Joy in believing
There are some, alas, in our community who do not seem to find
joy in their faith. They seem to find the Church and its teaching
negative and burdensome, as if it denied them space and freedom
and fulfilment and burdened them with guilt. That perception
could only come from a caricature of what the Church is and

teaches. We pastors too, who are such inadequate ministers of the Gospel, must take some of the blame. Certainly, none of the fault lies with Christ or with his Gospel.

For Christ's Gospel is Good News, 'good spiel', a message to be preached with enthusiasm and received with joy. Karl Barth once remarked that Christian pastors should no longer say to their people, 'You are bound to believe', but rather, 'You are permitted to believe, you are privileged to believe'.

No words recur more often in the New Testament than 'love', 'freedom', 'joy'. For the New Testament message which the Church proclaims is that each woman and each man amongst us is personally loved by God with a love which is unconditional, which is boundless, which is infinite and therefore knows no bounds and no limits and has no end. That love is everlasting, and therefore never-ending, and therefore always new. So real, and, we could say, so 'down to earth', is his love for us that he sent his only Son to earth to be one of us, to be close to us. So now we can see God's beauty reflected in the face of Christ, we can feel God's love pulsating in the human heart of Christ. If we hold on to Christ, or rather if we allow Christ to hold on to us and to lead us by the hand, then nothing, in this life or in the next, nothing in the past, nothing now and nothing ever to happen in the future, can separate us from the love of God which is made visible in Christ Jesus (cf. Romans 8:38-9).

There are no lengths to which God will not go to convince us of his love for us. We need only look at the Crucifix to see what God is prepared to do for us, what he is willing to go through for us. 'It wasn't in fun', said Angela of Foligno, 'that God loved us.' The crucifix shows how much we all mean to God, how precious we each are in his eyes.

Again and again as a refrain there runs through the Old Testament and the New the words: 'Do not be afraid: I am with you'. To know God's love and his nearness is enough to set us free from fear, free from loneliness or lostness, free from the dread of being unwanted or unloved.

God's love is a patient, compassionate, forgiving love. We just cannot stop God from loving us. It is God's joy to forgive us, however badly and however often we offend. God never tires of forgiving and of giving us a new start. There is 'joy in heaven' every time we turn back to him and ask for his forgiveness. His forgiveness changes our past with all its shabbiness, lifts the load of guilt from our shoulders and frees us for a new future. In the last book of the New Testament, the Book of Revelation, we hear God saying to us:

> The world of the past is gone ... Now I am making the whole of creation new. (Rv 21:4, 5)

If we do feel burdened with a load of guilt this could only be because we have failed to come to Him to have our burden lifted. For Jesus has said:

> Come to me all of you who are tired from carrying heavy loads and I will give you rest. (Mt 11:25)

In another place he says with sadness:

> Yet you refused to come to me that you may have life. (Jn 5:40)

Vision of a New Ireland
The Church's whole message is therefore a message of love: God's incredible love for us and Christ's new commandment that we love one another as he has loved us. That is the blessed vision of peace which the Church wishes to share with all peoples in all generations. That vision gives meaning and purpose to life. It is that vision which shows us the unique value of every human existence, the dignity of each single human being, and the respect due to each one, regardless of race or class or address or income-bracket. That Christian vision is the ground of our sense of human rights, it is the foundation of our belief in justice for all, it is the source of our hope for a just, compassionate and caring society. It gives motivation and

courage for our struggle for reconciliation and for peace. It is the vision of a new world. It is the vision of a New Ireland.

We welcome today the recently elected President of Ireland, Mary Robinson. There is a sense of newness in the air in our country at this time. There is an intimation of a new future, of new possibilities, of new beginnings. But words like these are remarkably similar to the opening lines of each of the four Gospels. St Mark begins his Gospel on a note of almost breathless excitement:

> The beginning of the Good News about Jesus Christ the Son of God. (1:1)

Now is the opportunity for the Church in Ireland to rediscover that sense of excitement about the Good News of Jesus Christ. The New Testament is all about newness: a new testament, a new covenant, a new creation, a new heaven and a new earth, a new Israel, a new Jerusalem, a new people, a new law, a new commandment of love, a new song.

The Church is always new with the newness and the eternal youthfulness of Jesus Christ. This is an exciting time in the life of the Church. It is great to be a follower of Jesus Christ in his Church at this time. It is a privilege to be allowed to be a worker for his Kingdom.

Everything that is needed to make Ireland new and to give Ireland new life and new hope and new confidence is contained in the Good News of Jesus Christ, and will not be found without him. The whole meaning and purpose of the Church is to spread that Good News, to celebrate it, to help people to experience it, to share it with the poor and the excluded, the estranged and the alienated. The New Ireland will be based on a new discovery by all of us of the new depths of love which are to be explored anew in each generation in the mystery of Jesus Christ (cf. Ephesians 3:4).

The Church has no word to say to the world except Jesus Christ. It has nothing to give to the world except Jesus Christ. But he is the ultimate answer to all human needs and all human problems. In Christ all things are made new. Dostoevsky's Kirillov declares:

> Listen, that man was the loftiest of all on earth. He was that which gave meaning to life. The whole planet, with everything on it, is more madness without that Man. (*The Possessed,* trans. Constance Garnett, Heinemann, London, 1948)

Malcolm Muggeridge, towards the end of a long life and an unusual spiritual journey, wrote in his autobiography:

> I have conscientiously looked far and wide, inside and outside my own head and heart, and I have found nothing other than this man [Christ] and his word which offer any answer to the dilemmas of this tragic, troubled time. If his light has gone out, then as far as I am concerned, there is no light.

'Open wide the doors to Christ'

Pope John Paul introduced his pastoral ministry as Pope on 22 October 1978 with a homily in which he said:

> Do not be afraid! Open, open wide the doors to Christ!... Do not be afraid! Christ knows 'what is inside a person'. Only he knows! Today too often people do not know what they carry inside, in the deepest recesses of their soul, in their heart. Too often people are uncertain about the sense of life on earth. Invaded by doubts, they are led into despair. Therefore – with humility and trust I beg you and I implore you – allow Christ to speak to the person in you. Only he has the words of life, yes, eternal life (quoted in *Christifideles laici* 34).

The Church and the poor

To open wide the doors to Christ, as Pope John Paul urges us, is also to open the doors to the poor. The poor are near to the heart of the Church, they are the true riches of the Church. Jesus teaches that he regards everything done for the poor as being done for himself and everything refused to the poor as being refused to himself. But the poor are often turned away from the door of our society. A journalist has recently remarked how newspapers and the media in the 1990s are filled with the pictures and the stories of the beautiful, the rich and the famous, while all too often the living conditions and the life stories of the disabled, the poor and the homeless, the people of no property, are out of sight and out of mind. The bishop, as 'commissioned to continue the work of Christ the eternal pastor' (cf. *Decree on the Pastoral Office of Bishops in the Church, Christus Dominus* 1), must not fail to keep the poor constantly in his own mind and bring them before the mind of the public. The bishop must be strong on behalf of the weak; he must be a clear voice for the voiceless.

While being aware that not everything that is ideally desirable is economically or fiscally possible, the bishop must remind people that the economic recovery of recent years, for which due credit must be given to governments and to all concerned, has nevertheless left many people and many families in our society no better off, indeed in too many cases worse off than before. Can we genuinely speak of 'economic boom', while so many citizens of the nation are excluded from that 'boom'? Wealth does not 'trickle down' automatically to those at the bottom of the heap. A rising economic tide does not 'lift all boats', but leaves many stuck hopelessly and helplessly in the mudflats of poverty. Moral and political decisions are necessary on the part of government, and sacrifices are needed on the part of the beneficiaries of the 'boom', if the casualties of national prosperity are to be brought back to an acceptable level of human dignity and to be made full members of society. No government and no section of society can be satisfied with our record of recovery while unemployment remains high, and real poverty is still the fate of many.

The French theologian, Jacques Ellul, once spoke about 'the fashionable poor'. There are groups and problems for whom it is fashionable to campaign and to lobby, but there are other groups and problems which have no lobby and about which we hear and read too little. Rural poverty, the recurrence to an alarming degree in many areas of rural depopulation, mainly due to large-scale migration, the prospect of still greater flight from the land because of the economic weakness of small farmers, these are among the problems which affect the very structure of our society and which must be made to disturb the conscience of politicians and of citizens.

The Church and the alienated

To open the doors to Christ is to be confronted with people who have felt that the doors of the Church are closed to them, those who feel rejected in or by the Church. There are people and there are groups who feel estranged and alienated from the Church and who do not experience the Church as interested in them or as listening to them. A bishop, as a pastor who should take the Good Shepherd as his model, must go out to them too, he must offer dialogue to them too. There is no real dialogue without listening; and therefore the bishop must be a good listener. He must be open to learning from these people and to receiving from them, knowing always that Christ, in whose name he acts, and only Christ, knows and can judge the secrets of the heart, and knowing that, if he, the bishop, listens, Christ will hear and Christ will act through him and will speak the word which stills the storm and bids the angry waves be still.

The Church in dialogue

The Vatican Council reminds bishops that it is 'the mission of the Church to maintain a close relationship with the society in which she lives'. Bishops are exhorted by the Vatican Council to promote dialogue with the men and women of our time (*Christus Dominus* 13). Pope Paul VI gave a masterly outline, in his first encyclical, *Ecclesiam Suam,* published in 1964, of the qualities which must characterise the dialogue of the Church. He declared that the Church must 'strive constantly to put the message of which [she] is the custodian into the mainstream of human discourse'. Pope Paul stressed how we must approach those with whom we enter into dialogue, with love for their person, with respect for their sincerity, listening and not just refuting, persuading and not just dismissing.

The Church's dialogue must always be a dialogue of love. St Paul spoke of 'living by the truth and in love' (cf. Ephesians 4:15). He saw himself as an 'ambassador for Christ', and was conscious in preaching of 'God appealing through us' (cf. 2 Corinthians 5:20). Of his own ministry of preaching St Paul said:

> Since we have by an act of mercy been entrusted with this work of administration, there is no weakening on our part. On the contrary, we will have none of the reticence of those who are ashamed, no deceitfulness or watering down the word of God; but the way we commend ourselves to every human being with a conscience is by stating the truth openly in the sight of God. (2 Co 4:12)

If we are trying really to be a voice for Christ, letting Christ speak through us, then we can be serenely confident that Christ's truth will prevail. We will respect Christ's truth too much to speak it in anger or without love. St Matthew applies to Jesus himself the words of Isaiah:

> He will proclaim the true faith to the nations.
> He will not cry out or shout aloud,
> nor will anyone hear his voice in the streets.
> He will not break the bruised reed,
> Nor put out the smouldering wick
> till he has led the truth to victory.
> (cf. Matthew 12:18, 20)

St Paul solemnly charges his young disciple, Timothy:

> Before God and before Christ Jesus who is to be the judge of the living and the dead, I put this duty to you, in the name of his Appearing and of his Kingdom: proclaim the message and welcome or unwelcome, insist on it. Refute falsehood, correct error, call to obedience – but do all with patience and with the intention of teaching. (2 Tm 4:1, 2)

Like the Apostles, we bishops cannot stop proclaiming what we have seen and heard from Christ (cf. Acts 4:20). But we must try to proclaim it in such a way that it will be heard for what it really is, a word which is Good News, 'good tidings of great joy', a truth which liberates, a truth which heals the bruised and mends the broken and rekindles the flickering flame of a faith which has burned low. St Augustine reminds us that a statement is not necessarily true just because it is harsh: *Non ideo verum quia durum.* Christian dialogue can never be a dialogue of the deaf or a diatribe of the strident or a polemic of the angry.

The Church and ecumenism

The Vatican Council called the Church to dialogue with those outside our communion, who are nevertheless our brothers and sisters in Christ. Here in this land of ours the ecumenical imperative is particularly pressing. It is sometimes suggested that the momentum has gone out of the ecumenical movement and that ecumenism is now reduced again to merely cosmetic gestures. This is not true. Ecumenism is as much as ever in the strong current of the Church's concerns. But we must make this more visible, until the conviction becomes universally established among the whole people of God that one cannot be authentically Christian or Catholic without the ecumenical spirit.

I have been immeasurably heartened since my appointment by the multitude of messages I have received from Church leaders, clergy, lay men and women in the Protestant Churches, and by their promises of prayers and support. The large number of Protestant Church leaders and clergy and people present with us in this cathedral today touches me deeply. It brings forcefully home to me my duty as bishop to do all in my power to build on this good will and to explore with my brothers and sisters in other Churches all opportunities for Catholics and Protestants to work together for mutual understanding and respect, for the removal of reciprocal prejudices and for their replacement by reconciliation and Christian love.

The Church as peacemaker

Christ's parting gift to his Church was the gift of peace (cf. John 14:27). The Church receives that gift in order to pass it on to the world. That gift is desperately needed in the northern part of our land. Now and here, more than ever, a bishop must be a peacemaker. By a long tradition, the bishop has been called a 'Pontifex', a bridge-builder. Bridges are constantly being blown up in this country, but the bombing of physical bridges is a symbol and a cause of something still more tragic, the blowing up of bridges of the mind and the heart, the widening of the separation between the Protestant and the Catholic, the unionist and the nationalist communities. Dividing walls and security gates are grim evidence of a separation which is becoming institutionalised and which, so far as some social strata are concerned, is now not far from total.

Violence and sectarianism are two potent causes of this separation. Opposing and overcoming these twin evils must be a priority concern for all the Churches. We have biblical assurance that in Christ there should be no hostility and there should be no need for any dividing wall. St Paul says:

> [Christ] is the peace between us... [he] has broken down the barrier which used to keep them apart.... In his own person he killed the hostility. (cf. Ephesians 2:14,17)

It is only when we Catholics and Protestants open wide the doors to Christ that we will replace barriers by bridges and find that God's love can vaporise any wall.

St Paul in another place speaks of the veil that prevents the eyes of some from recognising the face of Christ. He says that only Christ himself can remove that blindfold. He says that this will happen when and only when the men and women with the blindfolds over their eyes turn to the Lord (cf. 2 Corinthians 3:15,16). There are people in both communities who keep blindfolds over their consciences which prevent them from seeing the moral enormity of their deeds of violence, and keep them from seeing the inviting finger of Christ calling them back to the love and compassion and mercy which wait for them in his Sacred Heart.

I appeal to these people in God's name to turn to Christ the Lord and to learn from him the meaning of true justice and the way to a just peace. I appeal to them to learn from Christ that love is the secret weapon of the only revolution that really works. St Paul says that our minds 'must be renewed by a spiritual revolution' (Ep 4:23-4). The peaceful revolution which transformed Eastern Europe was primarily a spiritual and a moral revolution and it has achieved by non-violent means what armed uprising could never achieve and what resort to arms, were it to occur, would totally destroy. We can take heart from it for our situation here at home. Violence continues because we, all of us, fail in so many ways to turn our lives towards Jesus Christ, to be converted.

I appeal particularly to republican activists, who were brought up in their childhood to listen to God and to the Church and who might be expected to listen to a Catholic bishop. I wish to say to them: 'The longer you continue with your campaign of violence, the more inglorious in the end will be the memory you will leave behind you and the further away from attainment will be any of your aims and objectives. If or when you call off your campaign, your aims and objectives become in principle attainable through the only means by which they ever could be attained, namely through peaceful political processes. You have no sane reason or justification, moral, rational or political, for continuing with your campaign of violence. You have every reason, religious, moral, rational and political, for calling off your campaign now. May Christ, who enlightens every man and woman coming into this world (cf. John 1:9) enlighten your minds and your consciences so that in his light you may, as St Patrick puts it, 'recover your senses for God' (*Letter to Coroticus*).

Mary of Graces
We turn to Mary, Queen of Peace, to intercede for us and for our country that we may receive Christ's gift of peace. In lovely words from the Irish, we say:

Blessed is she, the bright white Swan,
The first who really cared.
She is summer's milk and honey,
Who heard and kept God's word.

In words from the *Leabhar Breac,* we pray:

O Temple of the Divinity,
O Beauty of Virgins,
O Mistress of the clan,
O Fountain of the garden,

O Cleansing of the sins,
O Washing of the souls,
O Mother of the orphans,
O Solace of the wretched,
Destroy our wickedness and corruption.

In the words of other prayers from the Irish I make my own
prayer to Mary at this beginning of my new life in Armagh:

O Woman of the poor
Let me anger Him no more.

My very love
Whisper for me before God
That His will may be mine
And my will may be His.

A Mhuire na ngrás,
A Mháthair Mhic Dé,
Go gcuire tú
Ar mo leas me.

Garda na n-aingeal
Os mo chionn;

Dia romham
Is Dia liom.

Mary of Graces,
Mother of God's Son,
May you set me
On the right course.
May you save me
On sea and on land.
May you save me
From eternal loss.

Guard of angels,
Over my head;
God before me
And God with me.
Amen.

(ii) Meeting with the priests of Armagh
Homily preached in St Patrick's Cathedral
11 February 1991
during Mass concelebrated
with the clergy of the Archdiocese

This is my first meeting as Archbishop with the priests of Armagh as a body. I particularly wanted this first meeting between us to be a gathering together around the altar in concelebration of the Eucharist. St Thomas Aquinas stated that the first effect of the Eucharist is the building up of the body of Christ which is the Church. We, the bishop and the priests of the Church founded by St Patrick, have a shared task, which is the building up of the Church in Armagh, of which we and the laity together are the 'living stones, making a spiritual house' (1 P 2:5).

Mass concelebrated by the bishop and his priests in the cathedral church is a special expression and a particularly fertile source of the communion which is the Church in the world and the Church in a diocese. The Vatican Council, in its *Constitution on the Liturgy*, said:

> The bishop is to be considered as the High Priest of the flock from which the life in Christ of his faithful is in some way derived and upon whom it in some way depends.

> Therefore all should hold in the greatest esteem the liturgical life of the diocese centred around the bishop, especially in his Cathedral Church. They must be convinced that the principal manifestation of the Church consists in the full, active participation of all God's holy people in the same liturgical celebrations, especially in the same Eucharist, in one prayer, at one altar, at which the bishop presides, surrounded by the college of priests, and by the ministers (*Sacrosanctum Concilium* 41).

This is why the Mass of Chrism on Holy Thursday, concelebrated by the bishop and the priests of the diocese, is a high point of the liturgical life of the diocese each year, and why every priest who can should attend and concelebrate.

In a beautiful phrase in its *Constitution on the Church*, the Council called the diocesan Church an 'altar community'. The Council said:

> [In the local Church] the faithful are gathered together through the preaching of the Gospel of Christ, and the mystery of the Lord's supper is celebrated 'so that, by means of the flesh and blood of the Lord, the whole brotherhood of the Body may be welded together'. In each altar community, under the sacred ministry of the bishop, a manifest symbol is to be seen of that charity and 'unity of the mystical body, without which there can be no salvation'. In these communities ... Christ is present, through whose power and influence the One, Holy, Catholic and Apostolic Church is constituted. For a 'sharing in the body and blood of Christ has no other effect than to accomplish our transformation into that which we receive'. (*Lumen gentium* 26)

The more closely each one of us is united to Christ through being 'filled with every grace and blessing' at his altar, and thereby transformed into Christ, the more we shall be in deep communion of faith and love with one another, as we together carry on his work in the world. The more we shall thereby be giving joy to Christ, who prayed for us at the Last Supper:

> I pray for them;
> I am not praying for the world
> but for those you have given me,
> because they belong to you....
> Holy Father,
> keep those you have given me true to your name,
> so that they may be one like us....
> Now I am coming to you

and while still in the world I say these things
to share my joy with them to the full....
As you sent me into the world,
I have sent them into the world....
Father, may they be one in us,
as you are in me and I am in you,
so that the world may believe it was you who sent me....
With me in them and you in me,
may they be so completely one
that the world will realise that it was you who sent me
and that I have loved them as much as you loved me.
(Jn 14:9, 11, 13, 18, 21, 23)

Bishop and priests

The Second Vatican Council saw itself in certain respects as a continuation of the First Council of that name, and as completing its teaching. There is a certain limited truth in the remark that the First Vatican Council was the Council of the Papacy, and the Second the Council of the Episcopacy. Certainly, the theology of the episcopacy and the role and responsibility of the bishop were amply developed in Vatican II. But this was always situated in the context of the communion of bishops, priests, religious and lay people in the Church, and the communion of the whole people of God, through their bishop, with the Pope.

The responsibility of the bishop towards his priests is particularly strongly stressed. In the *Constitution on the Church*, the bishop is invited to

> treat the priests, his helpers, as his sons and friends, just as Christ calls his disciples no longer servants but friends. (*Lumen gentium* 28)

In the *Decree on the Pastoral Office of Bishops in the Church*, the bishop is again reminded of his special relationship with his priests. This document says:

His priests, who assume a part of his duties and concerns, and who are ceaselessly devoted to their work, should be the objects of [the bishop's] particular affection....

[He] should be solicitous for the welfare – spiritual, intellectual and material – of his priests, so that they may live holy and pious lives and may exercise a faithful and fruitful ministry....

A bishop should be compassionate and helpful to those priests who are in any kind of danger or who have failed in some respect. (*Christus Dominus* 16)

The bishops at the Council became aware, in the course of their deliberations, that they could be perceived as being overly preoccupied with their own place in the Church. Several bishops called for equal attention to be paid to the ministry of priests. Cardinal Conway was prominent among those who intervened in this sense and his intervention more than any other led to the addition of a special document on priests, the *Decree on the Ministry and Life of Priests*. This document says:

All priests share with the bishops the one identical priesthood and ministry of Christ. Consequently the very unity of their consecration and mission requires their hierarchical union with the order of bishops. This unity is best shown on some occasions by liturgical concelebration, and priests also affirm their union with the bishops in the Eucharistic celebration. Bishops, therefore, because of the gift of the Holy Spirit that has been given to priests at their ordination, will regard them as their indispensable helpers and advisers in the ministry and in the task of teaching, sanctifying and shepherding the People of God....

On account of this common sharing in the same priesthood and ministry, bishops are to regard their priests as brothers and friends and are to take the greatest interest they can in their welfare, both temporal and spiritual. For on their shoulders particularly falls the burden of sanctifying their priests: therefore they are to exercise the greatest care in the progressive formation of their diocesan body of priests. They should be glad to listen to their priests' views and even consult them and hold conference with them about matters that concern the needs of pastoral work and the good of the diocese. (*Presbyterorum ordinis* 7)

Priests, for their part, are asked 'to reverence [in the person of their bishop] the authority of Christ the supreme pastor'. They are invited to 'be attached to their bishop with sincere charity and obedience' (7). Priests are reminded that there was never greater need than in our day for close union of priests with their bishop and with one another, because of the complexity of pastoral problems and the diversity of pastoral needs. The document continues:

No priest is sufficiently equipped to carry out his own mission alone and as it were single-handed. He can only do so by joining forces with other priests, under the leadership of those who are rulers of the Church. (7)

In the light of the Council
I referred to these passages from the Council documents in my first address as bishop to the priests of my first diocese, Ardagh and Clonmacnois, on the evening of my episcopal ordination, 16 July 1967. I remarked then on how happy I felt that, since I was called to be bishop, it was in the aftermath of the Second Vatican Council, with all its rich theology of the Church as communion and of the episcopacy and the priesthood as part of that communion. I spoke of what a privilege and a joy it was to commit myself to serving the priests, and, with them, serving the whole People of God in that diocese, in the spirit of the Vatican Council, to which I wanted wholeheartedly to dedicate myself as bishop.

I renewed that commitment again in the first Mass I concelebrated with the priests of Down and Connor on 26 October

1982. I gladly renew that commitment with you, as we gather around this cathedral altar in Armagh today.

Survey of Armagh priests

I count myself doubly privileged that I begin my episcopal ministry in Armagh with the Report on the Survey of Armagh Priests 1990 to guide myself and you in the pastoral planning we are to share together in the Archdiocese in the coming years. This survey, as you know, was carried out among the priests throughout the year 1990 by a team of Jesuit Fathers. They were commissioned in January 1990 by the late Cardinal Tomás Ó Fiaich and by the Senate of Priests. The team began its round of personal interviews with priests exactly a year ago, on Ash Wednesday 1990.

The Jesuits met with a magnificent response from the priests of the diocese. Indeed, nearly all the priests (97%) agreed to be interviewed. The findings were presented in draft form to the priests of the Archdiocese at two well-attended meetings or 'Interim Report Days', held in Carrickmacross, in June 1990. The purpose of these meetings was to ascertain whether the priests accepted the Report as an accurate reflection of their own feelings and views and needs, as conveyed at the interviews. There were strong affirmations from the priests at both these meetings that the text did indeed correspond with their own thinking and that the priests of the Archdiocese accepted the findings as their own. In today's phrase, the priests of Armagh 'own' the survey.

Morale of priests

I feel it is a blessing to have in this survey a representative and reliable outline of the views of the priests about the present situation in our diocese, their discernment of its problems and needs, their vision of its mission, their hopes for its future. I am pleased to note that, as the Jesuit team put it, the morale of the priests is high. The Jesuits state:

> Virtually every priest and seminarian with whom we talked affirmed very positively that he was happy with his vocation

and believed strongly in the value of the priesthood. We were impressed by the commitment, approachability, a real concern for people, a desire and readiness to respond to people's needs, a remarkable conscientiousness in undertaking visitations and care of the sick, which characterise the clergy of the Diocese.

It was significant that many priests strongly resisted the notion, that partially gave rise to the survey, that the morale of the clergy is low.

While naturally pleased at this, I am not surprised. From my experience in two other dioceses and from my first observations in Armagh, I can say without hesitation that the diocesan priests of Ireland are a quite outstanding body of men. The bishops of Ireland are uniquely blessed in the priests who are their 'prudent cooperators' in the service of the Kingdom of God. I do not know if any bishops anywhere are so fortunate as the Irish bishops are in the quality of their priests and the faith, charity and loyalty of their people.

In all my experience in twenty-four years as bishop, I have been edified by the spirit of faith-filled obedience with which priests accept pastoral assignments, even unexpected and difficult ones. I have been inspired by their readiness to co-operate with new initiatives, their openness to change. Indeed, I doubt if any priests anywhere have come through the past quarter century of post-conciliar renewal with so much genuine regeneration, so little trauma, and so much fidelity to the spirit and the letter of the Council. In this Mass, I am thanking God for that and I am asking him to keep his blessing hand over us. In the words of St Paul:

> I am certain that the One who began this good work in you will see that it is finished when the Day of Christ Jesus comes. (Ph 1:6)

The Council and the signs of the times
The survey shows how remarkably the thinking of the priests

corresponds with the vision of the Council. Nearly every single recommendation in the survey is paralleled in the texts of the Council, as the passages I quoted earlier suffice to show. It is gratifying to note how much of the Council's teaching has entered the mainstream of the thinking of the priests.

It is also clear that the reading by the Council of the 'signs of the times' in the early 1960s and its insights into the profound cultural changes of the late twentieth century are verified by our own experience as we enter the 1990s. Truly, the Council was the work of the Spirit who 'renews the face of the earth'.

Partnership with the laity

It is gratifying to note the full acceptance by priests of the teaching of the Council and of the 1987 Synod of Bishops on 'The Vocation and Mission of the Laity in the Church and in the World'. There is strong consensus among the priests of the Archdiocese about the need for partnership in ministry between ourselves as ordained ministers and lay men and women. The Council left no doubt in anyone's mind about this. The *Constitution on the Church* declared:

> The pastors [of the Church] should recognise and promote the dignity and responsibility of the laity in the Church. They should willingly use their prudent advice and confidently assign duties to them in the service of the Church, leaving them freedom and scope for acting. Indeed, they should give them the courage to undertake works on their own initiative. They should with fraternal love consider attentively in Christ initial moves, suggestions and desires proposed by the laity. Moreover, the pastors must respect and recognise the liberty which belongs to all in the terrestrial city.
>
> Many benefits for the Church are to be expected from this familiar relationship between the laity and the pastors. The sense of their own responsibility is strengthened in the laity, their zeal is encouraged, they are more ready to unite

their energies to the work of their pastors. The latter, helped
by the experience of the laity, are in a position to judge more
clearly and more appropriately in spiritual as well as in
temporal matters. Strengthened by all her members, the
Church can thus more effectively fulfil her mission for the
life of the world (*Lumen gentium* 37).

The post-synodal document *Christifideles laici* confirmed this
teaching in a particularly challenging way. This is clearly a direction
in which the Spirit is moving the Church at this time, and we dare
not resist the Spirit. The Armagh Priests' Survey points the
Archdiocese in this same direction. I enthusiastically accept this as
a priority for myself. I already know from experience in two
dioceses what a vast resource the laity are for the Church and how
severely judged we would be if we were to leave that resource
unused or underused in the work of the Kingdom.

Facing problems realistically
The survey does not shirk our deficiencies and our lacks. It names
our failings openly and faces our problems honestly and
realistically. It enumerates in adequate detail the felt personal needs
of the priests of the Archdiocese, the parochial/pastoral needs we
have to tackle, the diocesan needs which we must meet together. It
outlines the priorities as the priests see them. It places the
Archbishop and priests together in face of our respective and our
shared responsibilities. The survey amounts to an outline pastoral
plan for the Archdiocese. It presents a challenge which will stretch
everyone to the full until the end of the century and even beyond.

I shall certainly not see the end of the century. But I do pledge
all the time that is left to me and all the energy that is left in me to
working with you to implement that pastoral plan.

Practical steps
At the last meeting of the Senate, the first I attended, I renewed the
mandate of the Senate. It was agreed that at the next meeting of
each area group of priests, the sole agenda will be the survey and

its recommendation. The clergy conferences over the coming year will all be devoted to the themes of the survey. To facilitate personal study of the survey by priests and group discussion of it, the text of the survey will be printed as soon as possible and circulated to the priests.

I take note for myself of the Jesuit team's conviction that 'progress… depends fundamentally on the following two premises':

a) That the Archbishop and the priests share the conviction of the need to work together with the laity to discover where the Holy Spirit is leading the diocese as a Particular Church (Canon 369) in this place and time.

b) That the Archbishop enables and actively participates in the discernment process, listening and learning from experience what are the providential realities of this diocese at this time and exercising his personal role as bishop from within this reality rather than from concepts alone.

I take to myself what is said about the Archbishop there, and I shall make it my best endeavour to see that I do not fail the challenge.

Forward in hope

In all this we have the consolation of knowing that we never walk alone in the vineyard of the Lord. It is his mission that we are continuing and he is with us as we work. The pericope which now concludes the Gospel of St Mark tells us:

> So the Lord Jesus, after he had spoken to them, was taken up into heaven; there at the right hand of God he took his place, while they, going out, preached everywhere, the Lord working with them and confirming the word by the signs that accompanied it. (Mk 16:19-20)

This is the great 'Sursum Corda' of the Apostolic Church. We find it again on the lips of St Stephen at his martyrdom:

> I can see heaven thrown open and the Son of Man standing
> at the right hand of God. (Ac 7:56-57)

However dark the clouds and however violent the storms on the earth's surface where we live and work, the Lord sits on high at God's right hand; he lives and reigns with the Father in the unity of the Holy Spirit for ever and ever. As the Abbot Vonier once put it, 'He has won all our battles for us long before we were born.' It is in the name of that Risen and Ascended Lord that we conclude every prayer in the liturgy. It is in confident hope in his triumph over all the powers of darkness and all the forces of evil that we carry on our ministry.

From his place in glory, he sends the Holy Spirit on the Church. He sent the Holy Spirit on each one of us at our ordination. He continues to send that Spirit on the people to whom we minister through our preaching of his Word and our celebration of his sacraments. The Fourth Eucharistic Prayer says:

> That we might live no longer for ourselves but for him,
> he sent the Holy Spirit from you, Father,
> as his first gift to those who believe,
> to complete his work on earth
> and bring us the fullness of grace.

So we can face our future task together in boundless hope. In the words of St Paul:

> May the God of hope bring you such joy and peace in your
> faith that the power of the Holy Spirit will remove all bounds
> to hope. (Rm 13:13)

Mary, help and hope of Christians

That same Holy Spirit came down upon Mary at the Annunciation, at the beginning of her ministry as Mother of Jesus and again at Pentecost, at the beginning of her ministry as Mother of the Church. Overshadowed and filled by the Spirit, Mary is the prototype of perfect discipleship and the model for all Christian ministry. We turn to her and ask for her motherly intercession in our priestly ministry. The Council's Constitution on the Church says:

> The Church in her apostolic work rightly looks to her who gave birth to Christ, who was conceived of the Holy Spirit and born of a virgin, in order that through the Church he could be born and increase in the hearts of the faithful. In her life the Virgin has been a model of that motherly love with which all who join in the Church's apostolic mission for the regeneration of mankind should be animated. (*Lumen gentium* 65)

The oldest known prayer to Mary dates from the third century. It is the prayer we know as *Sub Tuum Praesidium*. We make it our own today:

> We take refuge under your protection, O holy Mother of God. Do not reject our prayers in our times of need, but deliver us always from all dangers, O ever glorious and blessed Virgin. Amen.

(b) Appointment as Cardinal

(i) The 1991 Consistory
Homily in St Patrick's Church, Rome
30 June 1991

This Mass celebrated in St Patrick's Church gives us the opportunity to come together as the Irish family in Rome to celebrate in God's presence the sense of thankfulness and rejoicing and happiness which during this week has united us all. St Patrick's is commonly regarded as Ireland's national church in Rome and our congregation this morning is composed mainly of the Irish community in Rome, the priests and people who have come from the Archdiocese of Armagh, from Down and Connor, from Ardagh and Clonmacnois and elsewhere, to be with me here in Rome, and many other friends.

In the words of the liturgy, we pray:

> Father, hear the prayers of the family
> you have gathered here before you....
> In mercy and love unite all your children
> wherever they may be....

I spoke of St Patrick's as 'Ireland's national church'. But in an important sense, there are no national churches in the Holy Catholic Church. For us as Catholics, the Church is a worldwide Church and from Pentecost onwards, people 'from every nation under heaven [have proclaimed] the marvels of God' (Ac 2:5,11), united in one faith and in one communion of love.

The unity of faith and love of that huge multitude of believers of 'every nation, race, tribe and language' (Rv 7:9) is confirmed by their communion with the successor of St Peter, Bishop of Rome, His Holiness, the Pope. The word 'Roman' is not intended to qualify or restrict the word 'Catholic'; rather 'Roman' is the name for that which makes us at once 'one' and 'Catholic' across the world and 'apostolic' across the centuries. To be 'Roman' is to be continuous with the community of the Apostles themselves and in communion of faith with them, as they all were with Peter, chief of the Apostles and first Bishop of Rome.

In the Mass here in Rome we affirm once more our union of faith with Peter's successor, Pope John Paul, and therefore with the Church of every nation. We pray that we may grow in love together with him and all the bishops and clergy everywhere, and that as part of the pilgrim Church Catholic and Apostolic everywhere, we may be strengthened in faith and love with John Paul and the bishops and the entire people 'Christ has gained for his Father'.

In this renewing of our communion with Pope John Paul we are being faithful to the example and teaching of St Patrick and of St Malachy and of St Oliver Plunkett, the three great patron saints of the Archdiocese of Armagh. St Patrick was sent on his apostolic mission to Ireland by Pope Celestine and was most probably ordained bishop for that mission to Ireland in 432 by the Pope's special delegate for the Western Islands of Europe, St Germanus, Bishop of Auxerre. Later, in the year 441, as we read in the Annals of Ulster, Patrick was 'confirmed in the faith' by Pope Leo.

Centuries later, Malachy set out for Rome twice to seek from the hands of the Pope the Archbishop's pallium for himself and the Archbishop of Cashel; the first time in 1140, the second in 1148. On the way to Rome in 1140, Malachy called to Clairvaux. There he met the great St Bernard and the two saintly men became soul friends for life. This meeting also led to the introduction into Ireland by Malachy of the new Cistercian Order, whose first monastery in Ireland was at Mellifont, established in 1142.

The historical and spiritual links of Armagh and of Ireland with Rome are beautifully symbolised by the pallium which I received yesterday, as Archbishop of Armagh, from the hands of the Holy Father. The pallium is a scapular made of wool. It is woven from the wool of lambs which are presented to the Pope on the feast of St Agnes in January and then given into the care of the Benedictine Sisters of Santa Cecilia in Trastevere. The sisters weave the wool into the fabric from which the pallia are made. The pallia are placed in a silver urn and repose above the tomb of the Apostles, Peter and Paul, until their feast on 29 June, when they are placed by the Pope over the shoulders of that year's new archbishops. The symbolism of the pallium is manifold and impressive. It recalls Christ the Lord, the Good Shepherd and the Lamb of God; it recalls his mandate to Peter: 'Feed my lambs, feed my sheep … Confirm your brothers'. The pallium is worn by the Archbishop on all important liturgical occasions. When he dies, it is placed over the chasuble on his body and is buried with him. It places us in line of unity in faith with Saints Peter and Paul and with St Patrick, St Malachy and St Oliver Plunkett, the great patrons of our Archdiocese.

On his second journey to Rome for the pallium in 1148, Malachy called again at Clairvaux. He took ill there with fever and died in the arms of St Bernard on All Souls Day, 1148. His remains were interred in Clairvaux and later those of St Bernard were buried in the same grave. To this day the bones of both saints share a common grave in the Cathedral of Troyes. The late Cardinal Tomás Ó Fiaich brought back a major relic of St Malachy to his native Armagh in 1982.

Modern confessors of the faith
As I received the pallium from Pope John Paul's hands at the Mass in St Peter's Square yesterday, I was conscious of the venerable ninety-year-old Chinese Cardinal, Ignatius Gong Pin-mei, former Bishop of Shanghai, who spent thirty years of his life in prison simply because he would not renounce his communion in the obedience of faith with the Pope. He was put under intense pressure to join the so-called 'Patriotic Church' favoured by the Communist regime in China, under the pretence that he could remain Catholic but cease to be Roman. For this Bishop of Shanghai, in the distant Far East, the condition for being Catholic was to be in communion with Rome. Thirty years of barbaric conditions in a Red Chinese prison were not too high a price to pay for the 'joy and peace of believing' which he found in that communion with Rome.

As I received the pallium, I felt privileged to be close to another great confessor of faith of our time, Alexander Todea of Romania, one of the new Cardinals of this Consistory. Ordained priest and bishop secretly, Cardinal Todea endured fourteen years in prison for his faith and his loyalty to the Bishop of Rome. Early in this period, he managed to escape from prison, hoping to continue his clandestine ministry to his priests and people. He was soon rearrested and for further punishment he was assigned to what was regarded as the most humiliating and degrading job in the prison, cleaning the prisoners' latrines. He regarded this, however, as a blessing from God, firstly because, like the Apostles, he was glad to have the honour of suffering humiliation for the sake of the Name (Ac 5:41); and secondly because this job gave him permission to move throughout the whole prison, instead of being confined to his own sector. This meant that as he cleaned the latrines, he was able to hear the confessions of his fellow prisoners, pray with them, recount scripture passages for them and give them spiritual direction. Even cleaning latrines became an occasion for evangelisation, an opportunity for spreading the Good News of Jesus Christ. In the words of St Thérèse of Lisieux, popularised by Georges Bernanos, he found that 'everything is grace'.

Peace in Ireland
At the end of the ceremony of conferring the cardinalatial ring on the new cardinals, the Pope said to us:

> In the name of the Master and Lord we speak to you, dear brothers and say: 'Go out to your peoples and your Churches … be witnesses to Christ, build up the holy Church of God, bless all and bring the peace of Christ to everyone. The Lord Jesus Christ, Eternal Shepherd and King of all peoples of the earth will guide and will guard you and all of the flocks entrusted to your care'.

Part of a cardinal's task must be to bring the peace of Christ wherever there is war or violence. This charge has a special impact for an Irish cardinal. In fulfilment of it I must work ever harder to bring peace instead of violent conflict in Ireland. From Ireland's church in Rome, titular church of my two predecessors, Cardinal

William Conway and then Cardinal Tomás Ó Fiaich, I appeal to those engaged in violence. I appeal with all the 'passionate pleading' with which Pope John Paul pleaded with you in Drogheda twelve years ago. As one now called by the Pope to be Cardinal Primate of all Ireland, I appeal to you: Turn away from the path of violence. Pursue the struggle for justice which you believe in, but pursue it by the paths of peace, pursue it by the non-violent but efficacious strategies of political organisation and commitment to the real needs of people. You want to shape history; but, as a Mexican pilgrim, a great lover of Ireland, said to me here in Rome, there are other ways and better ways of shaping history and changing the course of history than the ways of war and violence. Here in Rome today we are praying that you will find those better ways.

The political talks
To the politicians now engaged in talks, I want to say that as well as the Irish, almost every one of the countless non-Irish persons I have met here in Rome asked me about the talks in Northern Ireland and whether they were likely to succeed. Politicians should know that there is great international good will accompanying them in their meetings and great worldwide support for their efforts to reach accommodation. There is much prayer across the Christian world for the success of these talks. There will be great disappointment among Christians across the world if the talks fail. Those who would bring about their failure would bear a grave responsibility before world opinion, and, I do not doubt, before God. May God prosper the work of their minds and their hands and give them courage to lead their respective communities in the paths of mutual understanding, reconciliation and peace.

Be faithful
The new cardinals are reminded frequently during the investiture ceremony of the new and greater bond of union between themselves and the Pope and their new responsibility of sharing in a closer way with him in the service of the Universal Church and in

concern for its fidelity in the truth of Christ and its growth in holiness and in love. I ask your prayers for me in these new responsibilities.

St Oliver Plunkett wrote in 1677, 341 years ago:

> The Irish are especially obliged to this [loyalty to the Pope] because of the great tenderness and compassion which the Holy Father has always had for them in their sufferings. I have no doubt but that he will have it as his special care, always to preserve and promote the holy faith in this country and remove all impediments and obstacles which could hold it back.

Earlier in 1669 he wrote:

> I shall not delay long, but shall go to my diocese where until my last breath I shall live in obedience to the Holy See and the service of souls.

What more fitting prayer could I find for whatever years lie ahead than the prayer of St Patrick?

> I now entrust my soul to God, who is most faithful and for whom I am an ambassador in my humble station. For God has no favourites and he chose me for this office to become one of his ministers, even if among the least of them.
>
> What return can I make to him for all his goodness to me? What can I say or what can I promise to my Lord since any ability I have comes from him? Suffice it for him to look into my heart and mind; for I am ready and indeed greatly desire it that he should give me his cup to drink, as he gave it to others who loved him. My only prayer to God is that it may never happen that I should leave his people which he won for himself at the end of the earth. I ask God for perseverance, to grant that I remain a faithful witness to him for his own sake until my passing from this life. (*Confessio*, 56-8)

On the road with Christ

Looking back on my life up to now, particularly my life as priest and bishop, I think of it as a pilgrimage. Again and again, particularly in the Gospel of St Luke, we find references to Jesus as being 'on the road'. The public life of Jesus is represented as a journey, a journey which took Jesus along the roads of Palestine, from village to village, gathering people together to listen to the Father's word, inviting people to follow him on that journey. The journey leads up to Jerusalem: St Luke says: 'They were on the road going up to Jerusalem' (Lk 19:28). The word 'up' is significant: it refers indeed to the journey up to Jerusalem, but also hints at the journey up to Calvary and the Passion, and beyond that again up to the Father, in the Resurrection and the Ascension.

On that journey, Jesus is always found to be out in front, inviting others to follow and waiting for them to catch up with him. Jesus walks ahead, but there is a certain look, a look of eagerness or even impatience on his face, because the work of the Kingdom will not wait. On one occasion the disciples, following him along the road, become conscious of some change in the atmosphere. Anxiously they look at Jesus, and they see the look of intensity and urgency upon his face. 'His face was as the face of one going up to Jerusalem' (Lk 9:53). Jesus took Twelve aside to tell them what was going to happen to him and how much he depended on them to be with him in that hour of trial. He said:

> You are the people who stood faithfully by me in my trials and now I confer a kingdom on you. (Lk 22:28)

We are the people who must stay faithful to Jesus in his trials in today's world. The priest, the bishop, has to share in the sufferings of Jesus, which continue in his people. The priest, the bishop, must be on the side of the poor, the oppressed, the sorrowing; he must even be in some sense on the side of the sinner, to bring the sinner to trust in God's mercy and forgiveness. The priest has to be ready for opposition, for resistance, for criticism. Cardinal Newman once said:

If the Church is not being criticised by the world, it is because she is no longer preaching the Gospel of Christ.

We have got to be prepared to be rejected, criticised and opposed. We take courage from the words of Jesus:

> If you belong to the world, the world will love its own. But you do not belong to the world. I have chosen you out of the world.

Keeping the faith

At my age, I cannot expect many more years of life or active ministry. I can only pray and ask you, my friends, to pray that I may stay faithful to the end and may never lose the sense of enthusiasm for the following of Christ and for his Gospel with which one starts on the road with Jesus Christ in youth. I ask you to pray that, despite all the shortcomings, St Paul's farewell wish may be granted to me:

> As for me, my life is already being poured out on the altar, and the hour for my departure is upon me. I have run the great race, I have finished the course, I have kept the faith. (2 Tm 4:6)

And finally, to you, my friends, I repeat the words of St Paul:

> We are always bound to thank God for you, my friends beloved by the Lord. From the beginning of the time God chose you to find salvation in the Spirit who consecrates you and in the truth you believe. It was for this that he called you through the Gospel we brought, so that you might come to possess the splendour of our Lord Jesus Christ.... And may our Lord Jesus Christ himself and God our Father, who has shown us such love, and in his grace given us such unfailing encouragement and so sure a hope, still encourage and strengthen you in every good deed and word. (2 Th 2:13-17)

May the Mother of Our Lord Jesus Christ, Mary, Virgin of Faith and of faithfulness, help us all by her prayers to trust unreservedly in the unchanging faithfulness of God who remembers the mercy he promised to the children of Abraham for ever.

(ii) Homily at Mass of Thanksgiving in
St Patrick's Cathedral, Armagh
Friday, 5 July 1991

What return shall we make to the Lord for all his goodness to us? God has blessed us in so many ways here in this country of ours, here in this Archdiocese, here in this Cathedral, here in this parish. What return shall we make? What return can we make, except to bless his Holy Name, to give thanks to him, to praise him and sing his praises to others, to love him and make him loved. As Pope John Paul so often repeats: Praised be Jesus Christ; *Laudetur Jesus Christus.*

In the words of the wonderful first chapter of St Paul's Letter to the Ephesians:

> Blessed be God, the Father of Our Lord Jesus Christ, who has blessed us with all the spiritual blessings of heaven in Christ. (cf. Ephesians 1:3)

As we say in one of the great hymns of praise in the Book of Revelation:

> Praise and glory and wisdom,
> thanksgiving and honour and power and strength
> to our God for ever and ever. Amen. (Rv 7:12)

First of all we praise God for the privilege of being chosen to know him through Jesus Christ his Son. We thank God for the privilege and the joy of believing. We praise God for the Good News brought to us by Jesus Christ. We praise God for giving us the privilege of praising him. We thank God for allowing us to thank him. We thank God for the gift of prayer, and we pray that he may always allow us to pray. We thank him for being God, so wonderful a God, so glorious a Lord, so majestic a King, so loving a Father, so caring a Shepherd, so incredible a Saviour, so cruelly crucified for us, so radiantly risen for us, so victoriously living and reigning for us in the glory of the Father. In the words of the Gloria of the Mass: 'We give you thanks, O God, for your great glory'.

We thank God for the great heritage of faith we have received in our country and in our Archdiocese. We thank God for once again, through the Supreme Pastor of his Church, Christ's Vicar on earth, choosing an Archbishop of Armagh to be a Cardinal. Unworthy though I know myself to be, with a full sense of my age and my limitations, I feel proud of this appointment and have joy in it, most of all because it has brought honour and rejoicing to our Archdiocese and, so I have been made to feel by the messages I have received and the crowds who have welcomed me, it has brought joy to many all over Ireland, north and south.

I have been particularly gratified by the many warm messages of congratulations and good wishes and assurance of prayers which I have received from clergy and people in the Protestant Churches. I received here in Rome a particularly warm message from the Archbishop of Canterbury, the Most Reverend George Carey, who pledged his prayerful support for any effort that I might continue to make for reconciliation and for peace, and particularly for collaboration between Archbishop Robin Eames and myself in that regard.

I confess that I have been completely overwhelmed by the welcome which I have received on my return from Rome to Ireland today. The courtesy which I received from Aer Lingus on the flight and at the airport, the reception given me by the Taoiseach and members of the Irish Government and Opposition and other dignitaries at the airport, the meeting with the President of Ireland, the reception at the Mansion House, the visit to the Apostolic Nuncio and the lunch at Archbishop's House in Dublin, all touched me deeply. The crowds along the way, particularly when I entered the Archdiocese at Drogheda, when I arrived in Dundalk, when I crossed into Armagh, when I arrived in Newtownhamilton, and then in Keady, and in each place the whole town if not the whole parish seemed to have turned out to greet me, all have left me filled with joy and thankfulness. Above all, the crowds which greeted me here in Armagh and which thronged the streets all the way from the outskirts of the City of Armagh until I arrived in the Cathedral precincts and back to Ara Coeli, will remain in my memory always. It was a 'Welcome Home' such as I never dreamt of and which has simply left me astonished, delighted, humbled and forever grateful.

Reconciliation
And now the future beckons us. The Lord Jesus Christ calls us now to face our responsibilities together in this Archdiocese and in this society at this time. He calls us above all, bishops, priests and people, to work for reconciliation. He sends us out into society as ambassadors for Christ to proclaim the message:

> Be reconciled with God.
> Be reconciled with one another.

It is not an easy task. Some might say it is an impossible task, so great have been the obstacles to reconciliation and so much greater have they been made by the bitter happenings of the past two decades. But let us not be discouraged. Let us pray for greater faith. All things are possible for God, nothing is impossible with the help of his grace. God is Master of the impossible. As Pope John Paul said in Drogheda, on that never-to-be-forgotten visit which he made to Ireland in 1979, the very year in which Cardinal Tomás Ó Fiaich was created Cardinal:

> We must attempt the impossible in order to avert the intolerable.

As we set our hands to the task, it is in God that we place our trust, and we say:

> Glory be to him whose power, working in us, can do infinitely more than we can ask or imagine; glory be to him from generation to generation in the Church and in Christ Jesus for ever and ever. Amen. (Ep 3:20-21)

May Mary, Mother of Hope, Mother of Pardon, Mother filled with holy Joy, obtain for us, by her intercession, the grace to be men and women of indomitable hope, of unbounded trust in God's mercy, of a holy joy the world cannot give and of a peace beyond human understanding.

(iii) Homily at Mass on the occasion of my first visit to Loughguile as Cardinal
Sunday, 21 July 1991

This is indeed a joyful day for me, as I stand at this open-air altar, beside the building where I once went to school, looking up at St Patrick's Church, where I served Mass as a boy and celebrated my first Mass, looking beyond it to my old home in Tully, and seeing beyond it again the heights of Drumkeel and, further still, the hill of Orra, or, to my right, 'Corkey Tops' and the hills where 'Knockagallon's purple tops look down on lone Kilwee', and I find crowding back to me in vivid recollection episode after episode of a life steeped in memories of Loughguile.

Some memories in particular stand out. I think of 10 June 1967, twenty-four years ago. That was the day when I made my first visit to Loughguile after having been named Bishop of Ardagh and Clonmacnois. On that day too, I received a wonderful reception from the people of Loughguile. Then, as today, I was conducted by a guard of honour of the hurlers of Loughguile Shamrocks. There was pride and joy in my heart at being at home among my own people. I remember the joy of my mother that day, but I remember also the uneasiness she felt at being thrust into the limelight, for this always brought out her essential shyness and humility. I remember also the occasional shadow of anxiety for her son that crossed her face as she faced separation from him and the lonely thought of his leaving her home for a new and untried future.

Ordination as priest
I also remember vividly today a date twenty-six years before that, the day when I celebrated my first Mass in Loughguile as a newly-ordained priest. I had been ordained in Maynooth on the previous day, 22 June 1941; I commemorated the Golden Jubilee of that date last month. Because of the difficult wartime conditions prevailing then, visitors were excluded and none of the ordinands could have members of his family present at the ordination. Exceptionally, however, the newly-ordained priests were permitted to return

home on ordination day in order to celebrate their first Mass in their home parish. With petrol rationing, transportation was difficult. I got a lift with a classmate as far as Dunloy, and was ferried home from there by a kind friend.

After a night when there seemed to be no desire for sleep and no need for sleep, I celebrated Mass in the Church of my boyhood, assisted by the curate of Loughguile at the time, the late Father Barney Mac Laverty (uncle of Bernard Mac Laverty, the writer). The Church was thronged. It was with great emotion that I celebrated Mass on the altar where I had been an altar boy. It was a special moment when, for the first time, I gave Holy Communion to my mother and to my brothers and sisters and friends and to my fellow-parishioners from Loughguile. It was with a real sense of privilege that I imparted my first blessing to each one after the Mass.

With the help of a great team of local ladies, my mother provided lunch for everyone in our home in Tully. Several sittings were needed for a multitude of people, who filled every room in our house for the occasion. I can still see my mother occasionally casting protective and anxious glances towards me, glances that expressed her joy and thankfulness at what had happened to me, but also her prayer that I would be all that a priest should be and all that she had prayed that I would be. In the days that followed, there was manifest in her at one and the same time her wish to have me near her, and yet her concern that I should visit friends all round the parish, and especially the old and the sick and the poor. Each day when I came back from my visits, there was the question: 'Did you visit so-and-so?' 'Surely you didn't pass such-and-such a house!' This refrain continued after each visit I made to Loughguile during her lifetime and 'reported' to her on the people I had visited (or failed to visit!) on the occasion. It was good training in the prime importance of pastoral visitation of homes!

A young priest in Loughguile
All my early years as priest saw my holidays spent entirely in Loughguile, where I called on homes all over the parish and was received with a welcome and a hospitality and a generosity which

came from the people's deep faith, their sense of the grace of priesthood, and their joy to see a son of the parish ordained. There were very few houses in Loughguile and Magherahoney that I did not visit during those years, and the bonds formed then were firm and lasting.

During all the years of my priesthood, up to the year of my appointment as bishop, there were very few Christmases when I did not celebrate Midnight Mass in Loughguile and have the privilege of preaching at these Masses. My late sister Margaret, then a teacher in the parish until her early death in 1961, trained and conducted the parish choir, which always excelled itself at Christmas. Christmas, therefore, for me has always been and remains to this day specially associated with Loughguile.

During nearly all those years, the late Canon George Clenaghan was Parish Priest of Loughguile (where he served for thirty years) and, even after I had left for Longford and could no longer be present at Loughguile's Christmas, he always invited me to send a message to the people for Christmas, and this was always read by him at Midnight Mass. His successors have kept up this practice.

After my mother's death, on 28 January 1974, I have returned each year to Loughguile on the Sunday nearest to the anniversary of her death.

Bishop of Down and Connor

Another very special day for me was that of my first visit to Loughguile following my nomination as Bishop of Down and Connor. I was coming back to Loughguile, not simply as its native son and priest, but now as its bishop. The people once more received me with joy and enthusiasm. As a boy, I had heard older people recall the scenes of jubilation when carriages and side-cars and pony-traps from the parish went to the nearest railway station at Killagan to greet Dr Henry Henry, a native of the parish who had been ordained Bishop of Down and Connor on 22 September 1895, and who was the only other Loughguile man to have become bishop, when he made his first visit to his native parish. There were no horse-drawn carriages for my return, but the enthusiasm and the joy of the welcome were none the less for that.

Supporting one another in the faith

As student, as priest and as bishop, I have at every stage felt inspired and empowered in my life and in my ministry by the faith of the people of Loughguile, and I have felt sustained by their prayers. We Irish priests and bishops are singularly blessed in knowing that, if we try to be the priests and bishops our people desire us to be and expect us to be, we shall at the same time be becoming the priests and the bishops the Lord wants us to be. That certainly has been the experience of my fifty years of priesthood and my twenty-four years of episcopate. I feel that today I must say to you, people of Loughguile, what St Paul said to his communities:

> We always mention you in our prayers and thank God for you all and constantly remember before God our Father how you have shown your faith in action, worked for love and persevered through hope in our Lord, Jesus Christ (1 Th 1:2-3).

> We feel we must be constantly thanking God for you, brothers and sisters, and quite rightly, because your faith is growing so wonderfully and the love you have for one another never stops increasing, and among the Churches of God we can take special pride in you for your constancy and faith under all the trials you have to bear (2 Th 1:3-4).

Mary, Mother of the High Priest

Thinking of my mother today naturally brings to my mind Mary, the Mother of Jesus, our great High Priest and the source of all priesthood. Mary conceived the Son of God spiritually before conceiving him physically; she conceived him in faith before conceiving him in her womb. My mother, like so many in her generation, would often have spoken of 'God's holy will'. The words, 'God's holy will be done' came often to her lips. That is the

meaning of Mary's fiat. Mary said, 'God's holy will be done', even
when she did not know what that will was going to entail for her.
She had some premonition of future suffering when she heard
Simeon's words at the Temple about the sword that was to pierce
her soul. It was only on Calvary that she knew the significance of
that sword. It was the price of her 'com-passion', her sharing in the
Passion of her Son; but surely, she saw it also as connected with her
son's dying commission to her to be the Mother of his Church, and
so to share in the tribulations and sufferings, as well as in the joys
and gladness of the followers of her Son throughout the ages to
come. To all this, Mary said 'Yes' on Calvary, as she had said 'Fiat'
at the Annunciation. That 'Yes' she spoke above all as Mother of the
great High Priest who is capable of feeling our weaknesses with us
and is tried in every way that we are (cf. Hebrews 4:15). He is the
High Priest who first learned obedience by being subject to Mary
and to Joseph at Nazareth, and was thus prepared to become
'obedient unto death, even death on the cross' (cf. Philippians 2:8).

Neither at the Annunciation nor during the 'hidden life' at
Nazareth nor even on Calvary did Mary fully understand the
meaning of God's plan. She lived by the night-light of faith as we
must try to do. Like many an Irish mother of the past and of the
present, she said, 'Welcome be the holy will of God', even when this
will ran counter to human expectations.

In union with Mary, we need to ask and should seek to know no
more than that; whatever the human appearances may be and
whatever suffering may be entailed, God's plan is a plan of love. In
the words of Mother Julian, 'Love is his meaning.' And so, with
Mary, we can repeat St Paul's hymn of praise:

> Blessed be God, the Father of our Lord Jesus Christ....
> He has let us know the mystery of his purpose,
> the hidden plan he so kindly made in Christ from the
> beginning...
> ...that he would bring everything together under Christ, as
> head, everything in the heavens and everything on earth.
> (Ep 1:9-10)

In this Mass, united with Mary and with all the angels and saints and with all those dear to us who, in Loughguile or elsewhere, have done God's will throughout the ages and are one with us now in the great communion of saints, we

> bend the knee at the name of Jesus and [our tongues] acclaim Jesus Christ as Lord, to the glory of God the Father. (Ph 2:10-12)

(iv) Taking Possession of Titular Church, St Patrick's, Rome
Homily at Mass on Sunday, 8 December 1991

The assigning to a cardinal of a titular church in Rome and his formal taking possession of it have an important symbolism and significance. By this act, the cardinal becomes formally a priest of the Diocese of Rome, a member of the clergy of this city of St Peter and St Paul, where Peter was the first bishop and where his successors, inheritors of the Petrine primacy and universal jurisdiction, have presided in charity over the Lord's Church since Peter's time. In the early Church, it was the prerogative of the clergy of Rome to designate the candidate who was to be ordained as bishop of the holy and apostolic see of Rome. That function in modern centuries devolves upon the college of cardinals; but it is entrusted to them precisely in their capacity as canonically members of the clergy of Rome. A new cardinal is not qualified to participate in a conclave for the election of a new pope before he has taken possession of his titular church in Rome. Hence the solemnity of today's ceremony, with its public reading of the Bull whereby the present Bishop of Rome, His Holiness Pope John Paul II, entrusts this Church of St Patrick in Rome to a new Irish cardinal as his titular church.

This fine church, built in fourteenth-century Lombardo-Gothic style, with its façade ingeniously and very satisfactorily inserted in the setting of the Augustinian College here, was begun in 1909 and completed in 1911. It took shape after a long and trying period of false starts, dating back to 1886. At that date, the Prior of the Irish Augustinians in Rome, Father Glynn, conceived the ambitious plan of building an Irish national church in Rome. The concept caught the imagination of many and a generous flow of contributions was expected. The foundation stone, set in earth taken from St Patrick's grave in Downpatrick, was laid on the feast of St Brigid, 1 February 1888. I remember the date as the year of the birth of my mother. But soon difficulties began to mount and the flow of subscriptions quickly dried up. The plans were too ambitious and the organisation for the raising of funds was too haphazard. The over-ambitious project had to be abandoned. For some years the Irish Augustinians had to withdraw from the property and, indeed, suspend their presence in Rome. This was in 1898.

Happily, this withdrawal was short-lived. By 1908, a new Prior resumed the building on a revised and less ambitious plan, and the new St Patrick's was dedicated on the feast of St Patrick in 1911. Many additions and improvements were incorporated in later years, including the fine shrines of St Brigid and of Blessed, now Saint, Oliver Plunkett.

These were completed in 1938, a time of suspense in Europe, just before the outbreak of the Second World War. When Italy entered the war and German troops arrived in Rome, St Patrick's was scheduled for the billeting of officers of the Wehrmacht. The buildings were saved by the flying of the Irish flag and by the declaration made by the Irish Ambassador, Dr T. J. Kiernan, in the presence of the German officer detailed to take over the building, that St Patrick's was immune as property of neutral Ireland. The officer observed the flag, listened in silence to the declaration, and then saluted and left. He did not return.

Previous cardinals
Since its beginning, St Patrick's Church has seen many great liturgical occasions, drawing together the entire Irish community in Rome. It has received the visits of many Irish cardinals. In 1893 Cardinal Logue had blessed a temporary chapel which preceded the present St Patrick's. Cardinal D'Alton wrote a foreword for the booklet published in 1956 to mark the tercentenary of the coming of the Irish Augustinians to Rome. He recalled the great missionary zeal which marked the Irish Augustinians and noted that they had sent out missionaries all over the English-speaking world, most notably to Australia, where an Irish Augustinian became the first Archbishop of Melbourne. Cardinal Conway and then Cardinal Ó Fiaich were each given St Patrick's as their titular church in Rome. I feel humbled and yet proud to follow in their footsteps as cardinal patron of this church.

I first made the acquaintance of this church and college in the Holy Year 1950, when, with many other Irish pilgrims, I stayed here for two weeks on my first pilgrimage to the Eternal City. I visited this church again in the Holy Year of 1975 with a diocesan pilgrimage from Ardagh and Clonmacnois, and yet again in the Marian Year of 1983, with a pilgrimage from Down and Connor.

The tombs of the Apostles

Today, as I become canonically a member of the presbyterium of the Bishop of Rome, I feel that I can listen in a new way, as indeed all Irish residents in Rome can listen, to St Paul's greeting to the Christian community of Rome:

> From Paul, a servant of Jesus Christ, who has been called to be an apostle and specially chosen to preach the Good News that God promised long ago through his prophets in the Scriptures.
>
> This news is about the Son of God who, according to the human nature he took, was a descendant of David; it is about Jesus Christ our Lord who, in the order of the Spirit, the Spirit of holiness that was in him, was proclaimed Son of God in all his power through his resurrection from the dead. Through him we received grace and our apostolic mission to preach the obedience of faith to all pagan nations in honour of his name. You are one of these nations, and by his call belong to Jesus Christ. To you all, then, who are God's beloved in Rome, called to be saints, may God our Father and the Lord Jesus Christ send grace and peace. (Rm 1:7)

Here in Rome, the very streets we tread, the very stones we touch, link us across the centuries with the holy Apostles, Peter and Paul. When we recite our Creed in St Peter's Basilica we are joining ourselves with St Peter and the Apostles in professing the faith which Peter proclaimed to the Jews and Paul to the Gentiles. It is as though Peter and Paul were calling us into the same communion of faith and love which they preached and lived. It is as though St

Paul were solemnly reminding us that 'there cannot be more than one Gospel', that we cannot 'change the Good News of Christ' or preach a version of the Good News different from the one preached by himself and by St Paul and the Apostles (cf. Galatians 1:6-8). It was as though St Peter were appealing to us to be careful not to let ourselves be 'carried away from the firm ground we are standing on', but instead to 'go on growing in the grace and in the knowledge of our Lord and Saviour, Jesus Christ' (2 P 3:17-18).

The Immaculate Conception
It is a beautiful coincidence that our liturgy today is celebrated on the Feast of the Immaculate Conception of Mary, the Mother of God. Mary is the supreme embodiment of that free gift of God's grace in Christ Jesus which is the great theme of St Paul's Letter to the Romans. Mary's *Magnificat* is her hymn of thanks and praise to the glory of God's grace. It is as though Mary were saying to us, 'Do not praise me, praise God; do not admire me, admire God.' Or rather, Mary is saying to us: 'In admiring my beauty as purest of God's creatures, admire God, whose grace made me immaculate; in praising my holiness, praise God, who is the source of all holiness; for it is from him that comes all my holiness, through Jesus Christ, his Son, who is also my child. All that I radiantly am, his grace has made me. It is by his grace that I have been preserved, pre-redeemed, from all stain of original sin. It is by God's grace alone that I have been made a "new creature" in Christ and the prototype and model of all who are called to be part of Christ's new creation, Christ's new world, which Jesus, my son, came to establish.'

In the beautiful series of ikons known as Mary the 'Hodigitria', Mary is shown as pointing to Christ, her Son. Mary's place in the plan of salvation is to point us towards Christ, to show us the way to Christ, from whom all her grace and beauty and glory come. Grignon de Montfort called her 'the echo of God'; for 'when we say "Mary", she answers "God..."'. Her *Magnificat* is a precursor of St Paul's great hymn in praise of God's grace, which opens his Letter to the Ephesians. The *Magnificat* is Mary saying:

> Blessed be God, The Father of our Lord Jesus Christ,
> who has blessed [me] with all the spiritual blessings of
> heaven in Christ.
> Before the world was made, he chose [me], chose [me] in
> Christ
> to be holy and spotless and to live through love in his
> presence
> ... for his own kind purposes
> to make us praise the glory of his grace,
> his free gift to us in the Beloved....
> to make his glory praised. (Ep 1:3-14)

Mary's Immaculate Conception, her whole being, is praise of the glory of God's grace, that grace which St Paul never tires of praising, that 'amazing grace' at which St Paul never ceases to marvel, God's 'abundant free gift', the 'free gift [we do] not deserve' (cf. Romans 16-17).

Mary's message to us is one of total trust in the power of this grace to cancel out all our sinfulness and to overcome all the sinfulness of the world. In this century, which has seen so much sin, so much hatred and cruelty, which has seen genocide and mass slaughter on a scale never before paralleled in human history, and in which senseless slaughter still continues, not least in our own country, we could become discouraged. We need to listen to Mary's voice:

> He that is mighty has done great things for me....
> His mercy is from age to age to those who fear him. (cf. Luke
> 49-50)

It is as though Mary were saying to us: 'All that God's grace has done for me is offered to you also. That same grace which preserved me from all trace of sin, can also cancel out your sins and all the sins of this world and of this century.'

The message Mary gives us by her whole being is the same as the message of St Paul to the Romans:

When sin abounded, grace did more abound.
However great the number of sins committed, grace was even greater. (cf. Romans 5:21)

Violence in Northern Ireland

The news reaching us in Rome these days about the continuing violence in the North of Ireland fills us Irish with sadness. At a time when Eastern Europe is struggling to consolidate in peace its new-found freedom and justice, and when Western Europe is feeling its peaceful way towards greater unity, the violent acts still occurring in our own country cause the Irish here to feel discouraged and ashamed.

What is happening in Northern Ireland at this time represents all that Europe is now striving to put behind it. One clear message which our experience is sending out is that violence is not a solution to any political problem. It is not a way to justice or to unity. Violence drives people and communities further apart. It causes hurts and wounds which take generations to heal and it leaves scars which become motives for further violence in decades to come.

Ireland could send a positive message to Europe at this time by a united effort of governments, politicians and people to overcome violence. Northern Ireland's problems are not unique. Our double-minority problems in Ireland are replicated many times over in many parts of Europe. To devise institutions which will guarantee justice and equality to both political and cultural traditions in Ireland is a historic challenge. Success in meeting it could make a positive contribution to the contemporary evolution of Europe.

The Churches must together set an example and give a lead in the work of reconciliation. At the ecumenical service of prayer held during the Synod of Bishops for Europe, the Holy Father made a passionate plea for the settling of disagreements 'through patient and sincere dialogue, under the guidance of the Holy Spirit'. For this we must work, for this we must pray, so that our country may save itself by Christian reconciliation and give inspiration to Europe by its example.

Those who even now are planning further acts of violence over the coming weeks, if they have respect for the Christian spirit which fills people at Christmas, if they want to respond to the wishes and the hopes of the vast majority of Irish people at this time, would cease their campaign at Christmas, so as to give peace at last the beginning of a chance.

'Courage: I am with you'

The 1991 Synod of Bishops for Europe is devoting much of its deliberations to the theme of the 'New Evangelisation of Europe', a mighty task which seems beyond our human capacity, if not even beyond the bounds of the humanly possible. There have been many references at the Synod to the text from the Acts of the Apostles, which recounts the heavenly summons received by St Paul to cross over from Asia Minor into Europe and begin the first evangelisation of Europe. The text reads:

> One night Paul had a vision. A Macedonian appeared and appealed to him in these words: 'Come across to Macedonia and help us'. Once he had seen the vision, we lost no time in arranging a passage to Macedonia, convinced that God had called us to bring them the Good News. (16:9-10)

The call is similar to that which brought St Patrick back to Ireland to bring the Good News to the Irish. After escaping from captivity in Ireland, Patrick heard a voice, that of a certain Victoricus, calling to him:

> We ask you, young man, come and walk once more amongst us.

He recognised this as the 'voice of the Irish', imploring him to come back and undertake the evangelisation of Ireland.

It is good for us in our troubled time to realise something of the state of Europe at the time when Patrick received that call and set out for Gaul to begin his preparation for that evangelisation. The year that Patrick left Slemish for Gaul opened on a New Year's night of terror and destruction. On that night, the first of the year 407, the barbarian tribes, as they were called by the Romans, poured across the Rhine to wreak savage destruction upon Christian Gaul. When Patrick and his Irish boat-crew landed in Southern Gaul, St Patrick tells us that they travelled for four weeks through 'a desert (a devastated countryside) without meeting any living thing' (*Confessio* 19). In 410, Rome itself, Eternal Rome, fell for the first time into the hands of the barbarians. Jerome wrote: 'The light of the world has been put out. …What is safe, if Rome is gone?' Such words of doom as these could hardly have been written in any subsequent age – until our own.

But the Lord had promised that he would be with his Church until the end of time. It was that faith that gave Patrick his indomitable courage and his unquenchable hope. His was the same faith and the same hope as that of St Augustine, who lay dying in his episcopal see at Hippo in North Africa in the year 430, two years before Patrick came to Ireland as Bishop. The Vandals were poised to sack Hippo. Roman and Christian civilisation, in Europe and in Africa, lay around the dying Augustine in ruins. But amid the ruins, Augustine had serenely written:

> Ours is the religion which constitutes the universal way of liberation for the soul, for no soul can be set free except by it. It is the royal road which alone leads to the Kingdom whose greatness does not sway with the vicissitudes of time but stands immovable on the solid ground of eternity…. This is the way which belongs, not to one nation only, but to all; … for the mediator himself said … that penance and the remission of sins would be preached in his name to all the nations. (*De Civitate Dei* X:32)

In that same time of the crumbling of civilisation, St Patrick spoke with the same confidence, and in very similar words:

> In Ireland I wish to wait for his summons…. For he has said:

'I am with you all days, even to the consummation of the world'. (*Confessio* 38-40)

We have the same reasons as St Augustine and St Patrick for being 'grounded and settled and immovable' (cf. Colossians 1:23) in our confidence in the victory of Christ's Gospel. Christ our Lord says to us today, as he said to the Apostles, to St Augustine and to St Patrick:

Behold I am with you all days, even to the consummation of the world. (Mt 28:20)

In the world you shall have distress; but have confidence, I have overcome the world. (Jn 16:33)

St Peter, in the Letter which bears his name, says:

The God of all grace, who called you to eternal glory in Christ, will see that all is well again. He will confirm, strengthen and support you. His power lasts for ever and ever. (1 P 5:10-11)

St Paul concludes his Letter to the Romans:

Glory to him who is able to give you the strength to live according to the Good News I preach and in which I proclaim Jesus Christ, the revelation of a mystery kept secret for endless ages but now so clear that it must be preached to pagans everywhere to bring them to the obedience of faith. This is all ... part of the way the eternal God wanted things to be. He alone is wisdom; give glory therefore to him through Jesus Christ for ever and ever. (16:24-7)

With Mary, therefore, let us again cry out:

My soul proclaims the greatness of the Lord,
my spirit exults in God my saviour.

May Mary intercede for us that we may put all our trust in the power of God's saving grace.

> A Mhuire na ngrás,
> A mháthair mhic Dé,
> guí orainn.
> Mary, Queen of Ireland, pray for us.
> Mary, Queen of Peace, pray for us.

And, in the beautiful words of the Irish tradition, we raise our eyes and our hearts above the dark clouds of these days and we pray:

> O Blessed Queen and Nurse of the Glorious King,
> This world bewilders me.
> Let me not fall into despair.
> And you, O Christ, carry my soul to the city of glory.
> Amen.

(c) Leavetakings

(i) Leavetaking Mass with Parishioners of
St Patrick's Parish, Armagh
23 November 1996

This is a moving moment for me: celebrating my last Mass in this great cathedral, which I have come to love so dearly over the past six years. This is Ireland's primatial cathedral, which, borrowing words used to describe the Basilica of St John Lateran in Rome, one can truly call the 'mother and head of all the churches' in Ireland. This coming Christmas will be the first in thirty years in which I shall celebrate Mass otherwise than as a bishop in my own cathedral, whether in St Mel's, Longford, or in St Peter's, Belfast, or in St Patrick's, Armagh. There is a great loneliness about that. I can describe it only as a kind of bereavement.

The bond between a bishop and his diocese and his cathedral is very real. I remember two occasions on which I celebrated Mass and preached in this cathedral before I came as Archbishop. The first was in 1987, for the tenth anniversary of the death of Cardinal Conway; the second was at the funeral of Cardinal Ó Fiaich. On each occasion I was nervous, I felt not 'at home', I was a stranger, a visitor. When I came as Archbishop, even as early as at my installation here on 16 December 1990, the feeling was totally different. There was still nervousness; but I was at home, among my own people. St Patrick spoke of 'the people whom God gave to him'. I am no St Patrick, but I know that feeling; I know the feeling of belonging to a people, the people of Armagh whom God gave into my pastoral care in the evening of my days.

The cathedral parish
From the very first day I came to you as Archbishop, you, the people of this cathedral parish, made me feel that I was welcome, that I was 'at home' among you, that we belonged to one another in the love of our one Lord. I assure you that my sense of belonging to you and to this Archdiocese will continue as long as I live. You know that a bishop celebrates Mass each Sunday for the people of

his diocese, as a parish priest does for the people of his parish; we know it as the *pro populo* Mass, the Mass for our people. My Sunday Mass will continue always to be offered for all the people of this Archdiocese of Armagh, and in a special way for the people of the cathedral parish; for the archbishop is your parish priest as well as your bishop. The same Lord will continue to be on my altar in Belfast who is here on this cathedral altar; in Christ, distance is abolished and separation does not exist. Close to him, we are close to one another and to all those who are dear to us. As the third Eucharistic Prayer puts it, we 'become one body, one spirit in Christ'.

The cathedral church has a very central place in the life and worship of a diocese. The people of the cathedral parish are called to be an example to the whole diocese in terms of liturgy and of adoration and prayer; in terms of pastoral care, co-operation of priests with one another and with the laity; involvement of the laity in partnership with priests in the work of the Church; spirit of unity and harmony of people with one another and with their priests; witness of Christian living; spirit of community; care of the sick, the old and the poor, pastoral care for young people; Catholic education; ecumenical spirit and outreach to Christians of other Churches; commitment to peace and justice. I thank God that you, the priests and people of Armagh, have lived up to that challenge. I have been proud of you on great and little occasions equally.

There have been great occasions over the past six years when the organisational ability and efficiency of all parish groups have been tested and have emerged triumphantly. I think of the ordination of your new Archbishop on 19 February 1995; the two installations, my own in 1990 and Archbishop Sean's on 3 November last; my return as Cardinal from the Consistory of June 1991; the Patrician week of 1995; the successive celebrations of the Week of Prayer for Christian Unity; the World Days of Peace on New Year's Day each year. On all of these, and on many other occasions, the co-operation of all parish groups and organisations, the calm and courteous efficiency of all those involved in the various aspects of the celebration, the friendliness of everyone, aroused universal admiration and were the subject of admiring comment from all. Many of these occasions were broadcast by television and radio and evoked much praise from the wider public.

I believe that you are entering now into a great new phase in the life of the Archdiocese and of the cathedral parish. You have a great and good new Archbishop, who has already endeared himself to everyone, and whose gentleness and kindness and goodness and holiness have already touched all of you. You have inaugurated your perpetual eucharistic adoration which will bring great blessings upon the whole parish. This has been primarily a movement of lay men and women; twelve hundred parishioners are involved in ensuring adoration of Our Lord in the Blessed Sacrament, seven days a week, without interruption by day or night. What a wonderful sign of living faith this is in a parish.

You have an active and enthusiastic parish pastoral council which unites priests, religious and lay people in partnership in a common commitment to make this indeed a vibrant Christian community, as befits the role of a cathedral parish. You have an Inter-Church forum for ecumenical exchange and sharing. You have a great spirit of charity and generosity and support for all good causes, at home and in the developing world and on the mission field. You have religious sisters and brothers working actively with you for the Kingdom of God, and to whom you give generous support. You have a very active branch of St Joseph's Young Priests Society, working and praying for increased vocations to the priesthood and religious life, and you are all aware that this is an acute and urgent need in the Church in Ireland today. You have the Apostolic Work, the Legion of Mary, the Scouts and Guides, the St John Ambulance, the Order of Malta, a host of Catholic organisations – I cannot name them all. You are about to introduce a Mass for young people, with music provided by young people themselves; you are developing Masses for children, with liturgy involving them as much as possible in the celebration. I welcome these developments very warmly and I congratulate priests and people on them. There are few causes dear to Christ, Our Lord, to which you are not already giving your urgent attention or at least your active consideration. You are well aware of the need for all of us to turn the modern world's crisis into Christ's opportunity. You are conscious of Christ's words, that the one who does not gather with him is part of the scattering of people away from him and from his Church, and you are determined instead to be gatherers for Christ of those who have strayed away (cf. Luke 11:23).

The testing of faith
The past six years have been difficult, painful years for bishops and priests and for you lay people. We have often had to lower our heads in shame at things done by a very small number of priests and even a brother bishop, which disgraced the Church. I want to thank you all for the support you gave to your bishops and to your priests during these trying times. This gave us new courage when we could have been tempted to discouragement. Your faith was tested, indeed it is continually being tested, in the changed culture through which we are living, a culture constantly critical of our faith and sometimes gratuitously insulting to the Church and its pastors.

As our secular knowledge increases and our technical skill advances at a phenomenal rate, so must our knowledge of the faith keep growing. A welcome feature of our time is the hunger for knowledge and further education among adults. People are flocking to self-improvement courses and to adult education classes in all sorts of subjects. Women are particularly to be commended for their enthusiasm for these courses and classes. All this is admirable. But there should be equal enthusiasm for ongoing formation in the faith and for adult religious education. We live in an age of appalling religious ignorance among many who are well educated in secular matters and who are often opinion-formers in media and in social circles. Deeper knowledge of the faith is not any longer merely desirable; it is essential in today's questioning and sceptical world. The new Catechism of the Catholic Church is a great resource for deepening our religious knowledge. It is a wonderful reference book which should be found in every home.

Christ the King

This is the last Sunday of the Church's year; next Sunday is the First Sunday of Advent. The Church has dedicated this Sunday to honouring Christ the King, with the feast of Our Lord, Jesus Christ, Universal King. The earliest creed of the Church is found in the words often used in the New Testament: 'Jesus Christ is Lord'. All of the rest of our faith is contained in this short formula. The Greek word for 'Lord' is Kurios. This was the same word as that used in New Testament times for the Roman Emperor, the August Emperor as he was called. The Emperor was the supreme source of all power and sovereignty and authority, whether political or religious, whether secular or sacred, throughout the world-wide empire of Rome. To call anyone Kurios except the August Emperor was a political crime as well as a religious abomination. The word is still used in the phrase, Kyrie Eleison, 'Lord, have mercy'. The Christian faith was therefore regarded by the Roman imperial regime as being treason as well as sacrilege. These charges have recurred in all totalitarian regimes throughout history.

The words 'Jesus is Lord' are not just a statement of faith about Jesus Christ; they are a call to live a life of which he truly is Lord. If I say, 'Jesus is Lord', or 'Jesus is King', then, to be honest and consistent, I must go on to make him Lord, to make him King, of my life and lifestyle, Lord and King of my choices and decisions. When faced with an important decision, career choice or lifestyle choice, how often do I say: 'What would Jesus want me to do in this situation?' I am simply being dishonest if I call him Lord but make no effort to seek and to do his will in my life. The word 'Church' may itself be derived from Kurios: it means the 'Kyrial' people, the people who have Jesus Christ as their King and Lord.

A loving Lord

Jesus is Lord. He is worthy of the highest praise our lips can utter. As the last Book of the Bible, the Apocalypse or Revelation, has it: Jesus Christ is worthy to receive 'all praise and honour and glory and power forever and ever' (Rv 5:12). But Jesus himself warned about people who honour him with their lips but whose heart is far from him (cf. Mark 7:6). The honour we give to Christ Our Lord and King will be tested by how we pray; but it will be tested also by how we live. Do I live in such a way as to make it clear to others that Jesus is my Lord?

Today's readings show that Jesus is King of love, and that we who call him Lord must live lives of love. The first reading shows him as the good and loving Shepherd who 'looks after the lost one, brings back the stray, makes the weak strong' (Ezk 24:16). That should be taken as the profile of a truly Christian community, as a criterion for belonging to the true Church of the Lord. That will be a major part of our final judgment by the Lord of love. Today's Gospel is St Matthew's well-known account of the Last Judgment, when Jesus identifies himself with the lost and the straying and the weak of the world, and says:

> In so far as you [looked after] one of the least of these brothers and sisters of mine, you did it to me.... In so far as you neglected to [look after] one of the least of these, you neglected to do it to me. (Mt 25:40, 45-46)

Jesus is King of peace. We who have him as our King must be men and women who pray and work for peace. The coming weeks and months are going to be decisive for the peace process. Peace is within our grasp, but the opportunity could be missed, and missing it would be a tragedy. We must pray very fervently at this critical time that peace may come and may be permanent.

May we all, as individuals, as families, as parish community, live lives which reflect the loving nature of Christ's kingship. Then we can be sure that our lives will be part of what Jesus in the end will hand over to his eternal Father, when he 'hands over the Kingdom to God the Father', and when 'God will be all in us all' (1 Co 15:24, 28).

So, my dear brothers and sisters in Christ, I want my farewell words to you to be the words of St Paul:

> Never give in ... never admit defeat; keep on working at the

Lord's work always, knowing that, in the Lord, you cannot be labouring in vain.

The grace of the Lord Jesus be with you.

My love is with you all in Christ Jesus. (1 Co 15:38; 16:23-4)

(ii) Leavetaking Mass with Religious Sisters
30 November 1996

I am very happy to have this opportunity of leavetaking with you, my dear Sisters, before I depart from Armagh for my new residence in Belfast. Our celebration of the Eucharist together is the most appropriate context for that leavetaking. The Eucharist is our constant point of departure for every new mission, every new day begun, in our service of the Lord. The Eucharist is our constant point of return, yesterday's mission accomplished and today's mission begun again; yesterday's mission failings forgiven, enthusiasm for today's mission renewed.

Your consecration to religious life, my consecration to ordained priestly and episcopal ministry, began alike in the Eucharist. Every day of your consecration, every day of my priestly ministry has been blessed by the Eucharist. From it, you and I have, day by day, drawn new life from the eucharistic Lord, as he draws life from the Father (cf. John 1:57). We have every day drawn from that Bread broken for the life of the world new energy for this day's labour, new strength to go on further, like Elijah, on our pilgrim journey towards the Mountain of God (cf. 1 Kings 19:8). The Eucharist is also food for tomorrow's journey; the word we translate as 'daily bread' could also be translated 'tomorrow's bread'; so the Eucharist should 'deliver us from all anxiety' about all our 'tomorrows'.

We need that deliverance from anxiety, for we are human, all too human in our feelings and our fears. Retirement is not as easy as I had sometimes fantasised. The French have the saying: 'to leave is to die a little'. In retiring there is a little dying. A rather free modern translation of the Anima Christi, has the words:

> Over each of our dyings
> shed your light and your love.

The bond between the bishop and his diocese is a very real and very profound one. It is much more than a merely juridical bond. It enters deeply into one's feelings and attitudes, and indeed into one's sense of identity. A bishop has a real sense of belonging in the diocese to which, his faith tells him, the Holy Spirit has appointed him (cf. Acts 20:28).

I think that the explanation of this lies deeper than just feelings or emotions. I think it can be explained only by the quasi-sacramental bond that exists between a bishop and the Church, which is embodied for him in the local church which is his diocese. Having served in three dioceses, I must say that in all three of them, for the duration of my appointment, I felt the same sense of total belonging in each. After leaving Down and Connor for Ardagh I felt that I belonged fully to Ardagh and that my native diocese of Down and Connor was no longer my home. After returning to Down and Connor, I felt more fully at home there than I had ever done before as a priest. Finally, having come to Armagh, my home was quite emphatically here; and I no longer belonged in Ardagh or in Down and Connor, however happy my memories of those two dioceses will always be. When retirement comes, there is a sense of not belonging anywhere, a kind of lostness and loneliness.

In the tradition of the Church from very early times, the relationship between a bishop and his diocese has been likened to a spousal relationship. St Paul writes to his Church in Corinth:

> I arranged for you to marry Christ, so that I might give you away as a chaste virgin to this one husband'. (2 Co 11:2)

St John addresses his Church in (presumably) Ephesus as follows:

> The Lady, the chosen one ... she whom I love in the Lord. (2 Jn 3)

The bishop's ring symbolises the spiritual marriage which unites a bishop and his diocese. When the union is broken by retirement, there is a feeling which can be compared to widowhood, with the bereavement and grieving which accompany that.

However, let me assure you that my bond with Armagh is not ended. I shall always feel that here is my home; my Sunday Mass

will always be offered for the Archdiocese of Armagh; here is where
I hope in my grave to await the resurrection. My house in Belfast
will always be open to anyone from Armagh who cares to call on
me, priest, religious or lay person, and I hope that many will. The
welfare of the Archdiocese will always be in my heart and in my
prayers. I hope that I shall always have a place in your prayers too
and that, as St Paul said to the Corinthians, you will 'make a place
for me in your hearts' (cf. 2 Corinthians 7:4).

The past six years
The past six years have been difficult years, often painful years, for
all of us. The scandals associated with a very small number of
priests and bishops, have brought great pain to many and have
tested the faith of all. But we knew that in our pain the Lord was
with us, sharing our pain, urging us, as he urged the disciples in
Gethsemane, to 'pray not to be put to the test' (cf. Luke 2:40). The
petition in the Lord's prayer, 'lead us not into temptation', can also
be translated as, 'do not put us to the test', or even, 'do not let us
fail in the test' (cf. Matthew 6:13). In these trials, we bishops and
priests were strengthened and sustained by the prayers and the
solidarity of our religious communities, and I want to thank you for
that. Truly we have carried one another's troubles and that is why
we were able to continue in obedience to the law of Christ (cf.
Galatians 6:3).

I believe that the Church will emerge, indeed is already
emerging, from these trials and sufferings, purified and
strengthened in faith. I believe that these humiliations have made
us more humble and penitent, and thereby more conscious of our
total dependence on God. That surely makes us more open to the
call with which Christ began his public ministry: 'Repent and
believe' (cf. Mark 1:15); 'Repent, for the Kingdom of heaven is close
at hand' (Mt 4:17).

I want to extend my thanks to you, Sisters. All through my life
as priest, and very specially through my life as bishop, I have been
inspired and helped by the truly sisterly relationship I have had
with religious Sisters. The special relationship of a bishop with his

diocese is found in a very special way in his relationships with religious women. I want to say to you what a comfort and strength it is for us bishops and priests in our priestly or episcopal ministry, and specifically in our celibate ministry, to enjoy the friendship and support of women who share happily with us the call to celibacy for the sake of the Kingdom, who share with us a desire for complete self-giving to the love of the Lord and for a life of holiness and prayer, who share with us a deep love for the Church, a total dedication to the work of Christ's Kingdom, and a desire to devote all our energies to making Christ known and loved. The holiness of Sisters has inspired me, their zeal has edified me and often shamed me, their prayers and friendship have supported me, their spiritual insights have enriched me. Without those whom I have liked to call 'my Sisters', my life as priest and my life as bishop would have been immensely impoverished. In your person, I thank all the Sisters with whom I have worked for all that you have meant in my life.

Religious life today
The present situation for religious women, like the present situation for priests, is humanly difficult. The extreme rarity of vocations, the comparative absence of young people in our ranks, the advanced age of many of us and the steady decline in numbers of active personnel, are all discouraging. I believe that Sisters are coming through this period with a wonderful resilience and high morale. I am constantly edified by the cheerfulness and joyfulness and lack of moroseness or pessimism which I find in religious communities. In this respect, you are an example to priests and perhaps even more to bishops. I believe that part of your special calling at this time in the history of the Church is precisely to be bearers of hope for the whole Church.

The call to holiness
Indeed, in a real sense all of us in the Church are called to be heralds of hope in a world where there is much hopelessness and lack of meaning and purpose in life. St Peter, in his first Letter, calls on us to

have our answer ready for people who ask us the reason for the hope that we all have. (cf. 1 Peter 3:15)

In the same passage, Peter gives us the reason for our hope by asking us to 'reverence the Lord Christ in our hearts' (1 P 3:15). Christ is the reason for our hope. God is the reason for our joy. One account of the life of St Columbanus tells of a disciple and companion of his called Tichuill. In spite of all the trials and travail of their missionary journeyings and all the dangers and hardships to which they were exposed, Tichuill was always smiling. Columbanus said to him, 'How is it, Tichuill, that you are always so happy?' Tichuill replied, 'Because they cannot take God away from me.'

Your vocation, my vocation, is to make Jesus Christ a living reality for those whose lives we touch. The only way to do this is for us to make Jesus Christ a living and loved presence in our own lives, to live in such a way that others will see in our own lives something of what Jesus Christ is like. We are called to live in such a way that we could say in truth:

To me to live is Christ. (Ga 2:20)

Our calling as persons consecrated to Jesus Christ is to lay our lives on the line for him; it is, as Pádraig Pearse said, to 'stake our lives on the truth of his word'.

Reasons for the hope that is in us can indeed be given in words, by solid arguments and convincing proofs. But arguments evoke contrary arguments, proofs invite disproofs, words generate more words without end. This was never more so than in the loquacious and disputatious world of the chat-show and the phone-in which is our modern world. It was in an off-moment that G. K. Chesterton said that people invented the radio and then found that they had nothing to say to one another. Not so. Radio gives people the chance to express any view they like on any subject they like and argue for every opinion that they choose; but it also gives other people the chance to express with equal passion every opposite view, to argue vehemently every contrary opinion. If the debate is truly open and if we, whom Christ calls 'the children of light', are willing and ready to take part, this open debate can be good. But it can also be confusing and it conduces towards that strange condition called 'anomie', or loss of conviction about everything, an ultimate loss of meaning and of hope. The increase in suicides of young people is a frightening sign of that loss of meaning and purpose in our society.

In our culture, the only statement which cannot be refuted by a contradictory argument is the statement of a person's life. A life wholly given up to Christ, a life wholly spent in his company, his love and his service, cannot be contradicted and cannot be ignored even by a sceptical world. That is the chief reason why the present decline in religious vocations is such a sad loss for the cause of Christ in our world. That a young woman or man should publicly commit her or his life to Christ and thereby show that they prefer Christ to everything else in the world and are prepared to give up freedom, career, money, and sexual love, for Christ's sake; that a man or a woman should live out that commitment faithfully all their lives long in chastity and poverty and obedience, that is what makes Christ real as no words will ever do; that is what demonstrates the truth of Christ's gospel as learned books and arguments alone will never do.

I suspect also that one cause of the decline in vocations is that our presentation of religious life, and sometimes our living of it, seem to concentrate less now on the person of the living Christ and to attach more weight to causes and ideals or ideologies. Causes such as justice, equality, ecology and liberation, are indeed worthy and noble; they are integral to the proclamation of Christ's gospel, but they lack that which gives religious vocation its unique and specific identity, namely the personal call of Christ:

Come, follow me. (Mk 1:18)

Go and sell what you own and give your money to the poor and then come and follow me. (Mt 19:21)

He or she that prefers father or mother ... or son or daughter to me is not worthy of me ... Anyone who loses his or her life for my sake will find it. (Mt 10:37-39)

All the other things, including love for the poor, peace, justice and the integrity of creation, will be added on; but Christ's commandment to 'seek first the Kingdom of God' is paramount, and Christ's call 'follow me' is the defining character of religious life. Our specific calling is to holiness, that is to a life immersed in Christ, 'hidden with Christ in God'. Our primary mission is to live a life of which it can be said:

Life to me means Christ. I live, now no longer I, but Christ lives in me. (Ga 2:20; cf. Philippians 1:21)

There is only Christ; he is everything; and he is in everything. (Col 3:10-11)

Mary ever faithful
Apart from faith in Christ, religious life is ultimately inexplicable and indefensible, and indeed simply absurd. Our understanding of our own religious vocation will develop in exact proportion to our growth in faith and union with Christ. Our model and our most powerful and prayerful help in that growth in faith is Mary the Virgin of faith and of faithfulness; Mary, whose life, as the Second Vatican Council recalled from St Ambrose, 'is a rule of life for all' (*Perfectae caritatis* 25). It is in the face of Mary that we shall see most clearly the image of Christ, which ought to be reflected in the whole manner of living of religious.

Saint Augustine was once saying goodbye to one of the congregations in his diocese. He said:

You are going to go away,
each one of you to his or her own home.
To have been together in the same light has been good,
to have rejoiced together has been good,

471

but when we part from one another
let us not part from God.

I want my last words to you to be taken from St Paul:

> I never stop thanking God for all the graces you have
> received through Jesus Christ. I thank him that you have
> been enriched in so many ways, especially in your teachers
> and preachers; the witness to Christ has indeed been strong
> among you, so that you will not be without any of the gifts
> of the Spirit while you are waiting for our Lord Jesus Christ
> to be revealed; and he will keep you steady and without
> blame until the last day, the day of Our Lord Jesus Christ;
> because God by calling you has joined you to his Son, Jesus
> Christ, and God is faithful. (1 Co 1:4-9)

(iii) Leavetaking Mass
with the Priests of the Archdiocese
Sunday, 15 December 1996

It is exactly six years tomorrow since, on 16 December 1990, I was installed in this cathedral as Archbishop of Armagh. Shortly afterwards, on 11 February 1991, I concelebrated Mass here for the first time with the priests of the Archdiocese. Leaving the ambo at the end of my homily, I forgot the step and nearly 'came a cropper'. It was an inauspicious beginning! However, Tom Hamill told me afterwards that the thing he remembers about that occasion was the adroit way in which I recovered my balance. So much for the homily I preached on that date!

The six years since then have passed very quickly. On Sunday, 8 December last, I was in Glasgow to take part in the silver jubilee celebration of the episcopal ordination of Cardinal Thomas Winning. Cardinal Tom is a good friend of mine and has been a good friend of Armagh. I recalled my last visit to Glasgow; it was on 8 May 1990. I was attending an ecumenical meeting. It was there that I received the terrible news of the sudden death of Cardinal Tomás Ó Fiaich. I felt shattered, as indeed everyone felt at the time. Little did I then know, of course, what impact that sad event was to have on my own later life.

Then came the arrival of the Cardinal's remains at the Airport Church in Dublin and the removal from there on 12 May and the journey with the cortège from Dublin to Armagh. I remember the funeral Mass on 15 May, at which I preached the homily as senior suffragan of the Northern Province. That experience was, frankly, an unnerving one for me. I felt a stranger, an outsider; the cathedral and the sanctuary were unfamiliar, I was not at home; I had acute attacks of nervousness. I had not the remotest idea that seven months later I would be back as Archbishop.

The bond between a bishop and the Church embodied in his diocese is a unique one. In the cathedral this bond is particularly close. In a strange way, my relationship with this cathedral was totally different at my installation here as Archbishop than it had been when I had come on 15 May for the funeral of Cardinal Tomás Ó Fiaich. For it was now clear that this was where the Lord called me and wanted me to be in the evening of my days. This cathedral and this Archdiocese were to be 'home' in the fullest sense. I remembered the words of the Lord:

> If a man serves me, he must follow me;
> wherever I am, my servant will be there too. (Jn 12:26)

> If you make my word your home,
> you will indeed be my disciples. (Jn 8:31)

This was where the Lord was waiting to be loved and served by me now. It was in Armagh that, as his disciple, I was to make my home in his word.

That sense of being at home was rooted in our faith and in what faith tells us about the nature of episcopacy; but it quickly developed into a deeply contented personal feeling of being at home among the priests, religious and people of Armagh. The relationship of a bishop with his priests is, I believe, the first index of the quality of his whole episcopal ministry. A bishop is helpless without the loyalty and support and co-operation of his presbyterium. No liturgical renewal will happen, no pastoral plan will work, no renewal programme will succeed, no team ministry will develop, no parental involvement in school catechesis, no lay involvement in the mission and work of the Church will come about without the commitment and the hard work of the priests. Often I feel that it is the priests who do the work and the bishop who gets the credit.

The priests of Ireland

I have served in three dioceses and have worked with a representative cross-section of the diocesan priests of Ireland, North and South. I believe they are among the finest body of priests to be found anywhere in the world. In spite of the undeniable and worrying decline in religious practice in the past couple of decades, the rate of religious practice in Ireland remains remarkably high in comparison with other countries.

I believe that the priests of Ireland can take legitimate satisfaction from this situation, despite all our anxieties about the future. Irish clergy certainly deserve, under God, a major share of the credit for the relatively strong state of the faith in Ireland today. Their personal witness of faith and love of God and of the Church have had a powerful impact on people. Their pastoral methods have been effective. New pastoral strategies are needed, and urgently needed, today; but the wise pastor of today will take out from the treasury of pastoral wisdom old things as well as new and new things as well as old (cf. Matthew 13:52).

The priests of Armagh

I venture now to identify some of the characteristics I have most admired in the Armagh clergy since I came to know you. There is great fidelity to prayer, assiduity in attending clergy retreats and days of recollection, a clear realisation of the primacy of holiness in the life of a priest.

There is a spirit of solidarity among the priests of Armagh and a great loyalty to the Archdiocese. These qualities are manifested in many ways: visits to sick confrères in hospital and to retired priests; attendance at priests' funerals; participation in diocesan liturgies and diocesan pilgrimages. There is a great loyalty to and support for your bishops. From the very first day I came to meet the chapter I have experienced your loyalty and your support and your friendship. Indeed I have never experienced anything else from any of you but friendship and support and loyalty. You will allow me to mention one or two of you in particular who can stand for all the rest. The Dean, Monsignor Frank McLarnon, has been a true friend and a trusted counsellor from the first day. Our friendship goes back a long way, indeed to Maynooth days, but it has deepened in the past six years. Frank has been a tower of strength to me. Next I mention Bishop Gerry Clifford. I always knew of his outstanding qualities of efficiency, discretion and loyalty as Executive Secretary of the Episcopal Conference, but I have appreciated these qualities even more since he became my auxiliary and my friend. I mention Monsignor Liam McEntegart, another true friend as well as a wise adviser and a tireless worker both as pastor of a busy parish and as a zealous promoter of vocations and a generous worker in so many diocesan services. These three can stand for all of you.

I can honestly say that I wanted to be and tried to be a friend to each one of you. This does not mean that there were not times when words or decisions of mine hurt one or other of you and caused one or other of you to feel that you or some other priest had been unfairly judged or unjustly treated. In so far as this is the case, I sincerely regret it and, before leaving you, I ask forgiveness.

I think of one occasion in particular when hurt was almost certainly caused to some. I speak of what has been called the '1995 clerical purge', when we had a large number of retirements. I now feel that this process may have been too rushed and the timing and manner of it might have been thought insensitive. I still believe that it was right, but it might have been more considerately handled. For this too I ask forgiveness.

Another characteristic of the Armagh clergy is your commitment to justice and to peace. You came through years of great tension and turmoil during the 'Troubles', standing by your people and sharing their pain, sometimes sharing the agony of persons very close to yourselves who were caught up in the conflict, comforting the bereaved, showing pastoral care to prisoners and their relatives, sometimes having your churches burned. Amidst all this stress and distress, you nourished the faith of our people and kept alive their hope and preached and prayed for peace and for a just society. I know that no one will mind if I name Monsignor Raymond Murray and Monsignor Denis Faul as fearless and tireless champions of justice and of human rights. Let them stand for all of you who came through these stressful years in a great spirit of faith and pastoral dedication.

The priests of Armagh have also a great sense of history and an enlightened sense of tradition, a love for the Irish language and a strong feeling for Irish spirituality; esteem for the *dúchas* is high among you. I have always regretted that I never had the opportunity to learn Irish, but Armagh's love for it inspired me.

I have to say that you, the priests of Armagh, are undemanding of your bishops. The Archbishop of Armagh has been Chairman of the Irish bishops' meetings since they first began and President of the Irish Episcopal Conference since it was first established. This makes great demands on the Archbishop's time and energy. He is also Chairman of the Trustees of Maynooth College, and Maynooth, particularly in recent years, has required much time and much travel. The Archbishop of Armagh is expected to have a national role as well as a diocesan one; the resultant mail and the extraordinary number and variety of problems which keep being referred to Armagh by all sorts of persons and groups by letter and by telephone demand much time from the Archbishop and much patience from his hard-working staff. Furthermore, the Archbishop is involved in various Roman Congregations, in Synods of Bishops, etc., in the service of the Universal Church. This requires much travel and frequent absences. There is also the ecumenical involvement, which is an essential pastoral duty of the Church at this time, and which is particularly necessary in Ireland. Then there is the constant commitment to the slow and arduous search for peace and for justice. All these extra-diocesan activities are necessary and important, but the pastoral care of the diocese unfortunately can suffer as a result, pastoral projects in the diocese can be postponed or neglected, decisions sometimes are not carried through, and the normal diocesan services rightly expected of a bishop are sometimes curtailed. The priests of Armagh understand all this and are extremely patient in respect of it. I want to thank you for the allowances you made for me in all of this and for your patience.

The future
We have come through very difficult years together since 1991. The scandals associated with a very few of our brethren brought great hurt and pain to innocent children and their families and brought humiliation to us all. Perhaps they were so shocking precisely

because they were rare and were so totally contrary to what people's long experience of good and holy priests had taught them to expect. I believe too that the whole awful experience has made us and the Church more humble, more penitent and, therefore, more conscious of our dependence on God's merciful love. Awareness of our fragility can make us more aware of our need for prayer, our own personal prayer, our prayer for one another, and our people's prayer for us. We must never forget the pain of the victims of child abuse; their pain is not a memory from the past but an open and raw wound in the present; it is not just their childhood that has been blighted but their adult lives which have been cruelly impaired. For many, it has alienated them from the Church. For all of us in the Church, all this has been extremely discouraging.

However, in spite of everything that might lead us to discouragement, I am full of hope for the future of our Church and of our Archdiocese. I leave Armagh with a heavy heart at departing; but I leave it with a heart lightened by the knowledge that Archbishop Seán Brady brings great qualities, both natural and supernatural, to his ministry among the priests, religious and people of Armagh. A sincerely humble, compassionate and gentle person, he has also the quiet strength of purpose, the firmness and steadiness of direction and the clarity of vision which will make him, in the words of one of the collects from the Missal, 'an ardent but gentle servant of the Gospel'. From my own experience I can guarantee him the support and loyalty and affection and prayers of the priests of Armagh. The spiritual heritage which generations of Armagh priests have bequeathed to us is indeed superb. In words based on Psalm 15, Archbishop Sean

> will keep the Lord ever in [his] sight;
> since God will be at his right hand,
> he shall stand firm (cf. Psalm 15:6, 8).

Retirement
Retirement is not easy. A cynic perhaps might say that we each believe that retirement is good and right for others, but that we see

no need for it in our own special case. Upsetting though it is, however, I believe that it is better to retire when one still has reasonable health and energy and when one is able to adapt to a new form of ministry in the Church. Retirement is never simply withdrawal from priestly or episcopal ministry; rather it is movement into a new way of serving God's Church. I hope to do this by writing and publishing material which I like to think might be of help to people, as they struggle to stay firm in their faith in Christ and strong in their Christian hope in the midst of the doctrinal and moral confusions of our time. Humanly speaking, however, there is loneliness and a kind of lostness in the first phases of retirement. I believe, however, that it is better that I should not continue to live in the Archdiocese in retirement. Archbishop Sean would have been happy and indeed anxious that I do so, but, all things considered, I feel it better that I move away. But please remember that, though I am going to live in Belfast, I am not 'going back to my own diocese'; for Armagh is 'my own diocese', and I am and remain an Armagh man. Please keep in touch with me sometimes and visit me sometimes. Above all, please, as St Paul said, 'keep a place for me in your hearts' (cf. 2 Corinthians 7:2) and in your prayers. I assure you that 'you have a permanent place in my heart' (Ph 1:7).

Priestly holiness
For his golden jubilee of priesthood this year, Pope John Paul has just published a little book of reflections on his own priestly vocation and ministry. He gives it the title *Gift and Mystery*. It is very personal and human, and is spiritually profound. The Pope repeatedly stresses that the priesthood is a special call to holiness and that the first ministry of the priest is the ministry of prayer. 'Christ needs holy priests', he cries; and he goes on to say:

> Today's world calls out for holy priests. In a world becoming more and more secularised, only a holy priest can become a transparent witness of Christ and of his Gospel.

The Pope writes:

> My own long experience in so many different situations has confirmed my deep conviction that an efficacious pastoral ministry and an authentic care of souls can grow only from the soil of priestly holiness.

There is no way to holiness except through prayer. Pope John Paul declares that:

> Prayer makes the priest and the priest makes himself priest by prayer.

Praying the Word of God, knowing the Word, living the Word, make the priest an efficacious preacher of the Word and an evangeliser such as the world and Ireland so greatly need today. Only thus can a priest be converted into the likeness of Christ and can then strengthen the faith of his brothers and sisters (cf. Luke 22:32).

The Pope recalls his own ordination and dwells particularly on the prostration of the ordinands on the ground. This, he says, is a sign of the submission to God's will and to the Church's needs which the priest freely undertakes. It is also a sign that, however lowly and helpless we priests as human beings are, we rest all our weight on the rock which is Christ; and this is how we in turn can help to provide a secure and solid ground for the pilgrimage of faith of our lay brothers and sisters in Christ.

The Marian thread

Pope John Paul devotes a section of his book to what he calls 'the Marian thread' in his priesthood. As Mary stood by Christ in his long and agonised dying on Calvary, so she stands by the altar on which we place 'the Victim whose death has reconciled us with God'. The Body which we hold and carry in our hands is the Body whose first nourishment in the womb came through Mary's bloodstream and which was then fed at Mary's breast. The Church,

St Thomas Aquinas says, 'makes' the Eucharist and the Eucharist 'makes' the Church. We can equally say, the priest 'makes' the Eucharist and the Eucharist 'makes' the priest. In one of the most powerful of her novels, *The Anteroom*, Kate O'Brien writes of a priest celebrating Mass in a sick-room:

> There was only in him as he spoke his Latin an entirely cold and calm understanding that God was in his hands.... He only said the words the Church ordained to him and was aware without cloud or pang or question of the everlasting miracle, the 'mystery of faith' ... [the Blood] which will be shed for you and for all.

Building our priesthood on that everlasting rock of faith, building the faith of our people on that rock, we need fear no storm or flood or wind of change in the years ahead. Rains will surely come down, floods will rise and gales will blow and hurl themselves upon the house of the Church; but

it will not fall; it is founded on rock. (cf. Matthew 7:25)

PART THREE

A FUTURE FULL OF HOPE

CHAPTER FIFTEEN

A FUTURE FULL OF HOPE

I know the plans I have in mind for you – it is the Lord who speaks – plans for peace, not disaster, reserving a future full of hope for you. (Jr 29:11)

After retrospect, prospect: the past is only prelude. I wish in this concluding chapter to clarify my own thinking about the future of the Church in Ireland by trying to identify some priorities for pastoral planning and action, as I see them, in this transition decade, bridging two centuries and two millennia. These have a common thread, that of evangelisation. Pope John Paul has called this the decade of the 'new evangelisation'. The Lambeth Conference of 1988 called this a 'decade of evangelism'. Both of these terms strike a positive note, a note of hope. This is how I myself see the future of the Church in Ireland. This is why I take my title for this chapter from the words of Jeremiah, conveying the word of God to his people at a time of exile and of great turmoil and depression and pessimism and fear about their future.

Church and State

I believe it important to begin this chapter with a look at relations between Church and State in today's Ireland. This question is often raised in public debate, and there are frequent calls for the 'separation of Church and State'. I believe that there is often misunderstanding of the present position of the Church in this regard, and confusion about what 'separation of Church and State' means. As leader of the Irish Episcopal Conference's delegation to the New Ireland Forum in February 1984, I made the following statement:

> The Catholic Church in Ireland totally rejects the concept of a confessional state. We have not sought and we do not seek a Catholic State for a Catholic people. We believe that the alliance of Church and State is harmful for the Church and harmful for the State.

Some seem to have read that statement as an undertaking by the Church to remain silent on all matters of legislation, leaving all our laws exclusively to politicians and effectively 'taking moral judgements out of social issues', as one writer has recently curiously demanded. No bishops in the world would accept that position. No democratic government in the world would attempt to enforce that position. It would be a denial of the fundamental democratic principle of religious liberty, which requires that the Churches have full freedom to proclaim the Gospel. There obviously can be laws which conflict with the moral and ethical principles of the Gospel, and the Church must have freedom to point this out. This does not mean that the Church expects civil legislation to conform to Church teaching, or demands that its moral teaching be incorporated into the laws of the State. Over the past thirty years, we have explicitly and repeatedly stated that we do not expect or demand any such thing. But the Church has the right and the duty to form and to inform the consciences of those citizens who are Catholics about the moral implications and the moral consequences of proposed laws or constitutional changes, leaving it to their duly informed consciences how to act and how to vote. We never instruct citizens how to vote; but many citizens are also committed to the Church and have a right to expect from their Church leaders clear guidance about moral issues which arise in the area of legislation. Separation of Church and State cannot entail separation of either legislator or voter from his or her conscience.

The Church has never claimed that the moral considerations which it puts forward are the only relevant considerations in a given piece of legislation, or that the Church's concerns are the only relevant concerns. The Church insists, however, that its moral considerations and concerns should not be excluded in any national debate about such issues. Such considerations are not matters of faith only; they are also open to reasoned conviction on the part of any citizen, and they are often accepted by people of different traditions on grounds of reason, rather than on grounds of faith. If something is true and good in itself, it does not cease to be true and good simply because the Catholic Church also teaches it. Only totalitarian regimes would hold that the legislature is above the moral law. Only totalitarian regimes try to prevent the Church from proclaiming the moral law.

As we said at the Forum for Peace and Reconciliation in 1996, the phrase 'separation of Church and State' has not a single and universally agreed meaning and there is no single and fixed model for its operation. It has in fact received a wide variety of interpretations and applications. Countries whose constitutions are founded on the principle of separation of Church and State show wide variation in the conclusions which they draw from this principle in terms of actual relationships between the Church and the State, for example, on such matters as support for Church schools, for Catholic health-care and welfare institutions, even salaries of clergy, etc. In many of these respects, the Church in Ireland has more 'separation' from the State than it has in other and more professedly 'secular' countries. Contrary to common assumptions, the independent Irish State has always had formal separation of Church and State. Efforts were made by small groups of Catholics in the 1930s to have the Catholic Church declared the official religion of the State. They received no public support and they failed. Ireland has never had and has never wanted a Catholic political party as such.

When the Prime Minister of France, Lionel Jospin, himself a Protestant, addressed Pope John Paul II at his departure from Paris on the occasion of the 1997 World Days of Youth, he had significant words to say about *laicité*, which is the official French version of the doctrine of separation of Church and State. He said:

> Frederic Ozanam, [founder of the Society of Saint Vincent de Paul] contributed … to the reconciliation of the Church and [the French Republic]. He thus encouraged the emergence of a French conception of *laicité*, respectful of religious liberty, which is an expression of freedom of conscience.

To invoke the principle of separation of Church and State in order to question or to deny the Church's right to intervene in public debate on issues of public morality would be to contravene the fundamental principles of democratic society, which are religious liberty and freedom of conscience.

In fact, separation of Church and State is a healthier condition for the Church than undue interdependence between politicians and churchmen. Political power and influence are not good for the Church. Servility and undue obsequiousness towards churchmen is not good for politicians. It is bad for the Church to be formally or even informally associated with any particular political party. The Vatican Council states that the Church 'must not in any way be confused with the political community nor bound to any political system' (*Gaudium et spes* 76).

Tensions, of course, can arise. When citizens take political decisions on the basis of consciences willingly and freely formed by the teaching of their Church, disagreements and even divisions at a political level can arise; but these are part of the democratic process; they are resolved, at the political level, by democratic debate and ultimately by the votes of citizens. It is important that communications between Church and government be open and transparent. Whatever may have happened in the past, it has been the policy of the Irish bishops over the past thirty years to release to the public the text of any submissions which they make to government, and, in any oral presentation which they make, to adhere strictly to the terms of their written submission.

However, separation of Church and State should not be seen as something negative, either by the State or by the Church. It does not imply hostility on the part of the Church towards the State or on the part of the State towards the Church. The Second Vatican Council, in its document on the Church in the Modern World, *Gaudium et spes*, expresses the Church's respect for the political community and speaks of the 'difficult but most honourable art of politics'; but it goes on to point out:

> The role and competence of the Church being what it is, she must in no way be confused with the political community nor bound to any political system. (75, 76)

Systematic or ideological opposition of the State to the Church would defeat the State's own interests, for the Church is the most powerful protagonist of the very values on which the State depends for its own well-being, such as the values of individual and social justice; respect for the right to life; social solidarity and concern for others, especially for the poor and the weak; respect for marriage and the family and their special place in society; respect for truth and fidelity to the pledged word, to contracts and to promises; respect for public institutions, for legitimate laws and for law enforcement agencies; payment of just taxes. All these matters are part of the Church's moral teaching; they are also formative of the moral consensus in society on which the State depends for its healthy functioning. There is room, therefore, for what the Council called 'wholesome, mutual cooperation' (cf. *Gaudium et spes* 76) between Church and State, each of them respecting the legitimate autonomy of the other within their respective spheres. The Church teaches these standards of conduct because they are true and good and are required by God's law, not in order to win favours from the State. Indeed, the Church has to be ever vigilant not to be used by the State for its own political purposes. In the Council's words, '[the Church] does

not lodge her hope in privileges conferred by the civil authority'
(*Gaudium et spes* 76).

The French bishops devoted their General Assembly in
November 1996 to the questions of the Church's role in the
contemporary situation of *laicité*, or secular State, and pluralism.
Monseigneur Claude Dagens, Bishop of Angoulême, presented a
paper on 'Proposing the Faith in Today's Society', which the bishops
approved as a Letter to be addressed to the Catholics of France. In
it, the author states:

> We are willing without any hesitation to situate ourselves as
> Catholics within the cultural and institutional context of
> today, marked as it is by ... the principle of *laicité* [separation
> of Church and State]. We reject any kind of nostalgia for past
> times, when the principle of [Church] authority seemed to
> be accepted without question. We have no desire to return
> [to such a past]. We believe that the present times are not
> any more unfavourable to the proclamation of the Gospel
> than past periods in our history. The critical situation in
> which we find ourselves today obliges us, on the contrary, to
> return to the sources of our faith and to become disciples
> and witnesses of God and of Jesus Christ in a more
> committed and more radical way than ever.

This sentiment is not different from that which the Irish
bishops' delegation expressed at the New Ireland Forum in 1984:

> The Catholic Church in Ireland has no power and seeks no
> power except the power of the Gospel which it preaches and
> the consciences and convictions of those who freely accept
> that teaching. The Catholic Church seeks only the freedom
> to proclaim the Gospel.

Liturgical renewal
I turn now to what I see as priorities for our proclamation of that
Gospel in today's Ireland. There can be little doubt but that the

Vatican Council saw the renewal of the liturgy as the key to its whole programme for the renewal of the Church, and as the primary instrument for the proclamation by the Church of the Good News 'to those who are near and to those who are far off'. That is surely the reason why the Council began its whole process with the drafting of its Constitution on the Liturgy, *Sacrosanctum Concilium*, and devoted much of its first session to debating this text. This lesson must not be lost on those who are charged today with responsibility for continuing the movement of conciliar renewal.

Much progress has been made in the area of liturgical renewal. We must salute and admire the immense work accomplished at all levels of the Church within the first two decades after the end of the Council. The renewal of rites, the new liturgical texts, the new Roman Missal, the new Lectionary, all represent a rich treasury. Yet, in a sense, those who laboured in those decades were merely giving us the tools for an ongoing task. There remains a huge programme still to be tackled of liturgical education of priests and of people.

The liturgy, with its copious use of Holy Scripture, has historically been and must again become the principal vehicle for formation in faith of all the members of the Church. The liturgy has been and is a privileged place of catechesis and of evangelisation. People sometimes contrast 'sacramentalisation' and evangelisation. But surely one of the principal ends and aims of evangelisation is precisely to lead people to the meaningful celebration and faith-filled reception of the sacraments, and, conversely, the preparation of people for the sacraments is a privileged instrument of evangelisation. The Rite of Christian Initiation of Adults is a supreme example of this truth.

The 'conscious, full and active participation' of the laity in the liturgy is declared by the Council to be the right and the duty of all the baptised. To promote this and to prepare people for this is a prime responsibility for bishops and priests, and must be a priority area (though by no means the sole area) for the involvement of laity in the life and mission of the Church. This must also be high on the agenda of diocesan and parish pastoral councils. The vitality and vibrancy of a parish can fairly be assessed by the quality of celebration of the liturgy by priests and the other ministers and by the laity, each performing their respective parts.

Again, great progress has been made in this regard, but much still remains to be done. Each parish should have a liturgical group, preferably a sub-group of its pastoral council, concerned with the liturgy in all its aspects, its preparation and its celebration, sharing in the composing of the intercessions, assisting in the preparation of readers and in the arrangements for extraordinary ministers of the Eucharist, offertory gift-bearers, leaders of intercessions; sharing in the preparation of the people for the responses and for congregational as well as choral singing, and helping in the liturgical formation of parishioners generally, always in collaboration with the priests of the parish.

A diocesan liturgy commission should organise programmes for the formation of such parish groups and of lay persons generally, working towards the continuing improvement of the quality of parish liturgical celebration throughout the diocese.

Ministry of music

Sunday Mass in the parish should be a community event and a joyful occasion. It is not for nothing that it is called a 'celebration'. Someone has said that the Church is the only organisation which makes it obligatory for its members to have a celebration once every week. It is sad that Sunday Mass should be felt by some to be just an obligation, a duty, and sadder still that is should be felt by some to be 'boring'. It is also sad that some should 'shop around' and travel far in search of the 'quickest Mass'.

One of the indispensable ways of making the Mass a celebration is music and singing, above all singing by the congregation. Few things can create unity in a gathering more than singing together. Any community of people who are happy to be together begin spontaneously to sing together. It is true that the joy of the Mass is of a different order than secular enjoyment; Mass is not 'happy-clappy' fun; but even spiritual joy lends itself to song. Singing at the principal parish Masses on Sunday should be the norm, not the exception. Indeed, in many, if not most, countries, singing at all Sunday Masses has become normal. In Ireland, to our shame, and greatly to the surprise of overseas visitors, this is not so.

Parish choirs have a vital part to play in the liturgy. It is right to speak of a 'ministry of music', shared by organist, choir leader, choir members, cantor, instrumentalists. They work hard and the community should appreciate and support their work. The task of choirs, however, like that of other liturgical ministers, is to serve the liturgy, not dominate it, to be part of the celebration, not to 'perform' for a silent audience. There are, of course, excellent liturgical chants and plainchant pieces which are difficult and require a degree of voice quality and training and practice which are beyond the capacity of the ordinary person 'in the pew' and which only the choir can render. Furthermore, the Church's rich treasury of plainchant and polyphony must not be allowed to be lost. But the choir should also allow and indeed encourage the congregation to sing. Priority should be given to the singing by the congregation of the people's responses. Good work, indeed some outstanding work, has been done by Irish composers in composing music for these and other liturgical chants, but much remains to be done. A new field for original composition will be opened up when the new translation of the Missal is published. It is good that a cantor lead the congregational singing, and that there be a short time left for 'practice' before Mass begins. Broadcast Masses could set a standard. Sadly, chants and music in broadcast Masses are sometimes deplorably banal, both musically and textually.

It has been sad to see the almost complete abandonment of plainchant pieces, once so familiar and always so beautiful and so conducive to prayer. No words and no music have been found to express the spirit of Advent and of Lent more appropriately than *Rorate Coeli* and *Attende Domine*. Pope Paul tried hard to revive such chants, publishing a collection of them, *Cantate Domino*, for general use. Past experience showed that many of these chants can be learned and used by whole congregations. The recent successes of plainchant CDs by monks are also encouraging.

Some of the music currently used in marriage liturgies is quite unacceptable for liturgical celebration, being either unbearably banal or irremediably secular or both. The couple should be invited to share in the selection of the readings and music for their wedding, but they must be helped to appreciate what is liturgically correct and what is not; and the intrusion of secular songs and other secular elements must be resisted, gently indeed, but firmly. It will be said that this is 'the couple's day', and this is true; but it is God's day first, for it is he who joins the couple together, and it is the Church's day, for it is a sacrament which is being celebrated.

The same applies for funerals. There is real danger of abuse here; for example, when orations are made in church by relatives or colleagues which are of a purely secular nature, or when secular songs are sung because the deceased 'liked them'. Sentimentality must not control liturgy. The feelings of mourners must certainly be treated with very great sensitivity, but priority of respect must be given to the sacred liturgy itself and its sacred and reverent character must be protected. This will become more difficult and more necessary if society becomes even more secularised and weddings and funerals come to be seen by some as secular rather than religious occasions.

I view with alarm a kind of 'creeping secularisation' in some liturgical occasions, particularly first communion, confirmation, weddings, funerals. The 'fashion parades' for children, especially at first communions, and the expense spent on these and on lavish 'parties', can verge on the scandalous. Weddings and funerals can have their sacred character eroded, especially on occasions when more and more 'unchurched' people are in attendance. Such occasions can become wonderful opportunities for evocation or revival or deepening of faith. We must not let their Christian meaning and message be obscured. I know how sensitive these occasions can be, and what difficulties can arise for priests. For all these reasons, greater understanding of liturgy among people must be promoted. Indeed, understanding of the faith, and even elementary knowledge of it, can no longer be taken for granted, and catechesis at all levels needs to be provided.

Church architecture and art

It is difficult to celebrate liturgy well in a space which is poorly designed for liturgical celebration. Some splendid architectural and artistic work has been done in Ireland in recent decades, both in church building and in the renovation of existing churches. But much inferior, and some bad, work has been done and continues to be done. On church refurbishment, the expedient, too often resorted to in the past, of separating the altar table from the old reredos and merely moving it forward to a new position, is, in my view, never successful. Whatever beauty the old altar-cum-reredos possessed depended on its being seen as a unit and seen in its original position and perspective. When that unity is broken and when the positioning and perspective are changed, the result is neither aesthetically pleasing nor liturgically correct. Concerns for heritage and for conservation are certainly legitimate but they need not conflict with and should not impede good liturgical celebration. Churches are built for liturgy and worship, not for conservation. Churches are not heritage centres.

Architects and artists (both are necessary and should work in partnership) must have a good liturgical formation as well as the skills, talents and training proper to their own profession. Education in liturgy is necessary for them too, and indeed should be part of their professional training, if they intend to get involved in church work. It is to be hoped that younger architects will interest themselves in church work and that they will acquire the interest in liturgy which is needed to equip them for their task. Good church architecture and good religious art have also their place in communicating a sense of God and of worship and in the work of the new evangelisation. Naturally, good church architecture includes also care for the ordinary needs of people, particularly for parents of small children, for wheelchair access, for the hearing-impaired, etc.

Understanding the Scriptures

Meaningful celebration of the liturgy, both for priests and for lay people, requires growing understanding of the Holy Scriptures.

Liturgy is scripture made prayer. One of the graces of liturgical renewal has been the greater exposure of the people to the Word of God as read in the liturgy. Much still remains to be done by both priests and people to enable us all to profit as we were intended to do from this wider exposure to God's Word. Selection and preparation of readers for parish liturgy has usually been carefully done. It is a never-completed task, but one which promises great growth in faith and prayer for all those concerned. The criterion for the selection of readers must be their ability to read Scripture audibly, intelligently and meaningfully. The passages to be read must be carefully prepared beforehand, with particular attention to the reader's understanding of the passage read and of its context. This requires appreciation of the use of Scripture in the liturgy. Readers and people should be helped to see the connection between the readings for a given day, particularly that between the Old Testament reading and the Gospel.

It is not only the readers, of course, who need to be helped to know the Scriptures: all possible efforts must be made to enable more and more people to understand the readings from holy Scripture and to assimilate them into their prayer and their lives. This leads on to greater familiarity with the Word of God as a whole, and this in turn will, by God's grace, lead to a deepening of people's prayer and a transformation of their lives. Proper appreciation of Scripture in the liturgy requires growing familiarity with the Bible as a whole, on the part of priests as well as of people. We must strive to promote the presence of the Bible in every home and its reading in every family.

Evangelising the active
The liturgy is, as I have said above, the primary instrument for evangelisation and for catechesis. The homily has a vitally important place here. We must be always open to new ways of making our homilies more faith-forming and more faith-evoking. Concern with presentation is essential; and much can be done to improve our language, our diction, etc. The advice and constructive criticism of kind friends, whether clerical or lay, can be most

helpful. Careful attention needs also to be given to sound amplification systems and to acoustics, which in Ireland are far too often deficient in ways which are inexcusable in the light of modern acoustic technology. It is debatable whether a bad homily is harder to endure than a good homily which cannot be heard! Competent acoustic specialists should be involved in the planning of churches. Nevertheless, our altars and ambos need not and should not look like broadcasting studios! Modern technology provides for excellent microphone systems which are inconspicuous and which do not detract from the sacred character and the liturgical design of altar and ambo. Modern technology also offers new audio systems for the hearing-impaired, and these should be provided in our churches.

Most important of all, so far as the homily is concerned, is its content and the conviction with which it is delivered. The purpose of the homily is, like the purpose of the Gospel itself, that people 'may believe that Jesus is the Christ, the Son of God, and that believing this [they] may have life through his name' (cf. John 20: 31), or, as St Luke puts it, that they 'may learn how well founded is the teaching that [they] have received' (Lk 1:4). The homily must be faith-nurturing and faith-developing. We to whom God has given the gift of faith must be continually striving to let our faith be deepened and strengthened by the living Word of God. Our faith is constantly under trial, constantly being questioned, challenged, criticised and resisted; and the resistance comes from within ourselves as much as it comes from the surrounding culture. A faith which is not growing may well be in the process of dying. A faith which is not being nourished cannot hope to survive. All of us are in some degree suffering from spiritual anorexia.

The faith of the preacher needs nourishing, no less than the faith of the congregation. The preacher must always be addressing the Gospel message to himself, evangelising himself, as much as addressing and evangelising the congregation. In an age of television, neglect by priests of serious reading of books in scripture studies and theology is a particular danger. For our comfort, however, we remember that it is always Christ who evangelises. It is Christ who speaks when his Word is being proclaimed and preached.

Our own personal struggle as priests to be Christ-like and to let Christ speak and act through us is an irreplaceable part of our preparation of a homily. Our own lives of prayer and faith are more potent ministers of the Word, and preach more compelling and grace-giving homilies, than our words can ever do. The most fundamental of the many services our people expect from us is the service of our own times of personal prayer. As Pope John Paul reminded us in Maynooth in 1979, we must not 'become so immersed in the work of the Lord that we neglect the Lord of the work'. Amid all the confusion about the very meaning of evangelisation today, we must pray and work for a spirit like the great evangeliser, St Paul. For Paul, 'there is only Christ; he is everything; he is in everything' (Col 3:11); 'to me to live is Christ' (Ph 1:21). The Church has only Christ to say to the world. The Church has only Christ to give to the world. If we do not 'say Christ' in our preaching and catechising, we are only a 'gong booming or a cymbal clashing' – much talk, many stories, but nothing that gives life or hope or joy or love.

So far as the preparation of homilies is concerned, there is great value in a preparation that is shared between the priests of the parish or the priests of neighbouring parishes. A special new dimension is added to the preparation when lay persons can also be involved. In the great liturgical seasons, particularly Advent, Lent and Easter, the shared preparation of a series of homilies by priests of adjoining parishes has been found to be very fruitful, particularly when it is followed by a 'sharing of pulpits' by the priests concerned. This provides a variety of voices and styles and thereby creates new interest and attentiveness on the part of parishioners.

A series of surveys of opinion in Ireland conducted over recent years has revealed a widespread malaise among the laity concerning homilies. If people were to find homilies poorly prepared and poorly presented, dull and 'boring', the danger is that even Mass-goers may drift away from Mass attendance. Attention to the quality of our preaching is one of the urgent challenges facing us at this time.

Adult religious education
Full churches can be a delusion unless we see them and use them as a unique opportunity for mutual sharing and deepening of faith and prayer between priests and people. In today's Ireland, faith-development is a condition of faith-survival. Faith today is constantly being challenged by a surrounding and pervasive and persuasive secular culture. Faith must become more profound, more mature and more enlightened if it is to stand up to the new challenges and respond to the new questionings. There is a huge catechetical deficit in many quarters in the Church today. Bishop Dagens, in the paper I quoted in the earlier part of this chapter, speaks of 'a certain loss of Catholic memory' in this generation. Adult religious education is no longer a luxury, it is a necessity. Religious education can no longer be thought to have been completed when the period of schooling is ended; it must be prolonged into late adolescence and through adult life. Catechesis is, indeed, a continuous process throughout the whole of life. Religious education must increasingly be parish-based and even neighbourhood-based. Faith is nurtured and matured in community.

Faith communities
Communities should increasingly be seen as the preferred context for growing in faith together. Among the most powerful agents for evangelisation and for Church renewal in the world today are basic Christian communities, associated particularly with Latin America, and the 'new communities' or 'communities of renewal', flourishing most of all in France, or communities like San Egidio, which has its origins in Rome. A strong accent on community living, permeated with faith and love, with welcome, warmth and sharing, is common to all these movements. This undoubtedly corresponds to a deep need in modern society. I have met many people, young and not so young, particularly in France, who have come, in their own words,

to meet the living Jesus Christ through contact with one or other of these communities. The new communities in general are marked by a fervent and unself-conscious faith, a great love for the Church and a spirit of communion with the Pope and the Holy See.

While we cannot slavishly copy Latin-American or continental European models of such communities, we can and must develop their equivalents in Ireland, in the form of parish and deanery groups based on parish or neighbourhood or common need or interest or whatever, for Scripture-sharing, faith-sharing and prayer. To borrow the title of Maura Hyland's excellent programme for young adolescents, growing in faith together is the task of adults and young people together. Her *Growing in Faith Together* programme, and many other community-based and community-fostering programmes of adolescent and adult religious education should be encouraged and promoted. In this regard, women's groups, increasingly a feature of our day, should be promoted, and not only for secular causes but also for religious and spiritual sharing and growth in faith. Great care must, however, be taken that communities and small groups do not become closed in on themselves, exclusive and elitist.

Pre-sacramental catechesis is widely developed across Ireland, with groups participating in pre-baptism, pre-first communion and pre-confirmation programmes. ACCORD is offering excellent pre-marriage programmes. There is also much advantage in having preparation for marriage and marriage-support programmes organised at parish level. Indeed, where possible, these should become part of the normal pre-sacramental catechesis in the parish community. The Christian community in the parish is a community of faith, a community which cares about the faith and the growth in faith of all of its members, a community whose members see it as their duty and their joy to support one another in believing. Surely the greatest act of Christian charity one can do for another is to be discreetly and quietly available to help another in situations which put faith to the test or to help another through a crisis of faith.

Evangelising the inactive

Catholics who are not actively practising their faith, or who are irregular and intermittent in their practice, are a reality now in most parishes in Ireland. They are sometimes called 'inactive Catholics'. Evangelisation of the inactive is a largely new problem in this country. Parish occasions and traditional pastoral methods for the most part leave such people untouched. Even an active and vibrant parish may be leaving a surprising number of its parishioners 'unchurched'. New pastoral strategies to meet this new situation need to be explored.

In the chapter on my fifty years of priesthood, I quoted statistics showing the increase in intermittent or irregular Mass attenders in Ireland. Some attend one or two or three times a month or even less. Many will come to Mass at Christmas or Easter or in November, who rarely come otherwise. Furthermore, many otherwise inactive Catholics will be present in church at funerals, weddings, first communions, confirmations. All of these occasions are special 'evangelising moments'. The meaningful celebration of the liturgy on these occasions, a carefully prepared homily, a tactful and compassionate word of welcome to the irregular attenders, can be a channel of grace. Indeed, every liturgical celebration must nowadays be seen as an 'evangelising moment'; for the dividing line between active and inactive Catholics runs in one respect or another not just through the average congregation but also through the personal lives of all of us. We are all of us lifelong converts 'under instruction'. We all need to be constantly re-evangelised, preachers and people, practising and non-practising. The inactive must be made to feel that they are not forgotten, not rejected; that the Church misses them and needs them and welcomes them back. In this sense, every parish community must try to be a welcoming community, an inviting community. In the United States they have invented the lovely term, 'a re-membering community'.

With a better educated and more critical laity, who have higher expectations and are more prone to disillusionment than formerly, we priests must remember that virtually everything we say or do as priests is in either an 'evangelising mode' or a 'contra-evangelising mode'. Whether we know it or not, people are being drawn to Christ or kept away from him by what we say or do not say, by how we behave and relate, in the most chance meetings or most secular occasions. Whether we realise it or not, the Church is being judged by what we say or do. In the words of the psalm, we should pray:

> Let not those who trust in you be put to shame through me, Lord of hosts. (Ps 68)

Cardinal Suhard deplored the 'untroubled irreligion' of many in our time. He called on priests to be men who, by their lives as well as by their ministry of word and sacrament, should stir up in all minds 'the healthy uneasiness which will prepare for the resurrection'.

But the task does not depend on priests alone. The parish as a whole must accept a responsibility for the evangelisation of its missing members. Each parish community must become in some sense an evangelising community. The depth of faith of parishioners, their prayer, the consistency between their faith and prayer and their life, are relevant to the attitudes of the inactive towards faith and the Church. Groups or communities of scripture-sharing and of prayer can play a role in bringing people to the faith as well as in deepening faith for their members and creating a sense of mission outreach in the community. The concept of 'faith-friends', which is an element in several new catechetical programmes for young people, could also be developed for adults.

Evangelisation of the culture
Evangelisation of the culture is also, as the Holy Father keeps insisting, essential. The Church must be present and active in the universities, the world of journalism and media, in the arts, literature and science, all the time 'thinking our times in a Christian perspective' (to adopt the title of a book by the late Professor Jacques Lerlercq of Louvain, *Penser chrétiennement notre temps*), but doing so in full respect for the legitimate autonomy of scholarship and literature and art and science, and measuring up fully to the

highest standards in the respective disciplines. Here is above all a field for lay Christian involvement, in which academics, writers, intellectuals and artists generally have an indispensable contribution to make.

Much new thinking and much praying must be done by us all to explore new ways of evangelisation. The task must not keep being postponed. It is urgent. Now is 'the acceptable time'. Each decade of religious 'inactivity' brings about a deeper secularisation, which in a generation can become humanly almost irreversible. There is scarcely any country in which evangelisation has better resources to draw upon and better chances of success than Ireland, and therefore there are few countries where failure to accept the challenge of evangelisation would be more inexcusable. This is one area where the only way to fail is not to try or to stop trying. I believe that no greater challenge than this faces the Church in Ireland at this time. Priests and laity may need to be released for this task and given special training and special resources to equip them for it. There is no time to be lost. In one sense time is no longer on our side; but in another sense, time is working for us, for it is Christ's time, and therefore the time of salvation and grace.

Schools of prayer
Evangelisation, whether of the active or the inactive, is closely linked with prayer. The vast majority of Irish people, even when they do not regularly practise their faith, still say that they believe in God and that they still pray. It may be that introducing the inactive to new and deeper forms of praying can be the way to bring them back to Mass and the sacraments and the active life of the Church. Religious communities of men and women can be a great resource in this regard. Recent documents from the Holy See have frequently invited religious communities, whether apostolic or contemplative, to become 'schools of prayer' for lay persons. Religious themselves are called to be 'specialists in prayer' in the Church and for the Church. The document, *Mutuae relationes*, jointly issued by the Holy See's Congregation for Religious and the International Conference of Major Religious Superiors, and

currently being revised for reissue, lays particular stress upon this aspect of religious life. Growth in prayer is for every Christian an essential condition for growth in faith and in Christian life; and in the spiritual life to stop growing is to start dying. The remarkable spread, all over Ireland, of the retreat movement, preached or directed, is one of the great signs of the action of the Holy Spirit in the Church of our time.

Evangelisation of youth

Several surveys of religious practice indicate that irregularity of practice is more marked among young people of post-secondary school age than in the population generally. Thank God, large numbers of young people and young adults are committed and active Catholics; but many are going through a period, the duration of which is unpredictable, of religious doubt or alienation from the Church, or at least feel that they have no longer any need for religion or the Church or think that the Church has no need, or no time, for them. Evangelisation of such young people must be a pastoral priority, for they are the future of the Church and of the country. 'Evangelising moments' for young people have to be found in their own 'youth culture'. No one appreciates this more than Pope John Paul, who is surely Christendom's most active and most effective evangeliser of young people today. Much can be learned from his choice of occasions for encounter and dialogue with young people and from his addresses to youth.

Pilgrimages, walks, rallies, fasts for famine relief, vigils of prayer, all have an attraction for young people and fit in with their culture. Youth Masses, with 'folk groups' providing the music and singing, and with maximum participation of young people themselves in all parts of the celebration, should be given an important place in parish life. A better quality and range of religious music in the 'folk' medium is now available than was formerly the case. The Taizé community has made a great contribution in this area. Chants in this medium are usually scripture-based and can serve also as an introduction to Scripture. Preparation for these youth liturgies and participation in them are important 'evangelising moments' for young people. Youth retreats, geared particularly to the needs and the questions and the difficulties of young people, can be very effective. Young people, however, do not always need religious services which are special to themselves, apart from ordinary parish services. They appreciate it, however, if occasionally the presence of young people is acknowledged and cognisance of it is taken in the course of a parish Mass or in a homily. Young priests have obvious advantages in ministry to youth; but older priests need not feel unequipped for this ministry: young people respond readily to the wisdom and experience and especially the holiness and charity of priests of older years.

Ministering to and with women

Women are, to an unprecedented degree, conscious nowadays of being a distinct group in society and in the Church. Questions like women's rights to equality in all spheres of life, including the religious sphere, are increasingly important. Questions about women's place in the Church are coming even from women who are not activists in any feminist movement and not even particularly 'feminist'. As is the case in every movement, there are some feminists whose extremism and militancy offend many, including women themselves; but the broad programme of mainstream feminism deserves and demands a positive response from the Church. We pastors must have the humility to recognise that over-reaction to feminist criticisms or dismissal of them on our part may be due to male prejudice or conditioning or to instinctive and unconscious assumptions of male superiority.

The question of 'inclusive language' has become a very sensitive one for many women. We may understandably regret this, because much great literature would have to be radically rewritten and in the process mangled if the full demands of 'inclusivists' were to be met. One can rightly regret also the fact that the words 'man' or 'men' are now being understood and 'heard' as standing for 'male' (*vir*), and no longer for 'human being' (*homo*). Awkward neologisms or circumlocutions have to be sought as terms for what males and females share together, their common humanity. This, I believe, can constitute an impoverishment of language and is often possible only by doing violence to the English language.

However this may be, it must be recognised that usage in English has changed, albeit partly through the influence of feminism, and has changed at least for the foreseeable future. Words like 'man', 'men', 'brothers' etc., are now 'heard' by women as excluding their sex, and this is understandably felt as an indignity and an injustice. Pastors must respond sensitively to this change of usage. Women need to be specifically mentioned and addressed; otherwise, as English is now heard, they are perceived as being excluded. The approach of the New Jerusalem Bible is commendable. Its authors state in their introduction:

> Considerable efforts have been made, though not at all costs, to soften or avoid the in-built preference of the English language, a preference now found so offensive by some people, for the masculine.

Somewhat similarly, the New Revised Standard Version states in its introduction the intention of being 'sensitive to the contemporary concern for inclusive language when referring to human beings'.

The last phrase is important. The question of the names used for God is much more profound and far-reaching than a matter of mere linguistic usage. It raises deep and fundamental questions which can touch on the very foundations of Christian faith. Calling God 'Father' is not, for Christians, the legacy of a patriarchal society. It is the very self-revelation of God in the human consciousness of Jesus Christ, who is truly God as well as truly man. As we remind ourselves in the introduction to the Our Father in the liturgy, we call God our Father because Jesus did so and allows and indeed commands his followers to do the same. The Church has always been conscious of the immense privilege of being allowed to use for God the special and intimate name which only Jesus used for him, 'Abba', 'Father'. Our use of the name would be a usurpation and a blasphemy unless we had first been admitted to a sharing in Christ's own filial relationship with the Person whom he knew and spoke to as 'Father'. The God whom we Christians are privileged to know is not just God as we choose to define and name him, but specifically the God and Father of Our Lord, Jesus Christ. Our God is God as Jesus reveals him and as Jesus names him.

Our prayer is our sharing in the prayer of Jesus Christ himself; our prayer is the expression of our baptised beings as sons and daughters of God our Father, through Jesus Christ, our Lord. This is the law of Christian prayer and it is the law of Christian faith. This is by no means to say that God is male. God reveals himself as having feminine qualities also. But the use of feminine names for God in the Church's official worship fails to express that unique experience of God which the Christian Church has received from Jesus Christ and which the Church itself shares through her union with Jesus Christ. Indeed it may gravely distort that experience. Profound issues of faith are at stake here. I confess to dismay at the levity with which some people take it on themselves to set aside in this connection the Christian *lex orandi,* the 'law of praying', which is also the Christian *lex credendi* or 'law of behaving'.

In dealing with women generally, we pastors must be prepared to listen to them, to learn from them, to seek their advice, not only in matters of special concern to women, but also in everything that concerns the life of the Church. We must ensure that women are equally involved with men in all services and ministries open to the non-ordained in the Church. We must ensure that there is equal representation for women and for men in all diocesan and parish pastoral councils and committees, composed of or open to the laity. Women have been and are the Church's most devoted members and most active workers; their place must become more visible and their voice more audible in the work of the Church.

Ministry to schools
Catholic schools remain a most essential instrument for the transmission of Christian faith and Christian values to the next generation. Ministry to schools is a vital part of the pastoral ministry of priests. Catholic teachers are themselves leading examples of the involvement of laity in the life and mission of the

Church; but they need affirmation and they need pastoral support in their task of religious and moral education. Theirs is often a difficult task, given the growing moral confusion in society and the increase in marriage and family breakdown, and the general weakening of the concepts and practice of authority and discipline. The task of teachers is difficult also because of the volume and speed of educational reform and curricular change. Visible support and help from the priest is essential. Regular school visitation by the priest is pastorally very productive and indirectly constitutes a valuable part of priestly ministry to the family and to youth as well as being a spiritual support to teachers.

Close co-operation between priests and teachers is particularly important in the preparation of young people and parents for the celebration of first penance and first communion and of confirmation. This co-operation is essential also in the context of pre-sacramental catechesis of parents of children preparing for these sacraments. It is a prime example of the partnership in ministry between priests and lay persons, which is so strongly urged upon us all at this time.

If schools are to carry out their religious or secular tasks successfully, they need support and co-operation from the parents and homes of the children, and indeed from the wider community. To promote this co-operation and this support is an important part of parish pastoral ministry. Religious and moral education should be a co-operative task of school, of home and family, of teachers, parents and priests; it must not be left unilaterally and exclusively to the school. The Church has always stressed that parents are the first teachers of the faith and that the home is both the first school of faith and the 'domestic Church'. We must work to put reality into these familiar terms.

School administration, however, becomes increasingly burdensome and time-consuming for priests. It requires skills for which priests are not normally trained. Many of these tasks can be shared with lay people, and their involvement is a further indication of the responsibility of the parish community, and not just the priest, for its schools.

The gift of faith is normally received in a community; it is nurtured and matured in community; it is transmitted within and by a community of faith. Every Christian community must be a faith-community; and by this very fact it must be an evangelising and missionary community. The post-synodal document on catechetics, published in 1978, stressed that the parish is the natural 'locus' for catechetics. The development of pre-sacramental catechesis of parents and of parish-based programmes for catechesis of adolescents is an important step towards realising this aim. It is not a question of parish-based versus school-based catechetics, but of both together, supporting and supplementing one another in partnership.

Ministry to marriage and the family
Among the greatest riches and blessings offered by the Church to society, and indeed to humanity, is that of Christian marriage. Marriage has always been seen by the Church as something deeply human, and yet transcending the merely human, something intrinsically sacred, even in its secular reality, and also sacral, and indeed explicitly sacramental. Christian marriage corresponds to and yet transcends the deepest intuitions and needs of the human heart, and fulfils the truest experiences and longings of human love. Marriage affirms but ennobles human sexuality and elevates and subsumes it into the mystery of Christ, thereby permeating it with the Christ-life of grace. Like all things precious, marriage needs to be guarded with care. In the modern world, Christian marriage is exposed to perhaps the greatest crisis in two thousand years of Christian history. Ministry to marriage and to the family is a basic form of pastoral ministry. The post-synodal document on the family, *Familiaris consortio*, published in 1987, says:

> The future of the world and of the Church passes through the family. (75)

> The future of humanity passes by way of the family. (86)

The work of the Catholic marriage advisory service, ACCORD, must be given every support, both at parish level and nationally. Ways should be explored of making pre-marriage preparation part of parish-based programmes of catechesis, not with the aim or the result of superseding the pre-marriage courses offered by ACCORD, but of supplementing them, particularly in their spiritual dimension. Marriage support services at diocesan and at parish level should be developed. Marriage and the family are subject to unprecedented challenge and stress in modern society and they need corresponding pastoral care. Crisis and even breakdown in marriage often come in the first years of marriage, and this is when support may be most needed. Married couples themselves are often in the best position to offer this support. Celebration of the liturgy of marriage has been greatly enriched in the post-conciliar years. Progress in this regard must continue.

Marriage is a privileged occasion for evangelisation and re-evangelisation, both of the couple themselves and their families and also of the community which assists at the wedding. There are few occasions which create a more favourable opportunity than does the marriage liturgy for linking people's life experience with God; for love between the sexes is one of humankind's deepest and most beautiful experiences and the liturgy links it with its source in God, who is Love itself and the source of human love. Love between man and woman may often be abused and debased because of human sinfulness, yet even then it is invariably experienced as carrying with it touches of the divine and traces of the hand of the Creator whose name is Love. Liturgical celebration of marriage offers unequalled opportunities for a loving encounter with God. The opportunity for evangelisation thus offered is all the more precious because at so many wedding celebrations nowadays there will inevitably be people who have lost touch with God and with the Church. As I have stressed above, great care is needed at this time to ensure that secular elements do not intrude into the liturgy of marriage, whether in music, posing for the camera at sacred moments, or otherwise.

Anniversaries of marriage should be given religious expression and should be liturgically celebrated, rather than being simply secular occasions. Marriage jubilees particularly should be liturgically celebrated, and can fittingly be marked by a parish celebration for all jubilarians in a parish, with perhaps special certificates being issued to mark the occasion.

Priestly visitation of homes is nowadays more important than ever, and yet in many respects more difficult than ever. When circumstances are suitable, it can help if house-to-house visitation of an area is announced in advance and is made the occasion for preparation in a neighbourhood community for a Mass to be celebrated in a house or in the Church, which all the families of the neighbourhood are invited to attend. The traditional custom of 'station Masses', still observed in many dioceses, has great pastoral value and can in today's society have even greater pastoral significance than in former times. 'House Masses' can be an appropriate modern expression of the community dimension which 'the stations' fostered. Indeed, decline in religious practice is invariably a concomitant of decline in the sense of community, and anything which strengthens community can help in building the sense of religious community as well.

Team ministry
Partnership in ministry, or 'collaborative ministry', are more than just vogue words today: they point to a community dimension in all ministry, which both corresponds to the *communio* which the Church is, and responds to one of the signs of the times in today's world. This partnership is desirable, first of all, between priests themselves, especially at parish or inter-parish level. 'Team ministry' is not a mere modish term: it can bring new vitality to a priest's individual ministry and new vibrancy to a whole parish. It is not, however, something which happens spontaneously. Even when priests in a parish have excellent personal relationships with one another, 'team ministry', in the real sense of the term, is not automatically guaranteed. It has to be patiently and perseveringly worked at. It calls for deliberate effort and planning. It requires regular dialogue and reflection on the problems and the

opportunities, the needs and the resources of the parish. It requires working towards a shared vision for the parish. It needs to be regularly reviewed; a sense of mutual accountability within the team needs to be developed. Above all, team ministry requires commitment to community prayer on the part of the priests involved. It is helped by the setting aside, from time to time, of days of prayer and reflection shared between the priests together.

Through team ministry, pastoral and homiletic or catechetical programmes can be planned together and shared. Pastoral planning for the parish can be organised in a more systematic and purposeful way, accountability for the parish plan can be shared and progress can be regularly reviewed and assessed.

The team spirit can be extended to neighbouring parishes, and then team ministry opens up new possibilities for shared preparation of homilies and for occasional inter-parish rotation of celebrants of Sunday Mass, interchange of pulpits, etc., so as to give people a variety of voices and insights. All this can contribute also to the development of the 'ministry of priests to priests' which is rightly desired by many priests today.

But collaborative ministry must also be extended to include lay parishioners. When laity are included, team ministry takes on new significance and new power to revitalise a parish. The whole conciliar and post-conciliar self-understanding of the Church points to collaboration of priests and lay persons in the Church's life and mission. For this to take effect, however, we priests need to imbue ourselves and form our people in the new vision of the Church as *communio* – communion of Pope, bishops, priests, religious, lay men and women, trying together to grow in faith and love, and trying to be one and be seen to be one, so that the world may believe. In this way, we can not only preach the mystery of God and his love, we can also witness to that mystery and in some sense be that mystery in our own lives.

For all these reasons, ongoing renewal for priests and bishops is essential. It is desirable that some of these renewal courses be shared with lay people; in this way the spirit of partnership of bishops and priests with lay people can be developed and a common vision of the Church and of the respective and complementary vocations of priesthood and laity in the Church can be formed.

Ministry of ecumenism

The growth in unity within the Church must motivate us also to pray and work for unity between the Churches. Ecumenism is not an optional extra for priests or for laity. It is a command of the Lord and a response to his own prayer. The ministry of reconciliation which bishops and priests have received from the Lord through the Apostles is incomplete unless we are working also for reconciliation between divided Christians. The relevance and urgency of the ministry of reconciliation in our society in the North of Ireland do not need to be emphasised.

Meetings of Church leaders are valuable and necessary; but meetings of clergy of different denominations at local level are also important. When trust is built up at clergy level, it then becomes easier to introduce various forms of contact at congregational level and, step by step, to reduce the gap of incomprehension and misunderstanding and sometimes suspicion and fear that divide communities. Christian ministry, particularly in today's world, is incomplete unless it includes an ecumenical dimension. In the North of Ireland, the cessation of violence and the recent Agreement must be followed by a long and systematic process of healing, repentance, reconciliation and forgiveness; and the more this can be planned and implemented by the Churches in unison, the better.

Justice and peace

Ever since priestly ordination I have felt that work for social justice was a vital part of priestly ministry and integral to the preaching of the Gospel. I have always felt that the Church's credibility in this half century in Ireland is bound up with its teaching and action on justice. Particularly since the 'Troubles' in the North broke out, I have felt that the Church's commitment to justice, to peace and to the poor would be a primary criterion of her relevance and credibility for the modern generation. At the same time, there has never been any doubt in my mind but that peace and justice are inseparable and that the only viable way to peace in the North is through working for justice for deprived communities and thus demonstrating that there are effective, non-violent ways of effecting change in the direction of justice, whereas violence only destroys the work of justice. The experience of the past thirty years has brought ample proof of this.

The problems of injustice and deprivation are by no means confined to the North. The poor are very much with us in all parts of Ireland. The gap between rich and poor has not lessened but widened. The plague of urban blight has not gone away in the age of the 'Celtic Tiger'. Chronic unemployment sets up ever new poverty traps. The Church must be in the forefront of action, at national and at local community level, both to seek for remedies to reduce poverty and unemployment and to do all it can to help the poor to sustain their dignity and self-worth despite the demoralising impact of social exclusion.

There has been a marvellous tradition in the Church in Ireland of being on the side of the poor. Wherever there were poor or marginalised groups, the Church was there to offer welcome and food and shelter, hope and love. Through a network of agencies, religious and lay, the Church built up an informal but wide-ranging welfare system, as well as an educational system, long before the State began to see either of these as its function. The Church in Ireland traditionally was a Church of the poor, making the 'preferential option for the poor', long before the term became familiar. The loyalty of the poor and the 'working class' to the Church became legendary. It is a great tragedy that this has waned in our time. Care for the poor, in circumstances where the gap between the 'haves' and the 'have-nots' grows steadily wider, and when new groups of poor are steadily increasing, must mark the Church today even more than in the past. This will be more difficult in future as, from shortage of personnel, religious communities increasingly have to withdraw from traditional apostolates and the laity will have to take over their works. This will be one of the great Christian challenges to lay men and women in the future, whether they work within or outside the public welfare systems. It must be remembered that delivery of health care and of social welfare are corporal and spiritual works of mercy, whether done by salaried professionals or by voluntary helpers. I am fully confident that our laity will respond to the challenge.

Church and media
Church people accuse the media of bishop-bashing or clergy-bashing. Media people accuse the Church of media-bashing. Each has some justification for so doing; but either way the exercise becomes somewhat tedious and unprofitable.

For the Church, it is much more important to see media both as an inseparable part of modern culture and as an essential instrument for communicating Gospel truths and values to that culture. We must try to find ways in which the Gospel message can be heard through all the modern media of mass communication. In the 1970s significant and innovative ways were explored by the Irish Episcopal Conference in the area of religious communication and some progress was made. It was then that the Catholic Communications Institute of Ireland was established, the Catholic Press and Information Office was put in place and the Communications Centre established. They have all given excellent service. But the media world is constantly changing and all our responses to it need to be kept under constant review.

It is now imperative that we identify lay men and women, including young people, well formed in their faith and imbued with love for the Church, and who have natural and acquired gifts of communication, and that we ask them to make themselves available for contributing to topics of current debate from the Church's point of view. These people should be given some training in communication skills, whether through print or audio-visual media. They should feel responsible for keeping themselves informed, doctrinally and factually, about a chosen range of relevant topics. They should then seek appropriate opportunities to participate in public discussion on matters of Church interest, for example by letters and articles in newspapers or by contributing to 'phone-in' radio or television programmes. They should also be willing to contribute to media programmes when invited to do so. There is no lack of opportunity, both in the electronic and in the print media, for making Christ's message heard and read. If we do not avail of these opportunities, we have ourselves to blame, in part at least, for the Church's bad press.

In today's great debates, which so often deal with profound moral and spiritual issues, the Church's voice must not be silent. This is most properly a lay person's area of involvement in the Church's mission. If, as Pope Paul VI desired, the Church's teaching is to find its way into 'the mainstream of public discourse', it is pre-eminently through the laity that this must be done. Pope John Paul II lays repeated stress on the need to evangelise modern culture. Again, it is primarily in the public forum of media that this must take place. It is sad that, especially in this age of the laity, there are too few writers, whether in the field of literature as such or in that of popular journalism, who find inspiration in their faith for creative writing or for informed comment. I am convinced that this will change, as people begin to see that the wells of a culture run dry unless renewed from a deeper spring, that of religious faith. What I have said applies at diocesan as much as at national level. The regional or provincial press and local radio offer many possibilities for diocesan and parish involvement and every effort must be made to avail of these.

A missionary Church
The Vatican Council insisted that the whole Church is of its very nature missionary. Every Christian, priest, religious or lay person shares in the calling of the Apostles to proclaim Christ as Saviour and Lord to the whole world and to announce his saving Gospel to every creature to the end of time. There are different ways of fulfilling this mandate, but no Christian man or woman can refuse to play his or her part. There is a danger that we Christians in Ireland can become so preoccupied with our own domestic problems and so weighed down by our difficulties or so

complacent in our country's new-found prosperity, that we neglect the missionary command of the Lord to 'Go out to the whole world and make disciples of all the nations'. Renewal of the Church in Ireland in past centuries and in modern times often came about through a renewal of missionary fervour. It has been rightly said that we keep the faith by giving it away to others, sharing it with those who do not believe in Christ. If this is the age of the laity, as in many ways it is, then the laity must become more conscious of their missionary calling and some of them should be ready to volunteer for work as lay missionaries overseas for some period of their lives.

To conclude what I have written in this chapter about the tasks facing the Church in Ireland in these closing years of the millennium, I wish to say two things. Firstly, many of these tasks are already being tackled in many dioceses across the country much more resolutely than I myself ever tackled them in my active ministry. Secondly, I have been conscious throughout of how much I myself have failed to do in all these regards. A critic might well retort: 'Those who can, do; those who can't, write'! I sometimes have the nightmarish fantasy that, at my judgment, I shall have brought before me in a flash all my homilies, addresses and writings, and shall hear a voice saying to me: 'This is what you preached to others. How did you live it yourself?' All I could say in reply would be: 'Have mercy on me, Lord, for, in spite of all my failings, I wanted to do your Will: *tuam in votis tenui voluntatem.*'

EPILOGUE

This is emphatically not a time for discouragement at how little we have done or for mere remorse for what we have failed to do. It is not a time for pessimism or fear about the future. The Holy Spirit has worked powerfully in the Church in our time, and continues to work mightily among the priests and lay persons who constitute the People of God. The fruits of the Second Vatican Council are only now beginning to mature. The fields are only ripening for harvest. The seeds of the Kingdom grow slowly, but they grow by their own God-given innate power 'even when we sleep'. Many of the Lord's parables of the Kingdom emphasise this God-given power of the seeds of the Kingdom to grow irresistibly, at their own pace and in their own time, and bear abundant fruit.

A little 'parable' from my own experience comes to my mind in this connection. When I went to Longford in 1967, the trees and shrubs around the bishop's residence needed 'thinning out', and in some cases replacement. It took only two or three days to cut down what had begun to decay, and two or three more to plant new trees and shrubs where needed. Thirty years later, the new trees and shrubs are still young and still growing. Cutting down is so fast and so final. Growing is slow and calls for careful tending and for long and patient waiting. But the thrill of greenness and newness of life and beauty abundantly repays the care and the patience. I see an analogy between this and the work of the Holy Spirit and the

Church, revealed significantly by the programme of the Second Vatican Council. A recent writer has said:

> Vatican II called both for a new opening to the world and for a re-vivifying return to the springs. The product was magnificent, but a generation has not been enough to digest it. (Robert Murray, *The Cosmic Christ*, 1992)

It is sometimes said that 'time is no longer on our side'. At a certain level, this is true. But at a deeper level, time is always on the Church's side, because all time is Christ's time and therefore is the Church's time. Someone has said: 'No one needs to save the Church; the Church saves us'. No one needs to save the Church, because the Lord saves his Church, the Holy Spirit renews the Church constantly and always leads it back to the joy of its youth and the love of its 'bridal days'. The Church can keep us young, regardless of our chronological age.

Cardinal Newman spoke of a second spring for the Church in England in his famous sermon with that title, preached in St Mary's, Oscott, in 1852, on the occasion of the First Provincial Synod of Westminster. I believe that the Church is having a second spring in Ireland at this time; but, adapting Newman's words, we can say that it is an 'Irish spring'. I quote the passage from Newman, substituting the word 'Irish' for 'English' in Newman's original text:

> Have we any right to think it strange, if, in this Irish land, the spring-time of the Church should turn out to be an Irish spring, an uncertain, anxious time of hope and fear, of joy and suffering – of bright promise and budding hopes, yet withal, of keen blasts and cold showers and sudden storms?

On a personal note, after nearly two years in retirement, I have to say that, as I have remarked elsewhere, retirement is not easy. The transition is abrupt from a life where one is at the centre of activity to one where the activity goes on perfectly well without one! The late Bishop William Philbin, after he retired, spoke of being 'weightless in space'. In retirement, a bishop or priest does not 'belong' anywhere and does not feel 'needed' by anyone. One has no parish or church or congregation or pastoral charge. Mail is mostly bills and 'bumph'. Looking back, I can see that as bishop I was not as sensitive in respect of retired priests and bishops or as attentive to their feelings and needs as I should have been. I have myself been extremely fortunate in the generosity shown towards me by the Archdiocese of Armagh and its concern for my welfare.

Ageing is not romantic; though I do not share the pessimism of Qoheleth (or Ecclesiastes), who speaks of 'evil days' when 'day is darkening at the windows ... when to go uphill is an ordeal and a walk is something to dread ... before the silver cord has snapped or the golden lamp has been broken or the pitcher shattered at the spring or the pulley cracked at the well' (11: 1-6). I have found that the secret of a satisfactory retirement is to keep active: an active retirement can be a happy and fulfilled retirement. I thank God that I still find the days and weeks too short for all the things I want to write and do and, sadly, too short for all the leeway in personal prayer which I have still to make up after so many years of activism or even 'workaholism'.

If I may continue on a personal note, I must at my age obviously hear echoing in my ears the words of St Paul to Timothy, his young disciple:

> As for me, my life is already being poured away as a libation, and the time has come for me to be gone. (2 Tm 4:6)

Yet I confess to a great impatience to do so much more for the Lord and for his Church. I feel a great sense of urgency about going out through all the doors which are opening for the Church at this time, and, along with this, I feel a great hope and confidence for all that lies ahead for the Church in Ireland. The impatience, I know, can be self-indulgent and even dangerous. It is not what 'I do' for the Church that matters, but what the Lord makes of me, what the Lord does for his Church, and what the Church does for me.

Humanly, however, I find myself wishing that I were beginning my life and my priesthood all over again now, rather than approaching the end. For this is a great time to be alive and especially to be young in the Church. At times, I find myself envying today's young priests and wishing that I were young again with them and facing today's new challenges with their energy and enthusiasm. The Church seems to me in so many ways to be healthier and more alive now than when I was young. If asked about my decision to be a priest, 'Would you do it over again?', my answer would be unhesitatingly, 'Yes'; but I would try to do it better; and I would prefer to do it amid the changes and challenges of the twenty-first century rather than in what at times were the excessive clericalism, the caution, the fussiness about rubrics, rules and petty regulations, and sometimes the routines and the complacencies of the early and middle twentieth century. As the end of the earthly phase of life draws near for me, I once more sincerely say to the Lord, with Dag Hammerksjöld:

> For all that has been, Lord, thanks.
> To all that will be, Lord, yes.

But my last wish and prayer and hope would still be the same as St Paul's:

> Life to me is not a thing to waste words on, provided that when I finish my race I have carried out the mission the Lord Jesus gave me – and that was to bear witness to the Good News of God's grace. (Ac 20:24)

I pray, and I would like my friends to pray, that when I die, my life might have been such as not to belie these words.

APPENDIX

PRAYERS

I append the text of some prayers which I have found helpful, especially at times of upheaval, anxiety and apprehension in my life. They may be helpful to others.

First is the well known 'Prayer of Abandonment' of Charles de Foucauld.

> Father,
> I abandon myself into your hands;
> do with me what you will.
> Whatever you may do I thank you:
> I am ready for all, I accept all.
>
> Let only your will be done in me,
> and in all your creatures.
> I wish no more than this, O Lord.
>
> Into your hands I commend my soul:
> I offer it to you
> with all the love of my heart,
> for I do love you, Lord,
> and so I need to give myself,

to surrender myself into your hands,
without reserve,
and with boundless confidence,
for you are my Father.

Second is a prayer of Thomas Merton – A copy of it was found on the person of one of the three Maryknoll Sisters murdered with Jean Donovan by government forces in El Salvador in December 1980.

My Lord God, I have no idea where I am going.
I do not see the road ahead of me.
I cannot know for certain where it will end.
Nor do I really know my own self,
and the fact that I think I am following your will
does not necessarily mean that I am actually doing so.
But I believe that the desire to please you
does in fact please you
and I hope I have that desire in everything that I do.
I hope that I will never do anything apart from that desire.
And I know that if I do this
you will lead me by the right road
even though I may know nothing about it.
Therefore I will trust you always.
Even though I may seem to be lost and in the shadow of
    death
I will fear no evil, for you are ever with me
and you will never leave me to face my peril alone.

Third is a prayer of another martyr for Christ in our time, Father (now Saint) Rupert Meyer SJ.

Lord, as You will, so be it done to me,
and as You will, so will I do;
Help me only to know Your will.

Lord, when You will, the time is right,
and when You will, then I am ready;
today and for all times.

Lord, what You will, I gladly accept,
and what you will, is gain for me;
enough to know that I belong to you.

Lord, because You will it, it is good for me,
and because You will it, then I have courage.
My heart rests in Your hands.

Father Rupert Meyer was born in Stuttgart on 23 January 1876. He died in a Nazi concentration camp on 1 November 1945. He was canonised by Pope John Paul II on 3 May 1987 in the Olympic Stadium, Munich.

TABLE OF BIBLICAL REFERENCES

Note: Books of the Bible are listed in biblical order

Old Testament
Deuteronomy
  7:9, 298, 358, 403
1 Kings
  19:8, 465
Psalms
  15:6, 8, 478
  41:5, 392
  42:4, 343
  46:6-7, 392-393
  68, 502
  102, 85
Ecclesiastes (Qoheleth)
  11:1-6, 520
Wisdom
  4:13, 382
Isaiah
  6:8-9, 86
  41:10, 349
  43:1-4, 5, 349
  46:3-4, 356
Jeremiah
  1:4-5, 56
  1:7, 362
  29:11, 485
Ezekiel
  24:16, 463
  34:2-5, 317

New Testament
Matthew
  4:17, 467
  5:37, 350, 352
  6:13, 467
  7:25, 481
  10:37-39, 471
  11:25, 406
  12:18, 20, 411
  13:52, 475
  16:18, 403
  16:19, 333
  16:24, 326
  16:24-25, 327

16:25, 346
19:16-22, 346
19:21, 471
19:26, 335
20:6-7, 336
25:40, 463
25:41-46, 99
25:45-46, 463
27:20, 350
28:20, 456
Mark
  1:1, 407
  1:15, 467
  1:18, 470
  7:6, 463
  10:30, 334
  16:19-20, 426
Luke
  1:4, 497
  1:49-50, 452
  2:40, 467
  2:49, 334, 353
  4:14, 319
  5:15-16, 330
  9:57, 365
  9:62, 365
  11:23, 461
  18:8, 344
  18:27, 335
  21:33, 345
  22:28, 435
  22:32, 334, 363, 480
  22:40, 357
  24:13-35, 364
  24:29, 334
John
  1:7, 402
  1:9, 414
  1:57, 465
  5:40, 406
  6:47, 399
  8:31, 474
  10:3, 384

10:14, 384
11:26, 362
12:26, 474
12:32, 399
14:9, 11, 13, 18, 21, 23,
  418-419
15:4-9, 340-341
15:5, 335
16:21, 60
17:9-10, 24, 398
19:27, 331
20:31, 497
21:15-16, 362
21:16-17, 334
21:17, 365
21:18, 86
21:18-19, 364
21:22, 363
Acts of the Apostles
  1:26, 306
  2:5, 11, 429
  2:33, 320
  7:56-57, 427
  16:9-10, 454
  18, 307
  20:24, 9, 324, 521
  20:26-27, 318, 367
  20:28, 326, 466
  20:31-32, 301, 367
  20:32, 290
  20:36, 304
  26, 307
Romans
  1:5, 362
  1:7, 450
  1:16, 322
  5:4-5, 323
  5:21, 277-278, 453
  8:38-9, 405
  12:11, 320
  13:13, 427
  15:13, 8, 309, 323
  16:1ff, 307

INDEX

Armagh clergy
characteristics of, 475-477
art. *see* Church art and architecture
Art D'Église, 109
Art Sacré, 109
arts, 502
ascetism, 89-90
Asia
Synod of Bishops for, 202
Athenagoras, Patriarch, 142, 185
Augustine, Saint, 112, 242, 283, 319, 412,
455, 456, 471-472
Augustinian College (Rome), 448
Auschwitz, 278-279
authority and obedience, 325-327, 366

B
B-Specials, 15
Ballinlea, 40
Ballintoy (Co. Antrim), 40
Ballybradden (Loughguile, Co. Antrim), 13,
16, 44
Ballycastle (Co. Antrim), 71, 215
Ballymena (Co. Antrim), 28, 82
Ballymoney (Co. Antrim), 34
Banagher (Co. Offaly), 65
Barth, Karl, 405
Baum, Gregory, 156
Bea, Cardinal Augustin, 123, 125, 128, 141,
174
Beckett, Mary, 57-58
Beckett, Samuel, 104-105
Behan, John, 197
Beijing (China)
Fourth World Conference of Women,
211
Belfast, 52, 218, 244
Ashton Development, 338
Church of the Good Shepherd, 351
community development, 249-252
Divis Flats, 250, 339
Falls Road, 93-94, 243, 315
housing, 250, 338-339
local enterprise centres, 338
North Howard Street Development, 338
rehabilitation in deprived communities,
249-252
Sacred Heart Parish (Oldpark), 94
St Peter's Cathedral, 243
unemployment, 338

urban deprivation, 244
Second World War air raids, 87
Belfast Jewish Institute, 141
Belfast Telegraph, 380
Belgian Episcopal Conference, 134
Bellot, Dom (Solesmes), 108
Benedict XV (Giacomo della Chiesa), 163-164,
178
Benedictines, 121, 357
Sisters of Saint Cecilia (Trastavere), 430
Vanves convent, 108-109, 171
Bernanos, Georges, 105, 141, 432
Bernard, Saint, 386, 430, 431
Bernardin, Archbishop, 184
Besse, Dom (Ligugé), 108
Bevilacqua, Cardinal (Philadelphia), 251
Bible, 496, 506
Biblical Institute (Rome), 122, 123
biblical studies, 167-168, 217
Bigo, Fr, SJ, 110
bigotry, 246, 321; *see also* sectarianism
Birkenau, 278, 279
Birmingham Six, 253
birth control, 147, 148, 152, 156-158, 177
Humanae vitae, 148, 149, 153, 157, 180
bishops, 417. *see also* Episcopal collegiality;
Irish Episcopal Conference; Synod of
Bishops
accessibility to lay people, 312
ad limina visits to Rome, 203-204
administrative efficiency, 312-313
aged and sick, care for, 312
alienated, responsibilities to, 410
authority, 325-327, 366
bond with diocese, 465-467, 473-474
complaints about, 204-205
consultation of priests, religious and
people, 264, 265-266, 314
criticisms of, 264
dialogue, promotion of, 410-411
divisions between, 206
ecumenism, 314
hearing the truth, 264-265
national problems, and, 266-267
nominations and appointments, 207-208
ordination, meaning of, 318-319
poor, responsibilities to, 408-410
priests, relationship with, 291-292, 311-
312, 419-421
priorities of a bishop, 310-314